NUCLEAR WAR SURVIVAL SKILLS

The purpose of this book is to provide Americans with information and instructions that will significantly increase their chances of surviving a possible nuclear attack. It brings together field-tested instructions that, if followed by a large fraction of Americans during a crisis that preceded an attack, could save millions of lives. The author is convinced that the vulnerability of our country to nuclear threat or attack must be reduced and that the wide dissemination of the information contained in this book would help achieve that objective of our overall defense strategy.

Underlying the advocacy of Americans learning these down-to-earth survival skills is the belief that if one prepares for the worst, the worst is less likely to happen. Effective American civil defense preparations would reduce the probability of nuclear blackmail and war. Yet in our world of increasing dangers, it is significant that the United States spends much less per capita on civil defense than many other countries. The United States' annual funding is about 50 cents per capita, whereas Switzerland spends almost $11 and, most importantly, the Soviet Union spends approximately $20.

In the first chapter the myths and facts about the consequences of a massive nuclear attack are discussed. As devastating as such an attack would be, with adequate civil defense preparations and timely warning much of the population could survive.

The information and instructions given in subsequent chapters tell the average citizen how to improve his and his family's chances of surviving a nuclear attack by working together to build expedient shelters and homemade life-support equipment. The reader is urged to make at least some of these low-cost preparations before a crisis arises. The main emphasis, however, is on survival preparations that could be made in the last few days of a worsening crisis.

This book includes chapters on psychological preparations, warning and communications, and evacuation. Because the greatest need would be for shelter that would provide good protection against fallout radiation and also would permit prolonged occupancy, much of the book deals with this subject. These chapters describe the building of expedient shelters, their ventilation and cooling, the purification and storage of adequate water, the processing and cooking of whole grains and legumes, fallout meters, protection against fires and carbon monoxide, and expedient furnishings for shelters. Other chapters cover sanitation and preventive medicine, medical advice for nuclear survivors lacking the help of doctors, improvised footwear and clothing, and advice on minimum preparations that can be made at low cost and should be made before a crisis arises.

One appendix of the handbook gives detailed, field-tested instructions for building six types of earth-covered expedient fallout shelters, with criteria to guide the choice of which shelter to build. The design features of several types of expedient blast shelters are described in another appendix. Two others contain instructions for making an efficient shelter-ventilating pump and a homemade fallout meter that is accurate and dependable. Both of these essentials can be made with inexpensive materials found in most households. Drawings are used extensively, as are photographs of people actually building and living in the various shelters.

This first-of-its-kind report is primarily a compilation and summary of civil defense measures and inventions developed at ORNL over the past 14 years and field-tested in six states, from Florida to Utah. It is the first comprehensive handbook of survival information for use by untrained citizens who want to improve their chances of surviving a possible nuclear attack.

Civil defense officials and others who realize the need for improved, field-tested instructions will find much new and useful information in *Nuclear War Survival Skills*. Information in the book is organized so that sections may be easily excerpted and reproduced for mass distribution through news media.

NUCLEAR WAR SURVIVAL SKILLS

CRESSON H. KEARNY

NWS RESEARCH BUREAU
COOS BAY, OREGON

35 34 33 32 31 30 29 28 27 26 25 24 23 22 21

Copies of this book may be purchased from the distributor for $10.95. All inquiries and catalog requests should be addressed to Caroline House Publishers, Inc., 920 West Industrial Drive, Aurora, Illinois 60506 — (312) 897-2050.

ISBN: 0-939002-02-7

LIBRARY OF CONGRESS
CATALOG CARD NO.: 81-82345

    Kearney, Cresson H.
      Nuclear War Survival Skills.

    Coos Bay, OR: Nuclear War Survival Research Bureau

    232 p.   810526
    8105

CONTENTS

FOREWORD

There are two diametrically opposite views on civil defense. Russian official policy holds that civil defense is feasible even in a nuclear war. American official policy, or at any rate the implementation of that policy, is based on the assumption that civil defense is useless.

The Russians, having learned a bitter lesson in the second world war, have bent every effort to defend their people under all circumstances. They are spending several billion dollars per year on this activity. They have effective plans to evacuate their cities before they let loose a nuclear strike. They have strong shelters for the people who must remain in the cities. They are building up protected food reserves to tide them over a critical period.

All this may mean that in a nuclear exchange, which we must try to avoid or to deter, the Russian deaths would probably not exceed ten million. Tragic as such a figure is, the Russian nation would survive. If they succeed in eliminating the United States they can commandeer food, machinery and manpower from the rest of the world. They could recover rapidly. They would have attained their goal: world domination.

In the American view the Russian plan is unfeasible. Those who argue on this side point out the great power of nuclear weapons. In this they are right. Their argument is particularly impressive in its psychological effect.

But this argument has never been backed up by a careful quantitative analysis which takes into account the planned dispersal and sheltering of the Russian population and the other measures which the Russians have taken and those to which they are committed.

That evacuation of our own citizens can be extremely useful if we see that the Russians are evacuating is simple common sense. With the use of American automobiles an evacuation could be faster and more effective than is possible in Russia. To carry it out we need not resort to the totalitarian methods of the iron curtain countries. It will suffice to warn our people and advise them where to go, how to protect themselves. The Federal Emergency Management Administration contains the beginnings on which such a policy might be built.

The present book does not, and indeed cannot, make the assumption that such minimal yet extremely useful government guidance will be available. Instead it outlines the skills that individuals or groups of individuals can learn and apply in order to improve their chances of survival.

This book is not a description of civil defense. It is a guide to "Stop-gap" civil defense which individuals could carry out for themselves, if need be, with no expenditures by our government. It fills the gap between the ineffective civil defense that we have today and the highly effective survival preparations that we could and should have a few years from now. However, if we go no further than what we can do on the basis of this book, then the United States cannot survive a major nuclear war.

Yet this book, besides being realistic and objectively correct, serves two extremely important purposes. One is: it will help to save lives. The second purpose is to show that with relatively inexpensive governmental guidance and supplies, an educated American public could, indeed, defend itself. We could survive a nuclear war and remain a nation.

This is an all-important goal. Its most practical aspect lies in the fact that the men in the Kremlin are cautious. If they cannot count on destroying us they probably will never launch their nuclear arsenal against us. Civil defense is at once the most peaceful and the most effective deterrent of nuclear war.

Some may argue that the Russians could evacuate again and again and thus, by forcing us into similar moves, exhaust us. I believe that in reality they would anger us sufficiently so that we would rearm in earnest. That is not what the Russians want to accomplish.

Others may say that the Russians could strike without previous evacuation. This could result in heavy losses on their part which, I hope, they will not risk.

Civil defense as here described will not eliminate the danger of nuclear war. It will considerably diminish its probability.

This book takes a long overdue step in educating the American people. It does not suggest that survival is easy. It does not prove that national survival is possible. But it can save lives and it will stimulate thought and action which will be crucial in our two main purposes: to preserve freedom and to avoid war.

Edward Teller

Edward Teller

ABOUT THE AUTHOR

When the U.S. Atomic Energy Commission authorized me in 1964 to initiate the Civil Defense Project at Oak Ridge National Laboratory, one of the first researchers I recruited was Cresson H. Kearny, the author of this book. Most of his life has been preparation, unplanned and planned, for writing this guide to help people not familiar with the effects of nuclear weapons improve their chances of surviving a nuclear attack. During the past 15 years he has done an unequaled amount of practical field work on basic survival problems, without always conforming with the changing civil defense doctrine.

After I returned to my professional duties at Princeton in 1966, the civil defense effort at Oak Ridge National Laboratory was first headed by James C. Bresee, and is now headed by Conrad V. Chester. Both have wholeheartedly supported Kearny's down-to-earth research, and Chester not only was a co-developer of several of the survival items described in this book, but also participated in the planning of the experiments testing them.

Kearny's concern with nuclear war dangers began while he was taking a degree in civil engineering at Princeton—he graduated summa cum laude in 1937. His Princeton studies had already acquainted him with the magnitude of an explosion in which nuclear energy is liberated, then only a theoretical possibility. After winning a Rhodes Scholarship, Kearny took two degrees in geology at Oxford. Still before the outbreak of World War II, he observed the very effective preparations made in England to reduce the effects of aerial attacks. He had a deep aversion to dictatorships, whether from the right or left, and during the Munich crisis he acted as a courier for an underground group helping anti-Nazis escape from Czechoslovakia.

Following graduation from Oxford, Kearny did geological exploration work in the Andes of Peru and in the jungles of Venezuela. He has traveled also in Mexico, China, and the Philippines.

A year before Pearl Harbor, realizing that the United States would soon be at war and that our jungle troops should have at least as good personal equipment, food, and individual medical supplies as do exploration geologists, he quit his job with the Standard Oil Company of Venezuela, returned to the United States, and went on active duty as an infantry reserve lieutenant. Kearny was soon assigned to Panama as the Jungle Experiment Officer of the Panama Mobile Force. In that capacity he was able to improve or invent, and then thoroughly jungle-test, much of the specialized equipment and rations

used by our jungle infantrymen in World War II. For this work he was promoted to major and awarded the Legion of Merit.

To take his chances in combat, in 1944 the author volunteered for duty with the Office of Strategic Services. As a demolition specialist helping to limit the Japanese invasion then driving into the wintry mountains of southern China, he saw mass starvation and death at close hand. The experiences gained in this capacity also resulted in an increased understanding of both the physical and the emotional problems of people whose country is under attack.

Worry about the increasing dangers of nuclear war and America's lack of civil defense caused the author in 1961 to consult Herman Kahn, a leading nuclear strategist. Kahn, who was at that time forming a nonprofit war-research organization, the Hudson Institute, offered him work as a research analyst. Two years of civil defense research in this "think tank" made the author much more knowledgeable of survival problems.

In 1964 he joined the Oak Ridge civil defense project and since then Oak Ridge has been Kearny's base of operations, except for two years during the height of the Viet Nam war. For his Viet Nam work on combat equipment, and also for his contributions to preparations for improving survivability in the event of a nuclear war, he received the Army's Decoration for Distinguished Civilian Service in 1972.

This book draws extensively on Kearny's understanding of the problems of civil defense acquired as a result of his own field testing of shelters and other survival needs, and also from an intensive study of the serious civil defense preparations undertaken by other countries, including Switzerland, Sweden, the USSR, and China. He initiated and edited the Oak Ridge National Laboratory translations of Soviet civil defense handbooks and of a Chinese manual, and gained additional knowledge from these new sources. Trips to England, Europe, and Israel also increased his information on survival measures, and this also contributed to the *Nuclear War Survival Skills*. However, the book advocates principally those do-it-yourself instructions that field tests have proved to be practical.

Eugene P. Wigner

Eugene P. Wigner

UNRESTRICTED INTRODUCTION

The scientific facts and the field-tested survival instructions given in this book have not been censored or otherwise restricted. However, as long as I was a civil defense specialist based at Oak Ridge National Laboratory, I was not permitted to criticize important Government policies, strategies, or politicans. Therefore, in order to be able to write and speak freely on these important matters, in late 1979 I retired from that Government-owned laboratory. Now to this Unrestricted Introduction I am free to state politically sensitive facts about America's civil defense weaknesses and needs.

WHY YOU AND YOUR FAMILY AND ALMOST ALL OTHER AMERICANS ARE LEFT UNPROTECTED HOSTAGES TO THE SOVIET UNION

Unknown to most of us, our Government continues to rely on a uniquely American strategic policy called Mutual Assured Destruction by its advocates, and MAD by its opponents. Almost unbelievably, Mutual Assured Destruction is the name that the civilian strategists in the Kennedy Administration gave to their new strategic policy intended to prevent nuclear war. MAD maintains that if both the United States and Russia do not or cannot adequately protect their people and industries, then neither will threaten nor attack the other. The influential minority of Americans who still have faith in Mutual Assured Destruction and who still control our strategic policies believe that if Americans and our vital industries were protected effectively, this would accelerate the arms race and increase the risk of war. No wonder that even a proposed small increase in funding for civil defense arouses stronger opposition than do most of the much larger increases in expenditures for weapons!

No nation other than the United States has advocated or adopted a strategy that purposely leaves its citizens unprotected hostages to its enemies. The rulers of the Soveit Union continue to prepare the Russians to fight, survive, and win a nuclear war. In contrast, influential Americans continue to demoralize us with exaggerated descriptions of nuclear war. Beginning with President Kennedy, all our Presidents have described nuclear war as "the end of mankind", or the like. This notwithstanding the fact that researchers on the effects of nuclear weapons know that although an all-out nuclear war between Russia and the United States would be the worst catastrophe in history, it would not be the end of mankind or of

civilization. Today an all-out Soviet attack would result in only about 3% of the area of our country suffering blast and fire damage severe enough to destroy homes and kill most of the occupants! Many millions of unprepared Americans would survive the very wide-spread radiation dangers from fallout and post-attack privations. Tens of millions of additional lives could be saved if even low-cost, realistic preparations were made -- especially realistic preparations for evacuating our cities and rapidly building good expedient shelters during a worsening crisis.

RUSSIAN PREPARATIONS TO SURVIVE AND WIN A NUCLEAR WAR

In contrast to American Presidents who have refused to support a serious civil defense effort, the rulers of the Soviet Union have spent billions of preparations to enable the big majority of Russians to survive a nuclear war - including building many permanent blast shelters. The Russians have learned from the devastating wars they have survived that people are the most important asset to be saved. Russian civil defense publications emphasize Lenin's justly famous statement:

"The primary productive factor of all humanity is the laboring man, the worker. If he survives, we can save everything and restore everything...but we shall perish if we are not able to save him." Strategists conclude that those in power in the Soviet Union will neither threaten nuclear war in a confrontation nor launch a nuclear attack until they have evacuated and sheltered most of their people.

The rulers of the Soviet Union know that the costly preparations that Russians have made to survive nuclear war have greatly strengthened their capabilities to win confrontations and extend Russian dominion without resorting to war. Small wonder that the Soviet negotiators of strategic arms limitation treaties have refused even to discuss the possibility raised by the Carter Administration of both the Soviet Union and the United States agreeing to limit their civil defense efforts.

Differing estimates of the Soviet Union's civil defense efforts indicate that its annual outlay for war survival and recovery preparations, if they were made at costs equivalent to those in the United States, would range from $8 to $20 for each Russian. Meanwhile, our Government continues to spend only about 50 cents yearly to protect each American against both the danger of nuclear war and natural disasters. Some democratic countries are much more realistic than America. Switzerland, according to the Swiss Civil Defense Magazine of November - December 1977, annually spends $10.85 per citizen on civil defense.

THE NEED FOR RELIABLE INSTRUCTIONS FOR BUILDING EXPEDIENT SHELTERS AND ESSENTIAL LIFE-SUPPORT EQUIPMENT

Our country's civil defense organization, the Federal Emergency Management Administration, is slowly working on urban evacuation plans called Crisis Relocation Planning. This promising official effort includes the preparation and field testing of instructions for making expedient shelters and a few expedient life-support items. For years it has been the policy of U.S. civil defense organizations to prepare abbreviated survival instructions for distribution to the public during a possible crisis. Official printed instructions for making a shelter or a survival item each have been limited to about a page. Field tests in 1977 of such abbreviated instructions have shown that typical American families, building shelters and homemade air pumps under simulated crisis conditions, have taken longer and made more mistakes than have smiliar families who followed the step-by-step, detained instructions given in this book. For example, 16 families each followed one-page instructions and built one of seven types of expedient shelters; each family found it necessary to spend a long time (an average of 88 minutes) studying the abbreviated instructions for building the assigned shelter. But even these inadequate instructions for good expedient shelters have not been readied for crisis distribution.

Ten of these 16 families attempted to follow the abbreviated instructions for making a homemade air pump of the type described in this book for ventilating and cooling shelters. Only four of the 10 succeeded in making a pump that worked. In contrast, almost all of the dozens of different families who have followed the step-by-step instructions given in this book for making a ventilating pump have succeeded.

Highly protective, earth-covered expedient shelters have not advocated or described in our official evacuation plan today, apparently because many urban Americans would be unable to build such shelters and because Washington officials under-estimate the intelligence and resourcefulness of typical Americans. The offical plans call for using existing buildings for shelters wherever buildings are available, even if a crisis were to last

two or more days, long enough to enable tens of millions of properly instructed citizens to build earth-covered expedient shelters giving much better protection.

Although civil defense specialists from Washington to Moscow know that people cannot survive in crowded, long-occupied shelters without adequate ventilation-cooling, to date the years-old instructions featured in this book for making an efficient homemade shelter-ventilating pump have not been given even to civil defense directors of towns and cities. Furthermore, some official civil defense pamphlets continue to picture expedient shelters that would collapse if built as specified or that would be death traps if occupied in warm or hot weather. An example is the door-covered trench shelter pictured in "In Time of Emergency", a survival pamphlet first published by the millions after the Cuban Missile Crisis and still stocked in large numbers for distribution during a crisis. This small, earth-covered trench shelter has only one opening, a hole at one end. A similar official pamphlet published in 1977, "Protection in the Nuclear Age", has a redrawn sketch of this same shelter. If during warm or hot weather a family were forced by heavy fallout to occupy this shelter for days, some members would die from heat prostration. It is immoral for any government to continue to advise its citizens to build shelters of types that its engineers have come to realize would be death traps if used as intended.

Nuclear War Survival Skills brings together field-tested instructions that have enabled untrained Americans to make expedient fallout shelters, air pumps to ventilate and cool shelters, homemade fallout meters, and other expedient life-support equipment. ("Expedient," as used in civil defense work, describes equipment that can be made by untrained citizens in 48 hours or less, while guided solely by field-tested, written instructions and using only widely available materials and tools.) Successive versions of these instructions have been used repeatedly and successfully by families working under simulated crisis conditions. These instructions have been improved repeatedly by Oak Ridge National Laboratory civil defense researchers over a period of eight years and are the heart of this book.

PRACTICALITY OF MAKING SURVIVAL PREPARATIONS DURING A CRISIS

The emphasis in this book is on survival preparations that can be made in the last few days of a worsening crisis. However, the measures put into effect during such a crisis can be very much more effective if plans and some preparations are completed well in advance. It is hoped that perons who read this book will be motivated at least to make the preparations outlined in Chapter 16, Minimum Pre-Crisis Preparations.

Well-informed persons realize that a nuclear attack is unlikely to be a Pearl Harbor type of attack, launched without warning. Strategists agree that a nuclear war would most likely begin after a period of days-to-months of worsening crisis. The most realistic of the extensive Russian plans and preparations to survive a nuclear war are based on using at least several days during an escalating crisis to get most urban dwellers out of the cities, to build or improve shelters in all parts of the Soviet Union, and to protect essential machinery and the like. Our satellites and other sources of intelligence would reveal such massive movements within a day; therefore, under the most likely circumstances Americans would have several days in which to make life-saving preparations. The Russians know that if they are able to complete evacuation and sheltering plans before the outbreak of nuclear war, the number of their people killed would be a small fraction of those who otherwise would die.

Nuclear weapons that could strike the United States continue to increase in both number and accuracy. The Soviet Union already has enough to target all American cities, major military targets, and long runways. The most modern warheads usually can hit within a few hundred yards of their precise targets. Because most Americans live in cities, their best chance of surviving a heavy nuclear attack is to get out of cities and into shelters away from probable target areas before the attack. Many American civil defense advocates believe it would be desirable for our government to build and stock permanent shelters, widely dispersed outside probable target areas. However, such permanent shelters would cost many billions of dollars and would be in competition with other more immediate needs requiring large expenditures of government funds. Therefore, field-tested instructions and plans are needed to enable both urban evacuees and rural Americans to build high-protection-factor expedient shelters and life-support equipment during a crisis.

WHY, EXOTIC WEAPONS ARE NOT DISCUSSED

Chemical and biological weapons and neu-

tron warheads are called "exotic weapons." Protective measures against these weapons are not discussed, because the purpose of this handbook is to help Americans improve their chances of surviving what is by far the most likely type of attack on the United States: a nuclear war.

Chemical weapons are inefficient killing agents compared to large nuclear warheads and bombs. Exterminating the unprepared population of a specified large area would require a delivered payload of deadly chemical weapons many thousands of times heavier than that needed if large nuclear weapons were employed.

Biological weapons are unreliable. Unless the meteorological conditions were favorable over the entire country at the same time, viruses and bacteria could not be effectively dispersed for spreading disease.

Neutron warheads are very small, yet extremely expensive. A 1-kiloton neutron warhead costs about as much as a 1-megaton ordinary warhead, but the ordinary warhead not only has 1000 times the explosive power but also can be surface-burst to cover a very large area with deadly fallout.

WHY THIS BOOK DOES NOT HAVE A CHAPTER ON SELF-DEFENSE

This book does not give advice on self-defense after a nuclear attack, for the following reasons:

There is no need to tell people that they may need their guns; even during my field-test evacuations, some families took along their firearms, although the Evacuation Check Lists that they were given made no mention of weapons.

Having trained both ordinary infantrymen and specialized jungle troops, I know that merely giving people a few pages to read will not enable them to become competent in the use of weapons or in defensive tactics.

The histories of great famines, from those in Ireland to famines I witnessed in China and India, belie the sensational forecasts of some "survivalists" who maintain that after a nuclear attack America will degenerate into a state of unprecedented anarchy, that we will behave like starving rats. In a famine, some people do rob and kill for food, and a very few become cannibals. But the big majority continue to maintain civilized values while they starve. And in America, where tens of millions of us have firearms, armed robbers would be killed off much sooner that they have been eliminated in starving lands where only a few people have guns.

RECOMMENDED ACTIONS BEFORE A CRISIS

During a crisis threatening nuclear attack, present uncertainties relative to the adoption and distribution of crisis information seem likely to continue. Thoroughly field-tested survival instructions may not be available to the majority of our people. Furthermore, even a highly intelligent citizen, if given the best possible instructions during a crisis, would not have time to learn basic facts about nuclear dangers and the reasons for various survival preparations. Without this understanding, a person cannot do his best at following any type of survival instructions.

A prudent citizen is advised to obtain and study the best instructions available before a crisis occurs. Better yet, he should make preparations, such as the low-cost ones described in this book, to increase his and his family's chances of surviving.

By following the instructions in this book, you and your family can increase the odds favoring your survival. If such instructions were made available and our government urged all Americans to follow them during a worsening crisis, additional millions would survive an attack. And the danger of an attack, even the threat of an attack, would be decreased if any enemy nation knew that we had significantly improved our defenses in this way.

HOW YOU AND OTHER REALISTIC AMERICANS CAN IMPROVE OUR CHANCES OF PREVENTING OR SURVIVING NUCLEAR WAR

Our Government's dependency on Mutal Assured Destruction is the principal roadblock to effective civil defense. As long as MAD for all practical purposes is our governing policy, most Americans will remain unprotected hostages to the Sovient Union.

An increasing number of well informed citizens have concluded that the MAD policy of keeping Americans hostage to our enemies is morally wrong and undermines our hopes for freedom and survival. For example, Bardyl R. Tirana, after his retirement in 1979 as the last

Director of Defense Civil Preparedness Agency (DCPA), wrote a most informative paper entitled "Civil Defense: the Unthinkable and the Non-doable." Tirana, who was one of our most conscientious and able national civil defense directors, expressed part of his frustration and anger in these words: "I do not understand or accept the morality of a policy which requires that the lives of innocent children, women and men, whether Soviet or American, be held hostage to the political power and authority of the leaders of either nation. I think it immoral for national leadership to fail to plan for national survival and population protection."

Bardyl R. Tirana, while Director of DCPA, told me that the decision to give the best available do-it-yourself survival instructions to his civil defense directors would have to be made at a higher level that his. Apparently up to now no such decision has been made; the Federal Emergency Management Administration (FEMA), that assumed responsibilities for civil defense after DCPA was abolished, has neither destroyed its life-endangering survival instructions nor made improved do-it-yourself instructions available to the public.

I am not alone in concluding that the best short-term hope for improving Americans' chances of surviving a nuclear attack is for private organizations to make widely available field-tested, do-it-yourself survival instructions, such as are given in this book, and for concerned citizens to use these instructions to the best of their abilities. Our best longer-term hope is that the increasing number of American leaders and other concerned citizens who realize the importance of civil defense will cause our Government to abandon its immoral, self-defeating Mutual Assured Destruction policy of leaving the American people unprotected hostages to our enemies, and to adopt more realistic strategies and policies. Only then will effective civil defense preparations be made an important part of U.S. capabilities to maintain peace through strength, or to save tens of millions from death if deterrence fails and nuclear war strikes.

You can do your part both by making preparations to improve your and your family's chances of surviving and by working against MAD and for greatly improved civil defense.

—Cresson H. Kearny
February 1980

Chapter 1

The Dangers from Nuclear Weapons: Myths and Facts

An all-out nuclear war between Russia and the United States would be the worst catastrophe in history, a tragedy so huge it is difficult to comprehend. Even so, it would be far from the end of human life on earth. The dangers from nuclear weapons have been distorted and exaggerated, for varied reasons. These exaggerations have become demoralizing myths, believed by millions of Americans.

While working with hundreds of Americans building expedient shelters and life-support equipment, I have found that many people at first see no sense in talking about details of survival skills. Those who hold exaggerated beliefs about the dangers from nuclear weapons must first be convinced that nuclear war would not inevitably be the end of them and everything worthwhile. Only after they have begun to question the truth of these myths do they become interested, under normal peacetime conditions, in acquiring nuclear war survival skills. Therefore, before giving detailed instructions for making and using survival equipment, we will examine the most harmful of the myths about nuclear war dangers, along with some of the grim facts.

● **Myth**: Fallout radiation from a nuclear war would poison the air and all parts of the environment. It would kill everyone. (This is the demoralizing message of *On the Beach* and many similar pseudo-scientific books and articles.)

● **Facts**: When a nuclear weapon explodes near enough to the ground for its fireball to touch the ground, it forms a crater. (See Fig. 1.1.) Many

ORNL-DWG 78-6264

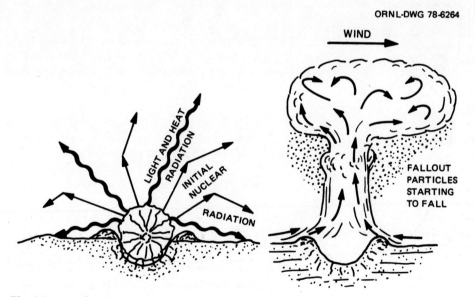

Fig. 1.1. A surface burst. In a surface burst, the fireball touches the ground and blasts a crater.

9

thousands of tons of earth from the crater of a large explosion are pulverized into trillions of particles. These particles are contaminated by radioactive atoms produced by the nuclear explosion. Thousands of tons of the particles are carried up into a mushroom-shaped cloud, miles above the earth. These radioactive particles then fall out of the mushroom cloud, or out of the dispersing cloud of particles blown by the winds—thus becoming fallout.

Each sand-like, contaminated particle continuously gives off invisible radiation, much like a tiny X-ray machine—while in the mushroom cloud, while descending, and after having fallen to earth. The descending radioactive particles are carried by the winds like the sand and dust particles of a miles-thick sandstorm cloud—except that they usually are blown at lower speeds and in many areas the particles are so far apart that no cloud is seen. The largest, heaviest fallout particles reach the ground first, in locations close to the explosion. Many smaller particles are carried by the winds for tens to hundreds of miles before falling to earth. At any one place where fallout from a single explosion is being deposited on the ground in concentrations high enough to require the use of shelters, deposition will be completed within a few hours.

The smallest fallout particles—those tiny enough to be inhaled into a person's lungs—are invisible to the naked eye. These tiny particles fall so slowly, from heights miles above the earth, that the winds carry them thousands of miles away from the site of the explosion before they reach the ground.

The air in properly designed fallout shelters, even those without air filters, is free of radioactive particles and safe to breathe except in a few rare environments—as will be explained later.

Fortunately for all living things, the danger from fallout radiation lessens with time. The radioactive decay, as this lessening is called, is rapid at first, then gets slower and slower. The dose rate (the amount of radiation received per hour) decreases accordingly. Figure 1.2 illustrates the rapidity of the decay of radiation from fallout during the first two days after the nuclear explosion that produced it. R stands for roentgen, a measurement unit often used to measure exposure to gamma rays and X rays. Fallout meters called dosimeters measure the *dose* received by recording the number of R. Fallout meters called survey meters, or dose-rate meters, measure the *dose rate* by recording the number of R being received per hour at the time of measurement. Notice that it takes about seven times as long for the dose rate to decay

ORNL-DWG 78-8265

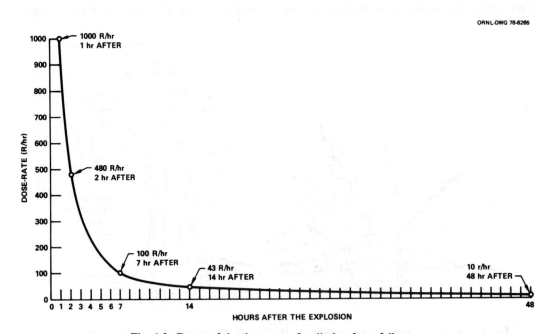

Fig. 1.2. Decay of the dose rate of radiation from fallout.

from 1000 roentgens per hour (1000 R/hr) to 10 R/hr (48 hours) as to decay from 1000 R/hr to 100 R/hr (7 hours). (Only in high-fallout areas would the dose rate 1 hour after the explosion be as high as 1000 roentgens per hour.)

If the dose rate 1 hour after an explosion is 1000 R/hr, it would take about 2 weeks for the dose rate to be reduced to 1 R/hr solely as a result of radioactive decay. Weathering effects will reduce the dose rate further; for example, rain can wash fallout particles from plants and houses to lower positions on or closer to the ground. Surrounding objects would reduce the radiation dose from these low-lying particles.

Figure 1.2 also illustrates the fact that at a typical location where a given amount of fallout from an explosion is deposited later than 1 hour after the explosion, the highest dose rate and the total dose received at that location are less than at a location where the same amount of fallout is deposited 1 hour after the explosion. The longer fallout particles have been airborne before reaching the ground, the less dangerous is their radiation.

Within two weeks after an attack the occupants of most shelters could safely stop using them, or could work outside the shelters for an increasing number of hours each day. Exceptions would be in areas of extremely heavy fallout such as might occur downwind from important targets attacked with many weapons, especially missile sites and very large cities. To know when to come out safely, occupants either would need a reliable fallout meter to measure the changing radiation dangers, or must receive information based on measurements made nearby with a reliable instrument.

The radiation dose that will kill a person varies considerably with different people. A dose of 450 R resulting from exposure of the whole body to fallout radiation is often said to be the dose that will kill about half the persons receiving it, although most studies indicate that it would take somewhat less.[1] *(Note: A number written after a statement refers the reader to a source listed in the Selected References that follow Appendix D.)* Almost all persons confined to expedient shelters after a nuclear attack would be under stress and without clean surroundings or antibiotics to fight infections. Many also would lack adequate water and food. Under these unprecedented conditions, perhaps half the persons who received a whole-body dose of 350 R within a few days would die.[2]

Fortunately, the human body can repair most radiation damage if the daily radiation doses are not too large. As will be explained in Appendix B, a person who is healthy and has not been exposed in the past two weeks to a total radiation dose of more than 100 R can receive a dose of 6 R each day for at least two months without being incapacitated.

Only a very small fraction of Hiroshima and Nagasaki citizens who survived radiation doses— some of which were nearly fatal—have suffered serious delayed effects. The reader should realize that to do essential work after a massive nuclear attack, many survivors must be willing to receive much larger radiation doses than are normally permissible. Otherwise, too many workers would stay inside shelter too much of the time, and work that would be vital to national recovery could not be done. For example, if the great majority of truckers were so fearful of receiving even non-incapacitating radiation doses that they would refuse to transport food, additional millions would die from starvation alone.

● **Myth**: Fallout radiation penetrates everything; there is no escaping its deadly effects.

● **Facts**: Some gamma radiation from fallout will penetrate the shielding materials of even an excellent shelter and reach its occupants. However, the radiation dose that the occupants of an excellent shelter would receive while inside this shelter can be reduced to a dose smaller than the average American receives during his lifetime from X rays and other radiation exposures normal in America today. The design features of such a shelter include the use of a sufficient thickness of earth or other heavy shielding material. Gamma rays are like X rays, but more penetrating. Figure 1.3 shows how rapidly gamma rays are reduced in number (but not in their ability to penetrate) by layers of packed earth. Each of the layers shown is one halving-thickness of packed earth—about 3.6 inches (9 centimeters).[3] A halving-thickness is the thickness of a material which reduces by half the dose of radiation that passes through it.

The actual paths of gamma rays passing through shielding materials are much more complicated, due to scattering, etc., than are the straight-line paths shown in Fig. 1.3. But when averaged out, the effectiveness of a halving-thickness of any material is approximately as shown. The denser a substance, the better it serves for shielding material. Thus, a halving-thickness of concrete is only about 2.4 inches (6.1 cm).

Fig. 1.3. **Illustration of shielding against fallout radiation.** Note the increasingly large improvements in the attenuation (reduction) factors that are attained as each additional halving-thickness of packed earth is added.

If additional halving-thicknesses of packed earth shielding are successively added to the five thicknesses shown in Fig. 1.3, the protection factor (PF) is successively increased from 32 to 64, to 128, to 256, to 512, to 1024, and so on.

● **Myth**: A heavy nuclear attack would set practically everything on fire, causing "firestorms" in cities that would exhaust the oxygen in the air. All shelter occupants would be killed by the intense heat.

● **Facts**: On a clear day, thermal pulses (heat radiation that travels at the speed of light) from an air burst can set fire to easily ignitable materials (such as window curtains, upholstery, dry newspaper, and dry grass) over about as large an area as is damaged by the blast. It can cause second-degree skin burns to exposed people who are as far as ten miles from a one-megaton (1 MT) explosion. (See Fig. 1.4.) (A 1-MT nuclear explosion is one that produces the same amount of energy as does one million tons of TNT.) If the weather is very clear and dry, the area of fire danger could be considerably larger. On a cloudy or smoggy day, however, particles in the air would absorb and scatter much of the heat radiation, and the area endangered by heat radiation from the fireball would be less than the area of severe blast damage.

Fig. 1.4. An air burst. The fireball does not touch the ground. No crater, no deadly local fallout. The blast effects, the thermal pulses of intense light and heat radiation, and the very penetrating initial nuclear radiation are the main dangers.

"Firestorms" could occur only when the concentration of combustible structures is very high, as in the very dense centers of a few old American cities. At rural and suburban building densities, most people in earth-covered fallout shelters would have nothing to fear from fire.

● **Myth:** In the worst-hit parts of Hiroshima and Nagasaki where all buildings were demolished, everyone was killed by blast, radiation, or fire.

● **Facts:** In Nagasaki, some people survived uninjured who were far inside tunnel shelters built for conventional air raids and located as close as one-third mile from ground zero (the point directly below the explosion). This was true even though these long, large shelters lacked blast doors and were deep inside the zone within which all buildings were destroyed. (People far inside long, large, open shelters are better protected than are those inside small, open shelters.)

Many earth-covered family shelters were essentially undamaged in areas where blast and fire destroyed all buildings. Figure 1.5 shows a typical earth-covered, backyard family shelter with a crude wooden frame. This shelter was essentially undamaged, although less than 100 yards from ground

Fig. 1.5. Undamaged earth-covered family shelter in Nagasaki.

zero at Nagasaki.[4] The calculated maximum over-pressure (pressure above the normal air pressure) was about 65 pounds per square inch (65 psi). Persons inside so small a shelter without a blast door would have been killed by blast pressure at this distance from the explosion. However, in a recent blast test,[5] an earth-covered, expedient Small-Pole Shelter equipped with blast doors was undamaged at 53 psi. The pressure rise inside was slight—not even enough to have damaged occupants' eardrums. If poles are available, field tests have indicated that many families can build such shelters in a few days.

The great life-saving potential of blast-protective shelters has been proven in war and confirmed by blast tests and calculations. For example, the area in which the surface-bursting of a 20-megaton weapon would wreck a 50-psi shelter with blast doors is about 17 square miles. Within this roughly circular area, practically all the occupants of wrecked shelters would be killed by blast, carbon monoxide from fires, or radiation. The same blast effects would kill most people who were using basements affording 5 psi protection, over an area of about 186 square miles.[6]

● **Myth:** Because some modern H-bombs are over 1000 times as powerful as the A-bomb that destroyed most of Hiroshima, these H-bombs are 1000 times as deadly and destructive.

● **Facts:** A nuclear weapon 1000 times as powerful as the one that blasted Hiroshima, if exploded under comparable conditions, produces equally serious blast damage to wood-frame houses over an area up to about 130 times as large, not 1000 times as large. However, the blast areas of multimegaton nuclear explosions are impressively large, and Americans concerned with survival should be aware of the destructive power of these huge weapons. For instance, a Soviet SS-9 missile reportedly can deliver a 20-megaton warhead. The explosion from such a weapon would release the same amount of energy as the explosion of 20 million tons of TNT. If a 20-megaton weapon were surface-burst (Fig. 1.1), the great majority of homes at least would be severely damaged to a distance of 10 to 11 miles from ground zero. Within a roughly circular area of about 350 square miles, homes would be severely damaged or completely destroyed.

In and close to the crater area of a large surface burst, even the best blast shelters would be obliterated or buried. In wet, hard rock, a 20-megaton contact surface burst would blast a crater about 550 feet deep. The ringlike, 200-foot-high hill of ejected rock around the crater would be almost a mile across.

If a weapon is air-burst (see Fig. 1.4) at the most advantageous height to produce on the maximum area overpressures that are at least as high as a desired overpressure, it will cover with the desired blast effect an area that is about twice as large as the same weapon would cover if it were surface-burst. A 20-megaton air burst over the center of a great city would cause severe damage to homes as far as 16 miles from ground zero. Nearer to ground zero, the blast damage would be worse. However, the air-bursting of weapons would not result in the often deadly fallout particles that reach the ground within 24 hours after a surface burst. Therefore, for Americans outside target areas, this would be a less dangerous attack than if weapons were surface-burst.

Although some strategists maintain that a limited attack is more probable than a massive one, the author believes it prudent to prepare for the worst possible attack. So let us suppose that an enemy strikes U.S. missile sites and other U.S. military targets with about 40% of its approximately 10,000 megatons of intercontinental nuclear weapons, with another 40% hitting American industries and cities with surface bursts. Most cities would be destroyed by warheads much smaller than 20 megatons. Such a massive attack could subject urban and suburban areas where some 140 million Americans live to blast effects sufficiently intense to destroy essentially all homes. Without well-supplied blast shelters, most urban Americans who would have remained in their cities would be killed by blast, fire, and very heavy fallout. Most Americans would greatly improve their chances of surviving a nuclear attack if they were to evacuate probable target areas before an attack and make or improve fallout shelters in dispersed locations outside these most threatened areas.

● **Myth:** So much food and water will be poisoned by fallout that people will starve and die even in fallout areas where there is enough food and water.

● **Facts:** If the fallout particles do not become mixed with the parts of food that are eaten, no harm is done. Food and water in dust-tight containers are not contaminated by fallout radiation. Peeling fruits and vegetables removes essentially all fallout, as does removing the uppermost several inches of stored grain onto which fallout particles have fallen. Water from many sources—such as deep wells and covered reservoirs, tanks, and containers—would not be contaminated. Even water containing dissolved radioactive elements and compounds can be made safe for drinking by simply filtering it through earth, as described later in this book.

● **Myth:** Most of the unborn children and grandchildren of people who have been exposed to radiation from nuclear explosions will be genetically damaged—will be malformed, delayed victims of nuclear war.

● **Facts:** The authoritative study by the National Academy of Sciences, *A Thirty Year Study of the Survivors of Hiroshima and Nagasaki,* was published in 1977. It concludes that the incidence of abnormalities is no higher among children later conceived by parents who were exposed to radiation during the attacks on Hiroshima and Nagasaki than is the incidence of abnormalities among Japanese children born to unexposed parents.

This is not to say that there would be no genetic damage, nor that some fetuses subjected to large radiation doses would not be damaged. But the overwhelming evidence does show that the exaggerated fears of radiation damage to future generations are not supported by scientific findings.

● **Myth:** Overkill would result if all the U.S. and U.S.S.R. nuclear weapons were used—meaning not only that the two superpowers have more than enough weapons to kill all of each other's people, but also that they have enough weapons to exterminate the human race.

● **Facts:** Statements that the U.S. and the Soviet Union have the power to kill the world's population several times over are based on misleading calculations. One such calculation is to multiply the deaths produced per kiloton exploded over Hiroshima or Nagasaki by an estimate of the number of kilotons in either side's arsenal. (A kiloton explosion is one that produces the same amount of energy as does 1000 tons of TNT.) The unstated assumption is that somehow the world's population could be gathered into circular crowds, each a few miles in diameter with a population density equal to downtown Hiroshima or Nagasaki, and then a small (Hiroshima-sized) weapon would be exploded over the center of each crowd. Other misleading calculations are based on exaggerations of the dangers from long-lasting radiation and other harmful effects of a nuclear war.

Chapter 2
Psychological Preparations

LEARNING WHAT TO EXPECT

The more one knows about the strange and fearful dangers from nuclear weapons and about the strengths and weaknesses of human beings when confronted with the dangers of war, the better chance one has of surviving. Terror, a self-destructive emotion, is almost always the result of unexpected danger. Some people would think the end of the world was upon them if they happened to be in an area downwind from surface bursts of nuclear weapons that sucked millions of tons of pulverized earth into the air. They might give up all hope if they did not understand what they saw. People are more likely to endure and survive if they learn in advance that such huge dust clouds, particularly if combined with smoke from great fires, may turn day into night—as have some volcanic eruptions and the largest forest fires.

People also should expect thunder to crash in strange clouds, and the earth to shake. The sky may be lit with the flickering purples and greens of "artificial auroras" caused by nuclear explosions, especially those that are miles above the earth.

FEAR

Fear often is a life-saving emotion. When we believe death is close at hand, fear can increase our ability to work harder and longer. Driven by fear, we can accomplish feats that would be impossible otherwise. Trembling hands, weak legs, and cold sweat do not mean that a person has become ineffective. Doing hard, necessary work is one of the best ways to keep one's fears under control.

Brave men and women who are self-confident admit their fears, even when the threat of death is remote. Then they plan and work to lessen the causes of their fears. (When the author helped Charles A. Lindbergh design a reinforced-concrete blast shelter for his family and neighbors, Lindbergh frankly admitted that he feared both nuclear attack and being trapped. He was able to lessen both of these fears by building an excellent blast shelter with two escape openings.)

TERROR

If the danger is unexpected enough or great enough, normal persons sometimes experience terror as well as fear. Terror prevents the mind from evaluating dangers and thinking logically. It develops in two stages, which have been described by Dr. Walo von Gregerz, a physician with much war experience, in his book *Psychology of Survival*. The first stage is apathy: people become indifferent to their own safety and are unable even to try to save themselves or their families. The second stage is a compulsion to flee.

Anxiety, fear, and terror can result in symptoms very similar to those caused by radiation injury: nausea, vomiting, extreme trembling, diarrhea. Dr. von Gregerz has described terror as being "explosively contagious." However, persons who learn to understand the nature of our inherent human traits and behavior and symptoms are less likely to become terrorized and ineffective in the event of a nuclear attack.

EMOTIONAL PARALYSIS

The most common reaction to great danger is not terror, but a kind of numbing of the emotions which actually may be helpful. Dr. von Gregerz calls this "emotional paralysis." This reaction allows many persons, when in the grip of great danger, to avoid being overwhelmed by compassionate emotions and horrible sights. It permits them to think clearly and act effectively.

ATOM BOMB SURVIVORS

The atomic explosions that destroyed most of Hiroshima and Nagasaki were air bursts and therefore produced no deadly local fallout. So we cannot be sure how people would behave in areas subjected to both blast and fallout from surface bursts. However, the reactions of the Japanese survivors are encouraging, especially in view of the fact that among them the relative number of horribly burned people was greater than is likely to be found among a population that expects a nuclear attack and takes any sort of shelter. Dr. von Gregerz summarizes: "In most cases the victims were, of course, apathetic and often incapable of rational action, but open panic or extremely disorganized behavior occurred only in exceptional cases among the hundreds of thousands of survivors of the two atomic bombing attacks." Also encouraging: ". . . serious permanent psychological derangements were rare after the atomic bomb attacks, just as they were after the large-scale conventional bombings."

HELP FROM FELLOW AMERICANS

Some maintain that after an atomic attack America would degenerate into anarchy—an every-man-for-himself struggle for existence. They forget the history of great human catastrophes and the self-sacrificing strengths most human beings are capable of displaying. After a massive nuclear attack starvation would afflict some areas, but America's grain-producing regions still would have an abundance of uncontaminated food. History indicates that Americans in the food-rich areas would help the starving. Like the heroic Russians who drove food trucks to starving Leningrad through bursting Nazi bombs and shells,[7] many Americans would risk radiation and other dangers to bring truckloads of grain and other necessities to their starving countrymen. Surely, an essential part of psychological preparations for surviving a modern war is a well-founded assurance that many citizens of a strong society will struggle to help each other and will work together with little regard for danger and loss.

Chapter 3

Warnings and Communications

IMPORTANCE OF ADEQUATE WARNING

When Hiroshima and Nagasaki were blasted by the first nuclear weapons ever to be used in war, very few of the tens of thousands of Japanese killed or injured were inside their numerous air raid shelters. The single-plane attacks caught them by surprise. People are not saved by having shelters nearby unless they receive warning in time to reach their shelters— and unless they heed that warning.

TYPES OF WARNINGS

Warnings are of two types, strategic and tactical.

● **Strategic warning** is based on observed enemy actions that are believed to be preparations for an attack. For example, we would have strategic warning if powerful Russian armies were advancing into western Europe and Soviet leaders were threatening massive nuclear destruction if the resisting nations should begin to use tactical nuclear weapons. With strategic warning being given by news broadcasts and newspapers over a period of days, Americans in areas that are probably targeted would have time to evacuate. Given a day or more of warning, tens of millions of us could build or improve shelters and in other ways improve our chances of surviving the feared attack. By doing so, we also would help decrease the risk of attack.

● **Tactical warning** of a nuclear attack on the United States would be received by our highest officials a few minutes after missiles or other nuclear weapons had been launched against our country. Radar, satellites, and other sophisticated means of detection would begin to feed information into our military warning systems almost at once. This raw

information would have to be evaluated, and top-level decisions would have to be made. Then attack warnings would have to be transmitted down to communities all over America.

Tactical warning (attack warning) of an out-of-the-blue, Pearl-Harbor-type attack would be less likely to be received by the average American than would an attack warning given after recognized strategic warning. However, the short time (only 20 to 40 minutes) that would elapse between missile launchings and the resultant first explosions on targets in the United States would make it difficult for even an excellent warning system to alert the majority of Americans in time for them to reach the best available nearby shelter.

Strengths and weaknesses of the present official warning system are summarized in the following two sections. Then the life-saving warnings that the first nuclear explosions would give, especially to informed people, are described.

OFFICIAL WARNING SYSTEM

The U.S. official warning system is designed to give civilians timely warning by means of siren signals and radio and television announcements. The National Warning System (NAWAS) is a wire-line network which is to provide attack information to official warning points nationwide. When the information is received at warning points by the officials who are responsible, they will sound local sirens and initiate radio and TV emergency broadcasts—if power has not failed. Officials at NAWAS warning points include many local civil defense directors. NAWAS receives information from our constantly improving military warning and communications systems.

SIREN WARNINGS

The Attack Warning Signal is a wavering, wailing sound on the sirens lasting three to five minutes, or a series of short blasts on whistles or horns. After a brief pause, it is repeated. This signal means only one thing: take protective action—go promptly to the best available shelter. Do not try to telephone for information; get information from a radio broadcast after you reach shelter. It is Federal policy that the Attack Warning Signal will not be sounded unless an enemy attack on the United States has been detected. However, since local authorities may not follow this policy, the reader is advised to check the plans in his community before a crisis arises.

The following limitations of attack warnings given by sirens and broadcasting stations should be recognized:

● Only a relatively small fraction of urban Americans could hear the sirens in the present city systems, especially if most urban citizens had evacuated during a crisis.

● Except in a crisis threatening the outbreak of nuclear war at any moment, most people who would hear the attack warning signal either would not recognize it or would not believe it was a warning of actual attack.

● A coordinated enemy attack may include the detonation of a few submarine-launched ballistic missiles (SLBMs) at high altitudes over the United States within two or three minutes of the launching of hundreds of SLBMs and intercontinental ballistic missiles (ICBMs). Such high-altitude bursts would produce electromagnetic pulse (EMP) effects primarily intended to knock out or disrupt U.S. military communications. These EMP effects also could knock out the public power necessary to sound sirens and could put most unprotected broadcasting stations off the air.

Radio warnings and emergency communications to the general public will be broadcast by the Emergency Broadcast System (EBS). This system uses AM broadcasting stations as the primary means to reach the public; selected FM and TV stations are included for backup. All stations during a crisis plan to use their normal broadcast frequencies.

EBS stations that are not put off the air by EMP or other effects of early explosions will attempt to confirm the siren warnings of a nuclear attack. They will try to give information to listeners in the extensive areas where sirens and whistles cannot be heard. However, EMP effects on telephones may limit the information available to the stations. The functioning EBS stations should be able to warn listeners to seek the best available nearby shelter in time for most of these listeners to reach such shelter before ICBMs begin to explode. Limitations of the Emergency Broadcasting System in 1979 include the fact that very few civilian radio stations are protected against EMP effects. Many of the protected stations would be knocked out by blast; most do not afford their operating personnel fallout protection that is adequate for continuing broadcasts for long in areas subjected to heavy fallout.

WARNINGS GIVEN BY THE ATTACK ITSELF

The great majority of Americans would not be injured by the first explosions of a nuclear attack. In an all-out attack, the early explosions would give sufficient warning for most people to reach nearby shelter in time. Fifteen minutes or more before big intercontinental ballistic missiles (ICBMs) blasted our cities, missile sites, and other extensive areas, most citizens would see the sky lit up to an astounding brightness, would hear the thunderous sounds of distant explosions, or would note the sudden outage of electric power and most communications. These reliable attack warnings would result from the explosion of submarine-launched ballistic missiles (SLBMs). These are smaller than many ICBMs. The SLBM warheads would explode on Strategic Air Command bases and on many civilian airport runways that are long enough to be used by our big bombers. Some naval bases and high-priority military command and communication centers would also be targeted.

The vast majority of Americans do not know how to use these warnings from explosions to help them save their lives. Neither are they informed about the probable strategies of an enemy nuclear attack.

One of the first objectives of a coordinated enemy attack would be to destroy our long-range bombers, because each surviving U.S. bomber would be one of our most deadly retaliatory weapons. Once bombers are airborne and well away from their runways, they are difficult to destroy. To destroy our bombers before they could get away, the first SLBMs would be launched at the same time that ICBMs would be fired from their silos in Europe and Asia. U.S. surveillance systems would detect launchings and transmit warnings within a very few minutes. Since some enemy submarines would be only a few hundred miles from their targets, some SLBMs would explode on American targets about 15 or 20 minutes before the first ICBMs would hit.

Some SLBMs would strike civilian airport runways that are at least 7000 ft long. This is the minimum length required by B-52s; there were 210 such runways in the U.S. in 1977. During a crisis, big bombers would be dispersed to many of these long runways, and enemy SLBMs would be likely to target and hit these runways in an effort to destroy the maximum number of bombers.

Unlike the more numerous, small, multiple warheads of most U.S. SLBMs, most Soviet SLBMs produce a megaton-range explosion. Within the first 10 minutes after the beginning of an attack, many runways 7000 feet or longer are likely to be cratered by a 1-megaton surface burst. Therefore, homes within about 4 miles of a runway at least 7000 ft long are likely to be destroyed before residents receive warning or have time to reach blast shelters away from their homes. Homes six miles away could be lightly damaged by such a warhead, with the blast wave arriving about 22 seconds after the warning light. Some windows would be broken 40 miles away. But the large majority of citizens would not be injured by these early SLBM attacks. These explosions would be life-saving "take cover" warnings to most Americans, if they have been properly informed.

Sudden power and communications failures caused by the electromagnetic pulse (EMP) effects of nuclear explosions also could serve as attack warnings in extensive areas. An EMP is an intense burst of radio-frequency radiation generated by a nuclear explosion. The strong, quick-rising surges of electric current induced by EMP in power transmission lines and long antennas could burn out most unprotected electrical and electronic equipment.

The usual means of protecting electrical equipment against surges of current produced by lightning are generally ineffective against EMP. The protective measures are known, but to date all too few civilian installations have been protected against EMP effects. Three or four nuclear weapons skillfully spaced and detonated at high altitudes over the United States would produce EMP effects that might knock out most public power, most radio and TV broadcasting stations lacking special protection against these effects, and most radios connected to long antennas. Nuclear explosions on or near the ground may produce damaging EMP effects over areas somewhat larger than those in which such equipment and buildings would be damaged by the blast effects.

HOW TO RESPOND TO UNEXPECTED ATTACK WARNINGS

Although a Pearl-Harbor-type of attack is unlikely, citizens should be prepared to respond effectively to unexpected warnings.

These warnings include:

● Extremely bright lights—more light than has been seen before. The dazzling, bright lights of the first SLBM explosions on targets in many parts of the United States would be seen by most Americans. One should not look to determine the source of light and heat, because there is danger of the viewer's eyes being damaged by the heat and light from a large explosion at distances as far as a hundred miles away, in clear weather. Look down and away from the probable source, and quickly get behind anything that will shield you from most of the thermal pulse's burning heat and intense light. A thermal pulse delivers its heat and light for several seconds—for more than 11 seconds if it is from a 1-megaton surface burst and for approximately 44 seconds if from a 20-megaton surface burst.

If you are at home when you see the amazingly bright light, run out of rooms with windows. Hurry to a windowless hallway or down into the basement. If you have a shelter close to your house, but separate from it, do not leave the best cover in your home to run outdoors to reach the shelter; wait until about two minutes after first seeing the light.

If outdoors when you see the bright light, get behind the best available cover.

It would be impossible to estimate the distance to an explosion from its light or appearance, so you should stay under cover for about two minutes. A blast wave initially travels much faster than the normal speed of sound (about 1 mile in 5 seconds). But by the time its overpressure has decreased to 1 pound per square inch (psi), a blast wave and its thunderous sound have slowed down and are moving only about 3% faster than the normal speed of sound.

If no blast or sound reaches you in two minutes, you would know that the explosion was over 25 miles away and you would not be hurt by blast effects, unless cut by shattered window glass. After two minutes you can safely leave the best cover in your home and get a radio. Turn the dial to the stations to which you normally listen and try to find information. Meanwhile, quickly make preparations to go to the best shelter you and your family can reach within 15 minutes—the probable time interval before the first ICBMs start to explode.

At no time after an attack begins should you look out of a window or stay near a window. Under certain atmospheric conditions, windows can be shattered by a multimegaton explosion a hundred miles away.

● The sound of explosions. The thunderous booms of the initial SLBM explosions would be heard over almost all parts of the United States. Persons one hundred miles away from a nuclear explosion may receive their first warning by hearing it about $7\frac{1}{2}$ minutes later. Most would have time to reach nearby shelter before the ICBMs begin to explode.

● Loss of electric power and communications. If the lights go out and you find that many radio and TV stations are suddenly off the air, continue to dial if you have a battery-powered radio, and try to find a station that is still broadcasting.

HOW TO RESPOND TO ATTACK WARNINGS DURING A WORSENING CRISIS

If an attack takes place during a worsening crisis, the effectiveness of warnings would be greater. Even if our government did not order an evacuation of high-risk areas, millions of Americans would already have moved to safer areas if they had learned that the enemy's urban civilians were evacuating or that tactical nuclear weapons were being employed overseas. Many prudent citizens would sleep inside the best available shelter and stay in or near shelter most of their waking hours. Many people would have made or improved family or small-group shelters and would have supplied them with most essentials. The official warning systems would have been fully alerted and improved.

During such a tense crisis period, neighbors or people sheltered near each other should have someone listen to radio stations at all times of the day and night. If the situation worsened or an attack

warning were broadcast, the listener could alert the others.

One disadvantage of waiting to build expedient shelters until there is a crisis is that many of the builders are likely to be outdoors improving their shelters when the first SLBMs are launched. The SLBM warheads may arrive so soon that the civilian warning systems cannot respond in time. To reduce the risk of being burned, persons working outdoors when expecting an attack should wear shirts, hats, and gloves. They should jump into a shelter or behind a nearby shielding object at the first warning, which may be the sudden cut-off of some radio broadcasts.

REMAINING INSIDE SHELTER

Curiosity and ignorance probably will cause many people to come out of shelters a few hours after an attack warning, if no blast or obvious fallout has endangered their area. This is dangerous, because several hours after almost all missiles have been launched the first enemy bombers may strike. Cities and other targets that have been spared because missiles malfunctioned or missed are likely to be destroyed by nuclear bombs dropped during the first several days after the first attack.

Most people should stay inside their shelters for at least two or three days, even if they are in a locality far from a probable target and even if fallout meter readings prove there is no dangerous fallout. Exceptions would include some of the people who would need to improve shelters or move to better shelters. Such persons could do so at relatively small risk during the interval between the ICBM explosions and the arrival of enemy bombers and/or the start of fallout deposition a few hours later.

Fallout would cover most of the United States within 12 hours after a massive attack. In such dangerous areas, people in shelters could rarely depend on information received from distant radio stations regarding changing fallout dangers and advising when and for how long they could go outside their shelters. Weather conditions such as wind speed would cause fallout dangers to vary with distance. If not forced by thirst or hunger to leave shelter, they should depend on their own fallout meter readings or on radiation measurements made by neighbors or local civil defense workers.

HOW TO KEEP RADIOS OPERATING

Having a radio to receive emergency broadcasts would be a great advantage. The stations that would still be on the air after an attack would probably be too distant from most survivors to give them reliable information concerning local, constantly changing fallout dangers. However, both morale and the prospects of long-range survival would be improved in shelters with a radio bringing word of the large-area fallout situation, food-relief measures, practical survival skills, and what the government and other organizations were doing to help. Radio contact with the outside world probably can be maintained after an attack if you remember to:

● Bring all of your family's battery-powered, portable radios with you to shelter, along with all fresh batteries on hand.

● Protect AM radios by using only their built-in short loop antennas. The built-in antennas of small portable radios are too short for EMP to induce damaging surges of current in them.

● Keep antennas of FM, CB, and amateur radios as short as practical, preferably less than 10 inches. When threatened by EMP, a danger that may continue for weeks after the initial attack because of repeated, high-altitude explosions, do not add a wire antenna or connect a short radio antenna to a pipe. Remember that a surge of current resulting from EMP especially can damage diodes and transistors, thus ending a radio's usefulness or reducing its range of reception.

● Keep all unshielded radios at least six feet away from any long piece of metal, such as pipes, metal ducts, or wires found in many basements and other shelters. Long metal conductors can pick up and carry large EMP surges, causing induced current to surge in nearby radios and damage them.

● Shield each radio against EMP when not in use by completely surrounding it with conducting metal if it is kept within six feet of a long conductor through which powerful currents produced by EMP might surge. A radio may be shielded against EMP by placing it inside a metal cake box or metal storage can, or by completely surrounding it with aluminum foil or metallic window screen.

● Disconnect the antenna cable of your car radio at the receiver—or at least ground the antenna when not in use by connecting it with a wire to the car frame. Use tape or clothespins to assure good metal-to-metal contact. The metal of an outside mirror is a convenient grounding-point. Park your car as near to your shelter as practical, so that after fallout has decayed sufficiently you may be able to use the car radio to get distant stations that are still broadcasting.

● Prevent possible damage to a radio from extreme dampness (which may result from long occupancy of some belowground shelters) by keeping it sealed in a clear plastic bag large enough so the radio can be operated while inside. An additional precaution is to keep a plastic-covered radio in an air-tight container with some anhydrite made from wallboard gypsum, as described in Appendix C.

● Conserve batteries, because after an attack you may not be able to get replacements for months. Listen only periodically, to the stations you find give the most useful information. The batteries of transistor radios will last up to twice as long if the radios are played at reduced volume.

Chapter 4

Evacuation

HIGHEST-RISK AND HIGH-RISK AREAS OF THE U.S.

The Soviet Union could deliver with increasing accuracy several thousand nuclear warheads and bombs on targets in the United States. These steadily improved weapons have at least 3 times the explosive power of all U.S. intercontinental weapons and therefore could produce 3 times as much fallout. If a massive all-out attack were launched, all important military installations, areas around airport runways longer than 7000 feet, and cities would be endangered by blast and fire. Much larger areas would receive fallout so heavy that persons would need to be inside good shelters to survive.

In response to these dangers, thoughtful Americans living in the highest-risk and high-risk areas should decide whether they would evacuate if, in a worsening crisis, the Soviets were to begin to evacuate their cities. The map on the following page (see Fig. 4.1 and its caption) shows highest-risk and high-risk fallout areas in the United States that might result from an attack delivering 6600 megatons, including 113 surface bursts of 20 megatons each on urban and industrial targets and a total of 3190 megatons surface burst on military targets. (The remaining 1150 megatons are air bursts; air bursts produce practically no local fallout.)

In regard to dangers from fallout radiation, highest-risk areas are those where a radiation dose of 10,000 R or more would be received by a person who remained outdoors continuously for the first two weeks. As will be explained later, to survive in such areas people would have to stay inside very good shelters for several weeks, or, after two weeks or more, leave very good shelters and drive in a few hours to an area relatively free of fallout dangers. A "very good" fallout shelter is one that reduces the radiation dose received by its occupants to less than 1/200th of the dose they would have received outdoors during the same period. If the two-week dose outdoors were 20,000 R, such a shelter with a protection factor of 200 (PF 200) would prevent each occupant from receiving a dose greater than 100 R—not enough to incapacitate. Even a completely belowground home basement, unless greatly improved as described in Chapter 5, would give entirely inadequate protection.

High-risk fallout areas are those where the two-week dose outdoors is between 5,000 and 10,000 R. In such areas, good fallout shelters would be essential, supplied at least with adequate water and baby food for two weeks. Furthermore, survivors would have to remain inside shelters for most of each day for several additional weeks.

The radiation dangers in the shaded areas of the map are shown decreasing as the distances from the explosions increase. This generally is the case, although sometimes rain or snow carries radioactive particles to the ground, producing "rainouts" of exceptionally heavy fallout farther downwind. Furthermore, this computer-drawn map made at Oak Ridge National Laboratory does not indicate the very dangerous fallout near the isolated surface bursts. Although the most dangerous fallout would be carried by high-altitude winds that usually blow from west to east, such simplified fallout patterns as those shown should be used only as rough guides to help improve chances of evacuating a probable blast area or very heavy fallout area and going to a less dangerous area. Wind directions are undependable; an enemy's targeting can be unexpected; weapons can miss. A prudent citizen, no matter

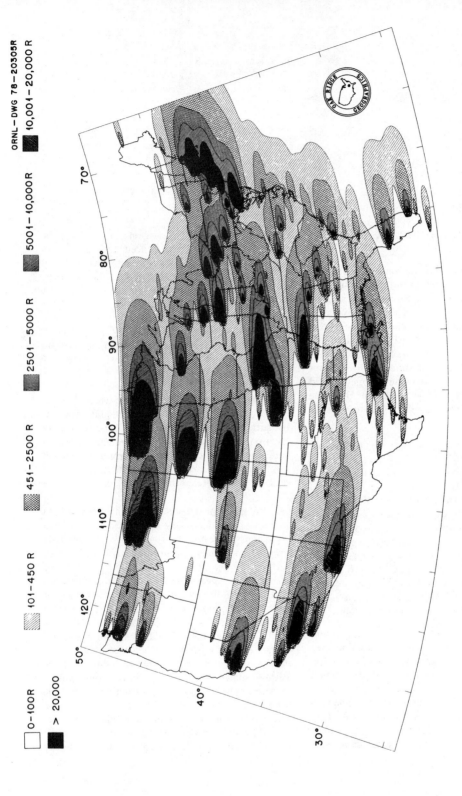

Fig. 4.1. Simplified fallout patterns showing total radiation doses that would be received by persons on the surface and in the open for the entire 14 days following the surface bursting of 5050 megatons on the targets indicated, if the winds at all elevations blew continuously from the west at 25 mph.

ORNL−DWG 78−20305R

0−100R

101−450 R

451−2500 R

2501−5000 R

5001−10,000 R

10,001−20,000 R

> 20,000

where he is, should try to build a shelter that gives excellent protection against fallout radiation.

Risk-area maps based primarily on blast dangers (see Fig. 4.2 and its caption) have been used extensively in planning urban evacuations and deciding what kind of shelters are needed in different communities. Note that the risk areas shown in Fig. 4.2 are smaller than the risk areas from fallout indicated in Fig. 4.1. A major disadvantage of all types of risk-area maps is the fact that poorly informed people often misinterpret them and conclude that if they are outside a mapped risk area, they are relatively safe from both blast and fallout dangers.

Another reason for not placing much reliance on risk-area maps such as Fig. 4.1 and Fig. 4.2 is that such available maps are based on the largest attacks that were considered possible several years ago. In the past few years the number of warheads and bombs that could strike the United States has increased greatly, although their total megatonage and capability to produce fallout have not. As a result, in 1979 many more targets in the United States might be hit than are indicated in Fig. 4.1 or Fig. 4.2, and the areas that could be free of fallout probably would be less extensive.

The areas of highest risk from blast and fire would be intercontinental ballistic missile (ICBM) sites, such as those around Great Falls, Montana and Tucson, Arizona. The surface-bursting of many large weapons on such sites would produce highest-risk fallout areas for a hundred miles downwind. In an all-out war, our largest cities also would be highest-risk areas. Several multi-megaton weapons would be needed to destroy each of these large urban and industrial areas. The areas near Strategic Air Command bases and Navy submarine bases are highest-risk areas, although smaller weapons would be adequate to destroy these targets.

High-risk areas would include major ports, runways over 7000 feet in length, and important aircraft and munitions factories. Less important cities, large oil refineries, steel mills, and the largest dams also would be high-risk areas, with heavy fallout to be expected downwind for a hundred miles or so.

WHETHER TO EVACUATE

Let's assume that cities of an enemy nation were being evacuated or that tactical nuclear weapons were beginning to be used in what had been an overseas conventional war involving the United States. In such a worsening crisis, most Americans could improve their survival chances by getting out of highest-risk and high-risk areas. Within a few years, the high-risk areas could include as many as 600 cities of more than 25,000 inhabitants. Similar-sized concentrations of urban evacuees might also become targets if the number of nuclear weapons continues to increase.

Persons who decide to evacuate from a *highest-risk* area should try to go at least 40 miles from the nearest probable aiming point for a large ICBM, such as the center of a big city. Even if several accurately delivered, large weapons were to destroy such a city, 40 miles away from its center should be far enough to avoid blast dangers, except possibly from flying, broken glass.[6]

If you are evacuating a *high-risk* area such as an average city or a location near an airfield or major factory, 20 miles from the anticipated ground zero should be the minimum distance to avoid most blast dangers.

Which way and how far one should go to reduce probable fallout dangers are more difficult questions to answer. Going westward, up-wind from the high-risk area relative to the generally west-to-east winds at high altitudes, usually would be most promising; next, going north or south. But if going in these generally favorable directions would result in moving into another high-risk area, or if these routes were to be blocked by a large body of water, then one would have to decide whether it would be practical to evacuate to a more distant area.

Studies of crisis relocation planning by the Defense Civil Preparedness Agency may result in official preparations to evacuate most urban citizens on the President's orders. If pre-crisis preparations for the movement, control, feeding, and health care of about 100 million Americans were to be completed and put into effect during a crisis, the decisions for those living in high-risk areas would be simplified. Also, the chances of surviving would be improved.

Whether or not such preparations are made, the following considerations may help you and your family make a more logical decision regarding evacuation:

Fig. 4.2. A Defense Civil Preparedness Agency map showing risk areas: (1) where minimum blast overpressures—those on the outer edges of the blast areas—are 2 pounds per square inch and/or (2) where the probability of very heavy fallout is calculated to be 50% or greater. Blast effects where overpressure is no greater than 2 pounds per square inch are severe enough to damage but not to destroy houses. This map is based on the same theoretical, 6600-megaton attack used in Fig. 4.1, except that all weapons are surface burst.

Favorable to Evacuation:	Unfavorable to Evacuation:
* You live in a highest-risk or high-risk area.	* You live outside a highest-risk or high-risk area and could build an expedient fallout shelter and make other survival preparations where you live.
* You have transportation (this means a car and enough gasoline), and roads are open to a considerably lower-risk area.	* You have no means of transportation or you believe that roads are likely to be blocked by the time you make your decision.
* You are in fairly good health or can evacuate with someone capable of taking care of you.	* You are sick, decrepit, or lack the will to try to survive if things get tough.
* Your work is not of the kind that your community depends on (such as a policeman, fireman, or telephone operator).	* You cannot suddenly leave your home area for several days without hurting others.
* You have some tools with which to build or improve a fallout shelter. You also have water containers, food, clothing, etc., adequate for life in the area to which you would go.	* You lack the tools, etc., that would be helpful—but not necessarily essential—to successful evacuation.

Instructions for building expedient fallout and blast shelters and for making expedient life-support equipment are given in following chapters. The reader is advised to study all of this book carefully before making up his mind regarding basic survival action.

THE NEED FOR AN EVACUATION CHECKLIST

A good flyer, no matter how many years he has flown, runs through a checklist covering his plane before taking off. Similarly, a citizen preparing under crisis pressures to do something he has never done before—evacuate—should use a checklist to be sure that he takes with him the most useful of his available possessions.

A family planning to use an expedient shelter or basement at or near home also should use the Evacuation Checklist to make sure needed survival items are not overlooked.

The family of six pictured in Fig. 4.3 used the Evacuation Checklist given below to select the most useful things that could be carried in and on their small car. They assembled categories of items in separate piles, then selected some items to take with them from each pile. They were able to leave their home 76 minutes after receiving the Evacuation Checklist. (Following chapters of this book include descriptions of this family's success in evacuating, building a Pole-Covered Trench Shelter, and living in it continuously for 77 hours.)

EVACUATION CHECKLIST

(Includes items for building or improving shelters)

Loading Procedure: Make separate piles for each category (except categories 1 and 5). Then load the car with some items from each category, taking as much as can be safely carried and being careful to leave room for all passengers.

A. THE MOST NEEDED ITEMS

Category 1. Survival Information: Shelter-building and other nuclear survival instructions, maps, all available small battery-powered radios and extra batteries, and a fallout meter such as a homemade KFM (see Appendix C).

Category 2. Tools: Shovel, pick, saw (a bow-saw is best), ax or hatchet, file, knife, pliers, and *any other tools specified in the building instructions for the shelter planned.* Also take work gloves.

Category 3. Shelter-Building Materials: Rainproofing materials (plastic, shower curtains, cloth, etc.) as specified in the instructions for the type of shelter planned. Also, unless the weather is very cold, a homemade shelter-ventilating pump such as a KAP, or the materials to build one (see Appendix B).

Category 4. Water: Small, filled containers plus all available large polyethylene trash bags, smaller plastic bags and pillow cases, water-purifying material such as Clorox, and a teaspoon for measuring.

Category 5. Peacetime valuables: Money, credit cards, negotiable securities, valuable jewelry, checkbooks, and the most important documents kept at home.

Category 6. Light: Flashlights, candles, materials to improvise cooking-oil lamps (2 clear glass jars of about 1-pint size, cooking oil, cotton string for wicks (see Chapter 11, Light), kitchen matches, and a moisture-proof jar for storing matches.

Category 7. Clothing: Cold-weather boots, overshoes, and warm outdoor clothing (even in summer, since after an attack these would be unobtainable), raincoats and ponchos. Wear work clothes and work shoes.

Category 8. Sleeping Gear: A compact sleeping bag or two blankets per person.

Category 9. Food: Food for babies (including milk powder, cooking oil, and sugar) has the highest priority. Compact foods that require no cooking are preferred. Include at least one pound of salt, available vitamins, a can and bottle opener, for each person one cup, bowl, and large spoon, and 2 cooking pots with lids (4-qt size preferred). Also, minimum materials for making a bucket-stove: a metal bucket, 10 all-wire coat hangers, a nail, and a cold chisel or screwdriver (see Chapter 9, Food).

Category 10. Sanitation Items: Plastic film or plastic bags in which to collect and contain excrement; a bucket or plastic container for urine; toilet paper, tampons, diapers, and soap.

Category 11. Medical Items: Aspirin, a first-aid kit, all available antibiotics and disinfectants, special prescription medicines (if essential to a member of the family), potassium iodide (for protection against radioactive iodine, see Chapter 13), spare eyeglasses, and contact lenses.

Category 12. Miscellaneous: Two square yards of mosquito netting or insect screen with which to screen the shelter openings if insects are a problem, insect repellents, a favorite book or two.

B. SOME USEFUL ITEMS (To take if car space is available):

1. Additional tools.

2. A tent, a small camp stove, and some additional kitchen utensils.

Fig. 4.3. Six members of a Utah family arriving at a rural shelter-building site 64 miles from their urban home.

EVACUATING BY CAR

The small car shown in Fig. 4.3 was skillfully loaded for a safe evacuation trip. To make room for supplies, the back seat was left at home. The load on top of the car included blankets, a small rug, and a small tent—all made of springy materials which kept the load from becoming compacted and working loose under the ropes tightened around it. The two loop-ended ropes went over the load and around the top of the car, passing over the tops of the closed doors.

USING MUSCLE POWER

Hazards of evacuation would include highways blocked by wrecks and stalled vehicles. If leadership and know-how were provided, the muscle power of people usually could quickly clear a highway. During a major Chinese evacuation before advancing Japanese armies in World War II, I observed Chinese, using only muscle power, quickly clear a mountain road of wrecks and other obstructions. Americans can do the same, if someone convinces

them that they can do it, as proved by a wintertime episode on Monarch Pass over the Continental Divide in Colorado. At least 100 vehicles were held up after a large wrecking truck overturned on the icy highway. The patrolmen were doing nothing until I told them how the Chinese handled such a situation. The patrolmen then called for volunteers from among the delayed motorists to lift the overturned truck back onto its wheels. In less than 15 minutes, about 50 people had combined their muscle power and opened Monarch Pass to traffic.

Citizens should take direct action to keep traffic moving during a crisis evacuation.

MAKING AN EXPEDIENT BLAST-PROTECTIVE SHELTER INSTEAD OF EVACUATING

Millions of Americans have homes within very large urban-industrial areas that probably would be subjected to blast and fire dangers. Many who live in the suburbs or adjacent towns in these metropolitan areas may find that their best survival strategy

29

is not to evacuate, but to build expedient earth-covered shelters at or very near their homes and to supply them with life-support essentials. This is a good idea, provided that (1) their homes are far enough away from probable aiming points to make such shelters practical, and (2) enough time, space, tools, materials, and supplies are available.

Consider the blast dangers from a 20-megaton surface burst and the effectiveness of expedient shelters for protection against blast. Wood frame buildings at the least would be severely damaged (usually collapsed) within about 10 miles from ground zero. This and worse destruction would result over a roughly circular area of approximately 315 square miles. In comparison, as has been indicated by test explosions conducted by Defense Nuclear Agency,[5] earth-covered expedient fallout shelters roofed with hollow-core interior doors would be undamaged if about 7.5 miles or more from ground zero of a 20-MT surface burst.

(Fallout shelters are designed for protection against radiation from fallout particles. Although fallout shelters lack blast doors and other means for keeping out blast, the better types would prevent their occupants from being killed by blast effects in extensive areas where people in houses would have little chance of surviving. In this book, an "expedient shelter" generally means an expedient fallout shelter.)

Persons who were farther than about four miles from ground zero of a 20-MT surface burst would survive in expedient or permanent blast shelters designed to give excellent protection against all blast, fire, and radiation effects where the overpressure is no higher than 15 psi. Thus 15-psi blast shelters would reduce the area of probable death to about 50 square miles—an 88% reduction. (See Appendix D, Expedient Blast Shelters.)

The photo (Fig. 4.4) shows a family with no adult male that built an expedient shelter that would give far better fallout, blast, and fire protection than almost any home. They succeeded, despite the necessity of working on cold November days with snow flurries. The top two inches of earth were frozen and the next two feet so dry that most of it had to be loosened with their dull pick. No member of this family had done any serious digging before, yet they

Fig. 4.4 This family completed a door-covered trench shelter in 34 hours. Earth placed on top of the doors gives good fallout protection. Though some blast and fire protection is also provided, this type of shelter is not recommended for blast areas.

built a shelter that would have given about 100 times as much protection against fallout radiation as would a typical small frame house and at least 25 times as much as a typical home basement.

In many areas, this and even better types of expedient fallout shelters affording considerable blast protection could be built by untrained families, following the written, field-tested instructions in this book. Furthermore, as shown in Appendix D, Expedient Blast Shelters, within a few days a small but significant fraction of the population could build expedient blast shelters complete with expedient blast doors and providing at least 15-psi blast protection.

Chapter 5
Shelter, the Greatest Need

ADEQUATE SHELTER

To improve your chances of surviving a nuclear attack, your primary need would be an adequate shelter equipped for many days of occupancy. A shelter that affords good protection against fallout radiation and weather would be adequate in more than 95% of the *area* of the United States. However, even in almost all areas not endangered by blast and fire during a massive nuclear attack, the fallout protection provided by most existing buildings would not be adequate if the winds blew from the wrong direction during the time of fallout deposition.

To remain in or near cities or other probable target areas, one would need better protection against blast, fire, and fallout than is provided by most shelters in buildings. Blast tests have proved that the earth-covered expedient fallout shelters described in this book can survive blast effects severe enough to demolish most homes.[5]

This chapter is concerned primarily with expedient shelters that give excellent protection against fallout radiation. These earth-covered fallout shelters could be built in 48 hours or less by tens of millions of Americans following field-tested, written instructions.[8] Expedient blast shelters are discussed in Appendix D. The special blast doors and other design features needed for effective blast protection require more work, materials, and skill than are needed for expedient fallout shelters.

If average Americans are to do their best when building expedient shelters and life-support equipment for themselves, they need detailed information about *what* to do and about *why* it is to their advantage to do it. We are not a people accustomed to blindly following orders. Unfortunately, during a crisis threatening nuclear war, it would take too long to read instructions explaining why each important feature was designed as specified. Therefore, only a few reasons are included in the step-by-step, illustrated instructions given in Appendix A for building 6 types of earth-covered expedient shelters during a crisis.

In this chapter, reasons will be given for designing a Pole-Covered Trench Shelter as specified in the Oak Ridge National Laboratory instructions given in Appendix A.2. The two pages of drawings and plans given at the end of Appendix A.2 show the parts of this shelter, except for the essential shelter-ventilating pump installed in its entrance trench. The following account of how an urban family, after evacuating, used these instructions to build such a shelter in less than 36 hours also includes explanations of various radiation dangers and of simple means to build protection against these dangers.

This family, like scores of other families recruited to build shelters or life-support equipment, was offered a sum about equivalent to laborers' wages if its members completed the experiment within a specified time. The test period began the moment the family received the written, illustrated instructions preparatory to evacuating by car, as mentioned in the preceding chapter. Like the other test families, this family was paid for all of its materials used. If a family worked hard and completed the project in half the specified time, it was paid a cash bonus. Throughout such tests workers were guided only by the written instructions, which were improved after each successive test.

The successful outcome of almost all the shelter-building experiments indicates that tens of millions of Americans in a nuclear war crisis would work hard and successfully to build earth-covered expedient shelters that would give them better protection against fallout, blast, and fire than would all but a very small fraction of existing buildings. However, this belief is dependent on two conditions: (1) that in a desperate, worsening crisis our country's highest officials would supply strong, motivating leadership; and (2) that Americans would have received—well in advance—shelter-building and other practical, tested survival instructions.

SHELTER AGAINST RADIATION

The family previously pictured evacuating by car (Fig. 4.2) drove 64 miles to build a shelter at the site shown in Fig. 5.1. Although the August sun was very hot in this irrigated Utah valley, the family members did not build in the shade of nearby trees. To avoid digging through roots, they carried the poles about 150 feet and dug their trench near the edge of the cornfield.

The father and the oldest son did most of the work of making the shelter. The mother and second son had health problems; the two youngest children were not accustomed to work.

The family followed an earlier version of the plans and instructions given in Appendix A for building a Pole-Covered Trench Shelter. Because the earth was firm and stable, the trenches were dug with vertical walls. If the earth had been less stable, it would have been necessary to slope the walls—increasing the width at the top of the main trench from $3^1/2$ to 5 feet.

Before placing the roof poles, the workers assured themselves a more comfortable shelter by covering the trench walls. They had brought a large number of the plastic garbage bags required in their home community and split some bags open to make wall coverings. Bed sheets or other cloth could have been used.

The room of this 6-person shelter was $3^1/2$ feet wide, $4^1/2$ feet high, and $16^1/2$ feet long. A small stand-up hole was dug at one end, so each tall occupant could stand up and stretch several times a day.

The trenches for entry and emergency exit were dug only 22 inches wide, to minimize radiation entering the shelter through these openings. One wall of these two narrow trenches was an extension of the

Fig. 5.1. Placing 9-foot poles for the roof of a Pole-Covered Trench Shelter.

room wall shown on the right in Fig. 5.1. The family sat and slept along the left wall, to be better shielded from radiation coming through the openings.

This shelter was designed so that its main trench could be enlarged to make a much more livable room without disturbing its completed roof. For this reason, the 9-foot roofing poles were placed off-center, with the two extra feet resting on the ground to the right of the main room.

Whenever practical, expedient shelters should be built so that they can be readily enlarged to make semi-permanent living quarters. After it becomes safe to emerge for limited periods, occupants could sleep and spend much of their waking time in such a rainproof dugout that affords excellent protection against continuing radiation. In cold weather, living in a dugout like this is more comfortable than living in a tent or shack. After the fallout radiation dose rate outdoors has decayed to less than about 2 R per hour, the small vertical entry could be enlarged and converted to a steeply inclined stairway.

The importance of giving inexperienced shelter builders detailed instructions is illustrated by the unnecessary work done by the young women shown in Fig. 5.2. They had agreed to try to build a Pole-Covered Trench Shelter, working unassisted and using only hand tools. Because the summer sun in Utah was hot, they selected a shady site under a large tree. The brief instructions they received included no advice on the selection of a building site. Cutting and digging out the numerous roots was very difficult for them and required several of the 22 hours they spent actually working.

Another disadvantage of making a shelter under trees is that more of the gamma rays from fallout particles on the leaves and branches would reach and penetrate the shelter than if these same particles were on the ground. Many gamma rays from fallout particles on the ground would be scattered or absorbed by striking rocks, clods of earth, tree trunks, or houses before reaching a belowground shelter.

Fig. 5.2. Two non-athletic college girls who completed a 4-person Pole-Covered Trench Shelter in 35$^1/_2$ hours, despite tree roots.

TYPES OF SHIELDING

Shelters provide protection against radiation by utilizing two types of shielding: **barrier shielding** and **geometry shielding.**

● **Barrier shielding** is shown by Fig. 5.3, a simplified illustration. (In a real fallout area, a man in an open trench would have fallout particles all over and around him.) The 3-foot thickness of earth shown (or a 2-foot thickness of concrete) will provide an effective barrier, attenuating (absorbing) about 99.9% of all gamma rays from *fallout*. (In the illustration, only a single fallout particle 3 feet from the edge of the trench is considered.) Only one gamma ray out of 1000 could penetrate the 3 feet of earth shown and strike the person in the trench. Rays from particles farther away than 3 feet would be negligible; rays from particles closer than 3 feet would be attenuated according to the thickness of earth between the fallout particle and the man in the trench.

However, the man in the trench would not be protected from "skyshine," which is caused by gamma rays scattering after striking the nitrogen, oxygen, and other atoms of the air. The man's exposed head, which is just below ground level, would be hit by about one-tenth as many gamma rays

as if it were 3 feet above ground (Fig. 5.3). Even if all fallout could be kept out of the trench and off the man and every part of the ground within 3 feet of the edges of the trench, skyshine from heavy fallout on the surrounding ground could deliver a fatal radiation dose to the man in the open trench.

Skyshine reaches the ground from all directions. If the man were sitting in a deeper trench, he would escape more of this scattered radiation, but not all of it. For good protection he must be protected overhead and on all sides by barrier shielding.

The barrier shielding of the Pole-Covered Trench Shelter shown in Fig. 5.4 was increased by shoveling additional earth onto its "buried roof." After father and son had mounded earth about 18 inches deep over the centerline of the roof poles, a large piece of 4-mil-thick polyethylene was placed over the mound. This waterproof material served as a "buried roof" after it was covered with more earth. Any rainwater trickling through the earth above the plastic would have run off the sloping sides of the "buried roof" and away from the shelter.

● **Geometry shielding** reduces the radiation dose received by shelter occupants by increasing the distances between them and fallout particles, and by

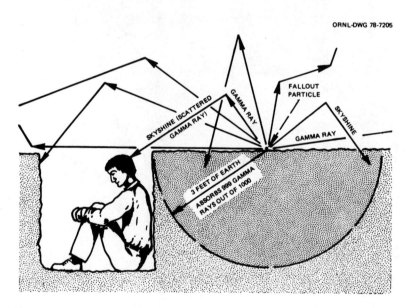

ORNL-DWG 78-7205

Fig. 5.3. Simplified illustration of barrier shielding and skyshine (scattered gamma radiation). An open trench provides poor protection.

Fig. 5.4. Increasing the barrier shielding over a Pole-Covered Trench Shelter.

providing turns in the openings leading into the shelter. Figure 5.5 is a sectional drawing of the shelter entry built by the Utah family.

The farther you can keep away from a source either of light or of harmful radiation, the less light or other radiation will reach you. If fallout particles are on the roof of a tall building and you are in the basement, you will receive a much smaller radiation dose from those particles than if they were on the floor just above you. Likewise, if either visible light or gamma rays are coming through an opening at the far end of a passageway, less will reach you at the other end if the passageway is long than if it is short.

Turns in passageways are very effective in reducing the amount of radiation entering a shelter through them. A right-angle turn, either from a vertical or horizontal entry, causes a reduction of about 90%.

Note: *Fallout* shelters need not provide additional shielding to protect occupants against initial nuclear radiation that is emitted from the fireballs of nuclear explosions. (See Figs. 1.1 and 1.4.) Large nuclear weapons would be employed in an attack on the United States. Initial nuclear radiation

would be so greatly reduced in passing through the miles of air between the fireball of a *large* nuclear explosion and fallout shelters far enough away to survive its blast effects, that occupants would not be endangered. (For a discussion of the more difficult shielding requirements of blast shelters that would enable occupants to survive blast effects much closer to explosions and therefore would be subjected to much larger exposures of initial nuclear radiation, see Appendix D, Expedient Blast Shelters.)

Figure 5.6 shows the completed shelter after it was occupied by the family of six just $32\frac{1}{2}$ hours after receiving the shelter-building instructions and beginning preparations to evacuate. (This family won a bonus for completion within 36 hours and also a larger bonus given if all members then stayed inside continuously for at least 72 hours.) To get a better idea of how six people can live in such a small shelter, look at the drawings at the end of Appendix A.2. In warm or hot weather, shelters, especially crowded ones, must be well ventilated and cooled by an adequate volume of outdoor air pumped through them. This family had built an efficient homemade air pump (a KAP) and used it as described in Chapter 6 and Appendix B.

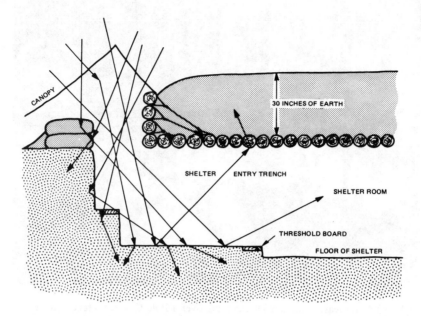

Fig. 5.5. Skyshine coming into a shelter through a vertical entry would be mostly absorbed while turning into and traveling down the entryway trench.

Fig. 5.6. Earth mounded over a $3^1/_2$-foot-wide Pole-Covered Trench Shelter. The canvas canopy would protect the vertical entry against both fallout and rain. (A smaller canopy over the air duct-emergency exit at the other end is obscured by the mounded earth.)

36

All of the earth excavated in digging the trenches was mounded over the roof poles, making a covering 30 inches deep. This shelter had a protection factor (PF) of over 300; that is, persons inside would receive less than 1/300th of the gamma-ray dose of fallout radiation that they would receive if they were standing outside in the open.

To have made the roof covering more than 36 inches thick would not have increased the protection against radiation very much, unless the entry trench and the air duct-emergency exit trench had been dug considerably longer. Field tests have shown that some families, given only 48 hours, cannot dig the longer trenches, cut the additional poles, and shovel on the additional earth necessary for a shelter that would offer significantly better protection than the shelter shown here. The Pole-Covered Trench Shelter and the other shelters described in Appendix A all have been built by untrained families within 48 hours, the minimum time assumed to be available to Americans before a possible attack if the Russians should begin to evacuate their cities.

EARTH ARCHING USED TO STRENGTHEN SHELTERS

Several types of expedient shelters can be made to withstand greater pressures if their roofs are built of *yielding* materials and covered with enough earth

to attain "earth arching." This arching results when the yielding of the roof causes part of the load carried by the roof to be shifted to the overlying earth particles, which become rearranged in such a way that an arch is formed. This arch carries the load to surrounding supports that are less yielding. These supports often include adjacent earth that has not been disturbed.

To attain earth arching, the earth covering the yielding roof must be at least as deep as half the width of the roof between its supports. Then the resultant earth arch above the roof carries most of the load.

(A familiar example of effective earth arching is its use with sheet metal culverts under roads. The arching in a few feet of earth over a thin-walled culvert prevents it from being crushed by the weight of heavy vehicles.)

Figure 5.7 shows how a flexible roof yields under the weight of 30 inches of earth mounded over it and how earth arching develops. After the arch is formed, the only weight that the yielding roof supports is the weight of the small thickness of earth between the roof and the bottom of the arch.

Protective earth arching also results if a shelter is covered with a material that compresses when loaded, or if the whole roof or the whole shelter can be pushed down a little without being broken.

Fig. 5.7. Earth arching over a yielding roof enables a shelter to withstand much greater pressures.

37

SHELTER AGAINST BETA AND ALPHA PARTICLES

In addition to the invisible, light-like gamma *rays,* fallout particles radiate two types of hazardous invisible *particles:* beta and alpha particles. These radiations would be minor dangers to informed people in fallout areas, especially to those who had entered almost any kind of shelter before the fallout began to be deposited in their area.

● Beta particles are high-speed electrons given off by some of the radioactive atoms in fallout. Only the highest-energy beta particles can penetrate more than about 10 feet of air or about $\frac{1}{8}$ inch of water, wood, or human body tissue. Any building that keeps out fallout particles will prevent injury from beta radiation.

The only frequently serious dangers are from (1) internal beta-radiation doses from fallout-contaminated food or drink, and (2) beta burns from **fresh** fallout particles. **Fresh** fallout particles are no more than a few days old and therefore very radioactive. If **fresh** particles remain for at least several tens of minutes in contact with the skin, beta burns are likely to result. If only thin clothing separates **fresh** fallout particles from the skin, a considerably longer time will elapse before their radiation causes beta burns.

In dry, windy weather, **fresh** fallout particles might get inside one's nose and ears, along with dust and sand, and could cause beta burns if not promptly washed off or otherwise removed.

Prompt washing will prevent beta burns. If water is not available, brushing and rubbing the fallout particles off the skin will help.

If a person is exposed outdoors where there is heavy, **fresh** fallout for a long enough time to receive a large dose of gamma radiation, the highest-energy beta radiation given off by **fresh** fallout particles on the ground may be a relatively minor danger to his eyes and skin. Even ordinary glasses give good protection to the eyes against such beta radiation, and ordinary clothing gives good protection to the skin.

Ordinary clothing will shield and protect the body quite well from all but the highest-energy beta particles given off by **fresh** fallout deposited on the clothing. Fallout-contaminated clothing should be removed as soon as practical, or at least brushed and beaten before entering a shelter room, to rid it of as many fallout particles as possible. (Fallout particles that are many days old will not cause beta burns unless large quantities are on the body for hours.)

Most of the knowledge about beta burns on human skin was gathered as a result of an accident during the largest U.S. H-bomb test in the tropical Pacific.[6] Winds blew the fallout in a direction not anticipated by the meteorologists. Five hours after the multimegaton surface burst, some natives of the Marshall Islands noticed a white powder beginning to be deposited on everything exposed, including their bare, moist skin. Unknown to them, the very small particles were fresh fallout. (Most fallout is sand-like, but fallout from bursts that have cratered calcareous rock, such as coral reefs and limestone, is powdery or flakey, and white.) Since the natives knew nothing about fallout, they thought the white dust was ashes from a distant volcanic eruption. For two days, until they were removed from their island homes and cared for by doctors, they paid practically no attention to the white dust. Living in the open and in lightly constructed homes, they received from the fallout all around them a calculated gamma-ray dose of about 175 R in the two days they were exposed.

The children played in the fallout-contaminated sand. The fallout on these islanders' scalps, bare necks, and the tops of their bare feet caused itching and burning sensations after a time. Days later, beta burns resulted, along with extreme discoloration of the skin. Beta burns are not deep burns; however, it took weeks to heal them. Some, in spite of proper medical attention, developed into ulcers. (No serious permanent skin injury resulted, however.)

For survivors confined inside crowded, unsanitary shelters by heavy fallout, and without medicines, beta burns could be a worse problem than were similar burns to the Marshall Islanders.

All of the Marshall Islanders unknowingly ate fallout-contaminated food and drank fallout-contaminated water for two days. Mainly as a result of this, radioactive iodine was concentrated in their thyroid glands, and thyroid abnormalities developed years later. (There is a simple, very low-cost means of attaining almost complete protection against this delayed hazard: taking minute prophylactic doses of a salt, potassium iodide. This will be discussed in Chapter 13.)

In dry, dusty, windy areas the human nasal passages usually filter out much dust. A large part of it is swallowed and may be hazardous if the dust is contaminated with fallout. Under such dry, windy conditions, beta burns also could be caused by large amounts of dust lodged inside the nasal passages. Breathing through a dust mask, towel, or other cloth would give good protection against this localized hazard. In conclusion: persons under nuclear attack should make considerable effort to protect themselves from beta radiation.

● **Alpha particles,** identical to the nuclei of helium atoms, are given off by some of the radioactive atoms in fallout. These particles have very little penetrating power: 1 to 3 inches of air will stop them. It is doubtful that alpha particles can get through unbroken skin; they cannot penetrate even a thin fabric.[6] Alpha particles are hazardous only if materials that emit them (such as the radioactive element plutonium) enter the body and are retained in bone, lung tissue, or other parts of the body. Any shelter that excludes fallout particles affords excellent protection against this radiation danger. Unless survivors eat or drink fallout-contaminated food or water in considerably larger quantities than did the completely uninformed natives of the Marshall Islands, danger from alpha particles would be minor.

PROTECTION AGAINST OTHER NUCLEAR WEAPONS EFFECTS

● **Flash burns** are caused by the intense rays of heat emitted from the fireball within the first minute following an explosion.[6] This thermal radiation travels at the speed of light and starts to heat or burn exposed people and materials before the arrival of the blast wave. Thermal radiation is reduced—but not eliminated—if it passes through rain, dense clouds, or thick smoke. On a clear day, serious flash burns on a person's exposed skin can be caused by a 20-megaton explosion that is 25 miles away.

A covering of clothing—preferably of white cloth that reflects light—can reduce or prevent flash burns on those who are in a large part of an area in which thermal radiation is a hazard. However, in areas close enough to ground zero for severe blast damage, the clothing of exposed people could be set on fire and their bodies badly burned.

● **Fires** ignited by thermal radiation and those resulting from blast and other causes especially would endanger people pinned down by fallout while in or near flammable buildings. The multiple dangers from fire, carbon monoxide, and toxic smokes will be discussed in a separate chapter.

● **Flash blindness** can be caused by the intense light from an explosion tens of miles away in clear weather. Although very disturbing, the blindness is not permanent; most victims recover within seconds

to minutes. Among the Hiroshima and Nagasaki survivors (people who had been in the open more than persons expecting a nuclear attack would be), there were a number of instances of temporary blindness that lasted as long as 2 or 3 hours, but only one case of permanent retinal injury was reported.[6]

Flash blindness may be produced by scattered light; the victim of this temporary affliction usually has not looked directly at the fireball. Flash blindness would be more severe at night, when the pupils are larger. Retinal burns, a permanent injury, can result at great distances if the eye is focused on the fireball.

People inside any shelter with no openings through which light can shine directly would be protected from flash burns and eye damage. Persons in the open with adequate warning of a nuclear explosion can protect themselves from both flash blindness and retinal burns by closing or shielding their eyes. They should get behind anything casting a shadow— quickly.

SKIN BURNS FROM HEATED DUST (THE POPCORNING EFFECT)

When exposed grains of sand and particles of earth are heated very rapidly by intense thermal radiation, they explode like popcorn and pop up into the air.[6] While this dust is airborne, the continuing thermal radiation heats it to temperatures that may be as high as several thousand degrees Fahrenheit on a clear day in areas of severe blast. Then the shock wave and blast winds arrive and can carry the burning-hot air and dust into an open shelter.[6,9] Animals inside open shelters have been singed and seriously burned in some of the nuclear air-burst tests in Nevada.[9]

Thus Japanese working inside an open tunnel-shelter at Nagasaki within about 100 yards of ground zero were burned on the portion of their skin that was exposed to the entering blast wind, even though they were protected by one or two turns in the tunnel.[4] (None of these Japanese workers who survived the blast-wave effects had fatal burns or suffered serious radiation injuries, which they certainly would have suffered had they been outside and subjected to the thermal pulse and the intense initial nuclear radiation from the fireball.)

Experiments conducted during several nuclear test explosions have established the amount of thermal radiation that must be delivered to exposed earth to produce the popcorning effect.[6] Large air bursts may result in exposed skin being burned by hot dust and heated air produced at overpressure ranges as low as 3 or 4 psi. However, calculations indicate that the large surface bursts most likely to endanger Americans would not result in the occupants of small, open shelters being burned by these effects—except at somewhat higher overpressures.

Protection is simple against the heated dust and very hot air that may be blown into an open shelter by the blast. When expecting an attack, occupants of an *open* shelter should keep towels or other cloths in hand. When they see the bright light from an explosion, they should cover their heads and exposed skin. If time and materials are available, much better protection is given by making expedient blast doors, as described in Appendix D. When occupants see the very bright light from a large explosion miles away, they can close and secure such doors before the arrival of the blast wave several seconds later.

ESSENTIAL LIFE-SUPPORT EQUIPMENT

Shelters can be built to give excellent protection against all nuclear weapon effects, except in places within or very close to cratered areas. But most shelters would be of little use in areas of heavy fallout unless supplied with enough life-support equipment to enable occupants to stay in the shelters until conditions outside become endurable. In heavy fallout areas most high-protection-factor shelters would be crowded; except in cold weather, most would need a ventilating pump to remove warmed air and bring in enough cooler outdoor air to maintain survivable temperature-humidity conditions. Means for storing adequate water is another essential life-support requirement. These and other essential or highly desirable life-support needs are covered in following chapters.

BASEMENT SHELTERS

The blast and fire effects of a massive, all-out attack of the magnitude possible in 1979 would destroy or damage most American homes and other buildings and endanger the occupants of shelters inside them. Outside the risk areas, the use of shelters inside buildings would not be nearly as hazardous. However, an enemy might also target some areas into which large numbers of urban Americans had evacuated before the attack.

Earth-covered expedient shelters in a blast area give better protection against injury from blast, fire, or fallout than do almost all basements. But during the more likely kinds of crises threatening nuclear war most urban Americans, including those who

would evacuate into areas outside probable blast areas, probably would lack the tools, materials, space, determination, physical strength, or time required to build good expedient shelters that are separate from buildings and covered with earth. As a result, most unprepared urban citizens would have to use basements and other shelters in existing structures, for want of better protection.

Shelters in buildings, including basement shelters, have essentially the same requirements as expedient shelters: adequate shielding against fallout radiation, strength, ventilation and cooling, water, fallout radiation meters, food, hygiene, etc. Sketches and short descriptions of ways to improve the fallout protection afforded by home basements are to be found in widely distributed civil defense pamphlets, including two entitled "In Time of Emergency," and "Protection in the Nuclear Age." In 1979, millions of copies of these pamphlets are stockpiled for possible distribution during a crisis. Unfortunately, most of such official instructions were written years ago, when the deliverable enemy megatonnage was a small fraction of what it is today. Official civil defense instructions available to average Americans in 1979 do not inform the reader as to what degree of protection against fallout radiation (what protection factor) is given by the different types of do-it-yourself shelters pictured. There is no mention of dependable ways to provide adequate cooling-ventilation, an essential requirement if even a home basement is to be occupied by several families in warm or hot weather. Outdated or inadequate information is given about water, food, the improvement of shelter in one's home, and other survival essentials.

No field-tested instructions at present are available to guide householders who may want to strengthen the floor over a home basement so that it can safely support 2 feet of shielding earth piled on it. In areas of heavy fallout, such strengthening often would be needed to safely support adequate overhead shielding, especially if the house were to be jarred by a light shock from a distant explosion. In the following paragraphs, a way to greatly improve the fallout protection afforded by a typical home basement is outlined. If improved in this manner, a basement would provide excellent fallout protection for several families.

First, earth should be placed on the floor above to a depth of about one foot. Earth can be carried efficiently by using sacks or pillowcases, using the techniques described in Chapter 8 for carrying water. If earth is not available because the ground is frozen or because of the lack of digging tools, other heavy materials (containers of water, heavy furniture, books, etc.) should be placed on the floor above. These materials should weigh enough to produce a loading of about 90 pounds per square foot—about the same weight as earth one foot thick. This initial loading of the floor joists causes them to carry some of the weight that otherwise would be supported by the posts that then are to be installed.

Next, a horizontal beam is installed so as to support all of the floor joists under their centers. Figure 5.8 shows a beam and one of its supporting posts. Such a supporting beam preferably is made by nailing three 2×6s securely together. (Three 2×4s would serve quite well.)

ORNL–DWG 78-18358

Fig. 5.8. Supporting beam and one of its posts installed to increase the load of shielding material that can be carried safely by the floor above a home basement.

Cut posts to fit exactly under the beam. If trees at least 4 inches in diameter are not available, make posts by nailing boards together. Position the two outermost posts within 2 feet of the ends of the beam. Space the posts at even intervals, with each post under a floor joist. A post under every third joist is ideal; this usually means a spacing between posts of about $4\frac{1}{2}$ feet. If the basement is 20 feet long, 5 posts are enough. Nail each post to the beam, and secure the bases of each with brace boards laid on the basement floor, as illustrated.

Finally, place a second 1-foot-thick layer of earth on the floor above. If the basement windows are protected with boards and if all but a part of one window and all the aboveground parts of the basement walls are covered with earth 2 feet thick, the basement shelter will have a protection factor of several hundred against fallout radiation.

Adequate ventilation and cooling should be assured by using a homemade air pump (a KAP), made and installed as described in Appendix B. Forced ventilation is especially necessary if more than one family occupies the basement in warm or hot weather.

More work and materials are required to improve a home basement in this manner than are needed to build a covered-trench shelter for one family. An earth-covered shelter separate from buildings will provide equally good protection against radiation, better protection against blast, and much better protection against fire.

If a family cannot build a separate, earth-covered shelter outdoors, often it would be advisable to make a very small shelter in the most protected corner of the basement. Such an indoor shelter should be of situp height (about 40 inches for tall people) and no wider than 3 feet. Its walls can readily be built of chairs, benches, boxes, and bureau drawers. Interior doors make an adequately strong roof. Expedient shielding materials, to be placed on the roof and the two exposed sides, can be ordinary water containers and bureau drawers, boxes, and pillow cases filled with earth or other heavy materials. Or, if heavy-duty plastic trash bags or 4-mil polyethylene film are available, make expedient water containers and use them for shielding. To do so, first line bureau drawers, boxes, pillow cases, trash cans, etc. with plastic. Place the lined containers in position to shield your shelter, then fill these expedient water containers with drinkable water (see Chapter 8).

As demonstrated by hot-weather occupancy tests of such very small indoor shelters, a small KAP or other air pump must be operated to maintain a forced flow of air through such a crowded shelter, to prevent intolerable temperature-humidity conditions. (See Chapter 6 for ventilation-cooling requirements, including the provision of an adequately large opening in each end of a shelter.) In some basements a second small KAP would be needed in hot weather to pump outdoor air through the basement. This KAP could be operated by pulling a cord from within the small shelter, using an improvised "pulley" as described in Appendix B.

PUBLIC SHELTERS

In the event of an unexpected attack, many unprepared Americans should and would take refuge in nearby marked public shelters. Throughout the populated areas that would not be subjected to blast, fire, or heavy fallout, the use of public shelters could save millions of lives. All persons concerned with survival should remember that the large majority of officially surveyed and marked shelters give better protection against radiation than most unimproved home basements.

Persons preparing to go to public shelters should be aware that many lack forced ventilation and that the blowers and fans of most forced ventilation systems would be stopped by loss of electric power due to electromagnetic pulse effects or by other effects of nuclear explosions on electrical systems. A blast wave at an overpressure range as low as 1 psi (144 pounds per square foot) would wreck most shelter-ventilating fans. In 1979, no water or food normally is stocked. A person who brought to a public shelter 10 large plastic trash bags and 10 pillow slips, to make 10 expedient water bags in which 60 gallons of water could be stored (as described in Chapter 8), would help both himself and dozens of other shelter occupants. If he hoped to share the basement in a strange family's home, his chances of being welcomed would be improved if he brought a small homemade shelter-ventilating pump and other survival items. The same small pump would be impractical in a large public shelter. An Oak Ridge National Laboratory study completed in 1978 found that if all citizens were to go to National Shelter Survey (NSS) shelters within one mile of their homes, 69% of those who found space would be in shelters rated for 1000 or more occupants.[10] The average number of shelter spaces in this largest class of public shelters is 3179. The prospect of living in an unequipped shelter crowded with this many unprepared people—each of whom would have only 10 square feet of floor space—is a strong motivation to work hard to build and equip a small, earth-covered shelter.

DECIDING WHAT KIND OF SHELTER TO BUILD OR USE

Before deciding what kind of shelter you and your family should build or use, it is best to read all of this book. Your final decision should include consideration of ways to provide life-support equipment discussed in following chapters. At this stage, however, the reader will find it helpful to review important reasons why different types of shelters offer the best hope of survival to different people, in different areas, and under different conditions.

This book is written primarily to improve the survival chances of people who cannot or do not build permanent shelters. The information which follows will help you select the best expedient or available shelter for your family.

SHELTER NEAR OR IN YOUR HOME

If your home is 20 or more miles from an average target such as most cities or a large industrial complex, or is 40 or more miles from a major target such as a great city, you are fortunate: you should build or use a shelter close to home. No one can foretell accurately which way the winds will blow or where weapons will explode, so, if practical, you should build a shelter that gives better protection against fallout, blast, and fire than shelters in buildings. Most people living outside targeted areas could build such a shelter in two days or less, using one of the designs of earth-covered expedient shelters detailed in Appendix A.

Even if you plan to evacuate, you should decide where you would take shelter nearby in case you were unable to do so. There is always a chance that an attack may be launched without warning, giving insufficient time to evacuate. Or the missile aimed at the area in which you live may miss its target. If your targeted home area were not hit, moderately heavy fallout might be the only danger; even an improved basement shelter would be adequate in that case.

EARTH-COVERED EXPEDIENT FAMILY SHELTERS

Advantages of earth-covered, expedient family shelters:

* Better protection against heavy fallout, blast, and fire than afforded by the great majority of shelters in buildings.

* The possibility of building in favorable locations, including places far removed from target areas, and places where it is impractical to build or to improve large group-shelters giving good protection.

* The opportunity for men, women, and children to work together to provide good protection in minimum time.

* A better chance to benefit from thoughtful preparations made in advance than would be the case in public shelters where water, food, etc. must be shared.

* Less risk of personality clashes, hysteria under stress, exposure to infectious diseases, and other problems that arise when strangers are crowded together for days or weeks.

Disadvantages of earth-covered, expedient shelters:

* It may be difficult to meet the requirement for time, space, people able to work hard, materials, and tools—and to get all these together at the building site.

* Building is difficult if heavy rain or snow is falling or if the ground is deeply frozen. (However, untrained Americans have built good fallout shelters with shielding provided by 5 or more feet of packed snow,[11] including a winter version of the Crib-Walled Pole Shelter described in Appendix A. The practicality of several Russian designs of snow-covered expedient shelters also has been demonstrated by winter construction tests in Colorado.[12])

* The fewer occupants of family shelters could not provide as many helpful skills as would be found in most public shelters, with tens-to-thousands of occupants.

* The lack of instruments for measuring changing radiation dangers. However, the occupants could make a homemade fallout meter by following the instructions in Appendix C, or buy a commercial instrument *before* a rapidly worsening crisis arises.

PUBLIC AND OTHER EXISTING SHELTERS

Advantages of the great majority of public and other existing shelters, most of which are in buildings:

* Their immediate availability in many localities, without work or the need to supply materials and tools.

* The provision of fair-to-excellent fallout protection—generally much better than citizens have available in their homes.

* The availability in some shelters of fallout meters and occupants who know how to use them and who can provide other needed skills.

* The chance for persons who are not able to carry food or water to a public shelter to share some brought by the more provident occupants.

Disadvantages of the great majority of public and other existing shelters available to large numbers of people:

* The location of most of them in targeted areas.

* Poor protection against blast, fire and carbon monoxide.

* Lack of water and means for storing it (in 1979) and lack of stocked food.

* No reliable air pumps, which are essential in warm or hot weather for supplying adequate ventilating-cooling air to maintain endurable conditions in fully occupied shelters—especially belowground.

* Uncertainties regarding the availability of fallout meters and occupants who know how to use them.

* No dependable lights, sanitary facilities, or other life-support equipment, with few exceptions.

* The crowding together of large numbers of people who are strangers to each other. Under frightening conditions that might continue for weeks, the greater the number of people, the greater would be the risks of the spread of infectious diseases and of hysteria, personality clashes, and the development of other conflicts.

BELOWGROUND EXPEDIENT FALLOUT SHELTERS

(Appendix A details two designs of belowground shelters, three designs of aboveground shelters, and one design that affords excellent protection built either below or aboveground).

Advantages of belowground, earth-covered expedient fallout shelters:

* They afford better protection than do aboveground, earth-covered types.

* Less time, work, and materials are required to build them than to build equally protective aboveground designs.

* If built sufficiently separated from houses and flammable woods, they provide much better protection against fire hazards than do shelters in buildings.

* If dug in stable earth, even types with unshored earth walls give quite good blast protection up to overpressure ranges of at least 5 psi—where most homes and buildings would be destroyed by blast or fire.

Disadvantages of belowground expedient fallout shelters:

* They are not practical in areas where the water table or rock is very near the surface.

* It is impractical to build them in deep-frozen ground.

* They are usually more crowded and uncomfortable than improved basement shelters.

EXPEDIENT BLAST SHELTERS

Advantages of expedient blast shelters:

* Occupants could survive uninjured in extensive blast areas where fallout shelters would not prevent death or injury.

* Blast doors would protect occupants from shock waves, dangerous overpressures, blast winds, and burns on exposed skin caused by the popcorning effect and heated air.

Disadvantages of expedient blast shelters are their requirements for more time, materials, tools, skill, and work than are needed for building fallout shelters.

WARNING

Do not build, in advance, an earth-covered **wooden** shelter. Except in very dry, cold areas wooden underground structures are soon dangerously weakened by boring insects, fungi and other organisms that rot wood. In warm, humid parts of the world, earth-covered shelters made of lumber or poles may, in a few months, be so weakened as to collapse.

You should obtain, in advance, low cost materials to make an earth-covered, high protection factor fallout shelter. In the event of a future crisis, there may not be time to procure these items. For the roofing materials, store 3/4″ exterior plywood. It bends more before it breaks than does lumber, and thus promotes protective earth-arching in the covering earth. To ensure that wood does not deteriorate during storage, keep it dry and well-ventilated (an air space under it to discourage termites).

SHELTER MANAGEMENT AND MORALE

A family or larger group confined inside a crowded shelter for days or weeks will have unprecedented need for leadership and meaningful, regular activities. The nearer the established shelter routines of sleeping, eating, cleaning, working, exercising, reading etc. can be made to approximate those of normal living, the better. Anxiety and tension are reduced if people are kept usefully busy. Thus, a manually operated shelterventilation pump makes for higher morale than does a motor-driven air pump. This occurs because shelter occupants are given useful work and also because they realize that a manual system is less likely to break down than is an electric-powered ventilation unit.

Chapter 6

Ventilation and Cooling of Shelters

CRITICAL IMPORTANCE

If high-protection-factor shelters or most other shelters that lack adequate forced ventilation were fully occupied for several days in warm or hot weather, they would become so hot and humid that the occupants would collapse from the heat if they were to remain inside. It is important to understand that the heat and water vapor given off by the bodies of people in a crowded, long-occupied shelter could be deadly if fallout prevents leaving the shelter.

When people enter an underground shelter or basement in the summertime, at first the air feels cool. However, if most shelters are fully occupied for a few days without adequate ventilation, the floors, walls, and ceilings, originally cool, will have absorbed about all the body heat of which they are capable. Some shelters will become dangerously hot in a few hours. Unless most of the occupants' body heat and water vapor from sweat are removed by air circulated through a typical shelter, the heat-humidity conditions will become increasingly dangerous in warm or hot weather. One of the most important nuclear war survival skills people should learn is how to keep occupied shelters adequately ventilated in all seasons and cool enough for many days of occupancy in warm or hot weather. Methods for keeping ventilating air from carrying fallout particles into shelters also are described in Appendix A and Appendix B.

MAKING AND USING AN EXPEDIENT AIR PUMP

The best expedient way to maintain livable conditions in a shelter, especially in hot weather, is to make and use a large-volume shelter-ventilating pump. Field tests have proved that average Ameri-

cans can build the expedient air pump described in Appendix B in a few hours, with inexpensive materials found in most households.

This simple pump was invented in 1962 by the author. I called it a Punkah-Pump, because its hand-pulled operation is somewhat like that of an ancient fan called a "punkah", still used by some primitive peoples in hot countries. (Unlike the punkah, however, this air pump can force air to move in a desired direction and is a true pump.) It was named the Kearny Air Pump (KAP) by the Office of Civil Defense following tests of various models by Stanford Research Institute, the Protective Structures Development Center, and General American Transportation Company. These tests confirmed findings first made at Oak Ridge National Laboratory regarding the advantages of the KAP both as a manually operated pump for forcing large volumes of outdoor air through shelters and as a device for distributing air within shelters and fanning the occupants. See Fig. 6.1.

The air pump instructions given in Appendix B are the result of having scores of families and pairs of untrained individuals, including children, build and use this air pump. They were guided by successively improved versions of these detailed, written instructions, that include many illustrations (see Appendix B). Some people who are experienced at building things will find these instructions unnecessarily long and detailed. However, shelter-building experiments have shown that the physically stronger individuals, usually the more experienced builders, should do more of the hard, manual work when shelters are built, and that those less experienced at building should do the lighter work—including making shelter-ventilating pumps. These detailed, step-by-step instructions have enabled people who never

Fig. 6.1. A 6-foot KAP tested for durability at Oak Ridge. After 1000 hours of operation during which it pumped air through a room at a rate of 4000 cubic feet per minute (4000 cfm), there were only minor tears in the plastic flaps.

Fig. 6.2. Behind the girl is the homemade air pump that made it possible for a family of six to live in a crowded trench shelter for more than three days. Outside the temperature rose to 93° F.

before had attempted to build a novel device of any kind to make serviceable air pumps.

(The air pump instructions given in Appendix B repeat some information in this chapter. This repetition is included both to help the reader when he starts to build an air pump and to increase the chances of the best available complete instructions being given to local newspapers during some future crisis. The instructions given in this book could be photographed, reproduced, and mass-distributed by newspapers.)

Figure 6.2 shows (behind the girl) a 20-inch-wide by 36-inch-high KAP installed in the entry trench of a trench shelter. The father of the Utah family described earlier had made this simple pump at home, using only materials and tools found in many homes—as described in Appendix B. He carried the pump on top of his car to the shelter-building site. The pendulum-like, flap-valve pump was swung from two cabinet hinges (not shown) screwed onto a board. The board was nailed to roof poles of the narrow entry trench extending behind the girl in the photograph. The pull-cord was attached to the pump frame below its hinged top and extended along one trench wall for the whole length of the shelter. Any

one of the six occupants could pull this cord and easily pump as much as 300 cubic feet per minute of outdoor air through the shelter and through the insect screens over both its entrances. (Without these screens, the numerous mosquitoes in this irrigated area would have made the family's shelter stay very unpleasant.)

During the 77 hours that the family continuously occupied their narrow, covered trench, the temperatures outside rose as high as 93° F. Without the air pump, the six occupants would have been driven from their shelter by unbearable temperature-humidity conditions during the day.[8]

The photo in Fig. 6.2 also shows how the air pump hung when not being operated, partially blocking the entry trench and causing a "chimney effect" flow of air at night. There was a 10-inch space between the air pump and the trench floor, and the resulting flow of air maintained adequate ventilation in the cool of the desert night, when outdoor temperatures dropped as low as 45° F. Cool outdoor air flowed down into the entry and under the motionless air pump, replacing the body-warmed air inside the shelter. The entering cool air continuously forced the warm air out of the shelter room at ceiling height through the emergency crawlway-exhaust trench at the other end. When the weather is cool, a piece of plastic or tightly woven cloth could be hung in the doorway of a well designed, narrow shelter, to cause a flow of fresh air in the same manner.

Numerous shelter occupancy tests have proved that modern Americans can live for weeks in an adequately cooled shelter with only 10 square feet of floor space per person.[13] Other tests, such as one conducted by the Navy near Washington, D.C. during an abnormally cool two weeks in August, 1962, have shown that conditions can become difficult even when summertime outdoor air is being pumped through a long-occupied shelter at the rate of 12 cubic feet per minute, per person.[14,15] This is four times the *minimum* ventilation rate for each occupant specified by the Defense Civil Preparedness Agency (DCPA) for American shelters: 3 cubic feet per minute (3 cfm). Three cfm is about three times the supply of outdoor air needed to keep healthy people from having headaches as a result of exhaled carbon dioxide. In hot, humid weather, much more outdoor air than 12 cfm per person must be supplied to a crowded, long-occupied shelter, as will be described in the following section and in Appendix B.

MAINTAINING ENDURABLE SHELTER CONDITIONS IN HOT WEATHER

The Navy test mentioned above showed how much modern Americans who are accustomed to air conditioning could learn from jungle natives about keeping cool and healthy by skillfully using hot, humid, outdoor air. While working in jungles from the Amazon to Burma, I observed the methods used by the natives to avoid unhealthful conditions like those experienced in the Navy shelter, which was ventilated in a conventional American manner. These jungle methods include the first five of the six cooling methods listed in this section. During 18 years of civil defense research, my colleagues and I have improved upon the cooling methods of jungle people, primarily by the invention and thorough field-testing of the homemade KAP described in Appendix B.

Even during a heat wave in a hot part of the United States, endurable conditions can be maintained in a fully occupied, belowground shelter with this simple pump, if the test-proven requirements listed below are ALL met.

Most basement shelters and many aboveground shelters also can be kept at livable temperatures in hot weather if the cooling methods listed below are ALL followed:

● Supply enough air to carry away all the shelter occupants' body heat without raising the "effective temperature" of the air at the exhaust end of the shelter by more than 2°F. The "effective temperature" of the air to which a person is exposed is equivalent to the temperature of air at 100% relative humidity that causes the same sensation of warmth or cold. "Effective temperature" combines the effects of the temperature of the air, its relative humidity, and its movement. An ordinary thermometer does not measure effective temperature. In occupancy tests of crowded shelters when the supply of outdoor air was hot and dry, shelter occupants have been surprised to find that they felt hottest at the air-exhaust end of their shelter, where the temperature reading was lower than at the air-intake end. Their sweaty bodies had acted as evaporative air coolers, but their body heat had raised the effective temperature, a reliable indicator of heat stress. If 40 cubic feet per minute (40 cfm) per person of outdoor air is supplied and properly distributed, then (even if the outdoor air is at a temperature which is typical of the hottest hours during a heat wave in a hot, humid area of the United States) the effective temperature of the shelter air will be increased no more than 2°F by the shelter occupants' body heat and water vapor. Except for a relatively few sick people dependent on air conditioning, anyone could endure air that has an effective temperature only 2°F higher than that of the air outdoors.

(There are exceptions to this ventilation requirement when the ceiling or walls of basement or aboveground shelters in buildings are heated by the sun to levels higher than skin temperature. In such shelters, more than 40 cfm of outdoor air per occupant must be supplied. However, if a shelter is covered by at least two feet of earth, it will be so well insulated that its ceiling and walls will not get hot enough to heat the occupants.)

● Move the air gently, so as not to raise its temperature. In the aforementioned Navy test, a high speed, electric ventilating pump and the frictional resistance of pipes and filters raised the temperature of the air supplied to the shelter by 3°F. Under extreme heat wave conditions, an air supply 3°F hotter than outdoor air could be disastrous—especially if considerably less than 40 cfm per occupant is supplied, and body heat raises the air temperature several additional degrees.

● Distribute the air quite evenly throughout the shelter. In a trench shelter, where air is pumped in at one end and flows out the other, good distribution is assured. In larger shelters, such as basements, ventilating air will move from the air-supply opening straight to the air-exhaust opening. Persons out of this air stream will not be adequately cooled. By using one or more additional, smaller KAPs (also described in Appendix B), fresh air can be distributed easily throughout large shelter rooms, and the occupants will be gently fanned.

● Provide occupants with adequate drinking water and salt. In extremely hot weather, this means 4 quarts of water per day per person and $^3/_4$ tablespoon (10 grams) of salt, including the salt in food.

● Wear as few clothes as practical. When the skin is bare, moving air can evaporate sweat more efficiently for effective cooling. Air movement can keep bare skin drier, and therefore less susceptible to heat rash and skin infections. In the inadequately ventilated Navy test shelter, 34 of the 99 initially healthy young men had heat rash and 23 had more serious skin complaints at the end of their sweaty two-week confinement, although their overall physical condition had not deteriorated.[15]

● Keep pumping about 40 cfm of air per person through the shelter both day and night during hot weather, so that the occupants and the shelter itself will be cooled off at night. In the Navy test, the ventilation rate of 7 to 12 cfm was not high enough to give occupants the partial relief from heat and sweating that people normally get at night.[15] In a National Academy of Sciences meeting on protective shelters, an authority stated: "Laboratory experiments and field investigations have shown that healthy persons at rest can tolerate daily exposures to ETs [effective temperatures] up to 90°F, provided they can get a good night's sleep in a cooler environment."[14] An effective temperature of 90°F is higher than the highest outdoor effective temperature during a heatwave in the South or in American deserts.

ADEQUATE VENTILATION IN COLD WEATHER

In freezing weather, a belowground shelter covered with damp earth may continue to absorb almost all of its occupants' body heat for many days and stay unpleasantly cold. In one winter test of such a fully occupied shelter, the temperature of the humid air in the shelter remained around 50°F.[16] Under such conditions, shelter occupants should continue to ventilate their shelter adequately, to avoid the following conditions:

● A dangerous buildup of carbon dioxide from exhaled breath, the first symptoms of which are headaches and deeper breathing.

● Headaches from the carbon monoxide produced by smoking. When the ventilation rate is low, smoking should not be permitted, even near the exhaust opening.

● Headaches, collapse, or death due to carbon monoxide from open fires or gasoline lanterns that release gases into the shelter air.

NATURAL VENTILATION

Enough air usually will be blown through an aboveground shelter if sufficiently large openings are provided on opposite sides and if there is any breeze. But if the weather is warm and still and the shelter crowded, the temperature-humidity conditions soon can become unbearable.

Adequate natural ventilation for belowground shelters is more difficult. Even if there is a light breeze, not much air will make a right-angle turn and go down a vertical entry, make another right angle turn, and then flow through a trench or other shelter partially obstructed by people and supplies.

In cool weather, occupants' body heat will warm the shelter air and make it lighter than the outdoor air. If a chimney-like opening or vent-duct is provided in the ceiling, the warmed, lighter air will flow upward and out of the shelter, provided an adequate air-intake vent is open near the floor. An Eskimo igloo is an excellent example of how very small ventilation openings, skillfully located in the ceiling and at floor level, make it possible in cold weather for chimney-type natural ventilation to supply the 1 cfm per person of outdoor air needed to prevent exhaled carbon dioxide from becoming dangerously concentrated.

In warm weather, chimney-type natural ventilation usually is inadequate for most high-protection-factor shelters that are fully occupied for days. And in hot weather, when as much as 40 cfm per occupant is required, body-warmed shelter air is no lighter than the outdoor air. Chimney-type ventilation fails completely under these conditions.

SAFE SHELTER VENTILATION
WITHOUT FILTERS

Numerous tests have shown that the hazards from fallout particles carried into shelters by unfiltered ventilating air are minor compared to the dangers from inadequate ventilation. A 1962 summary of the official standards for ventilating systems of fallout shelters stated: "Air filters are not essential for small (family size) shelters..."[17] More recent findings have led to the same conclusion for large fallout shelters. A 1973 report by the Subcommittee on Fallout of the National Academy of Sciences on the radioiodine inhalation problem stated this conclusion: "The opinion of the Subcommittee is that inhalation is far less of a threat than ingestion [eating or drinking], and does not justify countermeasures such as filters in the ventilating systems of shelters."[18]

In warm weather, it is essential to pump enough air through very small shelters like the one shown in Fig. 6.3. The photograph shows a man inside a Car-Over-Trench Shelter that provides fallout protection

Fig. 6.3. Pulling a small, stick-frame KAP to keep temperatures endurable for occupants of a Car-Over-Trench-Shelter.

about four times as effective as that given by the average home basement. The shelter was completed by piling earth inside and around the car that had been driven over the narrow trench. The shielding earth around the car's sides was piled against polyethylene film taped to the sides, to keep earth from going under the car. In warm or hot weather such a shelter cannot be occupied for long without forced ventilation.

Fallout particles that reach the earth within the first 24 hours after an explosion are so large and fast-falling that virtually all of them would be deposited on the ground. They would not fall into a properly designed shelter, especially one with a low-speed air intake. Particles small enough for a person to breathe into his lungs generally take several days to fall from where they are first carried, miles high in a mushroom cloud. By the time these small fallout particles are near the earth, the generally westerly winds blowing around the world at high altitudes would have carried them to Europe, or Asia, or back around the earth to North America. After days-to-weeks of wide dispersal and radioactive decay, such small particles would constitute a minor health hazard compared to other injurious conditions that would afflict an unprepared people subjected to a large-scale nuclear attack.

When sand-like fallout is being deposited, the occupants of small expedient shelters should decide whether to restrict or stop ventilation. If it is windy outside, some of the sand-like particles may be blown into a small open shelter. Ventilation should not be restricted long enough to cause serious overheating or headaches from exhaled carbon dioxide. As in a sand storm, breathing through a dust mask or towel would be helpful to avoid getting fallout particles into one's nose and mouth. Likewise, if a house is burning dangerously close to a separate, earth-covered shelter, closing the shelter's ventilation openings for an hour or two usually will prevent the entry of dangerous concentrations of carbon monoxide, carbon dioxide, or smoke. (Most houses will burn to the ground in less than two hours.)

When an attack is expected, an occupied shelter should be kept as cool as practical by pumping large volumes of outdoor air through it. This also will assure that the air is fresh and low in exhaled carbon dioxide. Then, if a need arises to stop or restrict ventilation, the shelter can be closed for longer than could be done safely otherwise.

Chapter 7

Protection Against Fires and Carbon Monoxide

RELATIVE DANGERS

Fire and its consequences probably would be the third-ranking danger to unprepared Americans subjected to a massive nuclear attack. Direct blast effects would be first, covering a large fraction of densely populated areas and killing far more people. Considerably fewer fatalities seem likely to result from the second-ranking danger, fallout radiation.

THE FACTS ABOUT FIRE HAZARDS

Firestorms would endanger relatively few Americans; only the older parts of a few American cities have buildings close enough together, over a large enough area, to fuel this type of conflagration. Such fires have not occurred in cities where less than about 30% of a large area was covered with buildings.[19]

In the blast area of Hiroshima, a terrifying fire storm that burned almost all buildings within an area of about 4.4 square miles resulted from many fires being ignited almost simultaneously. Many were caused by heat radiation from the fireball. Even more fires were due to secondary effects of the blast, such as the overturning of stoves. The buildings contained much wood and other combustible materials. The whole area burned like a tremendous bonfire; strong winds that blew in from all directions replaced the huge volumes of hot air that rose skyward from the intense fires.

Lack of oxygen is not a hazard to occupants of shelters in or near burning buildings or to those in shelters that are closed tightly to prevent the entry of smoke or fallout. Carbon monoxide, toxic smoke from fires, or high concentrations of carbon dioxide from shelter occupants' exhaled breaths would kill occupants before they suffered seriously from lack of oxygen.

FIRES IGNITED BY HEAT RADIATION

Figure 7.1 shows a wood-frame house after it was heated for one second by heat radiation from a small nuclear weapon exploded in a Nevada test. This test house had no furnishings, but the heat was intense enough to have ignited exposed upholstery, curtains, bedding, papers, etc. in a typical home.

Heat radiation will set fire to easily ignitable materials (dry newspapers, thin dark fabrics, dry leaves and dry grass) in about the same extensive areas over which blast causes moderate damage to frame houses. The blast wave and high-speed blast winds will blow out many flames. However, tests have shown that fire will continue to smolder within some materials such as upholstery and dry rotted wood, and after a while it often will burst into flame and will spread. The burning automobile pictured in Fig. 7.2 is an example of such ignition beyond the range of severe blast damage.

The number of fires started by heat radiation in areas where blast is not severe can be reduced by whitewashing the insides of window panes and by removing flammable materials from places in and around houses where heat radiation could reach them. Also, occupants of shelters in some homes that would be only slightly damaged by blast could move quickly to extinguish small fires and throw out smoldering upholstered articles before fallout is deposited.

Fig. 7.1. Heat radiation charred the paint on this house, which had been painted white to reflect heat rays. The charring instantaneously produced the smoke. However, precautions had been taken to prevent this typical U.S. house from being destroyed by fire, because the test was made to enable engineers to study the effects of blast, rather than fire. The house was demolished by the 5-psi overpressure blast that struck seconds later, but it did not burn.

Fig. 7.2. Thermal radiation from a nuclear explosion entered the car above through its closed windows and ignited the upholstery. The windows were blown out by the blast a few seconds later. However, the explosion was at such a distance that the blast wave was not severe enough to dent the car body.

Earth-covered shelters can be protected against heat radiation from nuclear explosions and other causes by painting any exposed wood and other combustible materials at shelter openings with a thick coating of slaked lime (old-fashioned white-wash). The World War II firebombing of Kassel was less effective than were similar raids on other German cities because the roof timbers of buildings had been so treated.[20]

Figure 7.3 illustrates the effectiveness of a thick coating of slaked lime in protecting a rough pine board against ignition by heat radiation. No flames from the burning logs touched the board. (Before this photograph was taken, the uppermost burning logs of a vertical-sided pile were removed so that the board could be seen clearly.)

Chinese civil defense instructions recommend coating exposed wood with both slaked lime and mud.[21] If only mud is available, a coating of it protects wood quite well. If kept damp, a mud coating is even more effective. (Simply keeping all exposed flammable materials damp is helpful.)

In blast areas, cloth or plastic canopies over the openings of expedient shelters usually would be ignited by the heat and certainly would be blown away by even moderate blast winds. If extra canopies and stakes could be made and kept inside the shelter, these replacements could be quickly erected after blast winds subside and before fallout begins—at least 15 minutes after the explosion. If no spare canopies were available, it would be best to keep the available canopies and their stakes inside the shelter, if it were not raining.

FOREST AND BRUSH FIRES

Unless forests or brushy areas are dry, it is difficult to start even scattered fires. Dangerous mass fires would be unlikely, except in blast areas where the heat radiation would be very intense. However, people building a shelter would do well to select a shelter site at least as far away from trees as the height of the tallest tree that could fall on the shelter—because of fire and smoke hazards in dry weather, and because digging a shelter among tree roots is difficult.

Fig. 7.3. Heat radiation had ignited the flaming half of the board on the ground, while the half near the shovel—painted white with a thick coating of slaked lime—had not even begun to smoke.

CAUSES OF FIRE

Figure 7.4 pictures the same house shown in Fig. 7.1 after it had been struck by the blast effects of a small nuclear test explosion at the 5-psi overpressure range. (If the house had been hit by the blast effects of a multimegaton weapon, with longer-lasting blast winds, it would have been wrecked about as completely at the 3-psi overpressure range. At the 3-psi overpressure range, the blast winds from an explosion 1000 times as powerful as the Nevada test explosion that wrecked this house would blow 10 times as long. This longer-duration, 100-mph blast wind would increase the damage done by the blast wave. The 3-psi overpressure range from a 20-megaton surface burst is about 10 miles from the center of the crater, and from a one-megaton surface burst, about 4 miles.[6])

If the blast-wrecked house shown in the illustration had had a furnace in operation when it was demolished, the chances of its being set on fire would have been high. In Hiroshima many of the first fires resulted from secondary effects of blast, especially the overturning of stoves, and not from heat radiation. Although the air burst produced no fallout, firefighters from undamaged, nearby communities were unable to reach most of the burning areas because of blast debris blocking the roads. Later they were kept from burning areas by the intense heat. Some water mains were broken, which made water unavailable for firefighting in certain areas.

In the event of an attack on the United States employing many surface bursts, fallout would prevent firefighting for days-to-weeks in a large part of the most populated regions.

The basements of many substantial buildings will withstand 5-psi blast effects and can prevent occupants from suffering serious injuries from blast. Most home basements can be reinforced with stout boards and posts so as to give good protection against blast effects up to considerably higher than 5 psi. But considering the dangers of fires in probable blast areas, it is safer to build an earth-covered shelter well removed from buildings than it is to seek protection in shelters inside buildings.

CARBON MONOXIDE AND TOXIC SMOKE

If an undamaged building is burning, people inside may be killed by carbon monoxide, toxic smoke, or fiery-hot air. Tests have shown that even fast-burning, rubble-free fires produce very high concentrations of carbon monoxide. If large-scale fires are burning near a shelter, the dangers from both carbon dioxide and carbon monoxide may continue for as long as $1\frac{1}{2}$ hours after ignition.[22] Therefore, the ventilation pipes or openings of a shelter should not be placed close to a building that might be expected to burn.

In the smoldering rubble of a large test fire, after 24 hours the carbon monoxide concentration was still more than 1% and the air temperature was

Fig. 7.4. Unburned wreckage of the same two-story, wood-frame house pictured in Fig. 7.1 after being wrecked by the 5-psi blast effects of a small nuclear test explosion.

1900° F. A carbon monoxide concentration of only 0.08% (8 parts CO in 10,000 parts of air) will cause headache, dizziness, and nausea in 45 minutes, and total collapse in 2 hours.

Realization of carbon monoxide dangers to persons in simple fallout shelters and basements may have led the writers of Soviet civil defense publications to define the "zone of total destruction" as the blast areas where the overpressure exceeds 7 psi and "residential and industrial buildings are completely destroyed ... the rubble is scattered and covers the burning structures," and "As a result the rubble only smolders, and fires as such do not occur."[23] Smoldering fires produce more carbon monoxide than do fiercely burning fires. Whether or not the occupants of basement shelters survive the direct blast effects is of little practical importance in those blast areas where the rubble overhead burns or smolders. So in the "zone of complete destruction," Russian rescue brigades plan to concentrate on saving persons trapped inside excellent blast shelters by the rubble.

About 135,000 Germans lost their lives in the tragic city of Dresden during three days of firebomb raids. Most casualties were caused by the inhalation of hot gases and by carbon monoxide and smoke poisoning.[20] Germans learned that when these dangers were threatening an air raid shelter, the occupants' best chance of survival was to run outside, even if the bombs were still falling. But in a nuclear war the fallout dose rate may be so high that the occupants of a shelter threatened by smoke and carbon monoxide might suffer a more certain and worse death by going outside. Instead, if they know from instrument readings and their calculations that they probably would receive a fatal dose before they could reach another shelter, the occupants should close all openings as tightly as possible. With luck, carbon monoxide in deadly concentrations would not reach them, nor would they be overcome by heat or their own respiratory carbon dioxide before the fire dangers ended.

Dr. A Broido, a leading experimenter with fires and their associated dangers, reached this conclusion: "If I were building a fallout shelter I would spend a few extra dollars to build it in my backyard rather than in my basement, locating the intake vent as far as possible from any combustible material. In such a shelter I would expect to survive anything except the close-in blast effects."[22]

This advice also applies to expedient shelters built during a crisis.

Chapter 8
Water

WATER AND SALT REQUIREMENTS

Painful thirst has been experienced by very few Americans. We take for granted that we will always have enough water to drink. Most of us think of "food and water" in that order, when we think of survival essentials that should be stored. But if unprepared citizens were confined in a shelter by heavy fallout, they soon would realize that they should have given first priority to storing adequate water.

For the kidneys to eliminate waste products effectively, the average person needs to drink enough water so that he urinates at least one pint each day. (When water is not limited, most people drink enough to urinate 2 pints. Additional water is lost in perspiration, exhaled breath, and excrement.) Under cool conditions, a person could survive for weeks on 3 pints of water a day—if he eats but little food and if that food is low in protein. Cool conditions, however, would be the exception in crowded belowground shelters occupied for many days. Under such circumstances four or five quarts of drinking water per day are essential in very hot weather, with none allowed for washing. For a two-week shelter stay, 15 gallons per person should be stored in or close to a shelter. This amount usually would provide for some water remaining after two weeks, to prevent thirst in case fallout dangers were to continue.

In a 1962 Navy shelter occupancy test lasting two weeks, 99 sailors each consumed an average of 2.4 quarts (2.3 liters) of water per day.[15] The test was conducted in August near Washington, D.C.; the weather was unseasonably cool. The shelter was not air-conditioned except during the last two days of the test.

When one is sweating heavily and not eating salty food, salt deficiency symptoms—especially cramping—are likely to develop within a few days. To prevent this, 6 or 8 grams of salt (about $\frac{1}{4}$ oz, or $\frac{1}{2}$ tablespoon) should be consumed daily in food and drink. If little or no food is eaten, this small daily salt ration should be added to drinking water. Under hot conditions, a little salt makes water taste better.

CARRYING WATER

Most families have only a few large containers that could be used for carrying water to a shelter and storing it in adequate amounts for several weeks. Polyethylene trash bags make practical expedient water containers when used as waterproof liners *inside* smaller fabric bags or pillowcases. (Plastic bags labeled as being treated with insecticides or odor-controlling chemicals should not be used.) Figure 8.1 shows a teenage boy carrying over 10 gallons (more than 80 pounds) of water, well balanced front and back for efficient packing. Each of his two burlap bags is lined with two 20-gallon polyethylene trash bags, one inside the other. (To avoid possible pinhole leakage it is best to put one waterproof bag inside another.)

To close a plastic bag of water so that hardly any will leak out, first spread the top of the bag until the two inner sides of the opening are together. Then fold in the center so that the folded opening is 4 thicknesses, and smooth (see Fig. 8.2). Continue smoothly folding in the middle until the whole folded-up opening is only about $1\frac{1}{2}$ inches wide. Then fold the top of the bag over on itself so the folded-up opening points down. With a strip of cloth or a soft cord, bind and tie the folded-over part with a bow knot, as illustrated.

Fig. 8.1. Carrying 80 pounds of water in two burlap bags, each lined with two larger plastic trash bags, one inside the other.

ORNL-DWG 78-7106

Fig. 8.2. Folding and tying the mouth of a water-filled plastic bag.

For long hikes, it is best to tie the water-holding plastic bags so that the openings are higher than the water levels inside.

To transport this type of expedient water bag in a vehicle, tie a rope around the fabric outer bag near its opening, so that the rope also encircles and holds the plastic liner-bags just below their tied-shut openings. The other end of this rope should then be tied to some support, to keep the openings higher than the water level.

To use two fabric bags or pillowcases to carry a heavy load of water contained in *larger* plastic liner-bags, connect the two fabric bags as shown in Fig. 8.1.

A small pebble, a lump of earth, or a similar object should be tied inside the opening of each bag before the two are tied together, to hold them securely. The bag that is to be carried in front should

have the pebble tied about 4 inches further down from the edge of its opening than the pebble tied in the bag to be carried in back. This keeps the pebbles from being pressed against the carrier's shoulder by a heavy load.

A pair of trousers with both legs tied shut at the bottoms can be used to carry a balanced load if pillowcases or other fabric bags are not at hand. Such a balanced load can be slung over the shoulder with the body erect and less strained than if the same weight were carried in a single bag-like pack on the back. However, trouser legs are quite narrow and do not provide room to carry more than a few gallons.

To prevent water from slowly leaking through the tied-shut openings of plastic bags, the water levels inside should be kept below the openings.

STORING WATER

When storing expedient water bags in a shelter, the water levels inside should be kept below the openings.

Not many expedient shelters would be large enough to store an adequate volume of water for an occupancy lasting two or more weeks. Plastic-lined storage pits, dug in the earth close to the shelter, are dependable for storing large volumes of water using cheap, compact materials. Figure 8.3 shows a cylindrical water-storage pit dug so as to have a diameter about two inches smaller than the inflated

ORNL-DWG 77-10423R

Fig. 8.3. Vertical section of cylindrical water-storage pit lined with two 30-gallon waterproof plastic bags. This pit held about 20 gallons.

diameter of the two 30-gallon polyethylene trash bags lining it (one bag inside the other). Before a plastic bag is placed in such a pit, the ends of roots should be cut off flush to the wall with a sharp knife, and sharp rocks should be carefully removed.

The best way to keep the upper edges of the pit-lining bags from slipping into the pit is shown in Fig. 8.3: Make a circular wire hoop the size of the opening of the bag, and tape it inside the top. In firm ground, the upper edges of double bags have been satisfactorily held in place simply by sticking six large nails through the turned-under edges of the bags and into the firm earth.

Figure 8.3 shows how to roof and cover a water storage pit so as to protect the water. The "buried roof" of waterproof material prevents any contamination of the stored water by downward-percolating rainwater, which could contain bacteria or small amounts of radioactive substances from fallout. The thick earth cover over the flexible roofing gives excellent blast protection, due to the earth arching that develops under blast pressure. In a large Defense Nuclear Agency blast test, a filled water-storage pit of the size illustrated was undamaged by blast effects at an overpressure range which could demolish the strongest aboveground buildings (53 psi).

A simpler way to store water is illustrated in Fig. 8.4. If the soil is so unstable that an unshored water storage pit with vertical sides cannot be dug, the opening of the bag (or of one bag placed inside another) can simply be tied shut so as to minimize leakage (see Fig. 8.4). Fill the bag with water, tie it, and place it in the pit. Then bury it with earth to the level of the water inside. A disadvantage of this method is leakage through the tied-shut openings due to pressure of loose earth on the bag. To lessen leakage, leave an air space between the filled bag and a roofing of board or sticks, so that the weight of earth piled on top of the roofing will not squeeze the bag. This storage method has another disadvantage: after the earth covering and the roof are removed, it is difficult to bail out the water for use—because as water is bailed out, the loose surrounding earth moves inward and squeezes the bag above the lowered water level.

Large volumes of water can be stored in plastic-lined rectangular pits. In order to roof them with widely available materials such as ordinary $^3/_4$-inch plywood or small poles, the pits should be dug no wider than 3 feet. Figure 8.5 pictures such a pit: 8 feet

Fig. 8.4. These two 30-gallon polyethylene trash bags, one inside the other, held 16 gallons of water. They were undamaged by 50-psi blast effects while buried in dry, very light soil. The plywood roof and the earth placed over the water bag were removed before this picture was taken.

Fig. 8.5. Post-blast view of plastic-lined water-storage pit undamaged at a 6.7-psi overpressure range. This pit held about 200 gallons.

long, 27 inches wide, and 30 inches deep. It was lined with a 10-foot-wide sheet of 4-mil polyethylene. The edges of this plastic sheet were held in place by placing them in shallow trenches dug near the sides of the pit and covering them with earth. Earth was mounded over the plywood roof to a depth of about 30 inches, with a "buried roof" of polyethylene. The earth cover and its "buried roof" were similar to the pit covering illustrated by Fig. 8.3. This rectangular pit contained about 200 gallons of water. No water leaked out after the pit had been subjected to blast effects severe enough to have flattened most substantial buildings. However, rectangular pits at higher overpressures failed, due to sidewall caving that caused leaks.

In a subsequent blast test by Boeing Aerospace Company, a plastic-lined water pit was undamaged at the 200-psi overpressure range. This storage pit had dimensions similar to the one pictured in Fig. 8.5, including the 4-ft-wide plywood roof, but the top of its lined pit was 2 feet below ground level, and the pit was completely filled with water. The roof of the pit was covered with 2 feet of earth.

Plastic garbage cans are usually watertight; most used metal garbage cans are not. If thoroughly cleaned and disinfected with a strong chlorine bleach solution, watertight garbage cans can serve for emergency water storage, as can some wastebaskets. If new plastic film is available, it can be used as a lining to waterproof any strong box. To lessen the chances of the plastic being punctured, rough containers first should be lined with fabric.

If shelter is to be taken in or near a building, water trapped in hot water heaters and toilet flush tanks or stored in tubs might be available after an attack.

SIPHONING

Pouring water out of a heavy water-storage bag is inconvenient and often results in spillage. Dipping it out can result in contamination. If a tube or piece of flexible garden hose is available, siphoning (see Fig. 8.6) is the best way. A field-tested method is described below. To prevent the suction end of the tube from being obstructed by contact with the plastic liner of the bag, tape or tie a wire "protector" to the end, as pictured later in this section.

Water can be siphoned from a covered water storage pit into a belowground shelter so that the siphon will deliver running water for weeks, if necessary. The Utah family mentioned earlier siphoned all they needed of the 120 gallons of water stored in a nearby lined pit. A field-tested method of siphoning follows:

Fig. 8.6. Using a tube to siphon water from a fabric bag lined with a larger plastic bag.

1. Dig the water storage pit far enough away from the shelter so that the covering mounds will not interfere with drainage ditches.

2. Use a flexible tube or hose which is no more than 25 feet long. For a single family, a flexible rubber tube with an inside diameter of $\frac{1}{4}$ inch (such as surgical tubing) would be best. A flexible $\frac{1}{2}$-inch hose of the type used with mobile homes and boats serves well. As indicated by Fig. 8.7, the tube should be long enough to extend from the bottom of the water pit to within about a foot of the shelter floor.

3. Make sure that the end in the water pit will not press against plastic and block the flow of water. This can be avoided by (1) making and attaching a wire "protector" to the end of the tube, as shown in Fig. 8.8, or (2) taping or tying the end to a rock or other object, to keep the end in the desired position.

4. Protect the tube by placing it in a trench about 4 inches deep. This small trench is best dug before roofing either the storage pit or the shelter. Be sure a roof pole or board does not crush the tube. Cover the tube with earth and tie it so that the end in

Fig. 8.7. Water siphoned into a belowground shelter.

Fig. 8.8. Two wire "protectors," each made of two pieces of coathanger wire taped to a $\frac{1}{2}$-inch flexible hose and a rubber tube. Shown on the right is a tube closed with a rubber band to stop a siphoned flow of water.

the storage pit cannot be accidentally pulled out of position.

5. To start the flow of water into the shelter, hold the free end of the tube at about the height of the surface of the water in the storage pit, while pulling gently on the tube so that the part in the shelter is practically straight. Exhale as much breath as you can, then place the end of the tube in your mouth, and suck hard and long. (The longer the tube or hose and the larger its diameter, the more times you will have to suck to start the flow of water.)

6. Without taking the tube out of your mouth, shut it off airtight by bending it double near the end.

7. Exhale, and suck again, repeating until you feel a good flow of water into your mouth while still sucking. Shut off the flow by bending the tube double before taking it out of your mouth.

8. Quickly lower the end of the tube (which is now full of water) and place the closed end in a container on the shelter floor. Finally, open the end to start the siphoned flow.

9. When you have siphoned enough water, stop the flow by bending the tube double. Keep it closed in the doubled-over, air-tight position with a strong rubber band or string, as shown in Fig. 8.8. To prevent loss of water by accidental siphoning, suspend the end of the tube a couple of inches higher than the surface of the water in the storage pit outside and close to where the tube comes into the shelter. (Despite precautions, air may accumulate in the highest part of the tube, blocking a siphoned flow and making it necessary to re-start the siphoning by repeating the sucking.)

DISINFECTING WATER

Water-borne diseases probably would kill more survivors of a nuclear attack than would fallout-contaminated water. Before an attack, if water from a municipal source is stored in expedient containers that could be unclean, it should be disinfected. For long storage, it is best to disinfect all water, since even a few organisms may multiply rapidly and give stored water a bad taste or odor.

Any household bleach solution, such as Clorox, that contains sodium hypochlorite as its only active

59

ingredient may be used as a source of chlorine for disinfecting. The amount of sodium hypochlorite, usually 5.25%, is printed on the label. (In recent years, perhaps as a precaution against drinking undiluted chlorine bleach solution, some household bleach containers show a warning such as "Not For Personal Use." This warning can be safely disregarded if the label states that the bleach contains only sodium hypochlorite as its active ingredient, and if only the small quantities specified in these and other instructions are used to disinfect water.) Add 1 scant teaspoonful to each 10 gallons of clear water, and stir. Add 2 scant teaspoonfuls if the water is muddy or colored. Wait at least 30 minutes before drinking, to allow enough time for the chlorine to kill all the microorganisms.[24] Properly disinfected water should have a slight chlorine odor.

To disinfect small quantities of water, put 2 drops of household bleach containing 5.25% sodium hypochlorite in each quart of clear water. Use 4 drops if the water is muddy or colored.[21] If a dropper is not available, use a spoon and a square-ended strip of paper or thin cloth about $1/4$ inch wide by 2 inches long. Put the strip in the spoon with an end hanging down about $1/2$ inch beyond the end of the spoon. Then when bleach is placed in the spoon and the spoon is carefully tipped, drops the size of those from a medicine dropper will drip off the end of the strip.

As a second choice, 2% tincture of iodine can be used. Add 5 drops to each quart of clear water, and let stand 30 minutes.[24] If the water is cloudy, add 10 drops to each quart. Commercial water purification tablets should be used as directed.

If neither safe water nor chemicals for disinfecting it are available during a crisis, store plenty of the best water at hand—even muddy river water. Most mud settles to the bottom in a few days; even in a crowded shelter ways often could be found to boil water. Bringing water to a boil for one minute kills all types of disease-causing bacteria.[21] Boiling for 10 to 20 minutes is required to kill some rarer infective organisms.

SOURCES OF WATER IN FALLOUT AREAS

Survivors of a nuclear attack should realize that neither fallout particles nor dissolved radioactive elements or compounds can be removed from water by chemical disinfection or boiling. Therefore, water should be obtained from the least radioactive sources available. Before a supply of stored drinking water has been exhausted, other sources should be located. The main water sources are given below, with the safest source listed first and the other sources listed in decreasing order of safety.

1. Water from deep wells and from water tanks and covered reservoirs into which no fallout particles or fallout-contaminated water has been introduced. (Caution: Although most spring water would be safe, some spring water is surface water that has flowed into and through underground channels without having been filtered.)

2. Water from covered seepage pits or shallow, hand-dug wells. This water is usually safe IF fallout or fallout-contaminated surface water has been prevented from entering by the use of waterproof coverings and by waterproofing the surrounding ground to keep water from running down outside the well casing. Figure 8.9 is taken from a Chinese civil defense manual.[21] It shows a well dug to obtain safe water from a fallout-contaminated source. If the earth is not sandy, gravelly, or too porous, filtration through earth is very effective.

3. Contaminated water from deep lakes. Water from a deep lake would be much less contaminated by dissolved radioactive material and fallout particles than water from a shallow pond would be, if both had the same amount of fallout per square foot of surface area deposited in them. Furthermore, fallout particles settle to the bottom more rapidly in deep lakes than in shallow ponds, which are agitated more by wind.

4. Contaminated water from shallow ponds and other shallow, still water.

5. Contaminated water from streams, which would be especially dangerous if the stream is muddy from the first heavy rains after fallout is deposited.

Fig. 8.9. A water-filtering well. This Chinese drawing specifies that this well should be dug 5 to 10 meters (roughly 5 to 10 yards) from a pond or stream.

The first runoff will contain most of the radioactive material that can be dissolved from fallout particles deposited on the drainage area.[25] Runoff after the first few heavy rains following the deposit of fallout is not likely to contain much dissolved radioactive material, or fallout.

6. Water collected from fallout-contaminated roofs. This would contain more fallout particles than would the runoff from the ground.

7. Water obtained by melting snow that has fallen through air containing fallout particles, or from snow lying on the ground onto which fallout has fallen. Avoid using such water for drinking or cooking, if possible.

WATER FROM WELLS

The wells of farms and rural homes would be the best sources of water for millions of survivors. Following a massive nuclear attack, the electric pumps and the pipes in wells usually would be useless. Electric power in most areas would be eliminated by the effects of electromagnetic pulse (EMP) from high-altitude bursts and by the effects of blast and fire on power stations, transformers, and transmission lines. However, enough people would know how to remove these pipes and pumps from wells so that bail-cans could be used to reach water and bring up enough for drinking and basic hygiene.

How to make a simple bail-can is illustrated in Fig. 8.10. An ordinary large fruit-juice can will serve, if its diameter is at least 1 inch smaller than the

ORNL-DWG 78-6691R

Fig. 8.10. Lower part of an expedient bail-can. The unattached, "caged" valve can be made of a material that does not have the springiness of soft rubber.

diameter of the well-casing pipe. A hole about 1 inch in diameter should be cut in the center of the can's bottom. The hole should be cut from the inside of the can: this keeps the inside of the bottom smooth, so it will serve as a smooth seat for a practically watertight valve. To cut the hole, stand the can on a flat wood surface and press down repeatedly with the point of a sheath knife, a butcher knife, or a sharpened screwdriver.

The best material for the circular, unattached valve shown in Fig. 8.10 is soft rubber, smooth and thin, such as inner-tube rubber. Alternately, the lid of a can about $^3/_4$ inch smaller in diameter than the bail-can may be used, with several thicknesses of plastic film taped to its smooth lower side. Plastic film about 4 mils thick is best. The bail (handle) of a bail-can should be made of wire, with a loop at the top to which a rope or strong cord should be attached.

Filling-time can be reduced by taping half-a-pound of rocks or metal to the bottom of the bail-can.

REMOVING FALLOUT PARTICLES AND DISSOLVED RADIOACTIVE MATERIAL FROM WATER

The dangers from drinking fallout-contaminated water could be greatly lessened by using expedient settling and filtration methods to remove fallout particles and most of the dissolved radioactive material. Fortunately, in areas of heavy fallout, less than 2% of the radioactivity of the fallout particles contained in the water would become dissolved in water.[25] If nearly all the radioactive fallout particles could be removed by filtering or settling methods, few casualties would be likely to result from drinking and cooking with most fallout-contaminated water.

● Filtering

Filtering through earth removes essentially all of the fallout particles and more of the dissolved radioactive material than does boiling-water distillation, a generally impractical purification method that does not eliminate dangerous radioactive iodines. Earth filters are also more effective in removing radioactive iodines than are ordinary ion-exchange water softeners or charcoal filters. In areas of heavy fallout, about 99% of the radioactivity in water could be removed by filtering it through ordinary earth. To make the simple, effective filter shown in Fig. 8.11, the only materials needed are those found in and

61

POROUS
CLOTH

WATER

6 TO 7
in.

CLAYEY
SOIL

1½ in.

PEBBLES

NAIL
HOLES
IN CAN

STICKS
OVER
PAN

FILTERED WATER

EXPEDIENT FILTRATION

Fig. 8.11. Expedient filter to remove radioactivity from water.

around the home. This expedient filter can be built easily by proceeding as follows:

1. Perforate the bottom of a 5-gallon can, a large bucket, a watertight wastebasket, or a similar container with about a dozen nail holes. Punch the holes from the bottom upward, staying within about 2 inches of the center.

2. Place a layer about 1½ inches thick of washed pebbles or small stones on the bottom of the can. If pebbles are not available, twisted coat-hanger wires or small sticks can be used.

3. Cover the pebbles with one thickness of terrycloth towel, burlap sackcloth, or other quite porous cloth. Cut the cloth in a roughly circular shape about 3 inches larger than the diameter of the can.

4. Take soil containing some clay—almost any soil will do—from at least 4 inches below the surface of the ground. (Nearly all fallout particles remain near the surface except after deposition on sand or gravel.)

5. Pulverize the soil, then gently press it in layers over the cloth that covers the pebbles, so that the cloth is held snugly against the sides of the can. Do not use pure clay (not porous enough) or sand (too porous). The soil in the can should be 6 to 7 inches thick.

6. Completely cover the surface of the soil layer with one thickness of fabric as porous as a bath towel. This is to keep the soil from being eroded as water is poured into the filtering can. The cloth also will remove some of the particles from the water. A dozen small stones placed on the cloth near its edges will secure it adequately.

7. Support the filter can on rods or sticks placed across the top of a container that is larger in diameter than the filter can. (A dishpan will do.)

The contaminated water should be poured into the filter can, preferably after allowing it to settle as described below. The filtered water should be disinfected by one of the previously described methods.

If the 6 or 7 inches of filtering soil is a sandy clay loam, the filter initially will deliver about 6 quarts of clear water per hour. (If the filtration rate is faster than about 1 quart in 10 minutes, remove the upper fabric and recompress the soil.) After several hours, the rate will be reduced to about 2 quarts per hour.

When the filtering rate becomes too slow, it can be increased by removing and rinsing the surface fabric, removing about ½ inch of soil, and then replacing the fabric. The life of a filter is extended and its efficiency increased if muddy water is first allowed to settle for several hours in a separate container, as described below. After about 50 quarts have been filtered, rebuild the filter by replacing the used soil with fresh soil.

● Settling

Settling is one of the easiest methods to remove most fallout particles from water. Furthermore, if the water to be used is muddy or murky, settling it before filtering will extend the life of the filter. The procedure is as follows:

1. Fill a bucket or other deep container three-quarters full of the contaminated water.

2. Dig pulverized clay or clayey soil from a depth of four or more inches below ground surface, and stir it into the water. Use about a 1-inch depth of

dry clay or dry clayey soil for every 4-inch depth of water. Stir until practically all the clay particles are suspended in the water.

3. Let the clay settle for at least 6 hours. The settling clay particles will carry most of the suspended fallout particles to the bottom and cover them.

4. Carefully dip out or siphon the clear water, and disinfect it.

● Settling and Filtering

Although dissolved radioactive material usually is only a minor danger in fallout-contaminated water, it is safest to filter even the clear water produced by settling, if an earth filter is available. Finally—as always—the water should be disinfected.

POST-FALLOUT REPLENISHMENT OF STORED WATER

When fallout decays enough to permit shelter occupants to go out of their shelters for short periods, they should try to replenish their stored water. An enemy may make scattered nuclear strikes for weeks after an initial massive attack. Some survivors may be forced back into their shelters by the resultant fallout. Therefore, all available water containers should be used to store the least contaminated water within reach. Even without filtering, water collected and stored shortly after the occurrence of fallout will become increasingly safer with time, due particularly to the rapid decay of radioactive iodines. These would be the most dangerous contaminants of water during the first few weeks after an attack.

Chapter 9

Food

MINIMUM NEEDS

The average American is accustomed to eating regularly and abundantly. He may not realize that for most people food would not be essential for survival during the first two or three weeks following a nuclear attack. Exceptions would be infants, small children, and the aged and sick, some of whom might die within a week without proper nourishment. Other things are more important for short-term survival: adequate shelter against the dangers from blast and fallout, an adequate supply of air, and enough water.

The average American also may not realize that small daily amounts of a few unprocessed staple foods would enable him to survive for many months, or even for years. A healthy person—if he is determined to live and if he learns how to prepare and use whole-grain wheat or corn—can maintain his health for several months. If beans are also available and are substituted for some of the grain, the ration would be improved and could maintain health for many months.

The nutritional information given in this chapter is taken from a July, 1979 publication, *Maintaining Nutritional Adequacy During a Prolonged Food Crisis.*[26] This book brings together from worldwide sources the nutritional facts needed to help unprepared people use unaccustomed foods advantageously during the prolonged crisis that would follow a heavy nuclear attack. The practical know-how which will be given in this chapter regarding the expedient processing and cooking of basic grains and beans is based on old ways which are mostly unknown to modern Americans. These methods have been improved and field-tested by civil defense researchers at Oak Ridge National Laboratory.

LOSS OF HIGH-PROTEIN ANIMAL FOODS

A massive nuclear attack would eliminate the luxurious, complicated American system of food production, processing, and distribution. Extensive, heavy fallout and the inability of farmers to feed their animals would kill most of the cattle, hogs, and chickens that are the basis of our high-protein diet. The livestock most likely to survive despite their owners' inability to care for them would be cattle on pasture. However, these grazing animals would swallow large numbers of fallout particles along with grass, and many would drink contaminated water. Their digestive tracts would suffer severe radiation damage.[27] Also, they would suffer radiation burns from fallout particles. Thus in an outdoor area where the total dose from gamma radiation emitted within a few days from fallout particles on the ground might be only 150 R, most grazing animals probably would be killed by the combined effects of external gamma-ray radiation, beta burns, and internal radiation.[27]

PRECAUTIONS WHEN EATING MEAT

In areas where the fallout would not be enough to sicken animals, their meat would be safe food. In fallout areas, however, animals that have eaten or drunk fallout-contaminated food or water will have concentrated radioactive atoms and molecules in their internal organs. The thyroid gland, kidneys, and liver especially should not be eaten.

If an animal appears to be sick, it should not be eaten. The animal might be suffering from a sickening or fatal radiation dose and might have developed a bacterial infection as a result of this dose. Meat contaminated with the toxins produced by some kinds of bacteria could cause severe illness or death if eaten, even if thoroughly cooked.

Under crisis conditions, all meat should be cooked until it is extremely well done—cooked long past the time when it loses the last of its pink color. To be sure that the center of each piece of meat is raised to boiling temperature, the meat should be cut into pieces that are less than $1/2$-inch thick before cooking. This precaution also reduces cooking time and saves fuel.

SURVIVAL OF BREEDING STOCK

Extensive areas of the United States would not receive fallout heavy enough to kill grazing animals. The millions of surviving animals would provide some food and the fertile breeding stock needed for national recovery. The loss of fertility caused by severe radiation doses is rarely permanent. Extensive experiments with animals have shown that the offspring of severely irradiated animals are healthy and fertile.[27]

LIVING ON BASIC PLANT FOODS

Even if almost all food-producing animals were lost, most surviving Americans should be able to live on the foods that enable most of the world's population to live and multiply: grains, beans, and vegetables. And because of the remarkable productivity of American agriculture, there usually would be enough grain and beans in storage to supply surviving Americans with sufficient food for at least a year following a heavy nuclear attack.[28] The problem would be to get the unprocessed foods, which are stored in food-producing regions, to the majority of survivors who would be outside these regions.

Surprisingly little transportation would be needed to carry adequate quantities of these unprocessed foods to survivors in famine areas. A single large trailer truck can haul 40,000 pounds of wheat—enough to keep 40,000 people from feeling hunger pains for a day. More than enough such trucks and the fuel needed to carry basic foods to food-short areas would survive a massive nuclear attack.[28] It is likely that reasonably strong American leadership and morale would prevail so that, after the first few weeks, millions of the survivors in starving areas should receive basic unprocessed foods.

Eating food produced in the years after a large attack would cause an increase in the cancer rate, due primarily to its content of radioactive strontium and cesium from fallout-contaminated soil. Over the first 30 years following an attack, this increase would be a small fraction of the number of additional cancer deaths that would result from external radiation.[29] Cancer deaths would be one of the tragic, delayed costs of a nuclear war, but all together would not be numerous enough to endanger the long-term survival of the population.

LIVE OFF THE LAND?

Very few survivors of a heavy attack would be in areas where they could live off the land like primitive hunters and gatherers. In extensive areas where fallout would not be heavy enough to kill human beings, wild creatures would die from the combined effects of external gamma radiation, swallowed fallout particles, and beta burns on their bodies. Survival plans should not include dependence on hunting, fishing, or gathering wild plants.

FOOD FOR SHELTER OCCUPANTS

Most people would need very little food to live several weeks; however, the time when survivors of blast and fallout would leave their shelters would mark the beginning of a much longer period of privation and hard manual labor. Therefore, to maintain physical strength and morale, persons in shelters ideally should have enough healthful food to provide well-balanced, adequate meals for many weeks.

In most American homes there are only enough ready-to-eat, concentrated foods to last a few days. Obviously, it would be an important survival advantage to keep on hand a two-week supply of easily transportable foods. In any case, occupants of shelters would be uncertain about when they could get more food and would have to make hard decisions about how much to eat each day. (Those persons who have a fallout meter, such as the homemade instrument described in Chapter 10, could estimate when and for how long they could emerge from shelter to find food. As a result, these persons could ration their limited foods more effectively.)

During the first few weeks of a food crisis, lack of vitamins and other essentials of a well-balanced diet would not be of primary importance to previously well-nourished people. Healthful foods with enough calories to provide adequate energy would meet short-term needs. If water is in short supply, high-protein foods such as meat are best eaten only in moderation, since a person eating high-protein foods requires more water than is needed when consuming an equal number of calories from foods high in carbohydrates.

EXPEDIENT PROCESSING OF GRAINS AND SOYBEANS

Whole-kernel grains or soybeans cannot be eaten in sufficient quantities to maintain vigor and health if merely boiled or parched. A little boiled whole-kernel wheat is a pleasantly chewy breakfast cereal, but experimenters at Oak Ridge got sore tongues and very loose bowels when they tried to eat enough boiled whole-kernel wheat to supply even half of their daily energy needs. Even the most primitive peoples grind or pound grains into a meal or paste before cooking. (Rice is the only important exception.) Few Americans know how to process whole-kernel grains and soybeans (our largest food reserves) into meal. This ignorance could be fatal to survivors of a nuclear attack.

Making an expedient metate, the hollowed-out grinding stone of Mexican Indians, proved impractical under simulated post-attack conditions. Pounding grain into meal with a rock or a capped, solid-ended piece of pipe is extremely slow work. The best expedient means developed and field-tested for pounding grain or beans into meal and flour is an improvised 3-pipe grain mill. Instructions for making and using this effective grain-pounding device follow.

Improvised Grain Mill

The grain mill described can efficiently pound whole-grain wheat, corn, etc., into meal and flour—thereby greatly improving digestibility and avoiding the diarrhea and sore mouths that would result from eating large quantities of unground grain.

TO BUILD:

(1) Cut 3 lengths of pipe, each 30 inches long; $\frac{3}{4}$-inch-diameter steel pipe (such as ordinary water pipe) is best.

(2) Cut the working ends of the pipe off squarely. Remove all roughness, leaving the full-wall thickness. Each working end should have the full diameter of the pipe.

(3) In preparation for binding the three pieces of pipe together into a firm bundle, encircle each

piece of pipe with cushioning, slip-preventing tape, string or cloth—in the locations illustrated.

(4) Tape or otherwise bind the 3 pipes into a secure bundle so that their working ends are as even as possible and are in the same plane—resting evenly on a flat surface.

(5) Cut the top smoothly out of a large can. A 4-inch-diameter, 7-inch-high fruit-juice can is ideal. If you do not have a can, improvise something to keep grain together while pounding it.

ORNL- DWG 73-11449

SLIP-PREVENTING TAPE OR STRING AROUND EACH PIPE

2 in.

30 in.

TAPE OR STRING BINDING ALL 3 PIPES TOGETHER

8 in.

CAN

2 in.

1 in. OF GRAIN IN A CAN RESTING ON A HARD, SMOOTH, SOLID SURFACE

TO MAKE MEAL AND FLOUR:

(1) Put clean, dry grain ONE INCH DEEP in the can.

(2) To prevent blistering your hands, wear gloves, or wrap cloth around the upper part of the bundle of pipes.

(3) Place the can (or open-ended cylinder) on a *hard, smooth, solid* surface, such as concrete.

(4) To pound the grain, sit with the can held between your feet. Move the bundle of pipes straight up and down about 3 inches, with a rapid stroke.

(5) If the can is 4 inches in diameter, in 4 minutes you should be able to pound $\frac{1}{2}$ lb (one cup) of whole-kernel wheat into $\frac{1}{5}$ lb of fine meal and flour, and $\frac{3}{10}$ lb of coarse meal and fine-cracked wheat.

(6) To separate the pounded grain into fine meal, flour, coarse meal, and fine-cracked wheat, use a sieve made of window screen.

(7) To separate flour for feeding small children, place some pounded grain in an 18×18-inch piece of fine nylon net, gather the edges of the net together so as to hold the grain, and shake this bag-like container.

(8) To make flour fine enough for babies, pound fine meal and coarse flour still finer, and sieve it through a piece of cheesecloth or similar material.

As soon as fallout decay permits travel, the grain-grinding machines on tens of thousands of hog and cattle farms should be used for milling grain for survivors. It is vitally important to national recovery and individual survival to get back as soon as possible to labor-saving, mechanized ways of doing essential work.

In an ORNL experiment, a farmer used a John Deere Grinder-Mixer powered by a 100-hp tractor to grind large samples of wheat and barley. When it is used to grind rather coarse meal for hogs, this machine is rated at 12 tons per hour. Set to grind a finer meal-flour mixture for human consumption, it ground both hard wheat and feed barley at a rate of about 9 tons per hour. This is 2400 times as fast as using muscle power to operate even the best expedient grain mill. With its finest screen installed, this large machine can produce about 3 tons of whole wheat flour per hour.

Unlike wheat and corn, the kernels of barley, grain sorghums, and oats have rough, fibrous hulls that must be removed from the digestible parts to produce an acceptable food. Moistening the grain will toughen such hulls and make them easier to remove. If the grain is promptly pounded or ground into meal, the toughened hulls will break into larger pieces than will the hulls of undampened grain. A small amount of water, weighing about 2% of the weight of the grain, should be used to dampen the grain. For 3 pounds of grain (about 6 cups), sprinkle with about one ounce (28 grams, or about 2 tablespoons) of water, while stirring constantly to moisten all the kernels. After about 5 minutes of stirring, the grain will appear dry. The small amount of water will have dampened and toughened the hulls, but the edible parts inside will have remained dry. Larger pieces of hull are easier to remove after grinding than smaller pieces.

One way to remove ground-up hulls from meal is by flotation. Put some of the meal-hulls mixture about 1 inch deep in a pan or pot, cover the mixture with water, and stir. Skim off the floating hulls, then pour off the water and more hulls. Sunken pieces of hulls that settle on top of the heavier meal can be removed with one's fingers as the last of the water is poured off. To produce a barley meal good for very small children, the small pieces of hulls must again be separated by flotation.

Figure 9.1 illustrates sieving fine, dry barley-meal and the smaller pieces of hulls from the coarser

Fig. 9.1. Sieving ground barley through a window-screen sieve.

meal and the larger pieces. The sieve was made of a piece of window screen that measured 20 × 20 inches before its sides were folded up and wired to form an open-topped box.

To lessen their laxative effects, all grains should be ground as finely as possible, and most of the hulls should be removed. Grains also will be digested more easily if they are finely ground. The occupants of crowded shelters should be especially careful to avoid foods that cause diarrhea.

COOKING WITH MINIMUM FUEL

In areas of heavy fallout, people would have to remain continuously in crowded shelters for many days. Then they would have to stay in the shelters most of each 24 hours for weeks. Most shelter occupants soon would consume all of their ready-to-eat foods; therefore, they should have portable, efficient cook stoves. A cook stove is important for another reason: to help maintain morale. Even in warm weather, people need some hot food and drink for the comforting effect and to promote a sense of well-being. This is particularly true when people are under stress. The Bucket Stove pictured on the following pages (Figs. 9.2 and 9.3) was the most satisfactory of several models of expedient stoves developed at Oak Ridge and later field-tested.

● **Bucket Stove**

If operated properly, this stove burns only about $^1/_2$ pound of dry wood or newspaper to heat 3 quarts of water from 60°F to boiling.

Materials required for the stove:

* A metal bucket or can, 12- to 16-quart sizes preferred. The illustrations show a 14-quart bucket and a 6-quart pot.

* Nine all-metal coat hangers for the parts made of wire. (To secure the separate parts of the movable coat-hanger wire grate, 2 feet of finer wire is helpful.)

* A 6 × 10-inch piece of a large fruit-juice can, for a damper.

Construction:

With a chisel (or a sharpened screw driver) and a hammer, cut a $4^1/_2$ × $4^1/_2$-inch hole in the side of the bucket about $1^1/_2$ inches above its bottom. To avoid denting the side of the bucket when chiseling out the hole, place the bucket over the end of a log or similar solid object.

To make the damper, cut a 6-inch-wide by 10-inch-high piece out of a large fruit-juice can or from similar light metal. Then make the two coat-hanger-wire springs illustrated, and attach them to the piece of metal by bending and hammering the outer 1 inch of the two 6-inch-long sides over and around the two spring wires. This damper can be slid up and down, to open and close the hole in the bucket. The springs hold it in any desired position. (If materials for making this damper are not available, the air supply can be regulated fairly well by placing a brick, rock, or piece of metal so that it will block off part of the hole in the side of the bucket.)

To make a support for the pot, punch 4 holes in the sides of the bucket, equally spaced around it and about $3^1/_2$ inches below the bucket's top. Then run a coat-hanger wire through each of the two pairs of holes on opposite sides of the bucket. Bend these two wires over the top of the bucket, as illustrated, so that their four ends form free-ended springs to hold the cooking pot centered in the bucket. Pressure on the pot from these four free-ended, sliding springs does not hinder putting it into the stove or taking it out.

Bend and twist 4 or 5 coat hangers to make the movable grate, best made with the approximate dimensions given in Fig. 9.2.

For adjusting the burning pieces of fuel on the grate, make a pair of 12-inch-long tongs of coat-hanger wire, as illustrated.

To lessen heat losses through the sides and bottom of the bucket, cover the bottom with about 1 inch of dry sand or earth. Then line part of the inside and bottom with two thicknesses of heavy-duty aluminum foil, if available.

To make it easier to place the pot in the stove or take it out without spilling its contents, replace the original bucket handle with a longer piece of strong wire.

Operation:

The Bucket Stove owes its efficiency to: (1) the adjustable air supply that flows up through the burning fuel, (2) the movable grate that lets the operator keep the maximum amount of flame in contact with the bottom of the cooking pot, and (3) the space between the sides of the pot and the inside of the bucket that keeps the rising hot gases in close contact with the sides of the pot.

In a shelter, a Bucket Stove should be placed as near as practical to an air exhaust opening before a fire is started in it.

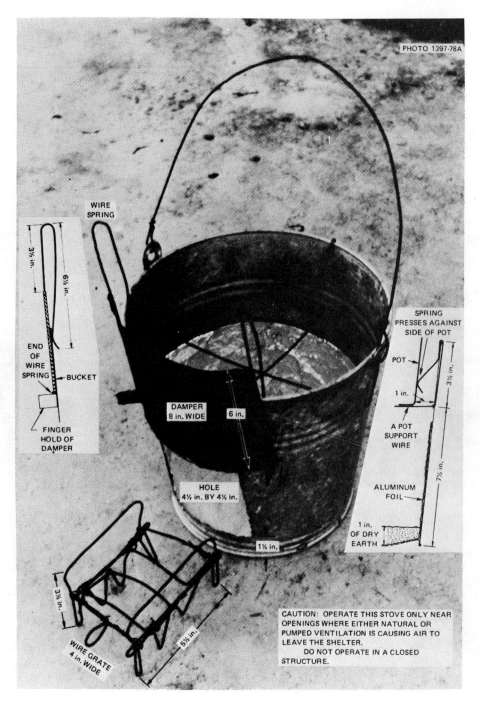

PHOTO 1397-78A

WIRE SPRING

3½ in.

6½ in.

END OF WIRE SPRING — BUCKET

FINGER HOLD OF DAMPER

DAMPER 8 in. WIDE

6 in.

SPRING PRESSES AGAINST SIDE OF POT

POT

1 in.

3½ in.

A POT SUPPORT WIRE

ALUMINUM FOIL

7½ in.

HOLE 4½ in. BY 4½ in.

1½ in.

1 in. OF DRY EARTH

WIRE GRATE 4 in. WIDE

3½ in.

5½ in.

CAUTION: OPERATE THIS STOVE ONLY NEAR OPENINGS WHERE EITHER NATURAL OR PUMPED VENTILATION IS CAUSING AIR TO LEAVE THE SHELTER.

DO NOT OPERATE IN A CLOSED STRUCTURE.

Fig. 9.2. Bucket-stove with adjustable damper and movable wire grate.

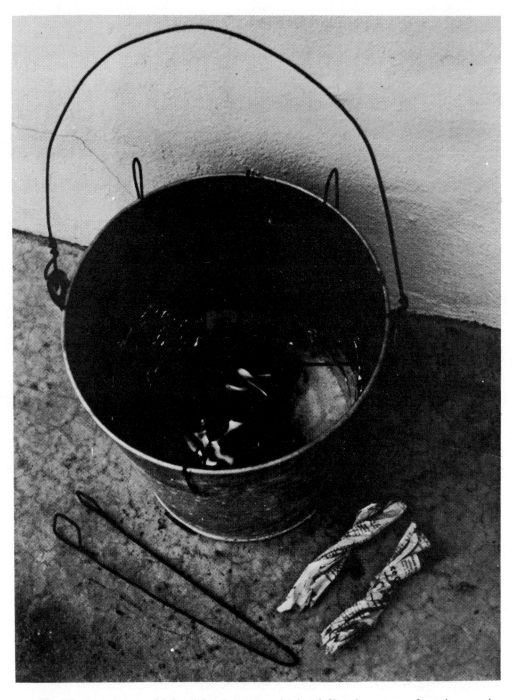

Fig. 9.3. **Bucket-stove with its sliding damper partly closed.** Foot-long tongs of coat hanger wire are especially useful when burning twisted half-pages of newspaper.

If wood is to be burned, cut and split dry wood into small pieces approximately ½ inch square and 6 inches long. Start the fire with paper and small slivers of wood, placing some under the wire grate. To keep fuel from getting damp in a humid shelter, keep it in a large plastic bag.

If newspaper is to be burned, use half-pages folded and twisted into 5-inch-long "sticks," as illustrated. Using the wire tongs, feed a paper "stick" into the fire about every half-minute.

Add fuel and adjust the damper to keep the flame high enough to reach the bottom of the pot, but not so high as to go up the sides of the pot.

To use the Bucket Stove for heating in very cold weather, remove the pot and any insulation around the sides of the bucket; burn somewhat more fuel per minute.

If used with the Fireless Cooker described on the following pages, a Bucket Stove can be used to thoroughly cook beans, grain, or tough meat in water. Three quarts of such food can be cooked with less fuel than is required to soft-boil an egg over a small campfire.

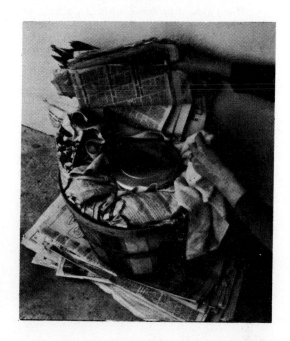

Fig. 9.4. Boiling-hot pot of food being placed in an expedient Fireless Cooker.

● Fireless Cooker

A Fireless Cooker cooks by keeping a lidded pot of boiling-hot food so well insulated all around that it loses heat very slowly. Figure 9.4 shows one of these simple fuel-saving devices made from a bushel basket filled with insulating newspapers, with a towel-lined cavity in the center. The cavity is the size of the 6-quart pot. A towel in this cavity goes all around the pot and will be placed over it to restrict air circulation. If the boiling-hot pot of food is then covered with newspapers about 4 inches thick, the temperature will remain for hours so near boiling that in 4 or 5 hours even slow-cooking food will be ready to eat.

The essential materials for making an effective Fireless Cooker are enough of any good insulating materials (blankets, coats, paper, hay that is dry and pliable) to cover the boiling-hot pot all over with at least 3 or 4 inches of insulation. A container to keep the insulating materials in place around the pot is useful.

Wheat, other grains, and small pieces of tough meat can be thoroughly cooked by boiling them briskly for only about 5 minutes, then insulating the pot in a Fireless Cooker for 4 or 5 hours, or

overnight. Whole beans should be boiled for 10 to 15 minutes before they are placed in a Fireless Cooker.

COOKING GRAIN AND BEANS WHEN SHORT OF FUEL OR POTS

● Cooking Grain Alone

When whole grains are pounded or ground by expedient means, the result usually is a mixture of coarse meal, fine meal, and a little flour. Under shelter conditions, the best way to cook such meal is first to bring the water to a boil (3 parts of water for 1 part of meal). Add 1 teaspoon (5 grams) of salt per pound of dry meal. Remove the pot from the fire (or stop adding fuel to a Bucket Stove) and quickly stir the meal into the hot water. (If the meal is stirred into briskly boiling water, lumping becomes a worse problem.) Then, while stirring constantly, again bring the pot to a rolling boil. Since the meal is just beginning to swell, more unabsorbed water remains, so there is less sticking and scorching than if the meal were added to cold water and then brought to a boil.

If any type of Fireless Cooker is available, the hot cereal only has to be boiled and stirred long enough so that no thin, watery part remains. This usually takes about 5 minutes. Continue to cook, either in the Fireless Cooker for at least 4 or 5 hours, or by boiling for an additional 15 or 20 minutes.

When it is necessary to boil grain meal for many minutes, minimize sticking and scorching by cooking 1 part of dry meal with at least 4 parts of water. However, cooking a thinner hot cereal has a disadvantage during a food crisis: an increased volume of food must be eaten to satisfy one's energy needs.

If grain were the only food available, few Americans doing physical work could eat enough of it to maintain their weight at first, until their digestive tracts enlarged from eating the very bulky foods. This adaptation could take a few months. Small children could not adjust adequately to an all-grain diet; for them, concentrated foods such as fats also are needed to provide enough calories to maintain growth and health.

● Cooking Grain and Beans Together

When soybeans are being used to supplement the lower quality proteins of grain and when fuel or pots are in short supply, first grind or pound the beans into a fine meal. To further reduce cooking time, soak the bean meal for a couple of hours, keeping it covered with water as it swells. Next put the soaked bean meal into a pot containing about 3 times as much water as the total volume of the bean meal and the dry grain meal. Gently boil the bean meal for about 15 minutes, stirring frequently.

Stop boiling and add the grain meal while stirring constantly. Again bring the pot to a boil, stirring to prevent sticking and scorching, and boil until the meal has swelled enough to have absorbed all the water. After salting, boil the grain-bean mush for another 15 minutes or more before eating, or put it in a fireless cooker for at least 4 or 5 hours.

Soybeans boiled alone have a taste that most people find objectionable. Also, whole soybeans must be boiled for a couple of hours to soften them sufficiently. But if soybeans are pounded or ground into a fine meal and then boiled with meal made from corn or another grain, they give a sweetish taste to the resulting mush. The unpleasant soybean taste is eliminated. If cooked as described above, soybeans and other beans or dried peas can be made digestible and palatable with minimum cooking.

100% GRAIN AND 100% BEAN DIETS

A diet consisting solely of wheat, corn, or rice, and salt has most of the essential nutrients. The critical deficiencies would be vitamins A, C, and D. Such a grain-based diet can serve adults and older children as their "staff of life" for months. Table 9.1 shows how less than $1\frac{3}{4}$ pounds of whole wheat or dry yellow corn satisfies most of the essential nutritional requirements of a long-term emergency ration. [The nutritional values that are deficient are printed in bold type, to make an easier comparison with the Emergency Recommendations, also printed in bold type. Food energy is given in kilocalories (kcal), commonly called calories (Cal).] Expedient ways of supplying the nutrients missing from these rations are described in a following section of this chapter.

Other common whole grains would serve about as well as wheat and yellow corn. At least $\frac{1}{6}$ oz of salt per day (about 5 grams) is essential for any ration that is to be eaten for more than a few days, but $\frac{1}{3}$ oz (about 10 g or $\frac{3}{4}$ tablespoon) should be available to allow for increased salt needs and to make grain and beans more palatable. This additional salt would be consumed as needed.

To repeat: few Americans at first would be able to eat the 3 or 4 quarts of thick mush that would be necessary with a ration consisting solely of whole-kernel wheat or corn. Only healthy Americans determined to survive would be likely to fare well for months on such unaccustomed and monotonous food as an all-grain diet. Eating two or more different kinds of grain and cooking in different ways would make an all-grain diet both more acceptable and more nourishing.

Not many people would be able to eat 27 oz (dry weight before cooking) of beans in a day, and fewer yet could eat a daily ration of almost 23 oz of soybeans. Beans as single-food diets are not recommended because their large protein content requires the drinking of more fluids. Roasted peanuts would provide a better single-food ration.

GRAIN SUPPLEMENTED WITH BEANS

People who live on essentially vegetarian diets eat a little of their higher-quality protein food *at every meal,* along with the grain that is their main source of nutrition. Thus Mexicans eat some beans along with their corn tortillas, and Chinese eat a little fermented soybean food or a bit of meat or fish with a bowl of rice. Nutritionists have found that grains

Table 9.1. Daily rations of 100% grain, beans, or peanuts[a]

	Wheat (dry)	Yellow Field Corn[b] (dry)	Emergency Recommendations	Soybeans (dry)	Red Beans (dry)	Peanuts (roasted)
Weight	790g (27.8 oz)	750g (26.4 oz)		645g (22.7 oz)	760g (26.8 oz)	447g (15.8 oz)
Energy, kcal	2600	2600	2600	2600	2600	2600
Protein, g	103	67	55[c]	220	171	117
Fat, g	15	29	30	114	11	218
Calcium, mg	324	165	400	1458	836	322
Magnesium, mg	1260	1100	200–300	1710	1240	782
Iron, mg	26	15.7	10	54.2	52.4	9.8
Potassium, mg	2920	2130	1500–2000	10800	7420	3132
Vitamin A, RE	0	368	555	52	15	0
Thiamin, mg	4.3	2.8	1.0	7.1	3.9	1.3
Riboflavin, mg	1.0	0.9	1.4	2.0	1.5	0.6
Niacin, mg	34.0	16.5[d]	17.0	14.2	17.5	76.4
Vitamin C, mg	0	0	15–30	0	0	0
Vitamin D, μg	0	0	0[e]	0	0	0

[a]Salt (1/3 oz, or 10 g, or 3/4 tablespoon) should be available. This would be consumed as needed.

[b]White corn supplies no Vitamin A, whereas yellow corn supplies 49 RE (retinol equivalent, a measure of Vitamin A value) per 100 g dry weight. Most corn in the United States is yellow corn.

[c]If a diet contains some animal protein such as meat, eggs, or milk, the recommended protein would be less than 55 g per day. If most of the protein is from milk or eggs, only 41 g per day is recommended.

[d]The niacin in corn is not fully available unless the corn is treated with an alkali, such as the lime or ashes Mexicans (and many Americans) add to the water in which corn kernels are soaked or boiled.

[e]Although adults do not need vitamin D, infants, children, and pregnant and lactating women should receive 10 μg (10 micrograms).

are low in some of the essential amino acids that the human body needs to build its proteins. For long-term good health, the essential amino acids must be supplied in the right proportions *with each meal* by eating some foods with more complete proteins than grains have. Therefore, in a prolonged food crisis one should strive to eat *at every meal* at least a little of any higher-quality protein foods that are available. These include ordinary beans, soybeans, milk powder, meat, and eggs.

Table 9.2 shows that by adding 7.0 oz (200 g) of red beans (or other common dried beans) to 21.1 oz (600 g) of either whole wheat or yellow corn, with salt added, you can produce rations that contain adequate amounts of all the important nutrients except vitamin C, vitamin A, vitamin D, and fat. If 5.3 oz (150 g) of soybeans are substituted for the red beans, the fat requirement is satisfied. The 600 g of yellow corn contains enough carotene to enable the body to produce more than half the emergency recommendation of vitamin A. The small deficiencies in riboflavin would not cause sickness.

Other abundant grains, such as grain sorghums or barley, may be used instead of the wheat or corn shown in Table 9.2 to produce fairly well-balanced rations. Other legumes would serve to supplement grain about as well as red beans. (Peanuts are the exception: although higher in energy (fat) than any other unprocessed food, the quality of their protein is not as high as that of other legumes.)

EXPEDIENT WAYS TO SUPPLY DEFICIENT ESSENTIAL NUTRIENTS

● Vitamin C

A deficiency of vitamin C (ascorbic acid) causes scurvy. This deadly scourge would be the first nutritional disease to afflict people having only grain and/or beans and lacking the know-how needed to sprout them and produce enough vitamin C. Within only 4 to 6 weeks of eating a ration containing no vitamin C, the first symptom of scurvy would appear: swollen and bleeding gums. This would be followed by weakness, then large bruises, hemorrhages, and

Table 9.2. Daily rations of whole wheat or yellow corn supplemented with soybeans or red beans. Recommended daily salt ration, including salt in food: $^3/_4$ tablespoon ($^1/_3$ oz, or 10 g).

	600g (21.1 oz) Whole wheat plus 200g (7.0 oz) Red beans (dry wt)	600g (21.1 oz) Whole wheat plus 150g (5.3 oz) Soybeans (dry wt)	Emergency Recommendations	600g (21.1 oz) Yellow corn[a] plus 150g (5.3 oz) Soybeans (dry wt)	600g (21.1 oz) Yellow corn plus 200g (7.0 oz) Red beans (dry wt)
Energy, kcal	2,666	2,585	2,600	2,693	2,774
Protein, g	123	129	55[b]	105	98
Fat, g	15	39	30	50	26
Calcium, mg	466	585	400	471	352
Magnesium, mg	1,286	1,358	200–300	1,280	1,208
Iron, mg	33.6	32.4	10	25.2	26.4
Potassium, mg	4,188	4,736	1,500–2,000	4,220	3,672
Vitamin A, RE	4	12	555	306	298
Thiamin, mg	4.3	5.0	1.0	3.9	3.2
Riboflavin, mg	1.1	1.2	1.4	1.2	1.1
Niacin, mg	30.4	29.1	17.0	16.5[c]	17.8
Vitamin C, mg	0	0	15–30	0	0
Vitamin D, μg	0	0	0[d]	0	0

[a]White corn supplies no vitamin A, whereas yellow corn supplies 49RE (retinol equivalent, a measure of vitamin A value) per 100g dry weight. Most corn in the United States is yellow corn.

[b]If a diet contains animal protein such as meat, eggs or milk, the recommended protein would be less than 55g per day. If all the protein is from milk or eggs, only 41g per day is required.

[c]The niacin in corn is not fully available unless corn is treated with an alkali, such as the lime or ashes added by Mexicans and Americans in the South and Southwest to the water in which they soak or boil corn kernels.

[d]Although adults do not need vitamin D, infants, children, and pregnant and lactating women should receive 10 μg (10 micrograms).

wounds that would not heal. Finally, death from hemorrhages and heart failure would result.

One good expedient way to prevent or cure scurvy is to eat sprouted seeds—not just the sprouts. Sprouted beans prevented scurvy during a famine in India. Captain James Cook was able to keep his sailors from developing scurvy during a three-year voyage by having them drink daily an unfermented beer made from dried, sprouted barley. For centuries the Chinese have prevented scurvy during the long winters of northern China by consuming sprouted beans.

Only 10 mg of vitamin C taken each day ($^1/_5$ of the smallest vitamin C tablet) is enough to prevent scurvy. If a little over an ounce (about 30 grams) of dry beans or dry wheat is sprouted until the sprouts are a little longer than the seeds, the sprouted seeds will supply 10 to 15 mg of vitamin C. Such sprouting, if done at normal room temperature, requires about 48 hours. To prevent sickness and to make sprouted beans more digestible, the sprouted seeds should be boiled in water for not longer than 2 minutes. Longer cooking will destroy too much vitamin C.

Usual sprouting methods produce longer sprouts than are necessary when production of enough vitamin C is the objective. These methods involve rinsing the sprouting seeds several times a day in safe water. Since even survivors not confined to shelters are likely to be short of water, the method illustrated in Fig. 9.5 should be used. First the seeds to be sprouted are picked clean of trash and broken seeds. Then the seeds are covered with water and soaked for about 12 hours. Next, the water is drained off and the soaked, swollen seeds are placed on the inside of a plastic bag or a jar, in a layer no more than an inch deep. If a plastic bag is used, you should make two loose rolls of paper, crumble them a little, dampen them, and place them inside the bag, along its sides. As shown in Fig. 9.5, these two dampened paper rolls keep the plastic from resting on the seeds and form an air passage down the center of the bag. Wet paper should be placed in the mouth of the bag or jar so as to leave an air opening of only about 1 square inch. If this paper is kept moist, the seeds will remain sufficiently damp while receiving enough circulating air to prevent molding. They will sprout sufficiently after about 48 hours at normal room temperature.

Fig. 9.5. Sprouting with minimum water.

Sprouting seeds also increases their content of riboflavin, niacin, and folic acid. Sprouted beans are more digestible than raw, unsprouted beans, but not as easily digested or nourishing as are sprouted beans that have been boiled or sauteed for a couple of minutes. Sprouting is not a substitute for cooking. Contrary to the claims of some health food publications, sprouting does not increase the protein content of seeds, nor does it improve protein quality. Furthermore, sprouting reduces the caloric value of seeds. The warmth generated by germinating seeds reduces their energy value somewhat, as compared to unsprouted seeds.

● Vitamin A

Well-nourished adults have enough vitamin A stored in their livers to prevent vitamin A deficiency problems for several months, even if their diet during that time contains none of this essential vitamin. Children would be affected by deficiencies sooner than adults. The first symptom is an inability to see well in dim light. Continuing deficiency causes changes in body tissues. In infants and children, lack of vitamin A can result in stunted growth and serious eye problems—even blindness. Therefore, a survival diet should be balanced with respect to vitamin A as soon as possible, with children having priority.

Milk, butter, and margarine are common vitamin A sources that would not be available to most survivors. If these were no longer available,

yellow corn, carrots, and green, leafy vegetables (including dandelion greens) would be the best sources. If these foods were not obtainable, the next best source would be sprouted whole-kernel wheat or other grains—if seeds could be sprouted for three days in the light, so that the sprouts are green. Although better than no source, sprouting is not a very satisfactory way to meet vitamin A requirements. The development of fibrous roots makes 3-day sprouted wheat kernels difficult to eat. And one must eat a large amount of seeds with green sprouts and roots to satisfy the recommended daily emergency requirements—up to $5\frac{1}{2}$ cups of 5-day sprouted alfalfa seeds. Survivors of a nuclear attack would wish they had kept an emergency store of multivitamin pills.

● Vitamin D

Without vitamin D, calcium is not adequately absorbed. As a result, infants and children would develop rickets (a disease of defective bone mineralization). A massive nuclear attack would cut off the vast majority of Americans from their main source of vitamin D, fortified milk.

Vitamin D can be formed in the body if the skin is exposed to the ultraviolet rays of the sun. Infants should be exposed to sunlight very cautiously, initially for only a few minutes—especially after a massive nuclear attack. Such an attack possibly could cause atmospheric changes that would permit more ultraviolet light to reach the earth's surface. In cold weather, maximum exposure of skin to sunlight is best done in a shallow pit shielded from the wind.

● Niacin and Calcium

Niacin deficiency causes pellagra, a disease that results in weakness, a rash on skin exposed to the sun, severe diarrhea, and mental deterioration. If a typical modern American had a diet primarily of corn and lacked the foods that normally supply niacin, symptoms of pellagra would first appear in about 6 months. Since corn is by far our largest crop—the U.S. production in 1974 was about 284 billion pounds—the skillful treatment of corn would be important to post-attack survival and recovery.

During the first part of this century, pellagra killed thousands of Americans in the South each year. These people had corn for their principal staple and ate few animal protein foods or beans. Yet

Mexicans, who eat even more corn than did those Southerners—and have even fewer foods of animal origin—do not suffer from pellagra.

The Mexicans' freedom from pellagra is mainly due to their traditional method of soaking and boiling their dried corn in a lime-water solution. They use either dry, unslaked lime (calcium oxide, a dangerously corrosive substance made by roasting limestone) or dry, slaked lime (calcium hydroxide, made by adding water to unslaked lime). Dry lime weighing about 1% as much as the dry corn is added to the soak water, producing an alkaline solution. Wood ashes also can be used instead of lime to make an alkali solution. The alkali treatment of corn makes the niacin available to the human body. Tables 9.1 and 9.2 show corn as having adequate niacin. However, the niacin in dried corn is not readily available to the body unless the corn has received an alkali treatment.

Treating corn with lime has another nutritional advantage: the low calcium content of corn is significantly increased.

• Fat

The emergency recommendation for fat is slightly over 1 ounce per day (30 g) of fat or cooking oil. This amount of fat provides only 10% of the calories in the emergency diet, which does not specify a greater amount because fats would be in very short supply after a nuclear attack. This amount is very low when compared to the average diet eaten in this country, in which fat provides about 40% of the calories. It would be difficult for many Americans to consume sufficient calories to maintain normal weight and morale without a higher fat intake; more fat should be made available as soon as possible. Increased fat intake is especially important for young children, to provide calories needed for normal growth and development. Oak Ridge National Laboratory field tests have shown that toddlers and old people, especially, prefer considerably more oil added to grain mush than the emergency recommendation of 10%.

• Animal Protein

Vitamin B-12 is the only essential nutrient that is available in nature solely from animal sources. Since a normal person has a 2 to 4-year supply of vitamin B-12 stored in his liver, a deficiency should not develop before enough food of animal origin would again be available.

Many adults who are strict vegetarians keep in good health for years without any animal sources of food by using grains and beans together. It is more difficult to maintain normal growth and development in young children on vegetarian diets. When sufficient animal sources of food are available, enough should be provided to supply 7 grams of animal protein daily. This could be provided by about 1.4 ounces (38 g) of lean meat, 0.7 ounce (20 g) of nonfat dry milk, or one medium-sized egg. When supplies are limited, young children should be given priority. Again: a little of these high-grade supplementary protein foods should be eaten with every meal.

• Iron

Most people live out their lives without benefit of an iron supplement. However, many pregnant and nursing women and some children need supplemental iron to prevent anemia. One tested expedient way to make more iron available is to use iron pots and pans, especially for cooking acid foods such as tomatoes. Another is to place plain iron nails (not galvanized nails) in vinegar until small amounts of iron begin to float to the surface. This usually takes 2 to 4 weeks. Then a teaspoon of iron-vinegar solution will contain about 30 to 60 mg of iron, enough for a daily supplement. The emergency recommendation is 10 mg per day. A teaspoon of the iron-vinegar solution is best taken in a glass of water. The iron content of fruit, such as an apple, can be increased by placing iron nails in it for a few days.

FOOD RESERVES

Russia, China, and other countries that make serious preparations to survive disasters store large quantities of food—primarily grain—both in farming areas and near population centers. In contrast, the usually large U.S. stocks of grain and soybeans are an unplanned survival resource resulting from the production of more food than Americans can eat or sell abroad. The high productivity of U.S. agriculture is another unplanned survival asset. Providing enough calories and other essential nutrients for 100 million surviving Americans would necessitate the annual raising of only about 16% of our 1974 crop of corn, wheat, grain sorghum, and soybeans— if nothing else were produced. In 1974, the U.S.

production of corn, wheat, and grain sorghum totalled about 408 billion pounds, and that of soybeans was 68 billion pounds. A total of 2 pounds per person per day of these basic staples, in the proportions shown in Table 9.2, would be sufficient to provide the essentials of an adequate vegetarian diet weighing about 27 ounces. (Grain sorghum is not listed in Table 9.2; it has approximately the same food value as corn.) The remaining 5 ounces of the 2 pounds would feed enough chickens to meet a survivor's minimum long-term requirement for animal protein.

If corn, wheat, grain sorghum, and soybeans were the only crops raised, the annual production would need to be 730 pounds per person. Our 1974 annual production would have supplied every adult, child, and infant in a population of 100 million with 4760 pounds of these four staples. This is more than 6 times enough to maintain good nutrition by Chinese standards.

Recovery from a massive nuclear attack would depend largely on sufficient food reserves being available to enable survivors to concentrate on restoring the essentials of mechanized farming. Enough housing would remain intact or could be built to provide adequate shelter for the first few crucial years; enough clothing and fabrics would be available. But if survivors were forced by hunger to expend their energies attempting primitive subsistence farming, many deaths from starvation would occur and the prospects for national recovery would be greatly reduced. In view of the crucial importance of large food reserves to the prospects for individual and national survival, it is to be hoped that U.S. food surpluses and large annual carry-overs will continue.

A BASIC SURVIVAL RATION TO STORE

A ration composed of the basic foods listed below in Table 9.3 provides about 2600 calories per day and is nutritionally balanced. It keeps better than a ration of typical American foods, requires much less space to store or transport, and is much less expensive. The author and some friends have stored enough of these basic foods to last their families several months during a crisis, and have eaten large quantities of these foods with satisfaction over the past 20 years. (A different emergency ration should be stored for infants and very small children, as will be explained in the following section.) Field tests have indicated that the majority of Americans would find these basic foods acceptable under crisis conditions. In normal times, however, no one should store this or any other emergency food supply until after he has prepared, eaten, and found its components satisfactory.

Unprocessed grains and beans provide adequate nourishment for many millions of the world's people who have little else to eat. Dry grains and beans are very compact: a 5-gallon can holds about 38 pounds of hard wheat. Yet when cooked, dry whole grains become bulky and give a well-fed feeling—a distinct advantage if it is necessary to go on short rations during a prolonged crisis.

This basic ration has two disadvantages: (1) it requires cooking, and (2) Americans are unaccustomed to such a diet. Cooking difficulties can be minimized by having a grain-grinding device, a

Table 9.3. A basic survival ration for multi-year storage

	Ounces per day	Grams per day	Pounds for 30 days full ration	Kilograms for 30 days full ration
Whole-kernel hard wheat	16	454	30.0	13.6
Beans	5	142	9.4	4.3
Non-fat milk powder	2	57	3.8	1.7
Vegetable oil	1	28	1.9	0.9
Sugar	2	57	3.8	1.7
Salt (iodized)	$1/3$	10	0.63	0.3
Total Weights	$26^1/_3$	748	49.5	22.5
Multi-vitamin pills:		1 pill each day		

bucket stove with a few pounds of dry wood or newspapers for fuel, and the know-how to make a "fireless cooker" by using available insulating materials such as extra clothing. The disadvantage of starting to eat unaccustomed foods at a stressful time can be lessened by eating more whole grains and beans in normal times—thereby, incidentally, saving money and improving a typical American diet by reducing fat and increasing bulk and fiber.

When storing enough of this ration to last for several months or a year, it is best to select several kinds of beans for variety and improved nutrition. If soybeans are included, take into account the differences between soybeans and common beans, as noted earlier in this chapter.

In many areas it is difficult to buy wheat and beans at prices nearly as low as the farmer receives for these commodities. However, in an increasing number of communities, at least one store sells whole-grain wheat and beans in large sacks at reasonable prices. Mormons, who store food for a range of possible personal and national disasters, are often the best sources of information about where to get basic foods in quantity, at reasonable cost. Soon after purchase, bulk foods should be removed from sacks (but not necessarily from sealed-plastic liner-bags) and sealed in metal containers or in thick-walled plastic containers for storage. Especially in the more humid parts of the United States, grain and beans should be frequently checked for moisture. If necessary, these foods should be dried out and rid of insects as described later in this chapter.

Vegetable oil stores as well in plastic bottles as in glass ones. The toughness and lightness of plastic bottles make them better than glass for carrying when evacuating or for using in a shelter. Since a pound of oil provides about $2\frac{1}{4}$ times as much energy as does a pound of sugar, dry grain, or milk powder, storing additional vegetable oil is an efficient way to improve a grain diet and make it more like the 40%-fat diet of typical Americans.

All multivitamin pills providing 5000 International Units (1500 mg retinol equivalent) vitamin A, 400 IU (10 mg) of vitamin D, and 50 to 100 mg of vitamin C, must meet U.S. Government standards, so the least expensive usually are quite adequate. Storage in a refrigerator greatly lengthens the time before vitamin pills must be replaced with fresh ones. Because vitamin C is so essential, yet very

inexpensive and long-lasting, it is prudent to store a large bottle.

It would be wise to have on hand ready-to-eat, compact foods for use during a week or two in a shelter, in addition to those normally kept in the kitchen. It is not necessary to buy expensive "survival foods" or the special dehydrated foods carried by many backpackers. All large food stores sell the following concentrated foods: non-fat milk powder, canned peanuts, compact ready-to-eat dry cereals such as Grape Nuts, canned meat and fish, white sugar, vegetable oil in plastic bottles, iodized salt, and daily multivitamin pills. If shelter occupants have a way to boil water (see Figs. 9.2 and 9.3, Bucket Stove), it is advisable to include rice, noodles, and an "instant" cooked cereal such as oatmeal or wheat—along with coffee and tea for those who habitually drink these beverages.

Parched grain is a ready-to-eat food that has been used for thousands of years. Whole-kernel wheat, corn, and rice can be parched by the following method: Place the kernels about $\frac{1}{4}$-inch deep in a pan, a skillet, or a tin can while shaking it over a flame, hot coals, or a red hot electric burner. The kernels will puff and brown slightly when parched. These parched grains are not difficult to chew and can be pounded to a meal more easily than can the raw kernels. Parched grain stores well if kept dry and free of insects.

EMERGENCY FOOD FOR BABIES

Infants and very small children would be the first victims of starvation after a heavy nuclear attack, unless special preparations are made on their behalf. Our huge stocks of unprocessed foods, which could prevent the majority of unprepared survivors from dying of hunger, would not be suitable for the very young. They need foods that are more concentrated and less rough. Most American mothers do not nurse their infants, and if a family's supply of baby foods were exhausted the parents might experience the agony of seeing their baby slowly starve.

Few Americans have watched babies starving. In China, I saw anguish on starving mothers' faces as they patted and squeezed their flat breasts, trying to get a little more milk into their weak babies' mouths. I saw this unforgettable tragedy in the midst of tens of thousands of Chinese evacuating on foot before a ruthless Japanese army during World War II. Years later, my wife and I stored several hundred pounds of milk powder while our five children were small. I believe that parents who fear the use of nuclear weapons will be glad to bear the small expense of keeping on hand the emergency baby foods listed in Table 9.4, below. (More detailed descriptions of these and many other foods, with instructions for their use, are given in an Oak Ridge National Laboratory report, *Maintaining Nutritional Adequacy During A Prolonged Food Crisis,* ORNL-5352, 1979. This report may be purchased for $6.50 from National Technical Information Service, U.S. Department of Commerce, 5385 Port Royal Road, Springfield, Virginia 22161.)

To make a formula adequate for a 24-hour period, the quantities of instant non-fat dry milk, vegetable cooking oil, and sugar listed in the "Per Day" column of Table 9.4 should be added to 4 cups of safe water. This formula can be prepared daily in cool weather or when a refrigerator is available. In warm or hot weather, or under unsanitary conditions, it is safer to make a formula 3 times a day. To do so, add $1/3$ cup plus 2 teaspoons (a little less than one ounce) of instant non-fat milk powder to $1^1/3$ cups ($^2/3$ pint) of boiled water, and stir thoroughly. Then add 1 tablespoon (about $1/3$ ounce, or 9 grams) of vegetable oil and 2 teaspoons of sugar, and stir. (If regular bakers' milk powder is used, $1/4$ cup is enough when making one-third of the daily formula, 3 times a day.) If baby bottles are not at hand, milk can be spoon-fed to an infant.

Especially during a war crisis, the best and most dependable food for an infant is mother's milk—provided the mother is assured an adequate diet. The possibility of disaster is one more reason

why a mother should nurse her baby for a full year. Storing additional high-protein foods and fats for a nursing mother usually will be better insurance against her infant getting sick or starving than keeping adequate stocks of baby foods and the equipment necessary for sanitary feeding after evacuation or an attack.

To give a daily vitamin supplement to a baby, a multivitamin pill should be crushed to a fine powder between two spoons and dissolved in a small amount of fluid, so that the baby can easily swallow it. If an infant does not receive adequate amounts of vitamins A, D, and C, he will develop deficiency symptoms in 1 to 3 months, depending on the amounts stored in his body. Vitamin C deficiency, the first to appear, can be prevented by giving an infant 15 mg of vitamin C each day (about $1/3$ of a 50-mg vitamin C tablet, pulverized) or customary foods containing vitamin C, such as orange juice. Lacking these sources, the juice squeezed from sprouted grains or legumes can be used. If no vitamin pills or foods rich in vitamin D are available, exposure of the baby's skin to sunlight will cause his body to produce vitamin D. It would be wise to wait about 30 days after an attack before exposing the baby to sunlight. After that, short exposures would be safe except in areas of extremely heavy fallout. As a further precaution, the baby can be placed in an open, shallow pit that will provide shielding from radiation given off by fallout particles on the ground. Initial exposure should be very short, no more than 10 minutes.

If sufficient milk is not obtainable, even infants younger than six months should be given solid food. Solid foods for babies must be pureed to a fine

Table 9.4. Emergency food supply for one baby.

Ingredients	Per Day		Per Month		Per 6 Months	
	Volumes and Ounces	Grams	Pounds	Kilograms	Pounds	Kilograms
Instant non-fat dry milk	1 cup + 2 tablespoons ($2^3/4$ oz)	8	6	2.72	32	15
Vegetable cooking oil	3 tablespoons (1 oz)	30	2	0.90	12	5.5
Sugar	2 tablespoons (0.7 oz)	20	1.3	0.60	8	3.6
Standard daily multi-vitamin pills	$1/3$ pill			10 pills		60 pills

texture. Using a modern baby food grinder makes pureeing quick and easy work. Under crisis conditions, a grinder should be cleaned and disinfected like other baby-feeding utensils, as described later in this section.

Several expedient methods are available: the food can be pressed through a sieve, mashed with a fork or spoon, or squeezed through a porous cloth. Good sanitation must be maintained; all foods should be brought to a boil after pureeing to insure that the food is safe from bacteria.

A pureed solid baby food can be made by first boiling together 3 parts of a cereal grain and 1 part of beans until they are soft. Then the mixture should be pressed through a sieve. The sieve catches the tough hulls from the grain kernels and the skins from the beans. The grain-beans combination will provide needed calories and a well-supplemented protein. The beans also supply the additional iron that a baby needs by the time he is 6 months old. Flours made from whole grains or beans, as previously described, also can be used; however, these may contain more rough material.

Some grains are preferable to others. It is easier to sieve cooked corn kernels than cooked wheat kernels. Since wheat is the grain most likely to cause allergies, it should not be fed to an infant until he is 6 to 7 months old if other grains, such as rice or corn, are available.

Small children also need more protein than can be supplied by grains alone. As a substitute for milk, some bean food should be provided at every meal. If the available diet is deficient in a concentrated energy source such as fat or sugar, a child's feedings should be increased to 4 or 5 times a day, to enable him to assimilate more. Whenever possible, a small child should have a daily diet that contains at least one ounce of fat (3 tablespoons, without scraping the spoon). This would provide more than 10% of a young child's calories in the form of fat, which would be beneficial.

If under emergency conditions it is not practical to boil infant feeding utensils, they can be sterilized with a bleach solution. Add one teaspoon of ordinary household bleach to a quart of water. (Ordinary household bleach contains 5.25% sodium hypochlorite as its only active ingredient and supplies approximately 5% available chlorine. If the strength of the bleach is unknown, add 3 teaspoons per quart.) Directions for safe feeding without boiling follow:

The Utensils (Include at least one 1-quart and one 1-pint mason jar, for keeping prepared formula sterile until used.)

1. Immediately after feeding, wash the inside and outside of all utensils used to prepare the formula and to feed the infant.

2. Fill a covered container with clean, cold water and add the appropriate amount of chlorine bleach.

3. Totally immerse all utensils until the next feeding (3 or 4 hours). Be sure that the bottle, if used, is filled with bleach solution. Keep container covered.

At Feeding Time

1. Wash hands before preparing food.

2. Remove utensils from the disinfectant chlorine solution and drain, but do not rinse or dry.

3. Prepare formula; feed the baby.

4. Immediately after feeding, wash utensils in clean water and immerse again in the disinfectant solution.

5. Prepare fresh chlorine solution each day.

STORAGE OF FOODS

Whole grains and white sugar can be stored successfully for decades; dried beans, non-fat milk powder, and vegetable oil can be stored for several years. Some rules for good storage follow:

• **Keep food dry.** The most dependable way to assure continuing dryness is to store dry grain in metal containers, such as ordinary 5-gallon metal storage cans or 55-gallon metal drums with gasketed lids. Filled 5-gallon cans are light enough to be easily carried in an automobile when evacuating.

Particularly in humid areas, grain which seems to be dry often is not dry enough to store for a long period. To be sure that grain is dry enough to store for years, use a drying agent. The best drying agent for this purpose is silica gel with color indicator. The gel is blue when it is capable of absorbing water and pink when it needs to be heated to become an effective drying agent again. Silica gel is inexpensive if bought from chemical supply firms located in most cities. By heating it in a hot oven or in a can over a fire until it turns blue again, silica gel can be used repeatedly for years.

The best containers for the silica gel used to dry grain (or to determine its dryness) are homemade cloth envelopes large enough for a heaping cupful of the gel. A clear plastic window should be stitched in, through which color changes can be observed. Put an envelope of silica gel on top of the grain in a 5-gallon can filled to within a couple of inches of its top. Then close the can tightly. Even a rather loose-fitting lid can be sealed tightly with tape. If after a few days the silica gel is still blue, the grain is dry enough. If the silica gel has turned pink, repeat the process with fresh envelopes until it can be seen that the grain is dry.

• **Keep grains and beans free of weevils, other insects, and rodents.** Dry ice (carbon dioxide) is the safest means still widely available to the public for ridding grain and beans of insects. Place about 4 ounces of dry ice on top of the grain in a 5-gallon metal container. Put the lid on somewhat loosely, so that air in the grain can be driven out of the can. (This will happen as the dry ice vaporizes and the heavy carbon dioxide gas sinks into the grain and displaces the air around the kernels.) After an hour or two, tighten the lid and seal it with tape. After one month, all insects in this carbon-dioxide atmosphere will have died from lack of oxygen.

• **Store foods in the coolest available place, out of the light.** Remember that the storage life of most foods is cut in half by an increase of 18°F (10°C) in storage temperature.[30] Thus 48 months of storage at 52°F is equivalent to 24 months at 70°F, and to 12 months at 88°F.

Illustrative of the importance of cool storage are my experiences in storing non-fat milk powder in an earth-covered, cool shelter. In steel drums I stored unopened 100-pound bags of compact, non-fat milk powder that I bought from bakeries. The cost per pound was much less than I would have paid for the largest packages sold in supermarkets. After 7 years storage at temperatures of about 50°F the year around, my milk powder was still good—as good as it would have been if stored in a normally air-conditioned and heated home for about 3 years.

• **Do not place stored metal containers directly on the floor.** To avoid possible condensation of moisture and the rusting that results, place containers on spaced boards. For long-term storage in damp permanent shelters or damp basements, use solid-plastic containers with thick walls.

• **Rotate stored foods.** Eat the oldest food of each type and replace it with fresh food. Although cooking oil and non-fat milk powder remain edible after several years of storage at room temperature, these and most other dry foods are more nourishing and taste better if stored for no more than 2 years. Most canned foods taste better if kept no more than one year. Exceptions are whole grains and white sugar, which stay good for decades if stored properly.

Chapter 10

Fallout Meters

THE CRITICAL NEED

A survivor in a shelter that does not have a dependable fallout meter—or that has one but lacks someone who knows how to use it—will face a prolonged nightmare of uncertainties. Human beings cannot feel, smell, taste, hear, or see fallout radiation. A heavy attack would put most radio stations off the air, due to the effects of electromagnetic pulse, blast, fire, or fallout from explosions. Because fallout intensities often vary greatly over short distances, those stations still broadcasting would rarely be able to give reliable information concerning the constantly changing radiation dangers around a survivor's shelter.

Which parts of the shelter give the best protection? How large is the radiation dose being received by each person? When is it safe to leave the shelter for a few minutes? When can one leave for an hour's walk to get desperately needed water? As the fallout continues to decay, how long can one safely work each day outside the shelter? When can the shelter be left for good? Only an accurate, dependable fallout meter will enable survivors to answer these life-or-death questions.

Civil defense experts have long recognized the central importance of having an adequate number of fallout meters and enough people trained to use them intelligently. In 1953 the National Academy of Sciences' Advisory Committee on Civil Defense concluded: "The final effectiveness of shelter depends upon the occupants of any shelter having simple, rugged, and reliable dose-rate meters to measure the fallout dose rate outside the shelter."

Note that *dose-rate* meters are specified. A dose-rate meter (also called a survey meter) is a fallout meter designed to measure the roentgens per hour (R/hr) of fallout radiation to which it is exposed. The other important type of fallout meter used in civil defense is a dosimeter, which measures the total dose (R) to which it has been exposed since being charged, or the dose between readings.

COMMERCIALLY AVAILABLE FALLOUT METERS

In 1979 an American does not have many choices if he wants to buy an off-the-shelf dose-rate meter suitable for measuring the high levels of fallout radiation that would result from a nuclear attack. Although inexpensive dose-rate meters and dosimeters have been under development by the military services and civil defense researchers for the past 10 years, they have not been produced commercially. Field tests of factory-produced models have not been completed at this writing.

An American instrument that satisfies most requirements of a wartime fallout meter is the Panoramic 470-A Survey Meter. This dose-rate meter is manufactured and sold by Victoreen Instrument Division, 10101 Woodland Avenue, Cleveland, Ohio 44104. It measures dose rates from 1 mR/hr to 1000 R/hr, is powered by 6 small batteries, and has modern integrated circuits that prolong battery life. The list price in 1979 was $810. Another American dose-rate meter is the RO-1 Survey Meter of Eberline Instrument Corp., P.O. Box 2108, Santa Fe, New Mexico 87501. This instrument measures dose rates from 0.2 mR/hr up to 500 R/hr and sold for $1125 in 1979.

A more rugged dose-rate meter, an instrument designed for wartime use that measures from 0.01 mR/hr to 300 R/hr, can be purchased from a Finnish manufacturer, Wallac Nuclear Instruments, P.O.

Box 10, 20101 Turku 10, Finland. Including import duties, the 1978 cost of the Wallac model RD-8 Universal Radiation Survey Meter was about $565. The author and an associate both have owned Wallac RD-8 rate meters for years, with no maintenance problems.

Commercially available dosimeters, which record the total dose received between readings, are not as expensive. In early 1978, high-range dosimeters retailed for about $70. A dosimeter sold by Dosimeter Corporation of America and by Victoreen Instrument Division measures doses up to 600 R. (Current price information can be obtained by writing to Dosimeter Corporation of America at P.O. Box 42377, Cincinnati, Ohio 45242 and to Victoreen Instrument Division, 10101 Woodland Avenue, Cleveland, Ohio 44104.)

A battery-powered charger must be used to operate all available dosimeters; one charger can be used for several of these instruments. A charger can be purchased from the same companies for about $70.

When the total dose shown on a dosimeter is observed to be increasing rapidly, a high-range dosimeter can be used to determine the dose rate, although this method is time-consuming. (If a 600 R dosimeter is exposed for 30 minutes and records a dose of 40 R, the dose rate is 40 R $\div \frac{1}{2}$ hr = 80 R/hr.)

Periodically, all commercially available fallout meters should be (1) supplied with fresh batteries, (2) checked with a radiation source (preferably each year) to see if they are still measuring radiation accurately, and (3) repaired if necessary.

The reader is advised to buy a good commercial dose-rate meter with which to quickly measure high levels of radiation, if he can afford one. A good commercial instrument, if properly maintained and calibrated, can be used for many years. However, the owner of a single expensive fallout meter would do well to make a KFM, the dependable homemade fallout meter described in Appendix C, for use as a back-up instrument in case of malfunction or breakage.

WARTIME RESERVES OF FALLOUT METERS

One important U.S. asset for surviving a nuclear war is the Defense Civil Preparedness Agency's supply of fallout meters. These instruments include approximately 660,000 dose-rate meters and about 2,900,000 dosimeters, all suitable for wartime use. In 1979 almost all these instruments are in good working condition. Unfortunately, most of them are in cities likely to be targeted, and are kept in existing shelters or stored in public buildings. If there were a sufficiently long, officially recognized period of warning before an attack, a large fraction of these fallout meters could be moved to locations outside areas of probable blast and fire damage and placed in officially designated fallout shelters.

It would be highly desirable for most families to have their own fallout meters. This is particularly true if they live in a region where chances of surviving a nuclear attack are good—or if in a crisis they plan to evacuate to such a favorable location.

A HOMEMADE DOSE-RATE METER

The only homemade fallout meter that is accurate and dependable was invented and thoroughly tested at Oak Ridge National Laboratory.[31] It is called the Kearny Fallout Meter (KFM); one is pictured in Fig. 10.1. This simple electrostatic instrument is made with common, inexpensive materials found in millions of homes, requires no

Fig. 10.1. A homemade KFM, an accurate dose-rate meter for measuring dose rates from 30 mR/hr (0.03 R/hr) up to 43 R/hr.

radioactive material to calibrate or check for accuracy, and needs no battery to operate. Detailed instructions that have enabled untrained citizens to make and use KFMs are given in Appendix C, along with an extra set of the cut-out patterns.

The preferred materials actually used in a KFM cost less than $2.00 in 1978. The materials to make a plastic "dry bucket," with a vinyl cover needed for charging a KFM in very humid conditions, cost about $3.50. In the unlikely event that a householder has to go out and buy all the materials needed for a KFM and its "dry bucket," it would cost less than $11.00. This sum will actually buy most of the materials for several KFMs. For example, only 39 square inches of ordinary aluminum foil is required to make the two "leaves" of this simple instrument. In 1979 ordinary (not "heavy duty") aluminum foil made in the United States weighed about 8.2 grams per 2 square feet. Variations in the weight of the foil used do not affect the accuracy of a KFM nearly as much as do changes in the dimensions of this instrument.

ADVICE ON BUILDING A KFM

The reader is urged to set aside several hours in the near future for making a KFM and for mastering its use. During field tests, average American families have needed about 6 hours to study the instructions given in Appendix C, to make this simple instrument, and to learn how to use it. These several hours may not be available in the midst of a crisis. Higher priority work would be the building of a high-protection-factor shelter, the making of a shelter-ventilating pump, and the storing of adequate water. In a crisis it might not be possible to obtain some needed materials for a KFM.

It is very difficult to concentrate on unfamiliar details during a nerve-racking crisis, or to do delicate work with hands that may become unsteady. The best time to build and learn to use a KFM is in peacetime, long before a crisis. Then this long-lasting instrument should be stored for possible future need.

Chapter 11
Light

THE NEED FOR MINIMUM LIGHT

Numerous disasters have proved that most people can remain calm for several days in total darkness. But some occupants of a shelter full of fearful people probably would go to pieces if they could see nothing and could not get out. It is easy to imagine the impact of a few hysterical people on the other occupants of a pitch-dark shelter. Under wartime conditions, even a faint light that shows only the shapes of nearby people and things can make the difference between an endurable situation and a black ordeal.

Figure 11.1 shows what members of the Utah family saw in their shelter on the third night of occupancy. All of the family's flashlights and other electric lights had been used until the batteries were almost exhausted. They had no candles at home and

Fig. 11.1. Night scene in a trench shelter without light.

failed to bring the cooking oil, glass jar, and cotton string included in the Evacuation Checklist. These materials would have enabled them to make an expedient lamp and to keep a small light burning continuously for weeks, if necessary.

At 2 AM on the third night, the inky blackness caused the mother, a stable woman who had never feared the dark, to experience her first claustrophobia. In a controlled but tense voice she suddenly awoke everyone by stating: "I have to get out of here. I can't orient myself." Fortunately for the shelter-occupancy experiment, when she reached the entry trench she overcame her fears and lay down to sleep on the floor near the entrance.

Conclusion: In a crisis, it is especially bad not to be able to see at all.

ELECTRIC LIGHTS

Even in communities outside areas of blast, fire, or fallout, electric lights dependent on the public power system probably would fail. Electromagnetic pulse effects produced by the nuclear explosions, plus the destruction of power stations and transmission lines, would knock out most public power.

No emergency lights are included in the supplies stocked in official shelters. The flashlights and candles that some people would bring to shelters probably would be insufficient to provide minimum light for more than a very few days.

A low-amperage light bulb used with a large dry cell battery or a car battery is an excellent source of low-level continuous light. One of the small 12-volt bulbs in the instrument panels of cars with 12-volt batteries will give enough light for 10 to 15 nights, without discharging a car battery so much that it cannot be used to start a car.

Making an efficient battery-powered lighting system for your shelter is work best done before a crisis arises. During a crisis you should give higher priority to many other needs.

Things to remember about using small bulbs with big batteries:

● Always use a bulb of the same voltage as the battery.

● Use a small, high-resistance wire, such as bell wire, with a car battery.

● Connect the battery after the rest of the improvised light circuit has been completed.

● Use reflective material such as aluminum foil, mirrors, or white boards to concentrate a weak light where it is needed.

● If preparations are made before a crisis, small 12-volt bulbs (0.1 to 0.25 amps) with sockets and wire can be bought at a radio parts store. Electric test clips for connecting thin wire to a car battery can be purchased at an auto parts store.

CANDLES AND COMMERCIAL LAMPS

Persons going to a shelter should take all their candles with them, along with plenty of matches in a waterproof container such as a Mason jar. Fully occupied shelters can become so humid that matches not kept in moisture–proof containers cannot be lighted after a single day.

Lighted candles and other fires should be placed near the shelter opening through which air is leaving the shelter, to avoid buildup of slight amounts of carbon monoxide and other headache-causing gases. If the shelter is completely closed for a time for any reason, such as to keep out smoke from a burning house nearby, all candles and other fires in the shelter should be extinguished.

Gasoline and kerosene lamps should not be taken inside a shelter. They produce gases that can cause headaches or even death. If gasoline or kerosene lamps are knocked over, as by blast winds that would rush into shelters over extensive areas, the results would be disastrous.

SAFE EXPEDIENT LAMPS FOR SHELTERS

The simple expedient lamps described below are the results of Oak Ridge National Laboratory experiments which started with oil lamps of the kinds used by Eskimos and the ancient Greeks. Our objective was to develop safe, dependable, long-lasting shelter lights that can be made quickly, using only common household materials. Numerous field tests have proved that average Americans can build good lamps by following the instructions given below (Fig. 11.2).

These expedient lamps have the following advantages:

● They are safe. Even if a burning lamp is knocked over onto a dry paper, the flame is so small that it will be extinguished if the lamp fuel being burned is a cooking oil or fat commonly used in the kitchen, and if the lamp wick is not much larger than $1/16$ inch in diameter.

● Since the flame is inside a jar, it is not likely to set fire to a careless person's clothing or to be blown out by a breeze.

● With the smallest practical wick and flame, a lamp burns only about 1 ounce of edible oil or fat in eight hours.

● Even with a flame smaller than that of a birthday candle, there is enough light for reading. To read easily by such a small flame, attach aluminum foil to three sides and the bottom of the lamp, and suspend it between you and your book, just high enough not to block your vision. (During the long, anxious days and nights spent waiting for fallout to decay, shelter occupants will appreciate having someone read aloud to them.)

● A lamp with aluminum foil attached is an excellent trap for mosquitoes and other insects that can cause problems in an unscreened shelter. They are attracted to the glittering light and fall into the oil.

● Two of these lamps can be made in less than an hour, once the materials have been assembled, so there is no reason to wait until a crisis arises to make them. Oil exposed to the air deteriorates, so it is best not to store lamps filled with oil or to keep oil-soaked wicks for months.

ORNL DWG 71-7240R

WARNING

DO <u>NOT</u> USE KEROSENE,
DIESEL FUEL, OR GAS-
OLINE – USE ONLY FATS
OR OILS OF THE KINDS
FOUND IN THE KITCHEN.

LOOP TO HANG LAMP
(LARGE ENOUGH FOR FINGER)

TO LIGHT LAMP, FIRST
MAKE MATCH LONGER
BY TAPING OR TYING
IT TO A STICK.
TO EXTINGUISH, DRIP
OIL ON WICK.

LIGHT WIRE

ATTACH ALUMINUM FOIL
⅔ AROUND JAR AND UNDER
ITS BOTTOM AND TO WIRES
TO ACT AS A REFLECTOR.
(NOT ILLUSTRATED)

CLEAN GLASS JAR
FREE OF LABELS

FLAME FROM END
OF WICK IS JUST
ABOVE OIL SURFACE

A FINE WIRE TIED IN
ITS CENTER AROUND
THE NAILS, WITH THE
ENDS OF THE WIRE
WOUND IN OPPOSITE
DIRECTIONS AROUND
THE COTTON-STRING-
WICK. USE COTTON
THAT IS SLIGHTLY
LESS THAN ⅛-in.
IN DIAMETER. USE
WINDOW SCREEN
WIRE OR OTHER
EQUALLY FINE WIRE.

FILL JAR NO MORE
THAN HALF-FULL
WITH COOKING OIL
OR FAT

BENT NAIL, TIED
OVER TOP OF ANOTHER
BENT NAIL, SO THE
BASE WILL NOT ROCK.

USE NAILS ABOUT ½-in.-
SHORTER THAN THE
DIAMETER OF JAR

KEEP EXTRA WIRE AND
WICK-STRING IN SHELTER

<u>WIRE – STIFFENED – WICK LAMP</u>

2½-in.-LONG SOFT PINE BLOCK,
OR ½-in. SHORTER THAN THE
INNER DIAMETER OF JAR

¾ in.
1 in.
⅜ in.   ⅜ in.
3/16 in.
⅜ in.   ⅜ in.   1 in.

MAKE NOTCH IN BLOCK BY
FIRST SAWING 5 EVEN
CUTS TO DEPTH, THEN
WHITTLE OUT NOTCH

ATTACH ALUMINUM FOIL
⅔ AROUND JAR AND
UNDER IT'S BOTTOM AND
TO THE WIRES, TO ACT
AS A REFLECTOR
(NOT ILLUSTRATED)

FILL JAR NO MORE
THAN HALF-FULL
WITH COOKING OIL
OR FAT

2½-in. LONG BLOCK,
½-in. SHORTER THAN
3-in.-DIAMETER OF
THIS GLASS JAR

1/16-in. TO 3/32-in. DIAMETER
WICK OF THIN COTTON
STRING OR TWISTED
COTTON THREADS –
SNUG WICK HOLE CAN
BE DRILLED WITH KNIFE
POINT FROM BOTH SIDES.

WARNING

DO <u>NOT</u> USE KEROSENE,
DIESEL FUEL, OR GAS-
OLINE – USE ONLY FATS
OR OILS OF THE KINDS
FOUND IN THE KITCHEN.

LOOP TO HANG LAMP
(LARGE ENOUGH FOR FINGER)

LIGHT WIRE

GLASS JAR

WHEN NOT IN
USE FOR DAYS,
KEEP WOOD
OUT OF OIL

OIL
SURFACE

<u>FLOATING WICK LAMP</u>

Fig. 11.2. Safe expedient lamps.

87

Chapter 12
Shelter Sanitation and Preventive Medicine

AN OUNCE OF PREVENTION

Should fallout force Americans to stay crowded into basements and expedient shelters for days or weeks, they should protect themselves against the spread of infectious diseases by taking both accustomed and unaccustomed preventive measures. Thousands of our jungle infantrymen in World War II learned to practice many of the health-preserving techniques described in this chapter. If modern medical facilities were temporarily unavailable, the prevention of diseases would become much more important to all of us.

The following infection-preventing measures are simple, practical, and require some self-discipline. The author has observed their practice and has used them while exploring and soldiering in a number of jungle, desert, and mountain regions. I also have used these measures while field-testing nuclear war survival skills in several states.

Basic first aid also would be of increased importance during a major confrontation or war. Good first aid booklets and instructions are available in practically all communities, so most first aid information will not be repeated here.

DISPOSAL OF HUMAN WASTES

To preserve health and morale in a shelter without a toilet or special chemicals for treatment of excrement and urine, human wastes should be removed before they produce much gas. A garbage can with a lid or a bucket covered with plastic will not hold the pressurized gas produced by rotting excrement. The following expedient means of disposal are listed in *increasing* order of effectiveness.

● Use a 5-gallon paint can, a bucket, or a large waterproof wastebasket to collect both urine and excrement. Use and keep it near the air-exhaust end of the shelter. Keep it tightly covered when not in use; a piece of plastic tied over the top keeps out insects and reduces odors. When such waste containers are full or begin to stink badly while covered, put them outside the shelter—still covered to keep out flies.

For some people, especially the aged, bringing a toilet seat from home would be justified. Padding on the edge of the bucket also helps those who have to sit down. An improvised seat of plywood or board serves well.

If only one container is available and is almost filled, periodically dump the wastes outside—unless fallout is still being deposited. Before an anticipated attack, people who plan to stay in a shelter should dig a waste-disposal pit if they do not have sufficient waste containers for weeks of shelter occupancy. The pit should be located about 3 feet from the shelter in the down-wind direction. This usually will be the air exhaust end of an earth-covered shelter. The pit should be surrounded by a ring of mounded, packed earth about 6 inches high, to keep surface water from heavy rains from running into it.

Quickly putting or dumping wastes outside is not hazardous once fallout is no longer being deposited. For example, assume the shelter is in an area of heavy fallout and the dose rate outside is 400 R/hr—enough to give a potentially fatal dose in about an hour to a person exposed in the open. If a person needs to be exposed for only 10 seconds to dump a bucket, in this 1/360th of an hour he will receive a dose of only about 1 R. Under war conditions, an additional 1-R dose is of little concern. If the shelter design does not permit an occupant to dispose of wastes without running outside, he can tie cloth or plastic over his shoes before going out, and remove these coverings in the entry before going back inside the shelter room. This precaution will eliminate the chance of tracking "hot" fallout particles into the shelter, and the small chance of someone getting a tiny beta burn in this way.

● Have all occupants only urinate in the bucket, and defecate into a piece of plastic. Urine contains few harmful organisms and can be safely dumped outside.

Two thicknesses of the thin plastic used to cover freshly drycleaned clothes will serve to hold bowel movements of several persons. Gather the plastic around the excrement to form a bag-like container. Tie the plastic closed near its upper edges with a string or narrow strip of cloth. Do not tie it so tightly as to be gas-tight. Each day's collection should be gently tossed outside. As the excrement rots, the gas will leak out of the tied end of the plastic covering. Flies will be attracted in swarms, but they will not be able to get into the plastic to contaminate their feet or to lay eggs. And because rotting excrement is so attractive to flies, shelter occupants will be bothered less by these dangerous pests.

● Use a hose-vented, 5-gallon can or bucket lined with a heavy plastic bag; cover tightly with plastic when not in use. Figure 12.1 shows this type of expedient toilet.

The vent-hose runs through a hole near the top of the paint can shown and is taped to seal it to the can. Such a hole can be quite easily cut with a chisel or a sharpened screwdriver. The hose is long enough to extend outside the shelter. Its outer end should be secured about 6 inches above ground level, to prevent water from running into it during a heavy rain. When a toilet-can is tightly covered, foul gases can escape through the hose to the outdoors.

With its opening tied shut, a large plastic trash bag containing as much as 30 pounds of wastes can be lifted out of a toilet-can and disposed of outside the shelter.

The 6-member Utah family described in preceding chapters used a home-like expedient toilet during their 77-hour shelter stay. Figure 12.2 pictures the toilet seat they took with them, placed on a hose-vented container in a hole in the ground. The toilet was at one end of the shelter. A person sitting on this

Fig. 12.1. A 5-gallon paint can used for a hose-vented toilet-can.

toilet could put his feet in the adjacent "stand-up hole" and be more comfortable.

The blanket shown hanging on the left in Fig. 12.2 could be drawn in front of the toilet for privacy. Behind the girl's head was the emergency crawlway-ventilation trench. When the toilet was being used, the shelter-ventilating KAP pumped air under the blanket-curtain and out the ventilation trench, resulting in very little odor in the rest of the shelter.

Vomiting is certain to cause both morale and health problems, especially for unprepared shelter occupants fearing this first dramatic symptom of radiation sickness. Nervousness, combined with the effects of unaccustomed food and water, will cause even some healthy persons to vomit. In a crowded shelter, the sight and smell of vomit will make others throw up. Plastic bags, well distributed throughout a shelter, are the best means to catch vomit and keep it

Fig. 12.2. The hose-vented expedient toilet used by the Utah family for over 3 days. (The unconnected telephone was brought along as a joke.)

off the floor. Buckets, pots, or a newspaper folded into a cone also will serve.

DISPOSAL OF DEAD BODIES

In large shelters which are occupied for many days, someone may die even when no occupants have been injured by blast, fire, or radiation. The sight or the sickly-sweet stink of a decaying human body is greatly disturbing. Some civil defense workers have theorized that the best way to take care of a corpse in a shelter until the fallout dose-rate outdoors is low enough to allow burial is to seal it in a large plastic bag. A simple test with a dead dog proved this idea impractical: gas pressure caused the bag to burst. One solution is to put the corpse outside as soon as the odor is evident. First, if possible, place it in a bag made of large plastic trash bags taped together and perforated with a few pinholes.

CLEAN WATER AND FOOD

Disinfecting water by boiling (preferably for at least 10 minutes) or by treating it with chlorine or iodine has been described in Chapter 8, Water.

When water is first stored, it should be disinfected by the addition of 1 scant teaspoon of ordinary household bleach for each 10 gallons.

To avoid contaminating water when removing small quantities from a container such as a waterproof bag, the simplest way is first to pour some into a pot or other medium-sized container, from which small amounts can be poured into individual cups. Dipping water with a cup runs more risk of contamination. The cleanest way to take small quantities of water out of a container is to siphon it with a flexible tube, as described in Chapter 8, Water.

Sanitary storage of food in expedient shelters is often difficult. Although almost any paper or plastic covering will keep fallout particles from food, shelter dampness can cause paper containers to break. Ants, roaches, and weevils can cut through paper or plastic coverings to reach food inside. Placing paper containers of food in plastic bags and suspending the bags from the ceiling of the shelter entryway gives good protection against bugs, and quite good protection against moisture for a few weeks. (Do not obstruct the air flow through an entryway if heat is a problem.) A small amount of insect repellent or grease smeared on the suspending string or wire will stop all crawlers. Metal and strong plastic containers with tight lids protect food best.

The hygienic preparation and serving of food in a shelter, especially in hot weather, require that all cooked food be eaten promptly. It is best to eat within half-an-hour after cooking. Canned foods should be consumed shortly after opening. The cleaning and disinfecting of utensils, bowls, etc., should be done promptly, to prevent bacteria from multiplying and to lessen the chances of ants and other insects being attracted into the shelter. Sugar should be mixed with cereals in the cooking pot, to avoid spilling.

In Oak Ridge National Laboratory shelter tests, only a few infants and toddlers have been included among the occupants. Feeding infants and small children over a piece of plastic would be one good way to keep the inevitable spillage from complicating shelter life.

To avoid using dishes, most foods can be served on squares of plastic. Spoons and such plastic "dishes" can be licked clean after eating, then disinfected by boiling or by dipping them into chlorine bleach solution containing one tablespoon of Clorox-type bleach to a quart of water.

A shelter occupant without a spoon can eat very thick grain mush in a sanitary manner by placing it on a piece of plastic held in his hand, forming it into a ball, and taking bites. Although Chinese peasants often eat wet-rice balls held in their bare hands, experiments have indicated—not unexpectedly—that Americans do not like to eat this way.

Cooking without oil or fat makes disinfecting utensils much easier when water and fuel are being conserved. Cereals and sugar are easy to wash off with a little water, without soap.

CONTROL OF INSECTS

Insect sprays used in high-protection-factor shelters are likely to cause more problems than they eliminate. Poisonous insecticides should be used with caution. Insect repellents on the skin and clothing are generally helpful, but not likely to be in sufficient supply to last for weeks or months. Some insect problems and simple means of controlling them are described below.

Mosquitoes would multiply rapidly after an attack, because normal control measures would not be in effect. Using insect screen or mosquito netting to cover the ventilation openings of a shelter is the best way to keep out mosquitoes, flies, and all larger insects. However, if the shelter has no air pump, it is impractical to use screens that obstruct the free movement of vital air—except in cold weather.

The fly population would explode after a nuclear attack. Radiation doses several times larger than doses that would kill people do not sterilize insects. In extensive rural areas where almost all people could have adequate shelter to be safe from fallout, most domestic animals and wild creatures would be killed. Trillions of flies would breed in the dead bodies.

Shelter occupants should make every effort to prevent flies from reaching disease-spreading human wastes.

Ants, especially in the warmer parts of the country, could drive people out of expedient shelters. The best prevention is to try to find a shelter-building site that is not near an ant nest. If shelter occupants are careful in storing food and eating, ants are less likely to become a problem.

Ticks and chiggers are usually found on grass and low bushes. To avoid carrying these pests into the shelter, do not bring grass or dead leaves into your shelter for bedding except in freezing weather. Cut leafy branches high above the ground: few pests live in tall vegetation.

PERSONAL POSSESSIONS

Toothbrushes are not boiled or otherwise disinfected after being used, because we all develop considerable resistance to our own infective organisms. For the same reason, each individual should have his own personal drinking cup, bowl, and spoon. They should be cleaned as well as possible and kept covered when not in use.

PREVENTION OF SKIN DISEASES

In crowded shelters, especially during hot weather, skin diseases are likely to be a more serious problem than is generally recognized. The importance of learning how to prevent skin diseases was made apparent by one of the very few shelter-occupancy tests to be conducted in the summer without air conditioning. This was a Navy test in which 99 men lived for 12 days in an underground shelter cooled only with outdoor summer air.[15] The incidence of skin complaints was high, even though medical treatment was available on a daily basis. The total number of reports to sick call was 560; 34 of these 99 healthy young men contracted heat rash and 23 had other skin complaints such as fungus infections. However, these sailors lived in an inadequately ventilated shelter and did not cleanse their sweaty skins or use the other methods listed below for preventing skin troubles.

Even in shelters that are skillfully ventilated with adequate outdoor air, skin diseases will be a serious problem—especially in hot weather—unless special hygiene measures are followed. Humid heat and heat rash increase susceptibility to skin diseases. Most of the following measures for preventing skin diseases have been practiced by jungle natives for thousands of years.

● Wash off sweat and dead skin. (When it is hot and humid, dead skin is continuously rubbing and flaking off and starting to decay.) Many jungle natives rinse their bodies several times a day. Bathing several times a day with soap is harmful in humid heat; the rapid loss of normal skin oils is one of the causes of skin diseases. Your skin can be kept fairly clean by rinsing off each day with just a cup of water, while rubbing gently with a very small cloth. A 6-inch square of bedsheet cloth serves well. So that you can dispose of the dirty water afterwards, wash yourself while standing on a piece of plastic with its edges held up slightly. (Place sticks or narrow boards under the edges.) Use about two-thirds of the precious water for the first rinse, starting from the face down and gently rubbing neck, armpits, stomach, groin, buttocks, and feet with a washcloth. Then use the remaining water to rinse off again, using bare fingers. If boiling water is available, sterilize washcloths every day by boiling them for a few minutes.

● Sleep as cool and bare as practical, to dry the maximum skin area.

● If practical, sit and sleep only where other members of your family do and avoid use of bedding by more than one family.

● Avoid infection from toilet seats by disinfecting with a strong chlorine solution and then rinsing, by covering with paper, or by not sitting down.

● Wash or disinfect clothing as often as practical, especially underwear and socks. Disinfecting clothing, not laundering it, is the most important health objective under difficult shelter conditions. Dipping clothing into boiling water disinfects it. Unless plenty of water is available for rinsing, do not disinfect clothing by putting it in a chlorine bleach solution.

● Wear shoes or sandals when walking about, to prevent fungus infections of the feet.

RESPIRATORY DISEASES

The spread of respiratory and other diseases transmitted by coughing and sneezing would be difficult to control in long-occupied shelters. Adequate ventilation would help in disease prevention. In small shelters, it would be better if persons who are sneezing or coughing could stay near the opening being used for air exhaust. In large shelters with many occupants, the risk of one or more of them having a disease that is easily spread obviously will be higher than in a small shelter.

Chapter 13
Surviving Without Doctors

A TEMPORARY RETURN TO SELF-HELP

Most doctors, hospital facilities, and medical supplies are located in cities. An all-out attack would destroy most of these modern blessings. Even if medical assistance were nearby, only a few of the survivors confined to shelters in areas of heavy fallout would be able to get needed medicines or the help of a doctor. For periods ranging from days to months, most unprepared survivors would be forced to live under medical conditions almost as primitive as those experienced by the majority of mankind for all but the past few decades of human history.

BENIGN NEGLECT

Life without modern medical help would be less painful and hazardous for those survivors who have some practical knowledge of what should be done—or not done—under primitive, unsanitary conditions. Information about first aid and hygienic precautions can be obtained from widely available Red Cross and civil defense booklets and courses. This knowledge, with a stock of basic first aid supplies, would reduce suffering and prevent many dangerous illnesses. However, first aid instructions do not include advice about what to do for serious injuries and sicknesses if no doctors or effective medicines are available.

Where There Is No Doctor,[32] the excellent self-help handbook recommended by Volunteers in Technical Assistance, gives much information that goes far beyond the scope of first aid. But even this handbook repeatedly recommends getting professional medical help whenever possible for serious injuries and illnesses.

Fortunately, the human body has remarkable capabilities for healing itself, especially if the injured or sick person and his companions practice intelligent "benign neglect." Such purposeful non-interference with the body's recuperative processes was called "masterful inactivity" by Colonel C. Blanchard Henry, M.D., a widely recognized authority on mass casualty evacuation and treatment. Colonel Henry was one of the first medical officers to visit Hiroshima and Nagasaki after their destruction and was an experienced analyzer of civil defense preparations in several countries.

The following is a brief summary of Colonel Henry's medical advice for nuclear war survivors living under primitive conditions and unable to get the help of a doctor or effective medicines.[33] (Additional advice, enclosed in brackets, is from a medical publication.[34])

● **Wounds:** Apply only pressure dressings to stop bleeding—unless an artery has been cut, as by a blast-hurled piece of glass. If blood is spurting from a wound, apply both a pressure dressing and a windlass-type tourniquet. Release the tourniquet pressure about every 15 minutes, to allow enough blood to reach the flesh beyond the tourniquet and keep it alive. There is a fair chance that clotting under the pressure dressing will stop blood loss before it becomes fatal.

● **Infected wounds:** Do not change dressings frequently. The formation of white pus shows that white corpuscles are mobilizing to combat the infection. In World War I, wounded soldiers in hospitals suffered agonies having their wounds cleaned and dressed frequently; many died as a result of such harmful care. In contrast, before antibiotics became available late in World War II, casts and dressings on infected wounds sometimes were not changed for weeks. (The author saw this treatment in China and India and smelled the stench resulting from such "benign neglect" of American soldiers' wounds—neglect that helped save limbs and lives.)

- **Pieces of glass deeply embedded in flesh**: Do not probe with tweezers or a knife in an attempt to extract them. Most glass will come out when the wounds discharge pus.

- **Burns**: Do not apply grease, oil or any other medicine to the burned area. Cover the area securely with a clean, dry dressing or folded cloth. Do not change the dressing frequently. [For most burns, the bandage need not be removed until the tenth to fourteenth day. Give plenty of slightly salted water: about 1 teaspoon (4.5 gm) of salt per quart (or liter), preferably chilled, in amounts of 1 to 3 liters daily.[34]]

- **Broken bones**: Apply simple splints to keep the bones from moving. Do not worry about deformities; most can be corrected later by a doctor. Do not attempt traction setting of broken bones.

- **Shock**: Keep the victim warm. Place blankets or other insulation material under him. Do not cover him with so many blankets that he sweats and suffers harmful fluid losses. Give him plenty of slightly salted water [about a teaspoon of salt in a liter (or quart) of water].

- **Heat prostration**: Give adequate fluids, including slightly salty water.

- **Simple childbirth**: Keep hands off. Wait until the mother has given birth. Do not tie and cut the cord unless a potent disinfectant is available. Instead, use the primitive practice of wrapping the cord and the placenta around the infant until they dry. Avoid the risk of infecting the mother by removing the rest of the afterbirth; urge the mother to work to expel it.

- **Toothache**: Do not attempt to pull an aching tooth. Decaying teeth will abscess and fall out. This is a painful but seldom fatal process—one which was endured by most of our remote ancestors who reached maturity.

VETERINARIAN ANTIBIOTICS

People who for decades have used antibiotics to combat their infections have not produced normal quantities of antibodies, and have subnormal resistance to many infections. People who have not been dependent on antibiotics have these antibodies. In the aftermath of a massive nuclear attack, most surviving Americans would be in rural areas; many would need antibiotics. A large part of their need could be met by the supplies of veterinarian antibiotics kept on livestock and chicken farms, at feed mills, and in small towns. Many animals are given more antibiotics in their short lives than most Americans receive in theirs. Hogs, for example, are given antibiotics and/or other disease-controlling medicines in their feed each day. In many farming areas, veterinary antibiotics and other medicines are in larger supply than are those for people. Realistic preparations to survive an all-out attack should include utilizing these supplies.

RADIATION SICKNESS

For the vast majority of Americans who would receive radiation doses from a massive attack, the help of doctors, antibiotics, blood transfusions, etc., would not be of life-or-death importance. Very few of those receiving acute doses (received within 24 hours) of less than 100 R would become sick, even briefly. All of those exposed to acute doses between 100 R and 200 R should recover.[6] If total doses this size or even several times larger are received over a period of a few months in small doses of around 6 R per day, no incapacitating symptoms should result. The human body usually can repair almost all radiation damage if the daily doses are not too large.

The majority of those with acute doses of less than about 350 R will recover without medical treatment. Almost all of those receiving acute doses of over 600 R would die within a few weeks, even if they were to receive the complex hospital treatments given to the very rare peacetime victims of large radiation doses. If all doctors and the equipment and drugs needed for such heroic treatments magically were to survive an attack—and persons suffering from radiation sickness could reach them—relatively few additional lives could be saved.

The most effective way to reduce losses of health and life from radiation sickness is to prevent excessive exposure to radiation. Adequate shelter and essential life-support items are the best means of saving lives in a nuclear war. The following information on radiation sickness is given to help the reader understand the importance of building a good shelter and to help him distinguish between symptoms of common illnesses and first symptoms of radiation sickness.

The first symptoms of radiation sickness are nausea, vomiting, headache, dizziness, and a general feeling of illness.[6] These symptoms begin several hours after exposure to acute doses of 100 R to 200 R, and within 30 minutes or less after receiving a fatal dose. A source of probable confusion is the fact that one or more of these symptoms is experienced by many people when they are first exposed to great danger, as in an air raid shelter during a conventional bombardment.

The occupants of a shelter might worry unnecessarily for weeks, mistaking their early emotional reactions for the initial phase of radiation sickness. This would be particularly true if they had no dependable instrument for measuring radiation, or if none of them knew how to use such an instrument.

The initial symptoms end within a day or two. Then follows the latent phase of radiation sickness, during which the patient experiences few, if any, symptoms. If the dose received was in the non-fatal range, the latent phase may last as long as 2 weeks.

In the final phase, the victim of serious or fatal radiation sickness will have reduced resistance to infections and is likely to suffer diarrhea, loss of hair, and small hemorrhages of the skin, mouth, and/or intestinal tract. Diarrhea from common causes may be confused with the onset of radiation sickness, but hemorrhages and loss of much hair are clear indications of having received serious, but not necessarily fatal, radiation exposure. The final phase usually lasts for one to two months. Any available antibiotics should be reserved for this critical phase of the illness.

Doses of 1000 R to 5000 R result in bloody diarrhea, fever, and blood circulation abnormalities, with the initial symptoms beginning within less than 30 minutes after exposure and the final phase occurring less than a day thereafter. Death results within 2 to 14 days. The victim of a dose of over 5000 R dies a hard death within 48 hours, due to radiation damage to the central nervous system.

Recovery from most cases of radiation sickness will be more likely for patients who receive a well balanced diet, rest, freedom from stress, and clean surroundings. But most patients, even without these advantages, will survive—as proved by the survival of thousands of Hiroshima and Nagasaki citizens who suffered serious radiation sickness. Nursing radiation victims is not hazardous. Even persons dying from a dose of 5000 R are not sources of dangerous radiation

by wartime standards, and radiation sickness is not contagious.

LIFETIME RISKS FROM RADIATION

The large radiation doses that many survivors of a nuclear attack would receive would result in serious long-term risks of death from cancer. But neither the lifetime risks from large wartime nor small peacetime radiation doses are as bad as many people believe. The risk estimates of reputable scientists vary widely. Joseph Califano, Secretary of the U.S. Department of Health, Education, and Welfare, gave testimony on April 4, 1979 that reflects an average of the reputable estimates. During an investigation of the Three Mile Island nuclear accident, Mr. Califano stated a "reasonable guess": if 10,000 people (a typical mixture of sexes and ages) are exposed to 1000 millirem (1 rem) of radiation, one additional fatal cancer will result.[35] (The "rem" is an abbreviation for "roentgen equivalent (in) man."[6] The rem takes into account the biological effects of different kinds of radiation. For external gamma-ray radiation from fallout, the numerical value of an exposure or dose given in roentgens is approximately the same as the numerical value given in rems or in rads, another unit in which radiation doses are given. Therefore, for simplicity's sake, this book gives both instrument readings (exposures) and doses in roentgens (R).)

This risk estimate can be applied to large wartime radiation doses from fallout: If 100 people each received a dose of 100 R (or 100 rem, or 100 rads), over a lifetime period it is probable that there would be *one more death* resulting from cancer than if these same people had not received this radiation dose.

The reader desiring good information on the long-term and worldwide effects of radiation is referred to two authoritative reports of the National Academy of Sciences, Washington, D.C. 20006: *The Effects on Populations of Exposures to Low Levels of Ionizing Radiation* (The BEIR Report made by the NAS Committee on the Biological Effects of Ionizing Radiation) (November 1972); and *Long-Term Worldwide Effects of Multiple Nuclear-Weapons Detonations* (1975).

From the standpoint of basic survival know-how, these and other complicated scientific studies show that after a nuclear attack people should:

* Provide the best protection against radiation for pregnant women and young children, since

fetuses and the very young are the most likely to be hurt by radiation.

* Persuade older people to do more of the essential work that necessitates receiving large radiation doses. A 65-year-old is less susceptible to radiation than a 20-year-old, and the older person probably will not live long enough to die of a cancer that takes 20 years or more to develop.

PREVENTION OF THYROID DAMAGE FROM RADIOACTIVE IODINES

There is no medicine that will effectively prevent nuclear radiations from damaging the human body cells that they strike. However, a salt of the elements potassium and iodine, taken orally even in very small quantities $1/2$ hour to 1 day before radioactive iodines are swallowed or inhaled, prevents about 99% of the damage to the thyroid gland that otherwise would result. The thyroid gland readily absorbs both non-radioactive and radioactive iodine, and normally it retains much of this element in either or both forms. When ordinary, non-radioactive iodine is made available in the blood for absorption by the thyroid gland before any radioactive iodine is made available, the gland will absorb and retain so much that it becomes saturated with non-radioactive iodine. When saturated, the thyroid can absorb only about 1% as much additional iodine, including radioactive forms that later may become available in the blood; then it is said to be blocked. (Excess iodine in the blood is rapidly eliminated by the action of the kidneys.)

An excess of ordinary iodine retained in the thyroid gland is harmless, but quite small amounts of radioactive iodine retained in the thyroid eventually will give such a large radiation dose to thyroid cells that abnormalities are likely to result. These would include loss of thyroid function, nodules in the thyroid, or thyroid cancer. Sixty-four Marshall Islanders on Rongelap Atoll were accidentally exposed to radioactive fallout produced by a large H-bomb test explosion on Bikini Atoll, about 100 miles away. Twenty-two of them developed thyroid abnormalities beginning nine years later.[6] In the two days before they were taken out of the fallout area, these completely uninformed natives, living essentially outdoors, had received estimated whole-body gamma-ray doses of about 175 R from the fallout all around them. They absorbed most of the radioactive iodine retained by their thyroid glands as a result of eating and drinking fallout-contaminated

food and water during their two days of exposure. (Because of unusual environmental conditions at the time of fallout deposition, some of the retained radioactive iodine may have come from the air they breathed.)

An extremely small and inexpensive daily dose of the preferred non-radioactive potassium salt, potassium iodide (KI), if taken $1/2$ hour to 1 day before exposure to radioactive iodine, will reduce later absorption of radioactive iodine by the thyroid to only about 1% of what the absorption would be without this preventive measure. Extensive experimentation and study have led to the Federal Drug Administration's approval of 130-milligram (130-mg) tablets for this preventive (prophylactic) use only.[36,37] A 130-mg dose provides the same daily amount of iodine as does each tablet that English authorities for years have placed in the hands of the police near nuclear power plants, for distribution to the surrounding population in the very unlikely event of a major nuclear accident. It is quite likely that a similar-sized dose is in the Russian "individual, standard first-aid packet." According to a comprehensive Soviet 1969 civil defense handbook,[38] this first-aid packet contains "anti-radiation tablets and anti-vomiting tablets (potassium iodide and etaperain)."

● **Prophylactic use of potassium iodide in peacetime nuclear accidents.**

In March 1979 no 130-mg potassium iodide tablets were available in the United States. Therefore, when the 1979 accident that killed no one occurred at the Three Mile Island nuclear plant in Pennsylvania, 259,000 small bottles of a saturated aqueous solution of potassium iodide were produced and rushed to the vicinity of the accident. An equal number of medicine droppers also was supplied.[39] It was not necessary to distribute this prophylactic medicine, however, because the plant's containment system prevented the discharge of hazardous quantities of radioactive iodine.

The following information and warnings concerning the use of potassium iodide were prepared by the U.S. Food and Drug Administration. This official advice would have been distributed along with small bottles of potassium iodide solution if the 1979 accident at the Three Mile Island nuclear plant had resulted in dangerous discharges of radioactive iodine.

PATIENT INFORMATION USE OF SATURATED SOLUTION OF POTASSIUM IODIDE (SSKI) FOR THYROID BLOCKING

Directions for Use: See label on bottle

Background: This product is available solely for public health protection in the event of a nuclear accident which releases into the environment radioactive iodine which may be inhaled or swallowed. Use of potassium iodide as directed reduces the accumulation of radioactive iodine in the thyroid gland. This is important because radiation may damage the cells of the thyroid gland in such a way that changes in the function or structure of the gland may occur even many years after exposure. You should take this product as soon as possible after being told to do so by your public health authority. While the length of time you will take this product will depend upon the directions from your public health authority, it is not expected to exceed about 10 days unless specifically directed otherwise.

Facts about Potassium Iodide: Potassium iodide has been used for many years in large doses (2 to 10 times the dose recommended here) to treat persons with asthma and other lung conditions. It is a relatively safe drug when taken as directed, but as with any drug, side effects may occur. Although side effects are unlikely because of the low dose and the short time you will be taking the drug, they are listed in this insert along with advice on what to do if they occur. It is important to emphasize that *larger doses are not necessary* for the drug to work properly. The larger the dose, the greater the risk of side effects; *therefore, do not exceed the recommended dose.*

Who Can Take Potassium Iodide? Unless you are *allergic* to iodide, you may take potassium iodide as directed. Even if you are taking a thyroid hormone drug product for an underactive thyroid gland, or taking an anti-thyroid drug for an overactive thyroid gland, you may still take potassium iodide. Pregnant women may also take it.

Side Effects: In general, the side effects of potassium iodide have been seen when higher doses of potassium iodide have been taken for a long time. You should be especially cautious not to exceed the recommended dose or take potassium iodide longer than instructed. There are two kinds of side effects: those not involving the thyroid gland and those involving the thyroid gland.

Side effects not involving the thyroid gland. The taking of iodide has been associated with skin rashes, swelling of the salivary glands ("iodide mumps"), and iodism (metallic taste, burning in the mouth and throat, soreness of the teeth and gums, skin rashes, symptoms of a head cold, and sometimes a gastric upset and diarrhea). Also, allergic reactions may produce symptoms such as fever and pains in the joints or, on rare occasions, swelling of various parts of the face and body with at times severe shortness of breath requiring immediate medical attention.

Side effects involving the thyroid gland: The taking of iodide has been associated with overactivity of the thyroid gland, underactivity of the thyroid gland, and enlargement of the thyroid gland (goiter). Goiter may occur also in infants born to mothers who took large doses of potassium iodide throughout pregnancy.

What To Do If Side Effects Occur:

For side effects not involving the thyroid gland: If any of these side effects occur, call your physician or public health authority for instructions. If the symptoms are minor, you may be advised to continue taking potassium iodide. If you have an allergic reaction, discontinue taking potassium iodide and seek immediate medical attention.

For side effects involving the thyroid gland: Because these side effects are very unlikely, with short term use, they pose no immediate problem. However, the taking of iodide has been associated with overactivity of the thyroid gland in elderly persons with heart disease. The symptoms of an overactive thyroid gland are very similar to those associated with anxiety and include nervousness, sweating, and rapid heartbeat. Because in an emergency some anxiety is likely, it is difficult to determine whether these symptoms are caused by anxiety or an overactive thyroid gland. An overactive thyroid, however, would only occur after you had taken potassium iodide for several days. Thus, if these symptoms are persistent and severe, and particularly if the heartbeat is not only rapid but irregular, you should call your physician or public health authority because medical attention is probably required.

If you do not have any potassium iodide, do not try to use tincture of iodine as a blocking agent. Elemental (free) iodine is ineffective as a blocking agent and is poisonous if taken in much larger quantities than the very small amounts consumed when you drink water that has been disinfected with iodine. Also you should not make a futile, harmful attempt to eat enough iodized salt to result in thyroid blocking.

- **For protection against radioactive iodine in fallout from a nuclear war fought outside the United States.**

Most strategists believe that a nuclear war fought by nations other than the United States is a more likely catastrophe than a nuclear attack on America. Several of the Soviet and Chinese nuclear test explosions have resulted in very light fallout deposition and some contamination of milk by radioactive iodine in many of the 50 states. However, serious contamination of milk, fruits, and vegetables could result if war fallout from many nuclear explosions were to be carried across the Pacific by the prevailing westerly winds. **The measured contamination of milk from a few cows in the United States indicates that protective measures would be taken.** The worst-contaminated milk produced in Tennessee and tested at Oak Ridge National Laboratory was from a cow that had grazed on a pasture near the laboratory onto which fallout from the Chinese test explosion of December 28, 1966 had been deposited.[40] Deposition of this fallout began in Tennessee on January 1, 1967. This cow's milk contained more radioactive iodine than is specified by the Food and Drug Administration's very conservative "Response level for Emergency PAG" (Protective Action Guide) as warranting protective action.[37] "An Emergency PAG establishes a level at which responsible officials should isolate food containing radioactivity to prevent its introduction into commerce, ..."[37]

If a nuclear war were to be fought in northern parts of Asia, or in Europe, or in the Middle East, a very small fraction of the fallout would come to earth on parts or all of the United States.[40] This fallout would not result in an overwhelming catastrophe to Americans, although the long-term health hazards would be serious by peacetime standards and the economic losses would be great.[40] The dangers from radioactive iodine in milk produced by cows that ate fallout-contaminated feeds or drank fallout-contaminated water would be minimized if Americans did not consume dairy products for several weeks after the arrival of war fallout. Safe milk and other baby foods would be the only essential foods that soon would be in very short supply. The parents of babies and young children who had stored potassium iodide would be especially thankful they had made this very inexpensive preparation, that can give 99%-effective protection to the thyroid. All members of families with a supply of potassium iodide could safely eat a normal diet long before those without it could do so.

The most dangerous type of radioactive iodine decays rapidly. At the end of each 8-day period it gives off only half as much radiation as at the start of that period. So at the end of 80 days it emits only about 1/1000 as much radiation per hour as at the beginning of these 80 days. Because of this rapid decay, a 100-day supply of potassium iodide should be sufficient if a nuclear war, either overseas or within the United States, were to last no more than a week or two.

The probability of most Americans being supplied with prophylactic potassium iodide during a major nuclear disaster appears low. Under present regulations the decision concerning whether to stockpile and dispense potassium iodide tablets rests solely with each state's governor.[41]

● Use for thyroid protection after a nuclear attack on the United States.

After a nuclear attack, very few of the survivors would be able to obtain potassium iodide or to get advice about when to start taking it or stop taking it. In areas of heavy fallout, some survivors without potassium iodide would receive radiation doses large enough to destroy thyroid function before modern medical treatments would again become available. Even those injuries to the thyroid that result in its complete failure to function cause few deaths in normal times, but under post-attack conditions thyroid damage would be much more hazardous.

● Ways to obtain potassium iodide for prophylactic use.

* *By prescription today.* With a prescription from a doctor, a U.S.P. saturated solution of potassium iodide can be bought at most pharmacies today. (In a crisis, the present local supplies would be entirely inadequate.) The saturated solution contains a very small amount of a compound that prevents it from deteriorating significantly for a few years. It is best stored in a dark glass bottle with a solid, non-metallic cap that screws on liquid-tight. A separate medicine dropper should be kept in the same place. An authoritative publication[36] of the National Committee on Radiation Protection and Measurements states: "Supplies of potassium iodide can be stored in a variety of places, including homes, ..."

In April of 1979, a 2-ounce bottle, containing about 2,000 drops of this 99-percent-effective prophylactic solution, sold for $2.35 in an economy drug store. This is enough for 500 daily doses—at a cost of less than half a cent per dose.

* *Possibly without prescription in future years.* If 130-mg potassium iodide tablets are produced in the United States and if they are made available in pharmacies, they will be sold over-the-counter and the buyer will receive accompanying written instructions for their prophylactic use.[37]

* *From chemical supply firms.* Chemical reagent grade potassium iodide is purer than the pharmaceutical grade. Individuals can buy it from some chemical supply firms; no prescription or other authorization is necessary. In 1979, one pound of the chemical reagent grade—enough for approximately 3,500 doses of 130 mg each—retailed for around $20. (Years ago the author bought a pound, enough for family and friends.)

For years of storage, crystalline or granular potassium iodide is better than a saturated solution. These dry forms are sold by prescription in some pharmacies. Dry potassium iodide should be stored in a dark bottle with a gasketed, non-metallic cap that screws on tightly. Two-fluid-ounce bottles, filled with dry potassium iodide as described below, are good sizes for a family. Separate medicine droppers should be kept with stored bottles.

● Practical expedient ways to prepare and take daily prophylactic doses of a saturated solution of potassium iodide.

To prepare a saturated solution of potassium iodide, fill a bottle about 60% full of crystalline or granular potassium iodide. (A 2-fluid-ounce bottle, made of dark glass and having a solid, non-metallic, screwcap top, is a good size for a family. About 2 ounces of crystalline or granular potassium iodide is needed to fill a 2-fluid-ounce bottle about 60% full.) Next, pour safe, room-temperature water into the bottle until it is about 90% full. Then close the bottle tightly and shake it vigorously for at least 2 minutes. Some of the solid potassium iodide should remain permanently undissolved at the bottom of the bottle; this is proof that the solution is saturated.

Experiments with a variety of ordinary household medicine droppers determined that 1 drop of a saturated solution of potassium iodide contains from 28 to 36 mg of potassium iodide. The recommended expedient daily doses of a saturated solution (approximately 130 mg for adults and children, and 65 mg for infants) are as follows:

* For adults and children, 4 drops per day of a saturated solution of potassium iodide.

* For infants less than 12 months old, 2 drops per day of a saturated solution of potassium iodide.

Potassium iodide has a very bad taste, so bad that a single crystal or 1 drop of the saturated solution in a small child's mouth would make him cry. Since many persons will not take a bad-tasting medication, especially if no short-term health hazards are likely to result from not taking it, the following two methods of taking a saturated solution are recommended:

* Put 4 drops of the solution into a glass of milk or other beverage, stir, and drink quickly. Then drink some of the beverage with nothing added. If only water is available, use it in the same manner.

* If bread is available, place 4 drops of the solution on a small piece of it; dampen and mold it into a firm ball the size of a large pea, about $3/8$ inch in diameter. There is almost no taste if this "pill" is swallowed quickly with water. (If the pill is coated with margarine, there is no taste.)

As stated before, 4 drops of the saturated solution provide a dose approximately equal to 130 mg of potassium iodide.

Protection of eyes and skin against possible injury by ultraviolet radiation

A nuclear war anywhere in the world that involves the detonation of thousands of megatons **may** result in a marked increase in the ultraviolet light in sunlight that reaches the ground, possibly for many months after the war ends. This **possible** increase in U.V. radiation is described, with proper emphasis on the uncertainties, in a report of the National Research Council, National Academy of Sciences: **Long-Term Worldwide Effects of Multiple Nuclear-Weapons Detonations** (1975).

Eyes could be protected by wearing U.V. sunglasses, or by wearing glasses covered with black or other opaque material except for two horizontal slits each 1/16 inch wide, or by using expedient eye coverings with slits--similar to those carved by Eskimos out of wood or bone to protect against snow blindness.

Skin could be easily protected by clothing, including gloves and a broad-brimmed hat. Protective creams also would be used.

Chapter 14

Expedient Shelter Furnishings

IMPORTANCE OF ADEQUATE FURNISHINGS

Throughout history, people have endured being crowded together while living and sleeping on hard surfaces. In times of war and privation, people have lived in such conditions for much longer periods than would be necessary for shelter occupancy due to fallout.[42] Realistic basement-shelter-occupancy tests conducted by research contractors for the U.S. Office of Civil Defense (now the Defense Civil Preparedness Agency) have shown that modern Americans can live and sleep for two weeks on a concrete floor. In some of these tests, only 8 square feet of floor space was provided for each person; only pieces of corrugated cardboard $3/16$-inch thick lessened the hardship of sleeping and sitting on concrete.[13]

Nevertheless, shelters should be adequately furnished whenever possible, for these reasons:

● More people can occupy a properly furnished shelter—for weeks, if necessary—if adequate additional ventilation is supplied for the additional occupants.

● Cleanliness, health, and morale are better if well-designed furnishings are used. More serious complications than discomfort are likely to result if occupants have to huddle together on a bare floor—especially if the floor is damp earth.

● Persons occupying a shelter made relatively comfortable by its furnishings are more likely to stay in the shelter long enough to avoid dangerous exposure to fallout radiation.

CHAIRS, BENCHES, AND BUNKS

The father of the previously described Utah family of six knew that the members of his family would be most uncomfortable and probably would have sore backs if they spent the required 72 hours of continuous shelter occupancy huddled on the floor. (Their shelter room was only $3\frac{1}{2}$ feet wide and $16\frac{1}{2}$ feet long.) So this family took with them from home four folding chairs and two pieces of plywood (each 21 inches wide by 6 feet long) tied as part of the load on top of the family car. Four small wooden boxes served as food containers during the drive to the shelter-building site. In the shelter, the boxes were used to support the ends of two narrow plywood bunks (Fig. 14.1).

The family's system of sleeping and sitting in shifts worked reasonably well. There were discomforts: the adults found the two plywood bunks too narrow, and the plywood was so hard that all the family members used their sleeping bags for padding rather than for needed warmth on chilly nights. The father and oldest son, whose turn to sleep was during normal waking hours, had trouble sleeping in such a small shelter while the lively 4-year-old son was awake.

Note that in the shelter pictured in Fig. 14.1 the earth walls are covered with plastic from trash bags. Covering earth walls with plastic or bed sheets makes for a cleaner shelter, with less earth falling in the faces of people who sleep on the floor. Bedsheets on the walls make a shelter brighter, but are flammable and a potential fire hazard. The plastic film prevented the

Fig. 14.1. Bunks and folding chairs furnished this Pole-Covered Trench Shelter. (Note the suspended transistor radio. Reception is good in all types of expedient shelters tested to date.)

Fig. 14.2. Benches with overhead bunks in a skillfully designed Small-Pole Shelter of Russian design. Three rural families in a wooded area of Tennessee built this expedient blast shelter in 48 hours, including the time spent felling trees and making furnishings.

earth walls from drying and crumbling as a result of the hot, dry desert air pumped through the shelter during the day.

Benches with overhead wooden bunks are shown in Fig. 14.2. These were installed in a Small-Pole Shelter 6 feet wide with a ceiling almost 7 feet high.

A well-designed expedient shelter should be as small as practical, with all space used very efficiently. The builders should make the heights and widths of benches and bunks as specified in the detailed shelter drawings, such as those for the Small-Pole Shelter given in Appendix A.3.

Serious difficulties can result from failure to use specific dimensions that may appear unimportant. For example, in field tests at Fort Bragg, N.C., 48

airborne infantrymen, working only with hand tools, cut pine trees and built two 24-man Small-Pole Shelters in less than 24 hours.[43] The men did not think it necessary to use the specific dimensions when they made the furnishings. As a result, they built the benches too high and the overhead bunks too far below the ceilings. This error forced the men to sit for hours in hunched positions. Even these able-bodied young men would have developed very sore backs and would have wanted very much to leave their shelters if they had been forced to sit in a bent-over position for days.

Figure 14.2 shows a good example of the importance of using dimensions which have been thoroughly field-tested when building essential parts of a shelter. Note the small air-exhaust opening above the girl lying on the overhead bunk at one end

OUACHITA TECHNICAL COLLEGE

of the shelter. This opening led to a small, chimney-like, air-exhaust duct made of boards, with its cross-sectional area as specified in Russian civil defense handbooks for natural ventilation of small expedient shelters. With such a small air-exhaust opening—only 4 square inches (10 square centimeters) per person—a fully occupied shelter of this size would soon become dangerously overheated in warm or hot weather, even though a good expedient shelter-ventilating pump (a KAP) were to be used.

BEDSHEET-HAMMOCK AND CHAIR

On the last night of the Utah family's shelter stay it was clear that the six members would win the cash bonus offered them for their 72-hour occupancy of the shelter starting immediately after they completed building it. Therefore, the author showed them that night how to make boat-shaped hammocks out of bedsheets. (Any strong cloth of the right size can be used.) They were shown how to hang these short, yet stable, hammocks securely from poles of the shelter roof. With three members sleeping in hammocks, two on the plywood bunks, and one on the floor, all six could sleep at the same time. Figure 14.3 shows part of this sleeping arrangement.

Fig. 14.3. Girl resting in a boat-shaped hammock. Her brother slept on the upper bunk of their $3\frac{1}{2}$-ft-wide trench shelter.

In a shelter this size without bunks, hanging four short hammocks at slight angles to the length of the trench would permit four occupants to sleep comfortably. An additional two persons could sleep

on the floor. In the Utah family's shelter, the floor was made comfortable by covering the damp earth with pieces of polyethylene cut from trash bags, then placing strips of shag rug over the plastic.

In shelters with ceilings at least 6 feet high, one hammock can be hung above another. In a Small-Pole Shelter that is 6 feet wide, a greater number of people can sleep or sit comfortably at the same time if Bedsheet-Hammocks and Bedsheet-Chairs are used rather than benches or a combination of benches and overhead bunks. Figure 14.4 shows how Bedsheet-Hammocks can be used like double-deck bunks.

Fig. 14.4. Bedsheet-Hammocks hung one above the other across the room of a Russian-type Small-Pole Shelter made of lumber.

Detailed instructions for making a Bedsheet-Hammock and a Bedsheet-Chair are given at the end of this chapter.

In an evacuation during a real crisis, carrying comfortable folding chairs and the materials to make wooden bunks would not be advisable. If the family car were loaded instead with an equivalent weight of additional food and clothing, the members' prospects of surviving would be improved. But in an actual crisis evacuation, a family planning to occupy a shelter with a strong roof should take along a bedsheet for each member. The other lightweight items described in the instructions for making a Bedsheet-Hammock and a Bedsheet-Chair also should be carried. By following the instructions at the end of this chapter, a comfortable hammock can be made and quickly converted to a comfortable suspended chair when not needed for sleeping.

Hammocks hung high off the floor and above other sleepers must be strong, securely suspended, and cupped so that it is impossible to fall out accidentally. This is why the instructions emphasize using a double thickness of bedsheet and folding the cloth so as to make the hammock boat-like, with high sides.

In a cold shelter, keeping warm in a hammock is somewhat difficult. Easily compressible materials, such as those used in a sleeping bag, are squeezed so thin under a person's body that they lose most of their insulating value. Pads of newspapers about an inch thick, protected by cloth coverings, will reduce heat losses. The best insulation is a quilt, fastened to the underside of a hammock by attaching it with rows of stitches every few inches and at right angles to each other.

Figure 14.5 shows a Bedsheet-Hammock that had been quickly converted into a Bedsheet-Chair and hung near a shelter wall. It occupies less than half the floor space used by the two hammocks shown in the preceding illustration. If a reclining seat is desired, the two support-points on the ceiling to which the chair-arm cords are attached can be located farther out from the wall.

Enough padding material should be placed in the bowl-shaped seat of a Bedsheet-Chair to make it rather flat. Extra clothing or a folded blanket can be used. The three cords suspending the chair should be adjusted for length so that the sitter's feet can rest on the floor and the edge of the chair seat does not press on the undersides of his thighs. (Such pressure cuts off circulation. During the London Blitz of World War II, many of the people who sat night after night in shelters on folding chairs with canvas seats

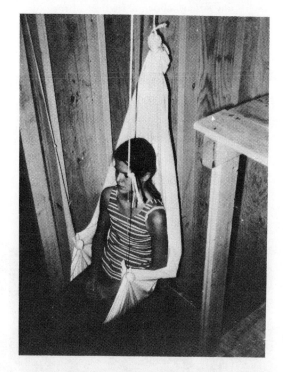

Fig. 14.5. A Bedsheet-Hammock converted into a comfortable suspended Bedsheet-Chair.

developed serious leg conditions. Authorities later prohibited bringing such chairs into shelters.)

CAUTION: To prevent skin infections and other diseases from spreading, a person's hammock or chair should not be used by others. This precaution is particularly important if the shelter is hot and its occupants are sweaty.

HOW TO MAKE A BEDSHEET-HAMMOCK AND CONVERT IT TO A SUSPENDED BEDSHEET-CHAIR

1. PURPOSE: To enable more people to occupy a shelter more comfortably.

2. ADVANTAGES:

* The hammock can be made in a few minutes, once you have the materials and the know-how.

* The only materials required are a strong double-bed sheet (or an equally large piece of

any strong fabric), a few feet of rope (or a piece of strong fabric from which expedient "rope" can be made quickly), a few large nails, and some wire.

* It is difficult to fall out of the hammock because its sides are each made about 8 inches shorter than its lengthwise mid-section, so as to produce a boat-like shape.

* It provides room for head and shoulders close to either end; thus it is practical to hang this hammock between supports that are as close together as 6 feet. See Fig. 14.6.

Before beginning work, someone should read aloud all of the instructions for making the hammock. This will help to avoid mistakes.

Fig. 14.6. The author lying in a Bedsheet-Hammock. (Note that he is pulling the operating cord of a homemade shelter-ventilating pump, a KAP.)

MAKING A BEDSHEET-HAMMOCK

A. How to fold and tie the bedsheet:

1. Select a strong double-bed sheet (one containing polyester is best) and use a ruler or tape measure to avoid guessing at measurements.

2. Fold the bedsheet lengthwise down its center line, so that pairs of corners are together.

3. With the sheet folded, mark the center of each of the two folded ends; then hold one end up.

4. Starting at one corner of one end of the folded bedsheet, make accordion-like pleats.

Make each pleat about 2 inches wide; make the left corner of each pleat about 1 inch lower than the left corner of the preceding pleat, when the sheet is being held as illustrated. Use your left hand to hold the completed pleats in place, while making new pleats with your right hand.

104

5. When one-half of the upper end of the sheet has been folded into pleats almost to the CENTER MARK, adjust the pleats so that the CENTER MARK is about 4 inches below the STARTING CORNER.

6. Continue making 2-inch pleats on past the CENTER MARK, but make the right corner of each pleat about 1 inch higher than the right corner of the preceding pleat. When the pleat-folding is completed, the STARTING CORNER and the other corner should be at the same height (4 inches) above the CENTER MARK.

7. Tie the hammock-supporting rope tightly around the end of the sheet about 3 inches below the edge with the CENTER MARK. (If a rope strong enough to support at least the weight of two men is not available, make an expedient "rope" by tearing a 16-inch-wide strip from a sheet or other strong cloth and then rolling this strip crosswise to its length to make a tight roll several feet long. Then tie string or small strips of cloth about 1 inch wide around it, spaced 4 to 6 inches apart, to keep the rolled-up cloth from unrolling.)

8. Bend the pleat-folded end of the sheet downward around the hammock rope, so that the knot of the hammock rope is uppermost.

9. To keep the sheet from being pulled through the encircling hammock rope, bind the doubled-over end of the sheet with cord (or with narrow strips of cloth) about 1 inch below the rope. Tie the binding cord at least four times around, knotting it each time around.

10. Repeat the procedure (4 through 9) with the other end of the double-folded sheet, thus producing a boat-shaped hammock with its two sides each about 8 inches shorter than its lengthwise center section.

105

B. How to hang the hammock:

1. To suspend a hammock from a strong wooden roof such as the poles of a Pole-Covered Trench Shelter, drive two strong nails (at least $3\frac{1}{2}$ inches long) into the wood at approximately 45° angles, crossing and touching each other. Bind the two nails together with wire. To prevent a hammock rope from being rubbed directly against fixed metal, make a loose loop of strong wire (best if doubled) through the crossed nails; tie the hammock rope to this free-moving wire loop.

2. To suspend the hammock from a wooden wall, use the same type of crossed-nails supports, with the nails driven in one above the other.

3. For comfort and safety, hang the hammock with the head end 18 inches higher than the center and with the foot end 24 inches higher than the center.

4. To make sure that the hammock is strong enough, two persons should place their open hands on its centerline and put all of their weight on the hammock.

5. To suspend hammocks and hammock-chairs from a pole roof that is not being built under fear of immediate attack, use loops of strong wire around the poles at the planned support points. (The correct placement of wire loops takes considerable time and delays completion of the shelter.) To reduce stresses and possible breakage, the loops should be loose, as illustrated.

ORNL-DWG 78-6321

1 1/2 in.

MAKING A SUSPENDED BEDSHEET-CHAIR

A Bedsheet-Hammock may be quickly converted into a comfortable Suspended Bedsheet-Chair so that a shelter occupant can sit comfortably, yet occupy less floor space during the daytime. Follow these steps:

1. Select one end of the hammock to be the top of the back of the chair.

2. From this end, measure 52 inches (4 ft 4 in.) along each side-edge of the hammock (see sketch), and mark these two spots.

3. About $2\frac{1}{2}$ inches in from these two marks (toward the centerline of the hammock), make two more marks.

4. To make an attachment point for a chair "arm", hold a pebble (or a lump of earth) under one of these last marks, pull the double-thickness cloth tight around the pebble, and tie it in place. (See illustration.) Repeat on the other side-edge of the hammock.

5. Tie the end of one rope (or "rope" made of 10-inch-wide strip of strong cloth) to one attachment point, and the end of another rope to the other attachment point.

6. Suspend the top of the back of the chair to a suspension point on the ceiling at least 4 inches out from the wall, and adjust the length of this suspending rope so that the chair arms will be about the same height from the floor as the arms of an easy chair (see sketch).

7. Suspend the arms of the chair from two suspension points 20 inches apart and 20 inches farther out from the wall than the suspension point of the back of the chair. (Study the illustration.)

8. Fold the unused end of the hammock up and back into the "seat" of the chair; fill the hollow of the seat with coats, a blanket, or anything else soft, to make it comfortable.

9. Adjust the lengths of all three suspending ropes so that the chair seat is the right height for the person sitting in it. When both feet are flat on the floor, the front edge of the seat should not press against the undersides of the thighs.

10. To simplify repeated conversion of the hammock to a chair, mark the spot on each of the 3

ORNL-DWG 77-17395

ATTACHMENT POINT

suspending ropes where each is tied to its suspension point on the ceiling; also mark the spot on each suspending rope for a chair arm where each is tied to its suspension point on a chair arm. If enough light rope or strong cord is available, the easiest and quickest way to connect and disconnect the arm supports is to suspend each arm with a double strand of rope, looped around an attachment point as illustrated by the sketch of the attachment point.

107

Chapter 15

Improvised Clothing and Protective Items

BASIC PRINCIPLES OF
COLD WEATHER CLOTHING

If Americans would learn to use skillfully the ordinary clothing, towels, cloth, newspapers, and paper bags in their homes, they could keep warm enough to stay healthy—even under much colder conditions than they believe endurable without specialized outdoor winter clothing. Efficient cold-weather clothing can be improvised if the following ways of conserving body heat are understood and used:

● **Trap "dead" air.** Covering enough of your body with a thick layer of trapped "dead" air is the basic requirement for keeping warm. Figure 15.1 shows how efficient body insulation works: Both the air warmed by close contact with the skin and the water vapor from evaporated perspiration flow outward into the insulating material. Any material that breaks up and separates air into spaces no more than $1/8$ inch

across has efficient cells of "dead" air. Air that is within $1/16$ inch of any surface—whether that of a filament of goose down or of a piece of paper—is slowed down by "sticking" to that surface and becoming hard to move. Trapped "dead" air moves outward very slowly, carrying heat away from the body at a slow rate—thus minimizing heat losses by convection.

● **Use windbreaker materials.** An outer wind-breaker layer of clothing that is essentially air-tight, such as a brown paper bag worn over a knit wool cap, prevents the escape of warmed air and results in an insulating layer of trapped "dead" air. A single layer of good windbreaker material also prevents cold outside air from being blown into the insulating material and displacing warmed air (Fig. 15.1).

The best windbreaker materials permit very little air to pass through them, while at the same time they allow water vapor to escape. Perspiration that cannot be felt or seen on cool skin continually evaporates, forming warm water vapor close to the skin. This moisture escapes outward through good insulating and windbreaker materials; as a result, underlying body insulation remains dry and efficient. Water vapor can pass readily through many sheets of newspaper or unglazed brown paper, although not enough wind can flow through a single sheet to be felt.

● **Prevent excessive heat losses by conduction.** Body heat also is lost by conduction—the direct flow of heat into a colder material. For example, if one sleeps in an excellent goose-down sleeping bag laid directly on cold ground, body weight will compress the down to a small fraction of an inch. This barrier to heat flow is too thin and will cause the body to lose heat rapidly to the cold earth. Likewise, the soles of

ORNL-DWG 77-18426

Fig. 15.1. Efficient body insulation.

ordinary shoes are such poor insulators that standing or walking on frozen ground sometimes results in frozen feet.

MINIMIZING HEAT LOSSES FROM HEAD AND NECK

The head and neck of the girl pictured in Fig. 15.2 are insulated almost as well as if she were wearing the hood of a skin-side-out Eskimo parka. She folded a large, fluffy bath towel and placed it over her head, neck, and the upper part of her body. A brown paper bag was worn over the towel. The edges of the face hole cut in the bag were taped to prevent tearing. A strip of cloth was tied around the part of the bag over her neck. Such a parka-like covering not only is the most efficient way to insulate the head and neck but also prevents air warmed by the body from escaping upward around the neck. The girl also is wearing a man's shirt large enough to cover and hold thick newspaper insulation around her body and arms.

Fig. 15.2. A bath towel and a paper bag used to efficiently insulate head, neck, and shoulders.

It is very important to prevent heat losses from the head and neck, which have many blood vessels near the skin surface. Heat losses from these vital parts cannot be sensed nearly as well as heat losses from other parts of the body. Furthermore, blood vessels near the surface in the head and neck do not automatically constrict to reduce heat losses, as they do in other parts of the body when heat is being lost faster than it can be supplied by metabolism. So when a person is in the cold—particularly when inactive—he should keep his hands, feet, and whole body

warmer by insulating his head and neck very well. (One difficulty in following this advice is that a well-covered head often will feel unpleasantly warm— even sweaty—before one's body temperature rises enough to increase the warming flow of blood to hands and feet.)

INSULATING THE WHOLE BODY

Occupants of freezing-cold shelters can keep warm enough to sleep without blankets by skillfully using ordinary indoor clothing plus paper and pieces of cloth to insulate their whole bodies. The girls pictured in Fig. 15.3 slept without a blanket in a frozen Door-Covered Trench Shelter while the night temperature outdoors dropped to 10° F. The shelter's ventilation openings were adjusted so that the inside temperature remained a few degrees below freezing, to prevent frozen earth from melting into icy mud. These girls had insulated themselves well. First, they covered their cotton shirts and pants with 10 thicknesses of newspaper wrapped around their bodies and tied with strips of cloth. Then around each arm and leg they wrapped and tied 8 sheets of newspaper, thus insulating their limbs with at least 16

Fig. 15.3. Girls wearing expedient clothing are prepared for sleeping in the freezing-cold trench shelter.

thicknesses. As an outer covering over their legs, they wrapped wide strips torn from a bedsheet. Their expedient foot coverings were of the type described in a following paragraph. Their heads and necks were insulated with towels covered with brown paper bags. Old cotton raincoats allowed water vapor to pass through and helped hold in place the insulating newspapers, which extended to cover the girls' bare hands.

The girls slept on newspapers spread about an inch thick over the gravel floor of the trench. When sleeping on cold or frozen ground, it is best to place newspapers or other insulation on top of a layer of small limb-tips or brush, so that drying air can circulate under the bedding. A sheet of plastic under bedding will keep it from being dampened by a wet floor but will not prevent it from being dampened after a few days by condensed water vapor from the sleeper's body.

Newspaper and other paper through which water vapor can pass are such good windbreaker materials that they can be used under any loose-fitting outer garment—even one through which air can pass quite readily. They also provide good insulation. Figure 15.4 shows the author coming out of an icy shelter at sunup. Many thicknesses of

newspaper covered my body and arms and extended like cuffs from my sleeves. A porous cotton bathrobe covered the newspapers and helped hold them in place. Because so little heat was lost through this clothing, plenty of warm blood continued to flow to my bare hands, ridding my body of excess heat by radiation.

IMPROVISED WINTER FOOTWEAR

Cold-weather footwear that is warmer than all but the best-insulated winter boots can be improvised readily. The trick is learning how to tie the several insulating layers securely in place, so that you could hike for miles in the snow if necessary.

For use in dry snow, first tie a porous insulating layer—such as two bath towels or 10 big sheets of newspaper—over each shoe. If you have no low-heeled shoes, make a paper sole by folding 3 large newspaper sheets to make a sole that has 72 thicknesses of paper. Then proceed in the following manner:

1. Place your foot and the sole on 10 newspaper sheets, as pictured in Fig. 15.5.

Fig. 15.4. The author emerges after a night's sleep in freezing-cold temperatures inside a Car-Over-Trench Shelter. Expedient clothing, primarily newspaper insulation, kept him warm without a blanket.

Fig. 15.5. Insulating a foot with a folded newspaper sole and 10 sheets of newspaper.

2. Fold all the sheets over the top of your foot while keeping the sole in the proper place, as indicated in Fig. 15.5.

3. Use a strip of cloth about 3 inches wide and 5 feet long to tie the papers in front of your ankle with a single overhand knot (half of a square knot). With the same strip, tie another single overhand knot over the tendon behind the ankle. Finally, tie a bow knot in front of the ankle.

4. Cover the insulating layer with a tough fabric, such as canvas or burlap sack material; secure with a second strip of cloth and tie as described above.

If the snow is wet, place a piece of strong plastic film or coated fabric outside the insulating layer, after securing it with the first strip of cloth. The outer protective covering should be tied over the water-proofing, with the second strip of cloth securing both it and the waterproofing. (When resting or sleeping in a dry place, remove any moistureproof layer in the foot coverings, to let your feet dry.) Figure 15.6 shows a test subject's waterproofed expedient foot-covering, held in place as described above, after a 2-mile hike in wet snow. His feet were warm, and he had not stopped to tighten or adjust the cloth strips.

Fig. 15.6. Expedient water-proofed foot-covering, over a newspaper sole and other newspaper insulation.

Persons who have not worked outdoors in icy weather seldom realize the importance of warm footwear for winter. Russian civil defense manuals direct urban citizens to take winter boots with them when they evacuate, even in summer.

KEEPING WARM WITHOUT FIRE

● If occupants of a cold room or shelter lack adequate clothing and bedding, all should lie close together.

● Always place some insulating material between your body and a cold floor. (Pieces of shag rug are excellent.) Plastic film should be placed under the insulating material if the ground is damp.

● Go to bed or put on all your body insulation before you begin to feel cold. Once the loss of body heat causes blood vessels in your hands and feet to constrict, it often is hard to get these vessels to return to normal dilation again.

● Do not jump up and down or wave your arms to get or to keep warm. The windchill factor is a measure of air movement over your skin; rapid body movements always cause some such air movement. If practical, lie down and cover up; then do muscular tension exercises by repeatedly tightening all your muscles so tight that you tremble.

● Prevent sweating and the dampening of insulation by taking off or opening up clothing as you begin to exercise, before you begin to sweat.

● If you are getting cold, don't smoke. Nicotine causes blood vessels to constrict and the flow of blood to hands and feet to be reduced.

● Don't drink an alcoholic beverage to warm yourself. Alcohol causes increased blood flow close to the skin surface, resulting in rapid loss of body heat. It is impossible for alcohol to make up for such loss for very long.

RAINWEAR

All that is needed to make serviceable, improvised rainwear is waterproof material and waterproof tape. Plastic film from large trash bags will do; 4-mil polyethylene is better; tough, lightweight, coated fabric is best. Fabric duct tape is the best widely available tape.

Figure 15.7 shows a pair of improvised rain chaps. Rain chaps are separate leg coverings, each with a loop to suspend it from one's belt and usually made large enough to be pulled on and off over the shoes and trousers. Rain chaps are better than waterproof trousers for working or walking while wearing a poncho or raincoat, because body movements cause drying air to be literally pumped under the chaps. This air keeps trousers and legs dry, and therefore warmer.

Fig. 15.7. Improvised rain chaps made of trash-bag polyethylene and freezer tape.

In the same way, a poncho or rain cape will allow plenty of air to reach the garments under them while one is working. When exercise is stopped, clothing underneath will stay dry and warm for some time.

SANDALS

Shoes are almost always in short supply for years following a disastrous war. Except in very cold weather, sandals can be made to serve quite well. The best sandal designs for hard work and serious walking have a strap around the heel and in front of the ankle, with no thong between the toes (Fig. 15.8).

Fig. 15.8. A Ho Chi Minh Sandal, excellent Vietnamese expedient footwear. Rubber bands cut from an inner tube have been inserted into a sole of auto-tire tread.

Such sandals also have the advantage of enabling one to wear socks and other foot insulation inside the straps.

CLOTHING TO PROTECT AGAINST BETA BURNS

If fresh and very radioactive fallout particles remain for long on the skin or extremely close to the skin, beta burns result. Any clothing that keeps fallout off the skin helps greatly. The best expedient protection is given by an outer layer of easily removable clothing similar to the improvised rainwear previously described, but fully covering the hair and neck and providing plastic trousers instead of chaps. Removable shoe coverings are highly advisable. All such protective coverings should be removed before entering a shelter, or removed in the entryway before going into the shelter room.

If a person has fallout particles on clothing that he must continue to wear, he should vigorously brush his outer clothing before entering a shelter room. If fallout particles are washed off, rinsed off, or otherwise removed from the skin within a few minutes, no beta burns will result.

A few days after a nuclear explosion, fallout particles are not radioactive enough to cause beta burns. In areas of heavy fallout, the danger from external doses of gamma radiation from fallout on the ground will continue much longer than will the risk of beta burns from some of these same fallout particles.

The gamma rays given off by fallout particles brought into a shelter on clothing or bodies would subject shelter occupants to gamma doses so small as to be of no significance by wartime standards. Nor would shelter occupants be endangered by radiation from the body of a person who, before reaching shelter, had received a gamma dose large enough to kill him many times over. Except in science fiction stories, the body of such a person does not become "radioactive."

FALLOUT MASKS

For the majority of Americans in most fallout areas, methods for filtering fallout particles out of the air they breathe would not be necessary.[18] Almost all fallout particles small enough to reach one's lungs would slowly fall to earth thousands of miles away from big nuclear explosions.

Persons living in dry, windy areas often wear dust masks and goggles to protect their noses and eyes from dust and sand particles. If fallout particles are mixed with dust and sand that is being blown into a shelter, then persons in windy areas who occupy small belowground expedient shelters should cover their noses and mouths with several thicknesses of towels or other cloth. Those who have dust masks should wear them, especially when working outside in dry, windy weather soon after fallout deposition. The danger would not be from getting radioactive particles in the lungs, but from the possibility of beta burns caused by fallout particles that would collect in the nasal passages, and from swallowed fallout particles. (Much of the substance continuously eliminated from the nasal passage is swallowed.)

Making a homemade dust and fallout mask is a low-priority survival task, even in a desert. The instructions for making the homemade mask given below are for an improved mask based on a Russian design (Fig. 15.9). This mask is the best of several

ORNL–DWG 78-11921

Fig. 15.9. A Russian-type homemade fallout mask. For most people, this would be a low-priority item.

homemade types, and the following instructions for making and using it have been field-tested.

AN INDIVIDUALLY-FITTED FALLOUT MASK

Materials Needed:

1. Three rectangular pieces of fluffy toweling (terry cloth preferred), each piece approximately 12 × 15 inches (or use 10 men's handkerchiefs).

2. Elastic. (The best expedient elastic is from the waistband of a man's undershorts.)

3. Clear plastic (from a photo album, billfold, plastic storm window, etc.).

4. Sewing materials.

Measurements:

1. Tie a string vertically around your head and face, passing it $1/2$ inch in front of each of your ears and making it quite tight.

2. Tie a second string horizontally around your head, crossing your forehead $1^1/4$ inches above the top of your eye sockets. These two strings should cross each other at points X and X^1, over your temples.

3. Measure the distance X-to-X^1 across your forehead and the distance X-to-X^1 going under your chin (around your lower jaw and next to your throat), as indicated by Fig. 15.9.

Construction:

1. Cut out 3 pieces of terry cloth, making the width of each piece equal to X-to-X^1 (the curved distance across your forehead), and the height of each piece equal to the distance X-to-Y plus $1/2$ inch—that is, equal to half the distance X-to-X^1 (measured under your chin) plus $1/2$ inch. See Fig. 15.9.

2. Cut the lower edge of each piece as illustrated.

3. Stitch the 3 pieces of terry cloth together, one on top of the other, thus making the mask three layers thick. Stitch around all four edges of the cloth rectangle and down the centerline.

4. Mark and cut out the eye holes, as illustrated. Make the mask's dimensions smaller for children.

5. Cut one rectangle of clear plastic measuring $5^1/2 × 2^1/4$ inches, and sew this plastic over the outside of the eye holes, stitching the plastic around its edges and down the centerline.

6. Fold the three pieces along their vertical center-line and stitch the lower side together, along the upper stitch line Y-to-Y^1. Stitch $1/2$ inch from the lower edge. Then sew a second row of stitches.

7. Sew on the elastic head bands, making them short enough to hold the mask tightly around your face. If the elastic is from the waistband of a man's undershorts, use a doubled elastic both over the top of your head and around the back of your head. Make these elastic pieces so short that you can just put all your fingers comfortably between the elastic and your head when the pieces are fully stretched. If using a weaker elastic, be sure to adjust the lengths to a tight fit, to prevent air leaks under the edges of the mask. Because of the thickness of material where the elastics are connected to the upper corners of the mask, it may be necessary to do this stitching by hand.

8. To keep fallout particles off your head and neck, sew a loose-fitting piece of bedsheet cloth (not illustrated) to the edges of the mask that fit around your face. This cloth should extend back over your head and down over your collar, over which it can be tied.

Use:

Put on the mask by first placing it over your chin, then pulling the back elastic down to fit around the back of your head.

CAUTION:

To avoid spreading infections, each mask should be labeled and worn by only one person.

Chapter 16
Minimum Pre-Crisis Preparations

Your chances of surviving a nuclear attack will be improved if you make the following low-cost preparations before a serious crisis arises. Once many Americans become convinced that a nuclear attack is a near certainty, they will rush to stores and buy all available survival supplies. If you wait to prepare until a crisis does arise, you are likely to be among the majority who will have to make-do with inadequate supplies of water containers, food, and materials. Furthermore, even if you have the necessary materials and instructions to make the most needed survival items, you and your family are not likely to have time to make all of them during a few days of tense crisis.

The following recommendations are intended primarily for the majority who live in areas likely to be subjected to blast, fire, or extremely heavy fallout. These people should plan to evacuate to a safer area. (Many citizens living outside high-risk areas, especially homeowners with yards, can and should make better pre-crisis preparations. These would include building high-protection-factor permanent shelters covered with earth.)

SHELTER

Keep on hand the tools and materials your family or group will need to build or improve a high-protection-factor expedient shelter: One or more shovels, a pick (if in a hard-soil area), a bow-saw with an extra blade, a hammer, and 4-mil polyethylene film for rainproofing your planned shelter. Also store the necessary nails, wire, etc. needed for the kind of shelter you plan to build.

Keep instructions for shelter-building and other survival essentials in a safe and convenient place.

VENTILATION-COOLING

Make a homemade shelter-ventilating pump, a KAP, of the size required for the shelter you plan to build or use.

WATER

Keep on hand water containers (including at least four 30-gallon untreated polyethylene trash bags and two sacks or pillowcases for each person), a pliable garden hose or other tube for siphoning, and a plastic bottle of sodium hypochlorite bleach (such as Clorox) for disinfecting water and utensils.

FALLOUT METER

Make one or two KFMs and learn how to use this simple instrument.

FOOD

Store at least a 2-week supply of compact, non-perishable food. The balanced ration of basic dry foods described in Chapter 9, Food, satisfies requirements for adults and larger children at minimum cost. If your family includes babies or small children, be sure to store more milk powder, vegetable oil, and sugar.

Continuing to breast-feed babies born during an impending crisis would greatly simplify their care should the crisis develop and worsen.

For preparing and cooking basic foods:

● Make a 3-Pipe Grain Mill like the one described in Chapter 9, Food, or buy a small hand-cranked grain mill, which grinds more efficiently than other expedient devices.

● Make a Bucket-Stove as described in Chapter 9. During evacuation, the stove can be used as a container. Store some kitchen-type wooden matches in a waterproof container.

● Keep essential containers and utensils on hand for storing and transporting food and for cooking and serving in a shelter.

SANITATION

A hose-vented 5-gallon can, with heavy plastic bags for liners, for use as a toilet. Include some smaller plastic bags and toilet paper with these supplies.

MEDICINES

● Any special medications needed by family members.

● Potassium iodide, a 2-oz bottle, and a medicine-dropper, for prophylactic protection of the thyroid gland against radioactive iodines. (Described in the last section of Chapter 13, Survival Without Doctors.)

● A first-aid kit and a tube of antibiotic ointment.

LIGHT

● Long-burning candles (with small wicks) sufficient for at least 14 nights.

● An expedient lamp, with extra cotton-string, wicks, and cooking oil as described in Chapter 11.

● A flashlight and extra batteries.

RADIO

A transistor radio with extra batteries and a metal box in which to protect it.

OTHER ESSENTIALS

Review the EVACUATION CHECKLIST (developed primarily for persons who make no preparations before a crisis) and add items that are special requirements of your family.

Instructions for Six Expedient Fallout Shelters

SHELTER-BUILDING INSTRUCTIONS

The following step-by-step instructions for building 6 types of earth-covered expedient shelters have enabled untrained families to build even the most difficult of these shelters in less than 2 days. The only families who took longer—up to 4 days—were the few who were delayed by very heavy rains. Each of these shelters has been built by several different families or groups of families. Only widely available materials and hand tools are required. They have been built under simulated crisis conditions in environments typical of large regions of the United States: covered-trench types have been built in forested clay hills of Tennessee, in a bare Colorado valley in snowy November, in an irrigated Utah valley in hot August. Most of the aboveground shelters were built by families in Florida, where the water table is within 18 inches of the surface.

All of these test families used instructions that contained general guidance to help inexperienced persons build almost any type of earth-covered shelter. In this appendix, general instructions which apply to all types of shelters will be given first, to avoid repetition. (However, if the instructions for building one type of shelter are reproduced separately, the pertinent parts of these general instructions should be given before the step-by-step instructions for building that shelter. For easy-to-read reproduction in a newspaper, the detailed shelter drawings first should be photo-enlarged about 50%.)

GENERAL INSTRUCTIONS FOR BUILDING AN EXPEDIENT SHELTER

1. Read all the instructions and study the drawings before beginning work. (Most families have found it helpful first to read the instructions aloud and then to discuss problems and work assignments.)

2. Sharpen all tools, including picks and shovels. Dull tools waste time and energy. If no file is available, tools can be sharpened by rubbing them hard on concrete or a rough stone.

3. Wear gloves from the start. Blisters can lead to serious infections, especially if antibiotics cannot be obtained.

4. Whenever practical, select a building site that:

   ● Will not be flooded if heavy rains occur or if a large dam farther up a major valley is destroyed by a nuclear explosion.

   ● Is in the open and at least 50 ft away from a building or woods that might be set afire by the thermal pulse from an explosion tens of miles away. (Keep well away from even a lone tree; it is hard to dig through roots.)

   ● Has earth that is firm and stable, if the planned shelter is to be a trench type with unshored (unsupported) earth walls. To make sure that the earth is firm and stable enough so that the walls will not cave in, make a "thumb-test" by digging an 18-in.-deep hole and trying to push your bare thumb into the undisturbed earth at the bottom. If you can push your thumb no farther than 1 in., the earth should be safe enough. If the earth does not pass the thumb-test, move to another location and repeat the test. Or build a belowground shelter with shored walls, or an aboveground shelter.

   ● Has a sufficient depth of earth above rock or the water table for a trench to be dug to the depth required. (To find out, try to dig a pit to the required depth before excavating the whole trench. Or, if you are quite sure there is no water-table problem, try driving down a sharpened rod or pipe to the required depth in several places along the planned length of the trench.)

5. If the shelter must be built on sloping ground, locate it with its length crosswise to the direction of the slope.

6. Before staking out the shelter, clear the ground of brush, weeds and tall grass over an area extending about 10 ft beyond the planned edges of the excavation. (If loose earth is shoveled onto tall plants, the earth will be difficult to shovel the second time when covering the completed shelter roof.)

7. Stake out the complete shelter, and then dig by removing layers of earth.

8. When digging earth that is too firm to shovel without first breaking it up, start picking (or breaking with a shovel) in a line across the center of the trench. Next, shovel out a narrow trench 6 or 8 in. deep all the way across the width of the trench. Then with pick or shovel break off row after row of earth all the way across the width of the trench, as illustrated.

ORNL–DWG 78-16212

9. When digging a trench, to avoid having to move the excavated earth twice more to get it out of the way, first pile all earth about 8 ft away from the trench. Later, pile additional earth you are excavating at least 3 ft away.

10. Never risk a cave-in by digging into lower parts of an earth wall. It is dangerous to produce even a small overhanging section of wall or to dig a small, cave-like enlargement of a shelter.

11. When making a "sandbag" of a pillowcase or sack to hold earth shielding in place around the sides of shelter openings or along the edges of a

shelter roof, fill it so that it will be only about two-thirds full after its opening is tied shut securely. Avoid dropping the sandbag.

12. If sufficient sandbags are not available, make earth-filled "rolls." Bed sheets or any reasonably strong fabric or plastic film can be used to make these rolls as described below. (To make a longer roll than the one illustrated below, several persons should make one together, standing side-by-side.)

To make an 8-in.-high earth-filled roll:

(1) Select a piece of cloth at least as strong as a new bed sheet, 2 ft longer than the side of the opening to be protected, and 5 ft wide.

(2) Place 2 ft of the width of the cloth on the ground, as illustrated.

ORNL–DWG 78-16213

(3) While using both hands to hold up and pull on 3 ft of the width of the cloth and pressing against the cloth with your body, have another person shovel earth onto and against the cloth.

(4) While still pulling on the cloth, pull the upper part down over the earth that covers the lower part of the cloth.

(5) Cover the upper part of the cloth with earth so as to form an earth-filled "hook" near the upper edge, as illustrated.

ORNL—DWG 78-16214

SLOPE EARTH TO DRAIN

DRAIN

CLOTH

FINISHED 8 in. ROLL

(6) If a greater thickness of rolls is needed, level the earth on top of a roll; then make another earth-filled roll on this level surface.

13. Cut and haul poles and logs more easily by doing the following:

(1) Take time to sharpen your tools before starting to work—no matter how rushed you feel.

(2) When sawing green trees that have gummy resin or sap, oil your saw with kerosene or diesel fuel. If you don't have these, use motor oil, grease, or even soap.

(3) When felling a small tree, the following method will help make a square cut, keep your saw from being pinched, and help make the tree fall in the desired direction: (a) Saw the tree about one-third through on the side toward which you want it to fall. (b) Then start sawing the opposite side, while another person pushes on the tree with a 10-ft push-pole, pressing the end of the push-pole against the tree about 10 ft above the ground. A push-pole with a forked end—or with a big nail on the end—is best.

(4) After a tree has been felled, trim off all limbs and knots so that the pole or log is smooth and will require no additional smoothing

ORNL—DWG 78-16210

LIMB CUT OFF, TO HOOK OVER THE SQUARE-CUT END OF THE POLE.

DESIRED POLE LENGTH

when you get ready to move it, or to use it for building your shelter. Make and use a measuring stick to speed up measuring and cutting poles and logs to the right lengths.

(5) It usually is best first to cut the poles exactly two or three times the final length of the poles to be used in the shelter.

(6) When you are ready to move the poles to the shelter site, drag them rather than trying to carry them on your shoulders. Shouldering them is more tiring, and you could injure yourself severely if you should trip.

To drag a log or several poles by hand: (a) Cut a stick 2 to $2\frac{1}{2}$ in. in diameter and about $3\frac{1}{3}$ ft long; (b) Tie a short piece of $\frac{1}{4}$-in. (or stronger) rope to the center of the stick; (c) Make a lasso-like loop at the free end of the rope, so that when it is looped around the log and two people are pulling (see illustration), the front end of the log is raised about 6 in. above the ground. The loop should be tightened around the log about 2 ft. from its end, so that the end of the log cannot hit the backs of the legs of the two people pulling it.

ORNL—DWG 78-16211

2 TO 2-1/2 IN. DIAMETER STICK 40 IN. LONG

ROPE

LOOP

CAUTION: If you drag a log down a steep hill, one person should tie a rope to the rear end of the log, and then follow the dragger, ready to act as the brake if needed.

(7) When you get the poles or logs to the location where you will build the shelter, cut them to the desired minimum diameters and specified lengths, and put all those of one specified

type together. Be sure that the diameter of the small end of each pole of one type is at least as large as the minimum diameter specified for its type. Make and use a measuring stick, as previously described.

14. Use snow for shielding material for aboveground shelters if the earth is so deep-frozen that digging is impractical. For a Ridge-Pole Shelter (see Appendix A.5), cover the entire shelter with 5 ft of wetted or well-packed snow. For a Crib-Walled Shelter (see Appendix A.6), fill the cribs and then cover and surround the entire shelter with snow at least 5 ft thick. With wetted or well-packed snow 5 ft thick, the protection factor is about 50. Families have completed these winter shelters within 2 days.

Several hundred pounds of snow can be moved at a time by sledding it on a piece of canvas or other strong material 6 to 8 ft wide. Attach a stick across one end of the material and tie a rope to the ends of the stick, so as to form a "Y" bridle on which a person can pull.

To keep the occupants of a snow-covered expedient shelter dry and tolerably warm in sub-freezing weather, provide sufficient ventilation openings to maintain inside temperatures at a few degrees *below* freezing. (See Chapter 14, Expedient Clothing.)

15. Make a reliable canopy over the shelter entry. By following the instructions given in Fig. A on the following page, you can make a dependable canopy that ordinary winds will neither tear nor blow down and that will not catch rainwater—even if you have no waterproof material stronger than 4-mil polyethylene film.

16. Take to your shelter enough window screen or mosquito netting to cover its openings. Except in freezing-cold weather, flies and mosquitoes would soon become a problem in most localities soon after an attack.

17. Work to complete (1) an expedient ventilating-cooling pump (a KAP) and (2) the storage of at least 15 gallons of water per person. This work should be accomplished by the time your shelter is completed. Especially in an area of heavy fallout during warm or hot weather, an earth-covered, high-protection-factor shelter when full of people would be useless unless adequately ventilated and cooled and provided with enough water.

18. In cold weather, restrict air flow through the shelter by hanging curtains of plastic or tightly woven fabric, or by otherwise partially obstructing its two openings. Always be sure to leave at least a few square inches open at the floor level of one opening and at the ceiling height of the other, to provide enough ventilation to prevent a harmful concentration of exhaled carbon dioxide. To prevent exhaled water vapor from wetting clothing and bedding and reducing its insulating value, keep the ventilation openings as wide open as possible without causing shelter temperatures to be intolerably cold.

FOR A 6-ft BY 6-ft CANOPY DRIVE TWO 4-ft STAKES ABOUT 6-½ ft. APART

IF IN SOFT OR SHALLOW EARTH, SECURE THE TOPS OF THE TWO 4-ft STAKES WITH GUY CORDS TO STAKES (NOT SHOWN)

ROPE OR CORD (OR A STRAIGHT *SMOOTH* STICK 7 FEET LONG) UNDER RIDGELINE OF CANOPY

TIE A STRING TO TIE-POINT IN CENTER OF END OF CANOPY

ENTER FROM THIS CORNER

TIE 27 in. ABOVE GROUND

ADJUSTABLE CORD *NOT* TIED TO STAKE, TIGHTENED BY LAST PERSON TO CRAWL UNDER CANOPY AND INTO VERTICAL SHELTER ENTRY

CORNER TIE-POINT

SIDE ABOUT 7 in. ABOVE GROUND

TIE CLOSE TO GROUND

TO COVER THE VERTICAL ENTRY HOLE OF A SHELTER, USE THIS CANOPY, THAT CAN BE MADE OF THIN PLASTIC TO WITHSTAND WIND AND RAIN FOR WEEKS

6 ft FINISHED

CUT OUT

3 in.

3 in.

4 in.

X

2 in.

3 in.

4 in.

3 in.

4 in.

CUT OUT

X

X

THREE TABS ON ONE END OF THE CANOPY (MAKE OTHER END THE SAME)

MARK AN "X" 2-¼ in. IN FROM CORNER

CUT SMOOTH CURVE

3 in.

4 in.

X

TAB AT CORNER

"NECK" TIED WITH STRING

¾ in. DIA. PEBBLE

"X" OUTERMOST

COMPLETED TIE-POINT

(IF TIE-POINTS ARE MADE AT THE CORNERS WITHOUT FIRST MAKING TABS, THE CANOPY WILL HAVE CUPPED-IN SIDES THAT CATCH WATER AND WIND.)

¾ in. DIA. IS THIS SMALL

DIRECTIONS:

1. CUT A PIECE OF PLASTIC 6-½ ft. BY 6-½ ft., TO MAKE A 6 ft. BY 6 ft. CANOPY. USE PLASTIC AT LEAST 4 MILS THICK.

2. TO MAKE DURABLE TIE-POINTS AT THE FOUR CORNERS AND AT THE CENTERS OF THE TWO ENDS, SMOOTHLY CUT TABS OUT OF THE SIDES – AS INDICATED BY SKETCH OF ONE END, ON RIGHT.

3. MARK AN "X" ON EACH TAB, AS SHOWN.

4. SELECT 6 PEBBLES OR LUMPS OF EARTH EACH ABOUT ¾ INCH IN DIAMETER.

5. WITH THE STRONG PIECE OF STRING THAT WILL BE USED TO CONNECT A TIE-POINT TO A STAKE, TIE A PEBBLE IN THE TAB SO THAT THE PEBBLE IS COMPLETELY COVERED AND THE "X" MARK IS OUTERMOST. SEE SKETCHES.

6. MAKE 6 TIE-POINTS IN THIS MANNER, EACH WITH A STRING ATTACHED.

7. PITCH THE CANOPY AS ILLUSTRATED ABOVE, WITH ITS TWO SIDES EACH ABOUT 7 INCHES OFF THE GROUND.

Fig. A. A dependable canopy to keep fallout and rain out of a vertical entry.

Door-Covered Trench Shelter

(See illustration at the end of Appendix A.1)

PROTECTION PROVIDED

Against fallout radiation: Protection Factor 250 (PF 250)—a person in the open outside this shelter would receive 250 times as much fallout radiation as he would if inside.

Against blast: Better protection than most homes, if built in very stable earth. Blast tests have indicated that this shelter would be undamaged up to at least the 5-psi overpressure range from large explosions. Without blast doors, the shelter's occupants could be injured at this overpressure range, although probably not fatally.

Against fire: Excellent, if sufficiently distant from fires producing carbon monoxide and toxic smoke.

WHERE PRACTICAL

In a situation where at least one hollow-core door per occupant is available. (A family evacuating in a pickup truck or large station wagon can carry enough doors, with doorknobs removed.)

In very stable earth, where neither the water table nor rock is less than $4\frac{1}{2}$ ft below the surface.

FOR WHOM PRACTICAL

For a family or other group with two or more members able to work hard for most of 36 hours.

CAPACITY

The shelter illustrated is roofed with **3 doors** and is the **minimum** length for **3 persons**. (If you have additional doors, or boards and sticks at least 3 ft long, make the entryway trenches 3 or 4 ft longer than illustrated—if not pressed for time.)

For each additional person, add an additional door. (If more than about 7 persons are to be sheltered, build two or more separate shelters.)

BUILDING INSTRUCTIONS

1. Before beginning work, study the drawings and read ALL of the following instructions.

2. Divide the work; CHECK OFF EACH STEP WHEN COMPLETED.

3. By the time the shelter is finished, plan to have completed (1) a ventilating pump (a KAP 16 in. wide and 28 in. high), essential for this shelter except in cool weather, and (2) the storage of at least 15 gallons of water per occupant (see Appendix B and Chapter 8).

4. Start to assemble materials and tools that are listed for the illustrated 3-person shelter.

   A. **Essential Materials and Tools for a 3-Person Shelter**

   - Three hollow-core doors.

   - A shovel (and a pick, if the earth is very hard).

   - Two to three square yards per person of waterproof materials for rainproofing the roof. Use materials such as 4-mil polyethylene film, shower curtains, plastic tablecloths, plastic mattress covers, or canvas.

   - Two pieces of plastic or tightly woven cloth (each about $6\frac{1}{2} \times 6\frac{1}{2}$ ft) to make canopies over the two shelter openings. Also sticks and cords or strips of cloth to support the canopies—as described in Fig. A of the introductory section of this appendix.

● Materials and tools for building a simple shelter-ventilating pump, a KAP 16 in. wide and 28 in. high. (See Appendix B.) Only in cold or continuously breezy, cool weather can tolerable temperatures and humidities be maintained in a crowded underground shelter without an air pump.

● Containers for storing adequate water. (See Chapter 8.)

B. Useful Materials and Tools

● Large cans, buckets, and/or pots with bail handles—in which to carry earth and later to store drinking water or human wastes.

● Two pillowcases and one bedsheet per person—to make "sandbags" around shelter openings and to cover trench walls. (If available, large sheets of 4-mil polyethylene are better than bedsheets, because they keep earth walls damp and stable. They also help keep shelter occupants dry and clean and prevent earth from falling into their eyes.)

● File, knife, pliers, hammer.

● Measuring tape, yardstick, or ruler.

● Expedient life-support items.

5. To save time and work, SHARPEN ALL TOOLS AND KEEP THEM SHARP.

6. Wear gloves from the start—even tough hands can blister and become painful and infected after hours of digging.

7. Check to be sure the earth is stable and firm enough so that a trench shelter with unshored (unsupported), **vertical** earth walls will be safe from cave-ins. (Interior doors are not strong enough to roof an earth-covered trench wider than 3 ft.)

As a test of the stability of earth, dig a small hole about 18 in. deep. Remove all loose earth from the bottom of the hole. Then make a "thumb test" by pushing your bare thumb into the undisturbed surface at the bottom of the hole. If you can push your thumb into the earth no farther than one inch, the earth should be suitable for this type of shelter. If the earth does

not pass the "thumb test," move to another location and try the test again. Continue to relocate and repeat until suitable earth is found, or build a shored-trench or aboveground shelter.

8. Prepare to dig a vertical-walled trench 4½ ft deep and 3 ft wide. To determine the length of the trench, add together the widths of all the doors to be used for roofing it, then subtract 8 in. from the sum. (To avoid arithmetical errors, it is best to lay all the doors side by side on the ground.)

9. Clear any brush, grass, or weeds that are more than a few inches high from the area where the trench will be dug. Also clear the ground around all sides of the trench, to a distance of about 8 ft from the sides and ends of the trench.

10. Stake out a rectangular trench 36 in. wide, with its length as determined above. Also stake out the entrance at one end, as illustrated in Fig. A.1 at the end of Appendix A.1, and the ventilation trench and opening at the other.

11. Dig the main trench, the entryway trench, and the ventilation trench. Place the excavated earth along both lengthwise sides of the trench, starting at the outside edges of the cleared space. Be sure that no earth is piled closer than 3 ft to the sides of the trench.

12. To be sure that unstable, unsafe earth is not encountered at depths below 18 in., repeat the "thumb test" each time the trench is deepened an additional foot. If the earth does not pass the test, do not dig the trench any deeper; try another location.

13. To keep each trench its full width as it is dug, cut a stick 36 in. long and another 18 in. long; **use them repeatedly from the start** to check the widths of the main trench and the entry trenches. Keeping the trenches full width will save much work and time later.

14. Carefully level and smooth the ground to a distance of 2½ ft from the sides of the trench, so that the doors will lie flat on the ground up to the edges of the trench.

15. If plenty of sheets, bedspreads, plastic, and/or other materials are available, cover the trench walls with them. Wall coverings should stop one inch from the floor of the trench to prevent their being stepped on and pulled down. Plastic wall coverings keep some types of damp earth walls from drying out and crumbling.

16. To rainproof the shelter and to prevent the roofing doors from being dampened and weakened, use available waterproof materials as follows:

  a. If the earth is *dry*, the easiest and best way to make a rainproof roof is to place the doors directly on the ground, with each of the end doors overlapping an end of the main trench by 4 or 5 in. (Be sure again to level the ground surface as you place each door, so that each lies flat against the ground all the way to the edges of the trench.) Next, mound dry earth over the doors. First place a few inches of earth on the doors near their ends; then mound it about 12 in. deep above the centerline of the trench. Slope the earth to both sides so as to just cover the ends of the doors. Next, smooth off the earth mound, being careful to remove sharp stones that might puncture rainproof materials. Then place waterproof material over the smooth mound, making the "buried roof" shown in Fig. A.1. Finally, carefully mound an additional 12 to 15 in. of earth on top of the buried roof, again placing it first over the doors near their ends. The earth over the trench should be at least 2 ft thick, so that effective earth arching will support most of the weight of the earth covering and will provide considerable protection if struck by blast.

  b. If the earth is *wet*, place the waterproof material directly on top of the doors, to keep them dry and strong. To make water run off this waterproof covering and to keep water from collecting on a horizontal surface and leaking through, slope the doors toward one side of the trench by first making one side of the trench about 3 in. higher than the other side. A way to raise one side—without increasing the distance the doors must span—is to place an earth-filled "roll" of bedsheets or other material along one edge of the trench. To keep the waterproof material used to cover the doors from sliding down the slope of the doors when earth is shoveled on, tuck the upper edge of the material under the higher ends of the doors. Finally, mound earth over the doors, first placing it near their ends. The mound should be at least 2 ft deep above the centerline of the roof and about 3 or 4 in. deep over both ends of the doors.

If more waterproof material is available than is required to make a buried roof (or to cover the doors) and to make the illustrated canopies over the two shelter openings, use this excess material to cover the wet ground on which the doors are placed.

17. To be able to place an adequate thickness of shielding earth all the way to and around the entryway and ventilation hole, stack improvised "sandbags" around these two openings before placing the earth on the roof. Or use cloth or plastic material to make "rolls" of earth, as illustrated in the introductory section of Appendix A.

18. Shovel earth around the rolls, sandbags, or other means used to raise the level of the earth around the two shelter openings. Slope this earth outward, and pack it, so that rainwater on the ground cannot run into the shelter.

19. Dig small drainage ditches around the completed shelter, to lead runoff water away.

20. To keep rain and/or sand-like fallout particles from falling into the shelter openings, build an open-sided canopy over each opening, as illustrated in Fig. A, shown in the introductory section of Appendix A.

21. Install the air pump (a KAP) in the shelter opening into which air is already naturally moving.

22. If the shelter has a KAP, protection against radiation can be increased by placing containers of water and of heavy foods, or bags of earth, so as to partially block the openings. This would still permit adequate air to be pumped through the shelter, except in very hot weather.

23. For seats, place water and food containers, bedding, etc., along the side of the trench that is farther from the off-center entry trenches. If the trench floor is damp, covering it with a waterproof material, tree limbs, or brush will help.

24. Fill all available water containers, including pits which have been dug and lined with plastic, then roofed with available materials. If possible, disinfect all water stored in expedient containers, using one scant teaspoon of a chlorine bleach, such as Clorox, for each 10 gallons of water. Even if only muddy water is available, store it. If

you do not have a disinfectant, it may be possible to boil water when needed.

25. As time and materials permit, continue to improve your chances of surviving by doing the following things if possible: (1) Make a home-made fallout meter, as described in Appendix C. (2) Make expedient lights.

Fig. A.1. Door-Covered Trench Shelter.

Pole-Covered Trench Shelter

PROTECTION PROVIDED

Against fallout radiation: Protection Factor 300 (PF 300)—a person in the open outside this shelter would receive 300 times more fallout radiation than he would if he were inside.

Against blast: Quite good protection if built in stable earth. Blast tests have indicated that this shelter, if built in stable earth, would not be seriously damaged by blast effects of large explosions at least up to the 7-psi overpressure range. (At 7 psi, most buildings would be demolished.) Without blast doors, occupants of the shelter could be injured, although probably not fatally.

Against fire: Excellent, if sufficiently distant from fires producing carbon monoxide and toxic smoke.

WHERE PRACTICAL

In wooded areas with small trees, for builders who have an ax or a bow saw, crosscut or chain saw, and digging tools. Or in any location where the necessary poles may be obtained.

In stable earth, where the water table or rock is more than $4\frac{1}{2}$ ft below the surface.

FOR WHOM PRACTICAL

For a family or other group with two or more members able to work hard for most of 2 days.

CAPACITY

The shelter illustrated is the minimum length recommended for 4 persons. For each additional person, add at least $2\frac{3}{4}$ ft to the length of the shelter room. If more than about 10 persons are to be sheltered, build 2 or more separate shelters.

BUILDING INSTRUCTIONS

1. Before beginning work, study the drawings and read ALL of the following instructions. Divide the work so that some people will be digging while others are cutting and hauling poles. CHECK OFF EACH STEP WHEN COMPLETED.

2. By the time the shelter is finished, plan to have completed: (1) a ventilating pump, and (2) the storage of at least 15 gallons of drinking water per occupant (see Appendix B and Chapter 8).

3. Start to assemble materials and tools. Those listed are for the illustrated 4-person shelter with a room 11 ft long.

A. Essential Materials and Tools

- Saw (bow saw or crosscut preferred) and/or ax for cutting poles to the lengths and diameters illustrated.

- Shovels (one for each two workers).

- Pick (if the ground is hard).

- Rainproof roof materials (very important in rainy, cold weather). At least 2 square yards of such material per person would be required; 3 square yards per person would be better. Shower curtains, plastic tablecloths, plastic mattress covers, canvas, and the like can be used. Also needed are 2 pieces of plastic or tightly woven cloth, each about $6\frac{1}{2} \times 6\frac{1}{2}$ ft, to make canopies over the two shelter openings.

- Materials and tools for building a simple shelter-ventilating pump, a KAP 22 in. wide and 36 in. long. (See Appendix B.) Only in cold or continuously breezy, cool weather can tolerable temperatures and humidities be maintained for days in a crowded underground shelter that lacks an air pump.

- Containers for storing adequate water. (See Chapter 8.)

B. Useful Materials and Tools

- Large cans, buckets, and/or pots with bail handles—in which to carry earth and later to store drinking water and human wastes.

- Two bedsheets and two pillowcases per person for covering cracks between roofing logs, making "sandbags," and improvising bedsheet-hammocks and bedsheet-chairs.

- A file.

- A measuring tape, yardstick, or ruler.

- Rope, or strong wire (100 ft)—to make earth-retaining pole walls close to the shelter openings (as explained in step 19) and for hammock supports, etc.

- Chain saw, pick-mattock, hammer, hatchet, pliers.

- Kerosene, turpentine, or oil—to keep hand saws from sticking in gummy wood.

- Expedient life-support items recommended in this book.

- Mosquito netting or window screen to cover the openings, if mosquitoes or flies are likely to be a problem.

4. To save time and work, SHARPEN ALL TOOLS AND KEEP THEM SHARP.

5. Wear gloves from the start—even tough hands can blister after hours of chopping and digging, and become painful and infected.

6. If possible, select a location for the shelter that is in the open and at least 50 ft from a building or woods. Remember that on a clear day the thermal pulse (flash of heat rays) from a very large nuclear explosion may cause fires as far away as 25 miles.

7. If the site chosen is on a steep slope, locate the shelter with its length crosswise to the direction of the slope.

8. Stake out the outlines of the trench, driving stakes as indicated in Fig. A.2.1 at the end of Appendix A.2. If more than 4 persons are to be sheltered, increase the length of the shelter room by 2 ft 9 in. for each additional person.

9. Clear the ground of saplings and tall grass within 10 ft of the staked outlines so that later the excavated earth can be easily shoveled back onto the completed shelter roof.

10. Start digging, throwing the first earth about 10 ft beyond the staked outlines of the trench. Less able members of the family should do the easier digging, near the surface. Those members who can use an ax and saw should cut and haul poles. See the introductory section of this appendix for the know-how to make this hard work easier.

11. Pile all excavated earth at least 2 ft beyond the edges of the trench, so roofing poles can be laid directly on the ground. To make sure that the trenches are dug to the specified full widths at the bottoms, cut and use two sticks—one 42 in. long and the other 22 in. long—to check trench widths repeatedly.

12. At the far end of the shelter dig the ventilation trench-emergency exit, making it 22 in. wide and 40 in. deep. This will help provide essential ventilation and cooling. In cold weather or when fallout is descending, canvas or plastic curtains should be hung in the two openings to control the air flow.

13. Make and install threshold boards, to keep the edges of earth steps and earth ledges from being broken off. (In damp earth, it is best to install threshold boards before roofing the shelter.) If boards are lacking, use small poles.

14. Unless the weather is cold, build a shelter-ventilating pump—a KAP 20 in. wide × 36 in. high. (If the weather is *cold*, building a KAP can be safely delayed until after the shelter is completed.) A KAP should be made before a crisis, or, if possible, before leaving home.

15. Obtain fresh-cut green poles, or, as a second choice, sound, dry, untreated poles. Use no poles smaller in diameter than those specified in the accompanying drawings. For ease in hauling, select poles no more than 50% larger in diameter than those specified.

16. Lay the poles side by side over the trench. Alternate the large and small ends to keep the poles straight across the trench. If roof poles 9 ft long are being used to roof a 5-ft-wide trench, be sure to place the roof poles so that their ends extend 2 ft farther beyond one side of the trench than beyond the other side. This will enable shelter occupants, after the stoop-in shelter is completed, to widen the shelter room 2 ft on one side. First, it can be widened to provide a 2-ft-wide sleeping ledge. Later, it can be further deepened to make space for additional expedient hammocks or for double-bunk beds of poles or boards built on each side of the shelter.

17. For ease and safety later when hanging expedient bedsheet-hammocks and bedsheet-chairs in the completed shelter, place **loose** loops around roof poles in the approximate locations given by the diagram on the second shelter drawing, Fig. A.2.2. Make these loose loops of rope, or strong wire, or 16-in-wide strips of strong cloth, such as 50% polyester bedsheet rolled up to form a "rope". (For making hammocks and seats, see Chapter 14. These are not essential, although decidedly useful.)

18. Cover the cracks between the logs with cloth, leaves, clay, or any other material that will keep dirt from falling down between the cracks. CAUTION: DO NOT try to rainproof this flat roof, and then simply cover it with earth. Water will seep through the loose earth cover, puddle on the flat roofing material, and leak through the joints between pieces of roofing material or through small holes.

19. Place 6-ft-long poles, one on top of the other, next to the entrances. This will keep earth to be placed on top of the entryway trenches from falling into the openings. Secure these poles with wire or rope. (See View A-A¹ in Fig. A.2.1.) If wire or rope is not available, make earth-filled "rolls" to hold the earth nearly vertical on the trench roof next to each opening. (See the introductory section of this appendix.)

20. Mound earth to a center depth of about 18 in. over the shelter roof (as shown in View B-B¹ in Fig. A.2.1) to form the surface of the future "buried roof." Be sure to slope both sides of the mound. Then smooth its surface and remove sharp roots and stones that might puncture thin rainproofing materials to be placed upon it.

21. Place the waterproofing material on the "buried roof." If small pieces must be used, lay them in shingle-like fashion, starting at the lower sides of the mounded earth.

22. Cover the buried roof with another 18 in. of mounded earth, and smooth this final earth surface.

23. Finish the entrances by placing some shorter poles between the two longer poles next to each entryway. Bank and pack earth at least 6 in. deep around the sides of the entrances, so that rainwater on the ground cannot run into the shelter entrances.

24. Dig surface drainage ditches around the outside of the mounded earth and around the entrances.

25. Place a piece of water-shedding material over each of the entrances, forming an open-ended canopy to keep fallout and rain from the shelter openings. (See Fig. A in the introductory section of Appendix A.) Almost all fallout would settle on these suspended canopies, rather than falling into shelter openings—or would fall off their edges and onto the ground like sand.

26. Hang the KAP from the roof of the trench opening into which outdoor air can be felt flowing, so that air will be pumped in the direction of the natural flow of air.

27. Fill all available water containers, including pits which have been dug and lined with plastic, then roofed with available materials. If possible, disinfect all water stored in expedient containers, using one scant teaspoon of a chlorine bleach, such as Clorox, for each 10 gallons of water. Even if only muddy water is available, store it. If you do not have a disinfectant, it may be possible to boil water when needed.

28. As time and materials permit, continue to improve your chances of surviving by doing as many of the following things as possible;

    (1) Make a homemade fallout meter, as described in Appendix C.

    (2) Make expedient lights.

    (3) Make and hang expedient bedsheet-hammocks and bedsheet-chairs, following the installation diagram shown in Fig. A.2.2.

    (4) Install screens of mosquito netting over the two openings, if mosquitoes or flies are a

problem. Remember, however, that screen or netting reduces the air flow through a shelter—even when the air is pumped through with a KAP.

(5) Dig a stand-up hole near the far end of the shelter. Make the hole about 15 in. in diameter and deep enough to permit the tallest of the shelter occupants to stand erect occasionally.

Fig. A.2.1. Pole-Covered Trench Shelter.

Fig. A.2.2. Pole-Covered Trench Shelter.

Appendix A.3
Small-Pole Shelter

PROTECTION PROVIDED

Against fallout radiation: Protection Factor 1000 (PF 1000), if the shelter is covered with at least 3 ft of earth. That is, a person in the open outside this shelter will receive a gamma ray dose 1000 times greater than he will receive inside the shelter. See drawings at the end of Appendix A.3.

Against blast: This shelter is excellent for preventing fatalities if it is built with strong expedient blast doors; it is still quite good if built without them. (These instructions are for fallout shelters. The instructions for making blast doors and other essentials for adequate blast protection are given in Appendix D.)

Against fire: Excellent, if sufficiently distant from fires that produce carbon monoxide and toxic smoke.

WHERE PRACTICAL

In wooded areas with small trees, for builders who have a saw (bow saw, crosscut, or chain saw) and digging tools. Any location is suitable if the necessary poles may be obtained there.

For belowground, semiburied, or aboveground construction. (However, aboveground construction requires the excavation and movement of so much earth that it is not practical for 2-day construction by families with only hand tools.)

FOR WHOM PRACTICAL

For families or other groups with most members able to work hard 12 hours a day for 2 days. (Most people do not realize how hard and long they can work if given a strong incentive.)

CAPACITY

The drawings and lists of materials given in these instructions are for a 12-person shelter. For each additional occupant beyond 12, add 1 ft to the length of the shelter room.

This shelter requires less work and materials per occupant if its room is sized for about 24 persons, because the entrances are the same regardless of the length of the room. (To make the shelter room twice as long, each of the horizontal, ladder-like braces on the floor and near the ceiling of the room can be made with two poles on a side, rather than one long pole on a side.)

If the room is sized for more than 24 people, management and hygiene problems become more difficult when it is occupied.

For 12 people to live for many days in this shelter without serious hardship, the benches and bunks must be built with the dimensions and spacings given in the illustration. Or, materials must be available for making and suspending 12 expedient bedsheet-hammocks that can be converted each day into 12 bedsheet-chairs.

BUILDING INSTRUCTIONS

1. Study both of the two drawings (Fig. A.3.1 and A.3.2 at the end of Appendix A.3) and read all of these instructions before beginning work. CHECK OFF EACH STEP WHEN COMPLETED.

2. By the time the shelter is finished, plan to have completed (1) a ventilating pump (a KAP 24 in. wide and 36 in. high), essential except in cold weather, and (2) the storage of at least 15 gallons of water per occupant.

3. Start to assemble the required materials. For building a **12-person** Small-Pole Shelter, the materials are:

- Green poles. No pole should have a small end of less diameter than the minimum diameter specified for its use by Figs. A.3.1 and A.3.2. The table below lists the number and sizes of poles needed to build a 12-person Small-Pole Shelter.

Pole Length	Minimum Diameter of Small End	Number of Poles Required	Width[b]
6 ft 2 in.	5 in.	2	–
3 ft 1 in.	5 in.	12	–
2 ft 4 in.[a]	5 in.	12	–
10 ft 8 in.	5 in.	–	7 ft
8 ft 8 in.	5 in.	–	7 ft
10 ft 6 in.	4 in.	4	–
7 ft 2 in.	4 in.	–	47 ft
5 ft 6 in.[a]	4 in.	12	–
6 ft 10 in.	4 in.	–	3 ft
6 ft 3 in.[a]	4 in.	8	–
2 ft 6 in.[a]	4 in.	16	–
2 ft 3 in.	4 in.	4	–
5 ft 2 in.	3½ in.	–	8 ft
3 ft 10 in.	3½ in.	4	36 ft
10 ft[c]	2 in.	12	–

[a]To be shortened to fit for crossbraces.

[b]Width equals the distance measured across a single layer of poles when a sufficient number of poles are laid on the ground side by side and **touching**, to cover a rectangular area.

[c]For supports during construction.

NOTE: The above list does not include flooring materials, to be placed between the poles of the ladder-like braces on the earth floor.

- Rainproofing materials: Preferably one 100-ft roll, 12 ft wide, of 6-mil polyethylene. The minimum amount needed is 200 sq. ft. of 4-mil polyethylene, or 200 sq. ft of other waterproof plastic such as tablecloths, shower curtains, and/or vinyl floor covering. Also include 100 ft of sticks for use in drainage ditch drains (½-in. diameter, any lengths).

- Nails, wire, and/or cord: Ten pounds of 40-penny nails plus 4 pounds of 16-penny nails are ideal. However, 7 pounds of 16-penny nails can serve.

- Boards for benches and overhead bunks, if bedsheet-hammocks are not to be used. (Boards are desirable, but not essential; small poles can be used instead.) 2 × 4-in. boards—70 feet for frames (or use 3-in.-diameter poles). 1 × 8-in. boards—100 feet (or use 1- to 2-in.-diameter poles).

- Materials to build a homemade ventilating pump (a KAP 24 in. wide and 36 in. high—see Appendix B) and to store at least 15 gallons of water per occupant (see Chapter 8).

4. Desirable muscle-powered tools for building a 12-person, Small-Pole Shelter are listed below. (Most builders have succeeded without having this many tools. A backhoe, chain saws, and other mechanized equipment would be helpful, but not essential.)

Tools	Quantity
Ax, long-handle	2
Bow-saw, 28-in.	2
(or 2-man crosscut saw)	1
Pick	2
Shovel, long-handle	3
Claw hammer	2
File, 10-in.	1
Steel tape, 10-ft	1

(Also useful: a 50-ft steel tape and 2 hatchets)

5. To help drain the floor, locate the shelter so that the original ground level at the entrance is about 12 inches lower than the original ground level at the far end of the shelter—unless the location is in a very flat area.

6. Stake out the trench for the entire shelter. Even in very firm ground, if the illustrated 12-person shelter is being built, make the excavation at the surface 9 ft 8 in. wide and 18 ft long (3 ft longer than the entire length of the wooden shelter). The sloping sides of the excavation are necessary, even in very firm earth, to provide adequate space for backfilling and tamping. (The trench illustrated in Fig. A.3.1 is 6 ft 4 in. deep, to minimize work when providing only for excellent fallout protection. For improved **blast** protection, the trench should be **at least** 7 ft deep.)

7. Check the squareness of the staked trench outline by making its diagonals equal.

8. Clear all brush, tall grass, and the like from the ground, to a distance of 10 ft all around the staked location—so that later you can easily shovel loose earth back onto the roof.

9. If the ground is unstable, excavate with sides that are appropriately less steep.

10. When digging the trench for the shelter, use a measuring stick 7 ft 8 in. long (the minimum

bottom width) to repeatedly check the excavation width.

11. When digging with a shovel, pile the earth dug from near ground level about 10 ft away from the edges of the excavation. Earth dug from 5 or 6 ft below ground level then can easily be piled on the surface only 1 to 5 ft from the edge of the excavation.

12. Finish the bottom of the excavation so that it slopes vertically $\frac{1}{2}$ in. per foot of length toward the entrance, and also slopes toward the central drain ditch. (Later, sticks covered with porous fabric should be placed in the ditches, to serve like a crushed-rock drain leading to a sump.)

13. While some persons are excavating, others should be cutting **green** poles and hauling them to the site. Cut poles that have **tops no smaller than the specified diameters for each type of pole** (not including the bark).

14. For ease in handling poles, select wall and roof poles with top diameters no more than 50% larger than the specified minimum diameters.

15. Sort the poles by size and lay all poles of the same size together, near the excavation.

16. Before the excavation is completed, start building the ladder-like, horizontal braces of the shelter frame. Construct these braces on smooth ground near the excavation. Place two straight poles, each 10 ft 6 in. long (with small-end diameters of 4 in.), on smooth ground, parallel and 6 ft 2 in. apart. Hold these poles securely so that their outer sides are exactly 6 ft 2 in. apart, by driving two pairs of stakes into the ground so that they just touch the outsides of the two long poles. Each of the four stakes should be located about one foot from the end of a pole. To keep the 10 ft 6 in. poles from being rotated during the next step, nail two boards or small poles across them perpendicularly as temporary braces, about 4 ft apart.

Then with an ax or hatchet, slightly flatten the inner sides of the two poles at the spots where the ends of the 6 cross-brace poles will be nailed. Next, saw each cross-brace pole to the length required to fit snugly into its place. Finally, toenail each cross-brace pole in place, preferably with two 40-penny nails in each end.

17. Place the lower, ladder-like horizontal brace of the main room on the floor of the completed excavation.

18. Build the frame of the main room. Near the four corners of the room, secure four of its wall poles in their final vertical positions by nailing, wiring, or tying temporary brace-poles to the inner sides of these 4 wall poles and to the inner sides of the two long poles of the ladder-like horizontal brace on the bottom of the excavation. To keep the two pairs of vertical wall poles exactly 6 ft 2 in. apart until the upper ladder-like horizontal brace is secured in its place, nail a temporary horizontal brace across each pair of vertical poles, about 1 ft below their tops.

19. To support the upper ladder-like horizontal brace, nail blocks to the inner sides of the four vertical wall poles, as shown in the lower right-hand corner of the pictorial view, Fig. A.3.2. If you have large nails, use a block about 3 in. thick and 6 in. long, preferably cut from a green, 4-in.-diameter pole.

20. In the finished shelter, DO NOT leave any vertical support poles under the long poles of the upper ladder-like horizontal brace; to do so would seriously reduce the usable space along the walls for benches, bunks, and occupants.

21. While some workers are building the frame of the main room, other workers should make the four ladder-like horizontal braces for the two entrances, then make the complete entrances. To keep the ladder-like horizontal braces square during construction and back-filling, nail a temporary diagonal brace across each one.

22. When the four wall poles and the two ladder-like horizontal braces of the main room are in place, put the remaining vertical wall poles in place, touching each other, until all walls are completed. When placing the wall poles, keep them vertical by alternately putting a butt and a top end uppermost. Wall poles can be held in position by backfilling and tamping about a foot of earth against their lower ends, or they can be wired in position until backfilled.

23. Be sure to use the two 5-in.-diameter poles (6 ft 2 in. long) by placing one next to the top and the other next to the bottom of each of the main doorways to the room. Study the drawings. Use braces, each 2 ft 3 in. long, to hold apart the top and bottom of each doorway—thus making sure that a 24-in.-wide air pump can swing in either doorway.

24. To prevent earth from coming through the cracks between wall poles, cover the walls with

cloth, plastic, rugs, roofing, or even cardboard. If none of these are available, use sticks, twigs, or grass to cover the wider cracks.

25. After all horizontal bracing and vertical wall poles are in place, begin backfilling, putting earth between the walls and trench sides. Pay particular attention to the order of filling. The earth fill behind all the walls must be brought up quite evenly, so that the earth fill behind one side is no more than 12 in. higher at any one time than the earth on the opposite side. Lightly **tamp the earth fill in 6-in. layers.** A pole makes a good tamper; do not use a mechanical tamper.

26. Next, lay the roof poles side by side, touching each other on top of the wall poles. Cover at least the larger cracks with plastic, roofing, boards, or sticks to keep earth from falling through. If the earth is sandy, cover the whole roof with some material such as bedsheets or plastic to keep sand from running through the cracks.

    CAUTION: Do not try to rainproof this flat roof and simply cover it with earth. If you do, water will seep straight through the loose earth cover, puddle on the flat roofing material, and leak through the joints between pieces of roofing material or through small holes.

27. Mound earth over the shelter, piling it about 15 in. deep along the centerline of the roof and sloping it toward the sides of the roof, so that the earth is only about 2 in. deep over the ends of the roof poles. (Preparatory to mounding earth onto the roof, place gradestakes in position so you will be able to know the locations and depths of roof poles as you cover them.) Continue these slopes to two side drainage ditches. Smooth this mounded earth with a rake or stick and remove any sticks or rocks likely to puncture the rainproof roofing material to be laid on it.

28. Place rainproofing material on top of the smooth, mounded earth—as shown in sections of the drawings in Fig. A.3.1—to make a "buried roof." Plastic film, such as 4-mil polyethylene, is preferable. Roofing material, plastic shower curtains and tablecloths, or canvas can also be used. Be sure to overlap adjoining pieces.

29. Place the rest of the earth cover over the shelter, being sure that the corners of the shelter have at least $2\frac{1}{2}$ ft of earth over them. Mound the dirt, smoothing its surface so that water will tend to run off to the surface drainage ditches which

should be dug all around the edges of the mounded earth.

30. Build the benches and overhead bunks. If boards are available, use them; if not, use small, straight poles. On each side, build a row of benches and bunks 9 ft long, centered in the shelter. In order to use the shelter space to the greatest advantage, make the heights and widths of the benches and bunks the same as the thoroughly tested heights (14 in. and 4 ft 5 in.) and widths (16 in. and 24 in.) given by Fig. A.3.2. Also be sure to space their vertical supports 3 ft apart—so two adults can sit between each pair of vertical bunk supports.

31. Narrow the ends of the overhead bunks so that the aisle between them is about 28 in. wide for a distance of 38 in. from each doorway. This allows room for installation and operation of an expedient air pump (a KAP) for prevention of dangerous overheating in warm weather.

32. Place a canopy (open on all sides) over each entrance, to minimize the entry of sand-like fallout particles or rain.

33. To improve the floor, lay small poles between the lower brace poles, so that the floor is approximately level. Or, use sticks covered with scrap boards.

34. Fill all available water containers, including pits which have been dug and lined with plastic, then roofed with available materials. If possible, disinfect all water stored in expedient containers, using one scant teaspoon of a chlorine bleach, such as Clorox, for each 10 gallons of water. Even if only muddy water is available, store it. If you do not have a disinfectant, it may be possible to boil water when needed.

35. As time and materials permit, continue to improve your chances of surviving by doing as many of the following things as possible;

    (1) Make a homemade fallout meter, as described in Appendix C.

    (2) Make expedient lights.

    (3) Make and hang expedient bedsheet-hammocks and bedsheet-chairs.

EXPEDIENT VENTILATION AND COOLING

(Those workers who are to work only on the shelter itself, if pushed for time, need not read this section before beginning their work.)

Install a KAP (one that is 24 in. wide and 36 in. high) near the top of the doorway through which you can feel air naturally flowing into the shelter room at that time. (If the direction of the natural air flow changes, move the KAP to the other opening.) To enable the KAP to efficiently pump fresh air from the outdoors all the way through the shelter, block the lower half of the doorway in which the KAP is installed with a quickly removable covering, such as a plastic-covered frame made of sticks. Be sure to connect the KAP's pullcord only 11 in. below its hinge line. This prevents excessive arm motions which would cause unnecessary fatigue.

In windy or cold weather, control the natural flow of air through the shelter by hanging adjustable curtains in the doorways at both ends, and/or by making and using trapdoors on the tops of the vertical entryways. For adjustable curtains, use pieces of plastic, each with a supporting stick attached to its upper edge. This allows for different-sized openings in the doorways: (1) an opening under the lower edge of the adjustable curtain at the air-intake end of the room, and (2) an opening over the top of the curtain at the air-exhaust end of the room. In cold weather, this arrangement usually will provide adequate chimney-type ventilation for the shelter without using an air pump.

Fig. A.3.1. Plan and Elevation of Small-Pole Shelter.

136

Fig. A.3.2. Pictorial View of Small-Pole Shelter.

Appendix A.4
Aboveground, Door-Covered Shelter

PROTECTION PROVIDED

Against fallout radiation: Protection Factor about 200 (PF 200) if covered with 30 in. of earth. (A person in the open outside this shelter would receive about 200 times more fallout radiation than if he were inside.) The drawing at the end of Appendix A.4 shows the earth cover only 20 in. thick, resulting in a PF of about 100.

Against blast: Better protection than most homes. Blast tests have indicated that this shelter would be undamaged at least up to the 5-psi overpressure range from large explosions. Without blast doors the shelter's occupants could be injured at this overpressure range, although probably not fatally.

Against fire: Fair, if the cloth in the entries is covered with mud and if the shelter is sufficiently distant from fires producing carbon monoxide and toxic smoke.

WHERE PRACTICAL

In locations where holes 14 inches deep can be dug quite easily, but the water table or rock is too close to the surface for a covered-trench shelter to be feasible.

FOR WHOM PRACTICAL

For a family or other group with two or more members able to work hard for most of 36 hours. Very little building skill is needed.

CAPACITY

The shelter illustrated in Fig. A.4 is the minimum length for 4 persons. It is roofed with 6 doors.

For each additional person, add another door. (If more than about 7 persons are to be sheltered, build 2 or more separate shelters.)

BUILDING INSTRUCTIONS

1. Before beginning work, study the drawing and read ALL of the following instructions. Divide the work so that some will be digging while others are building an air pump, storing water, etc. CHECK OFF EACH STEP WHEN COMPLETED.

2. By the time the shelter is finished, plan to have completed a ventilating pump (a 16-in.-wide by 24-in.-high KAP—essential except in cold weather) and the storage of 15 gallons of water per occupant. (See Appendix B and Chapter 8.)

3. Start to assemble the materials and tools needed. For the illustrated 4-person shelter, these are:

A. Essential Materials and Tools

- Six doors. Boards or plywood at least $^5/_8$-in. thick can be used to replace one or more of the doors.

- At least 4 double-bed sheets for each of the first four persons, and 3 double-bed sheets for each additional person to be sheltered—or enough pieces of fabric and/or of plastic to cover at least as large an area as the sheets would cover. (This material is for making aboveground shelter walls, to serve as sand bags.)

- Rainproofing materials (plastic film, shower curtains, plastic tablecloths, mattress protectors, etc.)—15 square yards for the first 4 persons and $2^1/_2$ square yards for each additional person.

- A shovel (one shovel for each two workers is desirable). A pick or mattock if the ground is very hard.

- A knife (the only essential tool for making a small shelter-ventilating KAP) and materials for a KAP 16 in. wide and 24 in. high. (See Appendix B.)

- Containers for storing water. (See Chapter 8.)

B. Useful Materials and Tools

- Two or more buckets, large cans and/or large pots with bail handles—to carry earth, and later to store water or wastes.

- Saw (or ax or hatchet)—to cut a few boards or small poles.

- Hammer and at least 15 small nails (at least 2½ in. long).

- Tape measure, yardstick, or ruler.

- Additional cloth and/or plastic—equivalent in size to 2 more double-bed sheets for each person.

- Additional waterproof material—2 more square yards per person.

- Pillowcases, or cloth or plastic bags—to serve as earth-filled sand bags. The more, the better.

4. To save time and work, sharpen all tools and keep them sharp.

5. Wear gloves from the start, to help prevent blisters and infections.

6. Select a building site where there is little or no chance of the ground being covered with water, and where the water table (groundwater level) is not likely to rise closer than 18 inches to the surface.

7. To avoid the extra work of digging among roots, select a site away from trees, if practical.

8. To lessen the dangers of fire and smoke from nearby houses or trees that might catch fire, locate your shelter as far as is practical from houses and flammable vegetation.

9. Before staking out your shelter, provide one door per person to roof the main room plus one additional door for each of the two entries. Be sure the door knobs have been removed. Use the two widest doors to roof the entries.

10. To be sure that all the walls will be in the proper positions to be roofed with the available doors, lay all the doors on the ground, touching each other and in the same relative positions they will have when used to roof the shelter. When all the roof doors are on the ground, side by side, determine the exact length of the shelter room. (Note that Fig. A.4 illustrates a shelter sized for only 4 persons.)

11. Stake out the shelter.

12. Make the earth-filled "rolls" that will form the aboveground walls of your shelter. To make walls out of the rolls:

(1) Use doors as vertical forms to hold the earth-filled rolls in place until the walls are completed. (These are the same doors that you will use later to roof the shelter.)

(2) Brace the door-forms with 36-in.-long braces (boards or sticks) that press against the doors, as shown in Fig. A.4. Nail only the upper braces, using only very small nails.

(3) After the forms for the two inner sides of the shelter have been finished, put parts of the long sides of bedsheets on the ground, as illustrated. (Or use other equally wide, strong cloth or plastic material.) About a 2-ft width of cloth should be on the ground, and the rest of each sheet should be folded up out of the way, over the outsides of the door-forms. Adjacent sheets should overlap about 1 ft when making a roll than is longer than one sheet.

(4) Shovel earth onto the parts of the sheet on the ground to the height of the rolls you are making, as shown. Note that the roll to be made on one side is 2 in. higher than the roll on the other side.

(5) Shape the surface of the shoveled-on earth as illustrated, to hold the "hooks" of cloth to be formed when the exposed sides of the sheets are folded down.

(6) Fold down the upper side of each sheet while pulling on it to keep it tight and without wrinkles. It should lie on the

prepared earth surface, including the small narrow trench, as illustrated in the first section of this appendix.

(7) Pack earth onto the part of the folded-down sheet that is in the narrow, shallow trench. Then, as shown in the sketches at the bottom of the accompanying drawing, fold back the loose edge over this small amount of packed earth to form a "hook." (The hook keeps the weight of the earth inside a roll from pulling the cloth out of its proper position.)

(8) Make a roll first on one side of the shelter, then on the other, to keep the heights of the earth **on both sides** of the shelter **about** equal. This will keep the unequal heights of earth from pushing the door-forms out of their vertical positions.

(9) Add additional earth on top of the rolls so that the height of the level earth surface, out to the full width of a roll, is the same as the height of the cloth-covered part of the roll that is against the door-form.

(10) When the roll walls have been raised to their planned heights on both sides of the shelter, remove the braces and the door-forms—being careful to keep the brace nails from damaging the doors.

(11) The door-forms of the side-walls of the shelter can be removed before building the end-walls.

13. When smoothing the earth surfaces of the final tops of the roll walls on both sides, check to see that they have the same slope as the lower sides of the roof doors will have after they are placed on the roll walls. (A slope is necessary so that rainwater reaching the waterproof covering to be placed over the doors will run off the lower side.) Study Fig. A.4.

14. After the side-walls have been completed (except for their ends that form the sides of an entry) and after the door-forms have been removed, use the same doors for forms to build the two 22-in.-wide entries.

15. Use earth-filled "sand bags" (made of pillowcases or sacks, and/or the tucked-in ends of earth-filled rolls) to make the outer ends of each entryway.

16. Make the two doorway frames if lumber, nails, and a saw are available. Make each frame as high as the wall on each side of it, and slope the top board of each frame so that it will press flat against the door to be supported. (If materials for a frame are lacking, place a single 2 by 4-in. board—or a pole about 6 ft. long—across the top of the entry, in the position shown in Fig. A.4 for the top of the doorway frame.)

17. After carefully removing all the temporary braces from the door-forms and the doors themselves, improve the slopes of the tops of all supporting walls so that the doors will be supported evenly and, without being twisted, will make contact with the smooth, sloping earth or cloth upon which they will rest.

18. If more than enough waterproof plastic or similar material is available to cover all the roof doors, also cover the tops of the walls on which the roof doors will rest. This will keep the doors from absorbing water from damp earth.

19. Dig the illustrated 14-in.-deep, 36-in.-wide trench inside the shelter. (If the water table is too high to dig down 14 in., in some locations the walls can be raised to a height of 38 in. by cutting turf sods and laying them on top of the walls. Another way the wall height can be increased is by making additional rolls.)

20. Place the roof doors in their final positions, and cover them with waterproof material (if available). Be sure the waterproof material is folded under the higher edges of the doors—to keep the material from slipping downward on the sloping doors as earth is shoveled onto the roof.

21. Extend the waterproof material on top of the doors a couple of feet beyond the lower ends of the doors—if enough material is available to cover all of the roof doors.

22. When shoveling the first layer of earth onto the rainproof material protecting the doors, avoid hitting and possibly puncturing it with rocks or sharp pointed roots in the earth.

23. To make earth arching more effective in supporting most of the earth to be placed on the roof doors, first mound earth on and near the ends of the doors.

24. Cover the roof with at least 20 in. of earth. Make sure that there also is a thickness of at least 20 in. of earth at the corners of both the room and entries.

25. To prevent surface water from running into the shelter if it rains hard, mound packed earth about 5 in. high just inside the two entries. Rain can be kept out by a small canopy or awning that extends 2 or 3 ft in front of the outermost edge of a doorway that roofs an entry.

26. If any waterproof material remains, use it to cover the floor of the shelter.

27. If the weather is warm or hot, install a 16-in.-wide by 24-in.-high air pump (a KAP). Attach its hinges to the board across the roof of the entry into which outside air is moving naturally at the time.

28. Cover all exposed combustible material with mud, earth, or other fireproof material, to reduce the chance of exposed cloth being ignited from a nuclear explosion or heat from a nearby fire.

29. Fill all available water containers, including pits which have been dug and lined with plastic, then roofed with available materials. If possible, disinfect all water stored in expedient containers, using one scant teaspoon of a chlorine bleach, such as Clorox, for each 10 gallons of water. Even if only muddy water is available, store it. If you do not have a disinfectant, it may be possible to boil water when needed.

30. As time and materials permit, continue to improve your chances of surviving by doing as many of the following things as possible;

    (1) Make a homemade fallout meter, as described in Appendix C.

    (2) Make expedient lights.

Fig. A.4. Aboveground, Door-Covered Shelter.

142

Appendix A.5
Aboveground, Ridgepole Shelter

PROTECTION PROVIDED

Against fallout radiation: Protection Factor 300 (PF 300) if covered with 24 in. of earth. (A person in the open outside this shelter would receive about 300 times more fallout radiation than if he were inside.) See the accompanying drawing at the end of Appendix A.5.

Against blast: Better protection than most homes. Blast tests have indicated that this shelter would be undamaged at least up to the 5-psi overpressure range from large explosions. Without blast doors, the shelter's occupants could be injured at this overpressure range, although probably not fatally.

Against fire: Good, if the shelter is sufficiently distant from fires producing carbon monoxide and toxic smoke.

WHERE PRACTICAL

In many wooded areas and wherever enough poles are available.

In locations where belowground expedient shelters are impractical because the water table or rock is too close to the surface for a covered-trench shelter.

FOR WHOM PRACTICAL

For a family or group with 5 or more members able to work hard for most of 48 hours, at least one of whom is able to saw and fit poles and use the hand tools listed on the following page.

CAPACITY

The shelter illustrated in Fig. A.5, is the minimum length for 5 persons. For each additional person, add 1 ft to the length of the ridgepole and shelter room. (If more than about 15 persons are to be sheltered, build 2 or more separate shelters.)

BUILDING INSTRUCTIONS

1. Before beginning work, study Fig. A.5 and read ALL of the following instructions.

2. Divide the work. CHECK OFF EACH STEP WHEN COMPLETED.

3. By the time the shelter is finished, plan to have completed a ventilating pump (a KAP 20 in. wide and 26 in high, essential for this shelter except in cool weather) and the storage of at least 15 gallons of water per occupant. (See Appendix B and Chapter 8.)

4. Start to assemble the materials. **For the illustrated 5-person shelter,** these are:

A. Essential Materials and Tools

● Poles. (Fresh-cut, green poles are best; sound, untreated poles are satisfactory.) See the following list for the number of poles required for a 5-person shelter.

Use	Pole Length	Minimum Diameter of Small End	Number of Poles Required	Width When All Are Laid on the Ground
For main room:				
Ridgepole	4 ft 9 in.	6 in.	1	
Column-posts	4 ft 3 in.	5 in.	2	
Footing log	8 ft 0 in.	6 in.	1	
Cross braces	6 ft 2 in.	3 in.	2	
Roof poles	9 ft 0 in.	4 in.	—	5 ft[a]
Vertical end-wall poles	5 ft 0 in.[c]	3½ in.	—	14 ft[b]
Slanting end-wall poles and extras	6 ft 6 in.[c]	3½ in.	—	18 ft[b]
For outer sections of entryways:				
Horizontal poles	8 ft 0 in.	3½ in.	4	
Cross braces (material for 16)	5 ft 0 in.[c]	3½ in.	6	
Wall poles	3 ft 4 in.	3 in.	—	32 ft[b]
Roof poles	2 ft 8 in.	2½ in.	—	12 ft[b]
For inner sections of entryways:				
Long, sloping poles	14 ft 0 in.	4 in.	4	
Cross braces	1 ft 8 in.[c]	4 in.	8	
Vertical support poles	4 ft 0 in.[c]	4 in.	8	
Roof poles	3 ft 0 in.	2½ in.	—	13 ft[b]

[a]This width equals the distance measured across the tops of a single layer of poles when a sufficient number of poles are laid on the ground side by side *with all the same ends in a straight line and touching*. (These poles will be placed butt-ends down to form the walls of the shelter room.)

[b]This width equals the distance measured across a single layer of poles when a sufficient number of poles are laid on the ground side by side and *touching, with large ends and small ends alternating so as to cover a rectangular area*.

[c]To be cut into the various lengths needed to close the ends of the main room and also to close a part of each entryway.

● A saw and an ax or hatchet, to cut green poles. (A bow saw or crosscut saw serves well and often is more dependable than a chain saw. Having an extra blade for a bow saw may be essential.)

● Two shovels (one shovel for each two workers is desirable). A pick will also be needed, if the earth is hard.

● Large buckets, cans, or pots with bail handles—in which to carry earth, and later to store water or wastes.

● A knife.

● A hammer and at least 80 nails (3 in. or longer). If these are not at hand, rope, wire, or strips of cloth can be used to lash poles together. At least 200 ft. of rope or strong wire will be needed, or two additional bedsheets for each person to be sheltered. (Other fabric of equal strength can be used.) The cloth can be cut or torn into foot-wide strips and twisted slightly to make "rope."

● Three double-bed sheets for the illustrated 5-person shelter or a piece of strong fabric or plastic of about the same size. One additional sheet for each additional 2 occupants. (If sufficient sheets or other material are not available, use many sticks and small poles, placed across the 9-ft side poles.)

● At least 2 square yards per person of rainproofing material (shower curtains, plastic tablecloths, plastic mattress covers, or the like)—essential in rainy, cold weather.

● Materials for building a ventilating pump, a KAP 20 in. wide and 26 in. high. (See Appendix B.)

● Containers for storing 15 gallons of water per occupant. (See Chapter 8.)

B. Useful Tools and Materials

● Additional saws, axes, hatchets, shovels, and large buckets or cans.

• A chain saw—if there is a person in the group who is skilled at operating one.

• Kerosene, turpentine, or oil—to keep a handsaw from sticking in green, gummy wood.

• A measuring tape, yardstick, or ruler.

• One bedsheet for each person to be sheltered, or a piece of strong fabric or plastic of about the same size.

• A total of 40 square yards of rainproofing materials for the illustrated 5-person shelter and $3\frac{1}{2}$ square yards for each additional person. (Even thin plastic will serve for the "buried roof.")

5. To save time and work, SHARPEN ALL TOOLS AND KEEP THEM SHARP.

6. Wear gloves from the start—even tough hands can blister after hours of digging and chopping and can become painful and infected.

7. Select a shelter location where there is little chance of the ground being covered with water if it rains hard. (If you are sure the water table will not rise to cover the floor of a shallow excavation, you can save work by first lowering the area of the planned main room by a foot or two. After the shelter is roofed, the excavated earth can be shoveled back to help cover the completed pole roof.) To avoid the extra work of cutting roots when excavating earth, select a site at least as far away from a tree as the tree is tall.

8. For a shelter that is completely aboveground, clear grass, weeds, etc. from the area where the shelter is to be built. (This reduces the possible problem of chiggers, ticks, etc.) Do not remove any earth at this stage.

9. Stake out the entire shelter. Check the squareness of the shelter room by making its diagonals equal. Then drive two lines of stakes to mark the outside edges of the completed earth covering. Place these stakes 4 ft outside the future positions of the lower ends of the roof poles.

10. Check the squareness of the future floor area inside the two lines marking where the two V-shaped, 4-in.-deep trenches will be dug, to secure the lower ends of the sloping side-poles of the room. These two parallel lines are 14 ft 6 in. apart. When the two diagonals joining the

ends of these two parallel lines are equal in length, the area between them has square corners.

11. While some persons are staking out the shelters, others should be cutting green poles and hauling them to the site. Cut poles that have tops with diameters (excluding bark) no smaller than the diameters specified on the illustration for each type of pole.

12. To make the hauling and handling of the longer poles easier, select poles with top diameters no more than 50% larger than the specified minimum diameters.

13. Sort the poles by length and diameter and lay all poles of each size together, near the excavation.

14. AS SOON AS POLES ARE BROUGHT TO THE SITE, SOME WORKERS SHOULD START BUILDING THE FOUR LADDER-LIKE HORIZONTAL BRACES FOR THE ENTRYWAYS—TO AVOID DELAYS LATER. Study the drawing. Then construct these braces on smooth ground near the excavation. Place two straight poles, each 8 ft long (with small-end diameters of $3\frac{1}{2}$ in.), on smooth ground, parallel and so that their outer sides are 3 ft apart. Hold these poles securely so that their outer sides are exactly 3 ft apart, by driving two pairs of stakes into the ground so that they just touch the outsides of the two long poles. Each of the four stakes should be located about one foot from the end of a pole. To keep the 8-ft poles from being rotated during the next step, nail two boards or small poles across them perpendicularly, as temporary braces, about 4 ft apart.

Then with an ax or hatchet, slightly flatten the inner sides of the two poles at the spots where the ends of the 4 cross-brace poles will be nailed. Next, saw each cross-brace pole to the length required to fit snugly into its place. Finally, toenail each cross-brace pole in place, preferably with two large nails in each end.

15. If more than 5 persons are to be sheltered, use 3 column-posts for 6 to 9 persons, and 4 column-posts for 10 to 14 persons.

16. For each additional person beyond 5, make the ridgepole and the footing log each 1 foot longer than shown in Fig. A.5.

17. After notching the footing log (see drawing), place it in a trench dug deep enough so that the bottoms of its notches are about 4 inches below the surface of the ground.

18. Carefully dig the 4-in.-deep, V-shaped, straight trenches in which the lower ends of the 9-ft wall poles will rest. Dig each of these two parallel trenches 7 ft 3 in. from the center line of the footing log.

19. Carefully notch a "V" only about $\frac{1}{2}$-in. deep in the top of each of the two outer column-posts. Then saw off the other ends so that each is 4 ft 3 in. long. (When they are placed on the notched footing log and the ridgepole is placed on them, the upper side of the ridgepole will be about 4 ft 4 in. above the ground.)

20. Place the two **outer** column-posts in their notches in the footing log, and secure the base of each column-post against sideways movement by placing two small-diameter, 4-ft horizontal poles just below the ground level on both sides, as illustrated. Then temporarily place and brace the ridgepole in position.

21. For shelters sized for more than 5 occupants, make and place the inner column-post, or posts. To avoid cutting a "V"-notched column-post too short, first carefully "V"-notch each remaining column-post, cut it about 1 in. too long, and trim it off to fit in its final position under the ridgepole.

22. If nails at least 4 in. long are available, nail sloping cross-braces to the inner sides of the column-posts. If nails are not available, notch slightly bowed cross-braces and the column-post as illustrated; then lash or wire them in position. (Strips of ordinary bedsheets, torn about a foot wide and twisted together slightly, can be made to serve as lashing "rope.") To hold the tops of the column-posts securely against the upper ends of the cross-braces, a tightened "rope" loop that encircles the tops of the column-posts can be used.

23. Next put four of the larger-diameter, 9-ft roof-poles in position, with the outsides of the outermost two roof poles each only about 1 in. from an end of the ridge pole.

24. Place the rest of the 9-ft roof-poles in position, making sure that all their small ends are uppermost, and that they are pressed together

and overlap on the ridgepole at least as far as illustrated. Pack earth between their lower ends. If the earth is clay, put small spacers of wood between the ends.

25. At each end of the shelter room, build extra shelter space and an entryway. First position two 14-ft poles with their upper ends resting on the outermost wall poles. Study Fig. A.5. Place the two 14-ft poles 20 in. apart, parallel, and equally distant from the centerline of the ridgepole. Nail four 20-in.-long spacer-poles between each pair of 14-ft poles, as illustrated. To make sure that the upper ends do not move before earth pressure holds them in place, tie the upper ends of the 14-ft poles together. Drive a stake against the lower end of each 14-ft pole, to keep it from slipping outward. Under the center of each 14-ft pole, place two supporting, vertical posts.

26. Dig. 4-in.-deep trenches for the lower ends of the sloping end-wall poles of the main room. These poles must be cut to length so that their upper ends will be about 4 in. above the outermost 9-ft roof pole against which they lean. Dig narrow, vertical trenches, about 8 in. deep, for all vertical wall poles that do not press against horizontal brace poles near the ground.

27. Start placing the sloping end-wall poles. First place the longest pole, then the shorter poles—all touching.

28. Across the open spaces between the 9-ft roof poles, place limbs and/or sticks roughly horizontally, as shown in the lower left-hand drawing. Be sure to use limbs or sticks that have diameters of at least $\frac{1}{2}$ in. and put them no farther apart than 6 in. Leave needles and leaves on the limbs. Do not leave sharp ends sticking upward. Do not place more than a 6-in.-thick mass of limbs and leaves over the side-poles. The thickness of the earth cover necessary for excellent fallout protection might be unintentionally reduced by making the limb cover too thick.

29. Place bedsheets (or 4-mil-thick polyethylene film or equally sturdy material) over the limbs and sticks to keep earth from falling through the roof.

30. To prevent sand or dry earth from falling between the cracks where the poles are side by side, cover these parts of the roof with cloth, plastic, or paper. If these materials are not

available, use sticks, leaves, and grass. (In tick or chigger season, avoid using grass or leaves from on or near the ground.)

31. After the entryways are completed, begin to cover the shelter with earth. **Starting from the ground up,** put on a full 1-ft thickness of earth cover. First raise its height about a foot on one side or end of the shelter, and then on the other—repeatedly. This is to prevent unequal loading from tipping the shelter or pushing it over. (Do not excavate any earth closer than 3 ft to the line of stakes marking the final outer edge of the completed, 2-ft-thick earth cover.)

32. Fill the spaces between the entryways and the main room only with earth. (An equal thickness of wood or other light material provides much less protection against radiation.)

33. Before placing the rainproofing material for the "buried roof," smooth the surface of the 1-ft-thick earth cover. This will prevent sharp rocks or sticks from puncturing the plastic or other rainproofing material. If you do not have sufficient waterproofing materials to cover the whole roof, use what is available to rainproof the central part, on both sides of the ridgepole.

34. To prevent rainwater on the ground outside from running into the entryways, make mounds of packed earth about 4 inches high across the entryway floors, about 2 ft from their outer ends.

Dig a shallow drainage ditch completely around the earth mounded over the shelter.

35. Unless the weather is cold, install your shelter-ventilating KAP in the entry into which you can feel air moving naturally.

36. Complete the storage of water and other essentials.

37. To prevent fallout or rain from falling onto the floor of the outer entryways, place a small awning (not illustrated) over each opening.

38. Fill all available water containers, including pits which have been dug and lined with plastic, then roofed with available materials. If possible, disinfect all water stored in expedient containers, using one scant teaspoon of a chlorine bleach, such as Clorox, for each 10 gallons of water. Even if only muddy water is available, store it. If you do not have a disinfectant, it may be possible to boil water when needed.

39. As time and materials permit, continue to improve your chances of surviving by doing as many of the following things as possible;

    (1) Make a homemade fallout meter, as described in Appendix C.

    (2) Make expedient lights.

    (3) Make and hang expedient bedsheet-hammocks and bedsheet-chairs.

Fig. A.5. Aboveground, Ridgepole Shelter.

Appendix A.6
Aboveground, Crib-Walled Shelter

PROTECTION PROVIDED

Against fallout radiation: Protection Factor 200 (PF 200) if the earth-filled cribs are built to the full width of 3 ft, as illustrated in Fig. A.6 at the end of these instructions. (A person in the open outside this shelter would receive about 200 times as much fallout radiation as he would if inside.) If earth is mounded to the top of the walls and 3 ft deep over the roof, the protection factor can be raised to PF 500 or better. See the accompanying drawing at the end of Appendix A.6.

Against blast: Better protection than most homes. Without blast doors, occupants could be injured—although probably not fatally—at lower overpressure ranges than those that would destroy this shelter.

Against fire: Poor, if the shelter is built as illustrated. The cloth and outer poles would be unprotected from thermal pulse and other possible sources of intense heat. However, if earth is mounded around the walls so as to cover all exposed cloth and wood, good fire protection would be provided.

WHERE PRACTICAL

The crib-walled shelter is practical in many wooded areas and whenever enough poles are available, or in locations where belowground expedient shelters are impractical because the water table or rock is too close to the surface for a covered-trench shelter.

FOR WHOM PRACTICAL

For a family or group with three or more members able to work very hard for most of 48 hours. An unskilled family with an ax or saw and materials found in most American homes can build this shelter. No nails are required. (Groups with the nails, tools, skill, and the number of workers required to build a Ridgepole Shelter are advised to do so; a Crib-Walled Shelter requires almost twice the total length of poles and more work to provide shelter for a given number of persons.)

CAPACITY

The shelter illustrated in Fig. 6.1 is the minimum length for 5 persons. For each additional person, add $1\frac{1}{2}$ ft to the length of the room. (If more than about 12 persons are to be sheltered, build 2 or more separate shelters.)

BUILDING INSTRUCTIONS

1. Before beginning work, study the drawing and read ALL of the following instructions.

2. Divide the work. CHECK OFF EACH STEP WHEN COMPLETED.

3. By the time the shelter is finished, plan to have completed a ventilating pump (a KAP 20 in. wide and 26 in. high, essential for this shelter except in cool weather) and the storage of at least 15 gallons of water per occupant. (See Appendix B and Chapter 8.)

4. Start to assemble materials and tools.

A. Essential Materials and Tools

● Poles. (Fresh-cut, green poles are best; sound, untreated poles are satisfactory.) For the illustrated 5-person shelter, the required poles are listed on the following page.

149

Use	Pole Length	Minimum Diameter of Small End	Number of Poles Required	Width When All Are Laid on the Ground[a]
Sides of longest crib	12½ ft	3 in.		7 ft
Sides of middle-sized crib	10 ft	3 in.		7 ft
Sides of shortest crib	7 ft	3 in.		7 ft
Ends of all cribs	3½ ft	3 in.		21 ft
Vertical poles at the corners of all cribs	3½ ft	2 in.	56	
Main roof	9 ft	3½ in.		12 ft
Entryway roofs	5 ft.	2½ in.		22 ft

[a] This width is the distance measured across a single layer of poles when a sufficient number of them are laid on the ground side by side and touching, with large ends and small ends alternating so as to cover a rectangular area.

- A saw (preferably a bow saw with an extra blade, or a crosscut saw) and/or an ax—for cutting green poles.

- A shovel (one for each two workers is desirable).

- A pick (if the ground is very hard).

- Two to five large cans, buckets, and/or pots with bail handles, in which to carry earth and to store water or wastes later.

- A knife.

- A minimum of 300 ft of wire at least as strong as clothesline wire. Second choice would be 300 ft of rope, or (third choice) 8 double-bed sheets that could be torn into 1-ft-wide strips and twisted slightly to serve as rope. For each additional person beyond 5, supply 20 ft of wire or rope or half a double-bed sheet.

- Rainproof roofing materials—at least 2 square yards per person. Such materials as plastic film, shower curtains, plastic table-cloths or plastic mattress covers can be used. These materials are essential for prolonged shelter occupancy in rainy, cold weather.

- Fifteen double-bed sheets (or equal square-yardage of other strong cloth or plastic).

- Materials for building a ventilating pump, a KAP 20 inches wide and 30 in. high. (See Appendix B.)

- Containers for storing 15 gallons of water per occupant. (See Chapter 8.)

B. Useful Materials and Tools

- Additional saws and shovels, chain saw, pick-mattock, hammer, hatchet.

- Kerosene, turpentine, or oil—to keep a hand-saw from sticking in gummy wood.

- A file.

- Two additional double-bed sheets per person, or equivalent square-yardage of other equally strong fabric or plastic.

- A measuring tape, yardstick, or ruler.

- Old newspapers (about 15 pounds).

- A total of 30 square yards of rainproofing materials for the illustrated 5-person shelter, and 3 square yards for each additional person to be sheltered. (Even thin plastic will serve to make a rainproof "buried roof.")

5. To save time and work, SHARPEN ALL TOOLS AND KEEP THEM SHARP.

6. Wear gloves from the start. Even tough hands can blister and become painful and infected after hours of digging and chopping.

7. Select a shelter location where there is little or no chance of the ground being covered with water by a hard rain.

8. If the building site is near the edge of a woods, pick a site at least 40 ft from the nearest trees—to avoid roots.

9. Clear off grass, weeds, etc., from the area where you plan to build the shelter—this also will help to avoid chiggers or ticks. Do not remove any earth.

10. Stake out the entire shelter, locating the 6 required cribs. BE SURE TO MAKE THE INSIDE LENGTH OF THE MAIN ROOM EQUAL TO THE NUMBER OF PERSONS TO BE SHELTERED MULTIPLIED BY $1\frac{1}{2}$ FT. The illustrated shelter is sized for 5 persons, and the poles listed are those required for this 5-person shelter.

11. While some persons are staking out the shelter, others should be cutting green poles and hauling them to the site. Cut poles with tops no smaller than the diameters specified. (Note: the specified diameters do not include bark.)

12. Select poles with small-end diameters no more than 50% larger than the specified minimum diameters, to make handling of the long wall and roof poles easier.

13. Sort the poles by length and diameter and lay all poles of each size together, near the excavation.

14. Use larger trees and poles, up to 6 in. in diameter, to make the $3\frac{1}{2}$-ft-long end-poles of the cribs (Fig. A.6). Do not use poles with small-end diameters of less than 3 in. for the side-wall poles of the cribs. For vertical brace-poles, use poles with diameters of at least 2 in., cut off at the height of the upper side of the uppermost horizontal poles against which they are tied.

15. Be sure to cut off all limbs so that the poles are quite smooth. Usually it is easier to drag smoothed poles to the building site before cutting them into the required lengths. Pull them by the small, lighter ends.

16. Determine if there are enough long poles to make the side-poles of the two cribs forming the sides of the shelter room without splicing two shorter poles together. If the shelter is being built for more than 7 persons, it will require side poles that are longer than $15\frac{1}{2}$ ft. Therefore, if a shelter for more than 7 persons is being built, it would be best to use 2 cribs placed end-to-end on each side of the shelter room, instead of a single crib as illustrated by Fig. A.6.

17. Place the lowermost four poles of each of the cribs in their final positions, so that all the bases of the crib-walls are in position on the ground. Use the thicker, heavier poles at and near the bottom of each crib. BE SURE THE ROOM IS LONG ENOUGH TO PROVIDE $1\frac{1}{2}$ FT OF ROOM LENGTH FOR EACH PERSON TO BE SHELTERED.

18. To build each crib:

    (1) Place two $3\frac{1}{2}$-ft end-poles on the ground. Put two of the side-poles on top of the two end-poles so that the ends of all four poles extend 3 in. (no more) beyond where they cross. The thicker poles should be used first to add stability.

    (2) Stack additional pairs of end-poles and side-poles to form the crib, keeping each wall of the crib vertical, until the tops of the uppermost side-poles are at least 42 in. above the ground. To keep the uppermost poles of the crib about level while the crib is being raised, alternate the large ends and small ends of poles.

    (3) Place a pair of small, vertical brace-poles in each of the four corners of the crib. The tops of the vertical brace-poles should be no higher above the ground than the upper sides of the crib's uppermost horizontal poles.

    (4) Tie each pair of vertical brace-poles together tightly at bottom, middle, and top. For tying, use 3-ft lengths of strong wire, rope, or slightly twisted, foot-wide strips of cloth at least as strong as cotton bed sheeting. Square knots with back-up overhand knots are best, but three overhand knots—one on top of the other—will hold.

    (5) If the crib is more than 8 ft long, place an additional pair of vertical brace-poles, with one in position at the outside center of each long crib-wall. Tie this pair of vertical brace-poles together permanently just above the ground, but not yet in the middle or near the top of the crib. Temporarily tie each of these center vertical brace-poles to the uppermost side-pole of the wall it touches.

    (6) Line the crib with cloth or plastic film, making sure that several inches of the lining hangs over the uppermost poles. So that the lining will not be pulled down when the crib is being filled with earth, tie the upper edge of

the lining to the uppermost wall pole about every 2 ft. First cut a small hole through which to thread a tie-string or a 2-in.-wide tie-strip of cloth. (If plenty of cloth and/or plastic is available for lining the cribs, secure the lining by simply wrapping a greater width of the upper edge of the lining around the uppermost crib wall-pole.)

(7) Permanently tie together the pair of vertical center brace-poles, using horizontal ties at their centers and just below the uppermost horizontal wall-poles of the crib. Use the strongest material you have for these horizontal ties across the center of the crib.

(8) Excavate earth 10 ft or so beyond the outer sides of the cribs. To save work, carry it in buckets and dump it inside the cribs. (Two children can carry a heavy bucket of earth by running a strong, 4-ft stick through the bail or handle of the bucket and tying the bail to the center of the stick before lifting.) Save earth closer to the cribs to put on the roof.

(9) Fill the lined crib with earth from which almost all grass, roots, and the like have been removed. Avoid placing hard lumps of earth in contact with the lining. Fill the crib so that the surface of the earth inside it is about 4 in. above the upper sides of the uppermost horizontal poles.

19. Line the narrow spaces between adjacent cribs with cloth or plastic; then fill these spaces with earth **a little at a time, tamping repeatedly so as to avoid leaving air spaces.**

20. Place the 9-ft roof poles over the main room. (If poles are unavailable and boards $1^1/_2$ in. thick are available, use two thicknesses of boards.) Use the strongest roof poles (or double-thickness boards nailed together) nearest the entryways. Then put shorter, 5- or 6-ft poles or boards over the entryways.

21. To keep earth from falling through the cracks between the roof poles, put sticks in the larger cracks and cover the roof with two or more thicknesses of cloth, plastic, or other material. Newspapers will do, if better materials are lacking.

22. Put earth on the roof to the depths shown for the illustrated "buried roof." Be sure to slope all sides and smooth this gently mounded earth surface so that the buried roof will shed water.

23. So that the earth cover near the outer edges of the roof will be a full 2 ft thick, make the earth cover slope steeply near the edges. Steep earth slopes can be made and kept stable by using large lumps of turf to make a steep bank, or by using earth-filled "rolls" of cloth or other material along the edges of a roof.

24. Put in place the waterproof material of the buried roof.

25. Pile on the rest of the earth cover, as illustrated, to **at least** a full 2-ft thickness.

26. Smooth the surface of the earth cover, including the sides, so that rain will run off. Do not walk on the finished roof.

27. To prevent rainwater on the ground outside from running into the entryways, make mounds of packed earth about 4 in. high across the entryway floors. Make the mounds about 2 ft from the outer ends of the floors. Dig a shallow drainage ditch completely around the shelter.

28. Unless the weather is cold, install your shelter-ventilating KAP in the entry into which you can feel the air moving naturally.

29. To prevent fallout or rain from falling onto the floor of the outer entryways, place small awnings (not illustrated) over the openings.

30. If time and energy are available, mound earth all around the shelter. Doing so will reduce fire hazards by covering flammable materials; it also will increase fallout protection.

31. Fill all available water containers, including pits which have been dug and lined with plastic, then roofed with available materials. If possible, disinfect all water stored in expedient containers, using one scant teaspoon of a chlorine bleach, such as Clorox, for each 10 gallons of water. Even if only muddy water is available, store it. If you do not have a disinfectant, it may be possible to boil water when needed.

32. As time and materials permit, continue to improve your chances of surviving by doing as many of the following things as possible:

(1) Make a homemade fallout meter, as described in Appendix C.

(2) Make expedient lights.

(3) Make and hang expedient bedsheet-hammocks.

Fig. A.6. Aboveground, Crib-Walled Shelter.

153

Appendix B

How to Make and Use a Homemade Shelter-Ventilating Pump, the KAP

I. THE NEED FOR SHELTER AIR PUMPS

In warm weather, large volumes of outside air MUST be pumped through most fallout or blast shelters if they are crowded and occupied for a day or more. Otherwise, the shelter occupants' body heat and water vapor will raise the temperature-humidity conditions to DANGEROUSLY high levels. If adequate volumes of outdoor air are pumped through typical belowground shelters in hot weather, many times the number of persons could survive the heat than otherwise could survive in these same shelters without adequate forced ventilation. Even in cold weather, about 3 cubic feet per minute (3 cfm) of outdoor air usually should be pumped through shelters, primarily to keep the carbon dioxide exhaled by shelter occupants from rising to harmful concentrations.

The KAP (Kearny Air Pump) is a practical, do-it-yourself device for pumping adequate volumes of cooling air through shelters—with minimum work. The following instructions have been improved repeatedly after being used by dozens of small groups to build KAPs—including families, pairs of housewives, and children. None of these inexpert builders had previously heard of this kind of pump, yet almost all groups succeeded in making one in less than 4 hours after assembling the materials. Their successes prove that almost anyone, if given these detailed and thoroughly tested instructions, can build a serviceable, large-volume air pump of this simple type, using only materials and tools found in most American homes.

If possible, build a KAP large enough to pump through your shelter at least 40 cubic feet per minute (40 cfm) of outdoor air for each shelter occupant. If 40 cfm of outdoor air is pumped through a shelter and distributed within it as specified below, even under heat-wave conditions the effective temperature of the shelter air will not be more than 2° F higher than the effective temperature outdoors. (The effective temperature is a measure of air's effects on people due to its heat, humidity, and velocity.) The 36-inch-high by 29-inch-wide KAP described in these instructions, if used as specified, will pump at least 1000 cfm of outside air through a shelter that has the airflow characteristics outlined in these instructions.

If more than 25 persons might be expected to occupy a shelter during hot weather, then it is advisable to build a larger KAP. The 72-inch-high by 29-inch-wide model described can pump between 4000 and 5000 cfm.

To maintain tolerable temperature-humidity conditions for people in your shelter during hot weather, you **must**:

● Pump enough outdoor air all the way through the shelter (40 cfm for each occupant in very hot, humid weather).

● Distribute the air evenly within the shelter. If the KAP that pumps air through the shelter does not create air movement that can be felt in all parts of the shelter in hot weather, one or more additional KAPs will be needed to circulate the air and gently fan the occupants.

● Encourage the shelter occupants to wear as little clothing as practical when they are hot. (Sweat evaporates and cools best on bare skin.)

● Supply the occupants with adequate water and salt. For prolonged shelter occupancy under heat-wave conditions in a hot part of the country, about 4 quarts of drinking water and $\frac{1}{3}$ ounce (1 tablespoon) of salt per person are required every 24 hours, including salt in food that is eaten. Normal American meals supply about $\frac{1}{4}$ ounce of salt daily. Salt taken in addition to that in food should be dissolved in the drinking water.

● Pump outdoor air through your shelter day and night in warm weather, so that both the occupants and the shelter are cooled off at night.

Almost all of the danger from fallout is caused by radiation from visible fallout particles of heavy, sand-like material. The air does **not** become radioactive due to the radiation continuously given off by fallout particles.

The visible fallout particles rapidly "fall out" of slow moving air. The air that a KAP pumps through a shelter moves at a low speed and could carry into the shelter only a very small fraction of the fallout particles that cause the radiation hazard outside. This fraction, usually not dangerous, can be further reduced if occupants take the simple precautions described in these instructions.

CAUTION

Before anyone starts to build this unusual type of air pump, ALL WORKERS SHOULD READ THESE INSTRUCTIONS AT LEAST UP TO **SECTION V, INSTALLATION**. Otherwise, mistakes may be made and work may be divided inefficiently.

When getting ready to build this pump, all workers should spend the first half-hour studying these instructions and getting organized. Then, after materials are assembled, two inexperienced persons working together should be able to complete the 3-foot model described in the following pages in less than 4 hours. To speed up completion, divide the work; for example, one person can start making the flaps while another begins work on the pump frame.

II. HOW A KAP WORKS

As can be seen in Figs. 1 and 2, a KAP operates by being swung like a pendulum. It is hinged at the top of its swinging frame. When this air pump is pulled by a cord as illustrated, its flaps are closed by air pressure and it pushes air in front of it and "sucks"

Fig. 1. Section through the upper part of a doorway, showing operation of a KAP.

ORNL-DWG 66-12319A

Fig. 2. KAP in doorway (with flaps open during its return stroke).

air in back of it. Thus a KAP pumps air through the opening in which it swings. This is the power stroke. During its power stroke, the pump's flaps are closed against its flap-stop wires or strings, which are fastened across the face of the frame.

When a KAP swings freely back as a pendulum on its return stroke, all its flaps are opened by air pressure. The pumped air stream continues to flow in the direction in which it has been accelerated by the power stroke, while the pump itself swings in the opposite direction (see Fig. 2). Thus the flaps are one-way valves that operate to force air to flow in one direction, where desired.

The KAP can be used: (1) to supply **outdoor** air to a shelter, (2) to distribute air within a shelter, and/or to fan the occupants.

1. To force **outdoor** air **through** a shelter, an **air-supply** KAP usually is operated as an air-intake pump by pulling it with a cord (see Fig. 1). (Only rarely is it necessary to operate a KAP as an air-exhaust pump by pushing it with a pole, as described in the last section of these instructions.)

2. To distribute air **within** a shelter and/or to fan the occupants, **air-distribution** KAPs may be hung overhead and operated as described later.

III. INSTRUCTIONS FOR BUILDING A KAP

In this section, instructions are given for making a KAP 36 inches high and 29 inches wide, to operate efficiently when swinging in a typical home basement doorway 30 inches wide. If your doorway or other ventilation opening is narrower or wider than 30 inches, you should make your KAP 1 inch narrower than the narrowest opening in which you plan to install it. Regardless of the size of the KAP you plan to build, first study the instructions for making the 36 × 29-inch model.

In Section VII you will find brief instructions for making a narrower and even simpler KAP, one more suitable for the narrow openings of small trench shelters and other small expedient shelters. Section VIII covers large KAPs, for large shelters.

A. Materials Needed for a KAP 36 inches High by 29 inches Wide

The preferred material is listed as first (1st) choice, and the less-preferred materials are listed as (2nd), (3rd), and (4th) choices. It is best to assemble, spread out, and check all your materials before beginning to build.

1. The pump frame and its fixed support:

● Boards for the frame:

(1st) 22 ft of 1 × 2-in. boards. (A nominal 1 × 2-in. board actually measures about $^3/_4$ × 1-$^3/_4$ in., but the usual, nominal dimensions will be given throughout these instructions.) Also, 6 ft of 1 × 1-in. boards. Soft wood is better.

(2nd) Boards of the same length that have approximately the same dimensions as 1 × 2-in. and 1 × 1-in. lumber.

(3rd) Straight sticks or metal strips that can be cut and fitted to make a flat-faced KAP frame.

● Hinges: (1st) Door or cabinet butt-hinges; (2nd) metal strap-hinges; (3rd) improvised hinges made of leather, woven straps, cords, or 4 eyescrews which can be joined to make 2 hinges. (Screws are best for attaching hinges. If nails are used, they should go through the board and their ends should be bent over and clinched—flattened against the surface of the board.)

● A board for the fixed horizontal support: (1st) A 1 × 4-in. board that is at least 1 ft longer than the width of the opening in which you plan to swing your pump; (2nd) A wider board.

● Small nails (at least 24): (1st) No. 6 box nails, about $^1/_2$ in. longer than the thickness of the two boards, so their pointed ends can be bent over and clinched); (2nd) other small nails.

2. The flaps (See Figs. 1, 2, 6, 7, and 8):

● Plastic film or other **very light,** flexible material—12 square feet in pieces that can be cut into 9 rectangular strips, each 30 × 5$^1/_2$ in.: (1st) polyethylene film 3 or 4 mils thick (3 or 4 one-thousandths of an inch); (2nd) 2-mil polyethylene from large trash bags; (3rd) tough paper.

● Pressure-sensitive waterproof tape, enough to make 30 ft of tape $^3/_4$ in. to 1 in. wide, for securing the hem-tunnels of the flaps: (1st) cloth duct tape (silver tape); (2nd) glass tape; (3rd) scotch tape; (4th) freezer or masking tape, or sew the hem tunnels. (Do not use a tape that stretches: it may shrink afterward and cause the flaps to wrinkle.)

3. The flap pivot-wires:

(1st) 30 ft of smooth wire at least as heavy and springy as coat hanger wire, that can be made into **very straight** pieces each 29 in. long (nine all-wire coat hangers will supply enough); (2nd) 35 ft of somewhat thinner wire, including light, flexible insulated wire; (3rd) 35 ft of smooth string, preferably nylon string about the diameter of coat hanger wire.

4. The pull cord:

(1st) At least 10 ft of cord; (2nd) strong string; (3rd) flexible, light wire.

5. The flap-stops:

● (1st) 150 ft of light string; (2nd) 150 ft of light, smooth wire; (3rd) 150 ft of very strong thread; (4th) 600 ft of ordinary thread, to provide 4 threads for each stop-flap.

● (1st) 90 tacks (not thumbtacks); (2nd) 90 small nails. (Tacks or nails are desirable but not essential, since the flap-stops can be tied to the frame.)

B. Tools

A hammer, saw, wirecutter pliers, screwdriver, scissors, knife, yardstick, and pencil are desirable. However, only a strong, sharp knife is essential for making some models.

C. Building a KAP 36 inches High by 29 inches Wide

A 36 × 29-in. KAP is most effective if operated in an air-intake or exhaust opening about 40 in. high and 30 in. wide. (If your shelter might have more than 25 occupants in hot weather, read all these instructions so you will understand how to build a larger pump, briefly described in Section VIII.)

NOTE THAT THE WIDTHS AND THICK-NESSES OF ALL FRAME PIECES ARE EXAGGERATED IN ALL ILLUSTRATIONS.

1. The frame

a. Cut two pieces of 1 × 2-in. boards, each 36 in. long, and two pieces of 1 × 2-in. boards, each 29 in. long; then nail them together(see Fig. 3). Use nails that do not split the wood, preferably long enough to go through the boards and stick out about $1/2$ in. on the other side. (To nail in this manner, first put blocks under the frame so that the nail points will not strike the floor.) Bend over nail points which go through.

Next, cut and nail to the frame a piece of 1 × 1-in. lumber 36 in. long, for a center vertical brace. (If you lack time to make or to find a 1 × 1-in. board, use a 1 × 2-in. board.) Figure 3 shows the back side of the frame; the flap valves will be attached on the front (the opposite) side.

Fig. 3. KAP frame (looking at the back side of the frame).

b. To make the front side smooth and flat so that the flaps will close tightly, fill in the spaces as follows: Cut two pieces of 1 × 2-in. boards long enough to fill in the spaces on top of the 36-in. sides of the frame between the top and bottom horizontal boards, and nail these filler boards in place. Do the same thing with a 1 × 1-in. board (or a board the size of that used for the center brace) as a filler board for the center brace (see Fig. 4).

If the frame is made of only one thickness of board $3/4$ in. to 1 in. thick, it will not be sufficiently heavy to swing back far enough on its free-swinging return stroke.

157

Fig. 4. Completing the frame.

2. The hinges

Ordinary door butt-hinges are best. So that the pump can swing past the horizontal position, the hinges should be screwed onto the front of the frame, at its top, in the positions shown in Fig. 4. (Pick one of the 29-in. boards and call it the top.) If you do not have a drill for drilling a screw hole, you can make a hole by driving a nail and then pulling it out. Screw the screw into the nail hole.

3. The pivot-wires and flaps

a. Make 9 flap pivot-wires. If you have smooth, straight wire as springy and thick as coat hanger wire, üse it to make **nine** 29-in.-long straight lengths of wire. If not, use wire from all-wire coat hangers or use strings. First, cut off all of the hook portion of each coat hanger, including the twisted part. If you have only ordinary pliers, use the cutter to "bite" the wire all around; it will break at this point if bent there. Next, **straighten** each wire **carefully.** Straighten all the bends so that each wire is straight within $\frac{1}{4}$ in., as compared to a straight line. Proper straightening takes 1 to 5 minutes per wire. To straighten, repeatedly grasp the bent part of the wire with pliers in slightly different spots, each time bending the wire a little with your other hand. Then cut each wire to a **29-in.** length. Finally, bend no more than $\frac{1}{2}$ in. of each end at a right angle and in the same plane—that is, in directions so that all parts of the bent wire will lie flat against a smooth surface. The bent ends are for secure attachment later (see Fig. 8).

b. Make 9 polyethylene flaps that will be the hinged valves of the KAP. First cut 9 strips,

making each strip 30 in. long by $5\frac{1}{2}$-in. wide (see Fig. 5). To cut plastic flaps quickly and accurately, cut a long strip of plastic 30 in. wide. Then cut off a flap in this way: (1) draw a cutting guideline on a wide board $5\frac{1}{2}$ in. from an edge; (2) place the 30-in.-wide plastic strip so that it lies on this board, with one of the strip's side edges just reaching the edge of the board; (3) place a second board over

Fig. 5.

the plastic on the first board, with a straight edge of this second upper board over the guideline on the lower board; and finally (4) cut off a flap by running a **sharp** knife along the straight edge of the upper board.

To form a hem along one of the 30-in. sides of a $5^1/_2 \times 30$-in. rectangular strip, fold in a **1-in.** hem. This makes the finished flap $4^1/_2$ in. wide.

To hold the folded hem while taping it, paper clips or another pair of hands are helpful. For each hem, use two pieces of pressure-sensitive tape, each about 1 in. wide and 16 in. long. Or make the hem by sewing it very close to the cut edge to form a hem-tunnel (see Fig. 5).

After the hem has been made, cut a notch with scissors in each hemmed corner of the flap (Figs. 6 and 8). Avoid cutting the tape holding the hem. Each notch should extend downward about $^1/_2$ in. and should extend horizontally from the outer edge of the flap to $^1/_4$ in. inside the inner side of the frame, when the flap is positioned on the frames as shown in Fig. 6.

ORNL-DWG 66-12324

Fig. 6. Sizes of notches in flaps.

Also cut a notch in the center of the flap (along the hem line) extending $^1/_2$ in. downward and extending horizontally $^1/_4$ in. beyond each of the two sides of the vertical brace (see Fig. 6). The notch MUST be wider than the brace. [However, if you are building a pump using wire netting for flap-stops (see Fig. 13), then do NOT cut a notch in the center of each flap.]

c. Take the 9 pieces of straightened wire and insert one of them into and through the hem-tunnel

of each flap, like a curtain rod running through the hem of a curtain. Check to see that each flap **swings freely** on its pivot-wire, as illustrated by Fig. 7. Also see Fig. 8.

ORNL-DWG 66-12325

Fig. 7. End view.

ORNL DWG 71-7005A

Fig. 8.

159

d. Put aside the flaps and their pivot-wires for use after you have attached the flap-stops and the hinges to the frame, as described below.

e. Using the ruler printed on the edge of this page, mark the positions of each pivot-wire (the arrowheads numbered 0, $3^5/_8$, $7^1/_4$ in.) and the position of each flap-stop (the four marks between each pair of numbered arrowheads on this ruler). All of these positions should be marked both on the vertical sides of the 36-in.-long boards of the frame and on the vertical brace. Mark the position of the uppermost pivot-wire (the "0" arrowhead on this ruler) $^1/_4$ in. below the top board to which the hinges have been attached (see Figs. 9 and 10).

4. The flap-stops

So that the flaps may swing open on only one side of the frame (on its front, or face), you must attach horizontal flap-stops made of strings or wires across the face of the frame. (See Figs. 10 and 11.) Nail or tie four of these flap-stops between the marked points where each pair of the horizontal pivot-wires for the flaps will be placed. Be careful not to connect any flap-stops in such a way that they cross the horizontal open spaces in which you later will attach the flap pivot-wires.

Fig. 11. Positions of pivot-wires and flap-stops.

If you have tacks (NOT thumbtacks) or very small nails, drive three in a horizontal line to attach each flap-stop—two in the vertical 36-in. sides of the frame and one in the vertical center brace (see Fig. 11). First, drive all of these horizontal lines of tacks about three-quarters of the way into the boards. Then, to secure the flap-stop string or thin wire quickly to a tack, wind the string around the tack and immediately drive the tack tightly into the frame to grip the string (see Fig. 11).

If you have no tacks or nails, cut notches or slots where the flap-stops are to be attached. Cut these notches in the edges of the vertical sides of the frame and in an edge of the center brace. Next, secure the flap-stops (strings or wires) by tying each

Fig. 9.

Fig. 10.

one in its notched position. This tying should include wrapping each horizontal flap-stop once around the vertical center brace. The stops should be in line with (in the same plane as) the front of the frame. Do not stretch flap-stops too tightly, or you may bend the frame.

5. Final assembly

a. Staple, nail, or tie the 9 flap pivot-wires or pivot-strings (each with its flap attached) in their positions at the marked $3^5/_8$-in. spacings. Start with the lowest flap and work upward (see Fig. 11). Connect each pivot-wire at both ends to the 36-in. vertical sides of the frame. **Also connect it to the vertical brace.** BE CAREFUL TO NAIL THE PIVOT-WIRES ONLY TO THE FRAME AND THE BRACE. DO <u>NOT</u> NAIL ANY PLASTIC DIRECTLY TO THE WOOD. All flaps must turn freely on their pivot-wires.

If any flap, when closed, overlaps the flap below it by more than 1 in., trim off the excess so that it overlaps by only 1 in.

b. Screw (or nail, if screws are not available) the upper halves of the hinges onto the horizontal support board on which the KAP will swing. (A 1-in.-thick board is best, $3^1/_2$ in. wide and at least 12 in. longer than the width of the doorway or other opening in which this KAP is to be installed.)

Be careful to attach the hinges in the <u>UN</u>usual, <u>OUT-OF-LINE POSITION</u> shown in Fig. 12.

CAUTIONS: Do NOT attach a KAP's hinges directly to the door frame. If you do, the hinges will be torn loose on its return stroke or on its power stroke.

If you are making a KAP to fit into a rectangular opening, make its frame 4 in. <u>SHORTER</u> than the height of its opening and <u>1 in.</u> <u>NARROWER</u> than the width of the opening.

c. For this 3-ft model, tie the pull-cord to the center brace about $12^1/_2$ **in. below the hinge line,** as shown in Fig. 12. (If you tie it lower, your **arm movements will waste energy.**) Use small nails or wire to keep the tie end from slipping up or down on the center brace. (For a more durable connection, see Fig. 22.)

Cut a slot in the flap above the connection of the pull-cord to the vertical brace, deep enough so that this flap will close completely when the KAP is being pulled. Tape the end and edges of the slot.

Fig. 12. Hinge is attached so pump can swing 180 degrees.

Labels in figure:
HORIZONTAL SUPPORT (<u>NOT</u> DIRECTLY ABOVE THE PUMP FRAME)
HINGE
12 ½ in.
FLAPS SHOULD OVERLAP ³/₄ in. TO 1 in.
BACK OF PUMP
PULLCORD ATTACHED ABOUT 1 in. ABOVE THE FOURTH FLAP FROM THE TOP
(THIS DRAWING IS NOT TO SCALE)

IV. MORE RAPID CONSTRUCTION

(Skip this section if you cannot easily get chicken wire and $1/_4$-in.-thick boards.)

If chicken wire and boards about $1/_4$ in. thick are available, use the chicken wire for flap-stops. By using these materials, the time required to build a given KAP can be reduced by about 40%. One-inch woven mesh is best. (Hardware cloth has sharp points and is unsatisfactory.)

Figure 13 illustrates how the mesh wire should be stapled to the KAP frame. Next, unless the KAP is wider than 3 ft, the front of the whole frame (except for the center brace) should be covered with thin boards approximately $1/_2$ in. thick, such as laths. Then the pivot-wires, with their flaps on them, should be stapled onto the $1/_4$-in.-thick boards. This construction permits the flaps to turn freely in front of the chicken-wire flap-stops.

With this design, the center of each pivot-wire should <u>NOT</u> be connected to the center brace, nor should the center of the flap be notched. However, pivot-wires that are attached this way must be made and held straighter than pivot-wires used with flap-stops made of straight strings or wires.

Fig. 13. Flaps attached $\frac{1}{4}$ inch in front of chicken wire used for flap-stops.

Note in Fig. 13 that each pivot-wire is held firm and straight by **2** staples securing each end. The wire used should be at least as springy as coat hanger wire. If string is used instead of wire, nylon cord about the diameter of coat hanger wire is best for the pivot-strings.

If the KAP is wider than 3 ft, its center vertical brace should also be covered with a $\frac{1}{4}$-in.-thick board, and each pivot-wire should be attached to it. Furthermore, the center of each flap should be notched.

V. INSTALLATION AND ACCESSORIES

A. Minimum Open Spaces Around a KAP

To pump its maximum volume, an air-supply KAP with good metal hinges should be installed in its opening so that it swings only about $\frac{1}{2}$ in. above the bottom of the opening and only $\frac{1}{2}$ in. to 1 in. from the sides of the opening.

B. Adequately Large Air Passageways

When using a KAP as an air-supply pump to force air through a shelter, it is essential to provide a **low-resistance** air passageway **all the way through** the shelter structure from an **outdoor** air-intake opening for **outdoor** air to a separate air-exhaust opening to the **outdoors** (see Fig. 14).

Fig. 14.

162

A low-resistance air passageway is one that is no smaller in cross-sectional area than half the size of the KAP pumping the air. For example, a 36 × 29-in. KAP should have a passageway no smaller than about $3\frac{1}{2}$ sq. ft. An air-supply KAP of this size will force at least 1000 cubic feet per minute (1000 cfm) through a shelter having such openings, if it is installed as illustrated in Fig. 14.

If smaller air passageways or air-exhaust openings are provided, the volume of air pumped will be greatly reduced. For example, if the air-exhaust opening is only $1\frac{3}{4}$ sq. ft ($\frac{1}{4}$ the size of this KAP), then this KAP will pump only about 500 cfm. And if the air-exhaust opening is only a 6 × 6-in. exhaust duct ($\frac{1}{4}$ sq. ft), then this same 36 × 29-in. KAP will pump only about 50 cubic feet per minute. This would not provide enough outdoor air for more than one shelter occupant in a well-insulated shelter under heat-wave conditions in the hottest humid parts of the United States. In contrast, when the weather is freezing cold and the shelter itself is still cold enough to absorb the heat produced by the shelter occupants, this same 6 × 6-in. exhaust duct and the air-intake doorway will cause about 50 cfm of outdoor air to flow by itself through the shelter without using any pump. The reason: body heat warms the shelter air, and the warm air rises if cold air can flow in to replace it. Under these **cold** conditions—provided the air is distributed evenly throughout the shelter by KAP

or otherwise—50 cfm is enough outdoor air for about 17 people.

To provide adequately large air passageways for air-supply KAPs used to ventilate shelters in buildings, in addition to opening and closing doors and windows, it may be necessary to build large ducts (as described below). Breaking holes in windows, ceilings, or walls is another way to make large, efficient air passageways.

Figure 15 illustrates how a 3-ft KAP can be used as a combined air-supply and air-distribution pump to adequately ventilate a small underground shelter that has an exhaust opening too small to provide enough ventilation in warm weather. (A similar installation can be used to ventilate a basement room having only one opening, its doorway.) Note how, by installing a "divider" in the doorway and entryway, the single entryway is converted into a large air-intake duct and a separate, large air-exhaust duct. To obtain the maximum increased volume of fresh outdoor air that can be pumped through the shelter—a total of about 1000 cfm for a 36 × 29-in. KAP—the divider should extend about 4 ft horizontally into the shelter room, as shown in Fig. 15. The 6 ft at the end of the divider (the almost-horizontal part under the KAP) can be made of plywood, provided it is installed so that it can be taken out of the way in a few seconds.

ORNL DWG 72-6630

Fig. 15. Ventilating a shelter when the air-exhaust opening is too small.

Note how the entry of fallout into a shelter can be minimized by covering the entryway with a "roof" and by forcing the slow-moving entering air to rise over an obstruction (the "wall") before it flows into the shelter. The sand-like fallout particles fall to the ground outside the "wall."

C. Adequate Distribution of Air Within the Shelter

To make sure that each shelter occupant gets a fair share of the outdoor air pumped through the shelter, **air-distribution KAPs** should be used inside most large shelters. These KAPs are used within the shelter, separate from and in addition to air-supply KAPs (see Fig. 16). Air-distribution KAPs can serve in place of both air-distribution ducts and cooling fans. For these purposes, one or more 3-ft-high KAPs hung overhead from the shelter ceiling are usually most practical. If KAPs cannot readily be hung from the ceiling, they can be supported on light frames made of boards or metal, somewhat like those used for a small child's swing.

KAP for every 25 occupants. In relatively wide shelters, these interior KAPs should be positioned so that they produce an airflow that circulates around the shelter, preventing the air that is being pumped into the shelter from flowing directly to the exhaust opening. Figure 16 illustrates how four KAPs can be used in this way to distribute the air within a shelter and to fan the 100 occupants of a 1000-sq.-ft shelter room. Avoid positioning an air-distribution KAP so that it pumps air in a direction greater than a right angle turn from the direction of airflow to the location of the KAP.

D. Operation with a Pulley

A small KAP—especially one with improvised hinges or one installed at head-height or higher—can be pulled most efficiently by running its pull-cord over a pulley or over a greased homemade "pulley" such as described in Figs. 17 and 18. A pulley should be hung at approximately the same height as the hinges of the KAP, as illustrated in Fig. 15. To make

ORNL DWG 72-7547

Fig. 16. The use of air-distribution KAPs.

You should make and use enough KAPs to cause air movement that can be felt in all parts of your shelter. Remember that if KAPs are installed near the floor and the shelter is fully occupied, the occupants' bodies will partially block the pumped airflow more than if the same KAPs were suspended overhead.

As a general rule, for shelters having more than about 20 occupants, provide one 3-ft air-distribution

ORNL DWG 71-7242

Fig. 17.

164

Fig. 18.

Fig. 19. Quick-removal bracket for KAP.

a comfortable hand-hold on which to pull downward, tie two or three overhand knots in a strip of cloth on the end of the pull-cord.

(Such a "pulley" can also be used to operate a bail-bucket to remove water or wastes from some shelters, without anyone having to go outside.)

E. Quick-Removal Brackets

The air-supply KAP that pumps air through your shelter is best held in its pumping position by mounting it in homemade quick-removal brackets (see Fig. 19) for the following reasons:

● A KAP provided with quick-removal brackets can be taken down easily and kept out of the way of persons passing through its doorway when it is not in use. It can be kept in a place where people are unlikely to damage it.

● By installing two sets of quick-removal brackets in opposite shelter openings, you can quickly reverse the direction in which the KAP pumps air, to take

advantage of changes in the direction of natural airflow through the shelter.

● If the KAP is installed on quick-removal brackets, in an emergency a person standing beside the KAP could grasp its frame with both hands, lift it upward a few inches to detach it, and carry it out of the way—all in 3 to 5 seconds. Being able to move the KAP quickly could prevent blast winds from wrecking the pump, which might also be blown into your shelter—possibly injuring occupants. In extensive areas where fallout shelters and their occupants would survive the blast effects of typical large warheads, more than 4 seconds would elapse between the time shelter occupants would see the extremely bright light from the explosion and the arrival of a blast wave strong enough to wreck a KAP or other pumps left exposed in a ventilation opening.

Note in Fig. 19 that the KAP's "fixed" support-board (a $3\frac{1}{2}$-in.-wide board to which its hinges are attached) is held in a bracket only 2 inches deep. To prevent too tight a fit in the bracket, be sure to place a $\frac{1}{32}$-in. shim or spacer (the cardboard back of a writing tablet will do) between two boards of the bracket, as illustrated. Also, make spaces about $\frac{1}{16}$ inches wide between the lower inner corners of the stop-blocks and the sides of the outer board. To prevent your hands from being cut, you should put tape over the exposed ends of wires near the frame's outer edges of a KAP that you want to be able to remove rapidly.

In a small expedient shelter, a small KAP can be quickly jerked loose if its "fixed" support-board is attached to the roof with only a few small nails.

VI. OPERATION AND MAINTENANCE

A. Pumping

Operate your 3-foot KAP by pulling it with an easy, swinging motion of your arm. To pump the maximum volume of air, you should pull the KAP toward you until its frame swings out to an almost-horizontal position. Then quickly move your hand so that the pull-cord is kept **slack during the entire, free-swinging return stroke.** Figure 24 in Section VIII, LARGE KAPs, illustrates this necessary motion.

Be sure to provide a comfortable hand-hold on the pull-cord (see Fig. 14). Blisters can be serious under unsanitary conditions.

To pull a KAP via an overhead pulley with minimum effort, sit down and pull as if you were tolling a bell—except that you should raise your hand quickly with the return stroke and keep it raised long enough so that the pull-cord remains slack during the entire return stroke. Or, if the pulley is not overhead, operate the KAP by swinging your extended arm back and forth from the shoulder.

B. Placement to Take Advantage of the Natural Direction of Air Flow

A KAP can pump more air into a shelter if it is installed so that it pumps air through the shelter in the direction in which the air naturally flows. Since this direction can be reversed by a wind change outdoors, it is desirable to provide a way to quickly remove your pump and reposition it so that air can be pumped in the opposite direction. This can be done in several ways, including making one set of quick-removal brackets for one air opening and a second set for the other.

C. Maintenance

To operate your KAP efficiently, keep the flaps in good repair and make sure that there is the minimum practical area of open spaces in and around the KAP through which air can flow back around the pump frame, opposite to the pumped direction. So keep at least some extra flap material in your shelter, along with some extra tape and the few tools you may need to make repairs.

VII. NARROW KAPs AND SMALL KAPs

A. Narrow KAPs

To swing efficiently in an entrance or emergency exit of an expedient trench shelter that is 22 in. wide, a KAP is best made 20 in. wide and 36 in. high. One of less height is not as efficient as a 36-in.-high model and has to be pulled uncomfortably fast. So, when ventilation openings can be selected or made at least 38 in. high, make your pump 36 in. high.

In a narrow trench shelter, it is best to have the pull-cord run the full length of the trench, along the trench wall that occupants will face when sitting. Then each occupant can take a turn pulling the pump without having to change seats.

Good metal hinges on a narrow KAP allow it to swing properly if pulled with the pull-cord attached to **one side** of the frame. (Pumps with improvised hinges and large pumps must be pulled from a connection point on their center vertical brace to make them swing properly.) Therefore, if you have small metal hinges and need a KAP no wider than 20 inches, build a rectangular frame **without** a vertical center brace. Make two pull-cord attachment points, one on each side of the frame and each 9 inches below the top of the frame. (For a small KAP, a satisfactory attachment point can readily be made by driving two nails so that their heads cross, and wiring them together.) Then if a change in wind direction outside causes the direction of natural air flow in the trench to become opposite to the direction in which air is being pumped, you can move your KAP to the opening at the other end of the trench. The pull-cord can easily be connected to the other side of the frame, and convenient pumping can be resumed quickly.

So that the horizontal support board can be nailed easily to the roofing poles or boards of an entry trench, it is best to use cabinet hinges. Screw them onto an **edge** of the support board, in the <u>UNusual, OUT-OF-LINE POSITION</u> shown in Fig. 20. This hinge connection allows the pump to swing a full 180 degrees. To facilitate moving the horizontal support board, connect it to the roof with a few small nails, so that it can be pulled loose easily and quickly.

ORNL–DWG 78–10358

ROOF POLES

HORIZONTAL SUPPORT BOARD

FLAPS

Fig. 20.

B. Small KAPs

If the only available opening in which a KAP can be installed is small, build a KAP to fit it. Use narrower boards to make the frame and make the flaps of thinner material, such as the polyethylene of large plastic trash bags. For pumps 24 inches or less in height, make the finished flaps only $3\frac{1}{2}$ inches wide and space their pivot-wires 3 inches apart. The flaps should overlap no more than $\frac{1}{2}$ inch. A KAP 24 inches high will pump enough outdoor air for only a few people, except in cold weather.

Small, yet efficient KAPs can be made even if the only materials available are straight sticks about $1\frac{1}{4}$ inches in diameter, strips of cloth to tie the frame together and to make the hinges and the pull cord, polyethylene film from large trash bags for the flaps, freezer or duct tape (or needle and thread) to make the flap hems, coat hanger wire or string for the pivot-wire, and string or ordinary thread for the flap-stops. A sharp knife is the only essential tool. Figure 21 shows a way to easily tie sticks securely together and to attach strings or threads for stop-flaps, when small nails and tacks are not available. The flap-stop strings or threads should be secured by wrapping them several times around each stick to which they are attached, so they will be gripped by the out-of-line knife cuts.

ORNL-DWG 78-21897

"U" NOTCH

GROOVE (ONLY ON UPPER SIDE)

STOP-FLAP
MADE OF STRING OR 4 THREADS

KNIFE CUTS TO SECURE FLAP-STOPS

Fig. 21. Sticks ready to be tied together to make a KAP frame.

VIII. LARGE KAPs

A. Construction

A 6-ft-high by 29-in.-wide model can be constructed in the same way as a 3-ft model—except that it should have both horizontal and vertical center braces (1 × 2-in. boards are best). To increase the strength of a 6-ft KAP, all parts of its double-thickness frame and its vertical center brace should be made of two thicknesses of 1 × 2-in. softwood boards, securely held together with clinched nails. Also, to increase the distance that the pump will swing back by itself during its return stroke, it is worthwhile to attach a 6-ft piece of 1 × 2-in. board (not illustrated) to the back of each side of the frame. Do NOT attach weights to the bottom of the frame; this would slow down the pumping rate.

This 6-ft-high pump requires 18 flaps, each the same size as those of the 36-in.-high KAP. The flaps on the lower part of a large KAP must withstand hard use. If $^1/_2$-in.-wide strips of tape are attached along the bottom and side edges of these lower flaps, then even flaps made of ordinary 4-mil polyethylene will remain serviceable for over 1000 hours of pumping. However, the **lower** flaps of large KAPs can advantageously be made of 6-mil polyethylene. The width and spacing of all flaps should be the same as those of the 36-in.-high model.

The pull-cord should be attached to the vertical center brace of a 6-ft KAP about $16^1/_2$ in. below the hinge line. A $^3/_{16}$-in. nylon cord is ideal.

To adequately ventilate and cool very large and crowded shelters in buildings, mines, or caves, KAPs larger than 72 × 29 in. should be used. You can take better advantage of large doorways, elevator shaft openings, etc., by "tailor-making" each large air-supply KAP to the size of its opening—that is, by making it as large as is practical. The frame and brace members should be appropriately strengthened, and one or more "Y" bridles should be provided, as described in the section below. A 7-ft-high × $5^1/_2$-ft-wide KAP, with a $^1/_4$-in.-diameter pull-cord attached 18 in. below its hinge line, and with two "Y" bridles for its two operators, pumped air at the rate of over 11,000 cubic ft per minute through a large basement shelter during tests.

To make a durable connection of the pull-cord to the center vertical brace: (1) Attach a wire loop (Fig. 22) about $16^1/_2$ in. below the hinge line. This loop can be made of coat hanger wire and should go around the center vertical brace. This fixed loop should be kept from slipping on the center brace by bending four 6-penny nails over it in front as illustrated, and two smaller nails in back. (2) Make a free-turning, triple-wire loop connected to the fixed loop. (3) Cover part of the free-turning loop with tape and tie the pull-cord to this loop. Tie the pull-cord tightly over the taped part.

ORNL DWG 72-8204

MAKE A 2-in. DIAMETER SNUG LOOP OF 3 TURNS OF COATHANGER WIRE.

PRESSURE SENSITIVE CLOTH TAPE

FUSED NYLON

PULL CORD

FOUR, 6-PENNY NAILS ON FRONT SIDE

Fig. 22.

B. Operation of Larger KAPs

A larger KAP can be pulled most easily by providing it with a "Y" bridle (see Fig. 23) attached to the end of its pull-cord.

Fig. 23. Y-bridle for pull-cord on KAP.

A man of average size and strength can operate a 6 ft × 29 in. KAP by himself, pumping over 4000 cubic feet per minute through a typical large shelter without working hard; tests have shown that he must deliver only about $\frac{1}{20}$ of a horsepower. However, most people prefer to work in pairs when pulling a 6-ft KAP equipped with a "Y" bridle, when pumping over 3000 cfm.

To pump the maximum volume of air with minimum effort, study Fig. 24 and follow the instructions given below for operating a large KAP.

Fig. 24.

1. Gradually start the pump swinging back and forth, moving your arms and body as illustrated and **pulling mostly with your legs and body.**

2. Stand at such a distance from the pump that you can pull the pump toward you until the forward-swinging pump **just touches the tightly stretched pull-cord**—and at such a distance that you can keep the pull-cord **slack** during the whole of the pump's free backswing.

3. To be sure you do not reduce the amount of air pumped, rapidly move your arms forward **as soon as the forward-swinging pump touches the tightened pull-cord.** Hold your arms forward until the pump again starts to swing toward you.

IX. SOLUTIONS TO SPECIAL PROBLEMS

A. Increasing the Usefulness of Shelters by Supplying 40 cfm per Planned Occupant

If a shelter is fully occupied for days during hot weather and is cooled both day and night by pumping through it and distributing at least 40 cubic feet per minute of outdoor air for each occupant—more than is required to maintain tolerable temperatures at night—these advantages result:

● The shelter occupants will be exposed to effective temperatures less than 2° F higher than the current effective temperatures outdoors, and at night will get relief from extreme heat.

● The floors, walls, etc. of a shelter so ventilated will be cooled at night to temperatures well below daytime temperatures. Therefore, during the day a considerable fraction of the occupants' body heat will flow into the floors, walls, and other parts of the shelter and less body heat will have to be carried out by the exhaust air during the hottest hours of the day. Thus daytime temperatures will be reduced.

● Since the shelter occupants will be cooler and will sweat less, especially at night, they will need less water than they would require if the shelter were ventilated at a rate of less than 40 cfm per occupant. (If the outdoor air is very hot and desert-dry, it usually is better to supply less than 40 cfm per occupant during the hottest hours of the day.)

● If the shelter were to be endangered by the entry of outside smoke, carbon monoxide or other poisonous gases, or heavy descending fallout under windy conditions, ventilation of the shelter could be temporarily restricted or stopped for a longer period than would be practical if the shelter itself were warmer at the beginning of such a crisis period.

• The shelter could be occupied beyond its rated capacity without problems caused by overcrowding becoming as serious as would be the case if smaller-capacity air pumps were to be installed and used.

B. Pre-Cooling Shelters

If the shelter itself is cooler than the occupants, more of the body heat of occupants can flow into its cool walls, ceiling, and floor. Therefore, it would be advantageous to pre-cool a shelter that may soon be occupied, especially during hot weather. KAPs (or other air pumps or fans) can be used to pre-cool a shelter by forcing the maximum volume of cooling outdoor air through the shelter and by distributing it within the shelter. A shelter should be pre-cooled at all times when the air temperature outdoors is lower than the air temperature inside the shelter. Then, if the pre-cooled shelter is used, the occupants will be kept cooler at a given rate of ventilation than if the shelter had not been pre-cooled, because the air will not have to carry all of their body heat out of the shelter.

C. Increasing the Effectiveness of a KAP

If you want to increase the volume of air that a KAP with good metal hinges can force through a shelter, install side baffles (see Fig. 25). Side baffles should be rigidly fixed to form two stationary "walls," one on each side of the swinging pump frame. They can be made of plywood, boards, doors, table tops, or even well-braced plastic. A space or clearance of $\frac{1}{2}$ to 1 in. should be maintained between the inner side of each baffle and the outer side of the swinging frame.

By installing side baffles you may be able to increase the volume of air your KAP will pump by as much as 20%, if it is in good repair and the openings around it are small.

ORNL-DWG 66-12334R

ALL UNUSED OPENINGS IN DOORWAY SHOULD BE COVERED

LENGTH OF KEARNY PUMP + 2 in.

1 in. CLEARANCE

SIDE BAFFLE

Fig. 25. Side baffles.

D. Operating a KAP as an Exhaust Pump

In some shelters, a KAP can be operated most effectively by using it as an exhaust pump. This can be done by pushing it with a push-pole attached to its center vertical brace. Push-pole operation is sometimes the best way to "suck" outdoor air into a shelter by pumping air out of the shelter in the natural direction of air flow; for example, up an elevator shaft or up a stairwell. This method is especially useful in those basement shelters in which air-intake openings are impractical for installing KAPs. This would be the case if the air-intake openings are small, exposed windows or holes broken in the ceiling of a shelter in a building.

To pump a large KAP most effectively with a push-pole, stand with your back to the KAP and grasp the push-pole with both hands. Using mostly your leg muscles, push the KAP by pulling the free end of its push-pole toward you.

Figure 26 shows an improvised, flexible connection of a push-pole attached to the center brace of a large KAP 28 in. from the top of its frame.

Fig. 26. Push-pole flexible connection.

E. Ventilating a Shelter with Only One Opening

Some basement rooms that may be used as shelters have only one opening, the doorway. A KAP can be used to ventilate such a shelter room if enough well-mixed and distributed air is moving just outside the doorway, or if air from outdoors can be pumped in by another KAP and made to flow in a hallway or room and pass just outside this doorway. Figure 27 indicates how to ventilate such a one-opening room by operating a 3-ft KAP as an air-intake pump in the upper part of the doorway.

Below such a doorway KAP, a "divider" 6 ft to 8 ft long can be installed. The divider permits exhaust air to flow out of the room without much of it being "sucked" back into the room by the KAP swinging above it. Plywood, reinforced heavy cardboard, or even well-braced plastic can be used to make a divider. It should be installed so that, in a possible emergency, it can be jerked out of the way in a few seconds.

When used with a divider, a 36 × 29 in. KAP can pump almost 1000 cubic feet of air per minute into and out of such a shelter room. Although 1000 cubic

feet of well-distributed air is sufficient for several times as many as 25 shelter occupants under most temperate climate conditions, it is enough for only about 25 people in a one-entry room under exceptionally severe heat-wave conditions. Furthermore, to make it habitable for even 25 people under such conditions, the air in this room must be kept from rising more than 2° F above the temperature outdoors. This can be done using a second air-supply KAP to pump enough outdoor air through the building and in some cases also using air-distribution KAPs in spaces outside the one-entry room. The KAP in the doorway of a one-entry room should supply 40 cfm per occupant of this room.

In order to prevent any of the used, warmed, exhaust air from the one-entry room from being "sucked" by the doorway KAP back into the room, a stiffened rectangular duct can be built so as to extend the exhaust-opening (in the lower part of the doorway) several feet outside the room. Such a duct can be built of plastic supported by a frame of small boards. It can be used to discharge the exhaust air far enough away from the KAP and "downstream" in the airflow outside the one-opening room so that no exhausted air can be "sucked" back into the room.

PULL-CORD PULLING

3-ft KAP

8-ft "DIVIDER" IN DOORWAY

Fig. 27. Use of a "divider" to ventilate a shelter with only one opening.

F. Installing a KAP in a Steel-Framed Doorway

If you need to install a KAP in a steel-framed doorway and it is not feasible to screw or otherwise permanently connect it to the doorway, you can attach the KAP by using a few boards and some cord, as illustrated by Figs. 28 and 29. The two horizontal boards shown extending across the doorway are squeezed tightly against the two sides of the wall in which the doorway is located by tightening two loops of cord, one near each side of the doorway. One loop is illustrated. A cord is first tightened around the two horizontal boards. Then the looped cord is further tightened by binding it in the center with another cord, as illustrated.

Two large "C" clamps serve even better than two looped cords. However, secure support for a swinging KAP still requires the use of a vertical support board on each side of the doorway, as illustrated.

CONCRETE WALL

STEEL DOOR FRAME

LOOPED CORD, TIGHTENED IN CENTER, HOLDING BOARDS TIGHT AGAINST DOOR FRAME

FIXED HORIZONTAL SUPPORT OF KAP, OR BOARD SUPPORTING THE QUICK-REMOVAL BRACKETS FOR A KAP

NOTCHED 1X4 in. SUPPORT BOARD EXTENDING DOWN TO FLOOR

Fig. 28.

172

Figure 29 shows a quick-removal bracket supported by two horizontal boards tightened across the upper part of a doorway by looped cords, as described above. Also, study Fig. 19 and its accompanying instructions.

ORNL DWG 72-6617

LOOPED CORD, TIGHTENED IN CENTER, HOLDING BOARDS TIGHT AGAINST STEEL DOOR FRAME.

VERTICAL SUPPORT BOARD EXTENDING DOWN TO FLOOR

BOARD FORMING A 2-in.-DEEP BRACKET, WITH AN APPROX. $\frac{1}{32}$-in. SHIM UNDER IT

QUICKLY REMOVABLE "FIXED" SUPPORT FOR KAP

BOARD THE SAME THICKNESS AS THE "FIXED" SUPPORT BOARD OF THE KAP

Fig. 29.

G. Building More Durable KAPs

If you are building KAPs in normal times, you may want to use materials that will make your pumps last longer, even though these materials are more difficult to obtain and are more expensive.

Durability tests have shown that the KAP parts that wear out first are the flaps and the pulleys. In 6-ft KAPs, the lower flaps are subject to hard use. Lower flaps made of 6-oz (per sq. yd), clear, nylon-reinforced, plied vinyl have lasted undamaged for over 1000 hours of full-stroke pumping, without having their edges reinforced. Lower flaps made of 6-mil nylon-reinforced polyethylene, without edge reinforcements, have lasted for 1000 hours with only minor damage.

The best pulley tested was a marine pulley such as that used on small sailboats, with a Delrin (DuPont) 2-in.-diameter wheel and $\frac{3}{16}$-in. stainless steel shaft. This pulley was undamaged after operating a 6-ft KAP for 324 hours. The pulley appeared to be good for hundreds of hours of further operation.

The best pulley-cords tested were of braided dacron or nylon.

H. Using Air Filters

To supply shelter occupants with filtered air usually would be of **much less** importance to their survival and health than to provide them with adequate volumes of outdoor air to maintain tolerable temperatures. However, filtering the entering air could prove worthwhile, provided:

● Your shelter is not in an area likely to be subjected to blast, or it is a blast shelter with blast doors and blast valves protecting everything inside.

● Work on filters is started *after* you have completed more essential work, including the building of a high-protection-factor shelter, making, installing, and testing the necessary number of KAPs, storing adequate water, making a homemade fallout meter, etc.

● You have enough low-resistance filters (such as fiberglass dust filters used in furnaces and air-conditioners) and other materials for building the necessary large, supported filter in front of your KAP.

● Your KAP can pump an adequate volume of air through the filter and shelter.

● The filter is installed so that it can be easily removed if shelter temperatures rise too high.

To prevent a filter used with a KAP from causing too great a reduction in the volume of air that the KAP can pump through your shelter, you must use **large areas of low-resistance filter material.** An example: In one ventilation test, a large basement shelter was used which had two ordinary doorways at its opposite ends. These served as its air-intake and its air-exhaust openings. A 72 × 29 in. KAP operating in one doorway pumped almost 5000 cubic feet per minute through the shelter. But when a filter frame holding 26 square feet of 1-in.-thick fiberglass dust filters was placed across the air-intake stairwell, the KAP could pump only about 3400 cfm through this filter and the shelter.

A HOMEMADE FALLOUT METER, THE KFM

HOW TO MAKE AND USE IT

FOLLOWING THESE INSTRUCTIONS MAY SAVE YOUR LIFE

The complete KFM instructions include patterns to be cut out and used to construct the fallout meter. At the end of the instructions are extra patterns on 4 unnumbered pages. The reader is urged to use these extra patterns to make KFM's in normal peacetime and to keep the complete instructions intact for use during a recognized crisis period.

If Xerox copies of the patterns are used, they should be checked against the originals in order to correct a few of the small changes in size that usually result from the copying process. Xerox copies of all the KFM patterns are satisfactory provided: (1) on the PAPER PATTERN TO WRAP AROUND KFM CAN, the distances between the 4 marks for the HOLES FOR STOP-THREAD are corrected--to eliminate the lengthening caused by xerox-type duplication; and (2) the dimensions of the FINISHED-LEAF PATTERN are corrected.

These instructions, including the heading on this page and the illustrative photos, can be photographed without additional screening and rapidly reproduced by a newspaper or printer. If you keep the KFM instructions intact, during a worsening crisis you may be able to use them to help your friends and thousands of your fellow citizens by making them available for reproduction.

I. The Need for Accurate and Dependable Fallout Meters

If a nuclear war ever strikes the United States, survivors of the blast and fire effects would need to have reliable means of knowing when the radiation in the environment around their shelters had dropped enough to let them venture safely outside. Civil defense teams could use broadcasts of surviving radio stations to give listeners a general idea of the fallout radiation in some broadcast areas. However, the fallout radiation would vary widely from point to point and the measurements would be made too far from most shelters to make them accurate enough to use safely. Therefore, each shelter should have some dependable method of measuring the changing radiation dangers in its own area.

During a possible nuclear crisis that was rapidly worsening, or after a nuclear attack, most unprepared Americans could not buy or otherwise obtain a fallout meter -- an instrument that would greatly improve their chances of surviving a nuclear war. The fact that the dangers from fallout radiation -- best expressed in terms of the radiation dose rate, roentgens per hour (R/hr) -- quite rapidly decrease during the first few days, and then decrease more and more slowly, makes it very important to have a fallout meter capable of accurately measuring the unseen, unfelt and changing fallout dangers. Occupants of a fallout shelter should be able to control the radiation doses they receive. In order to effectively control the radiation doses, a dependable measuring instrument is needed to determine the doses they receive while they are in the shelter and while they are outside for emergency tasks, such as going out to get badly needed water. Also, such an instrument would permit them to determine when it is safe to leave the shelter for good.

Untrained families, guided only by these written instructions and using only low cost materials and tools found in most homes, have been able to make a KFM by working 3 or 4 hours. By studying the operating sections of these instructions for about 1 ½ hours, average untrained families have been able to successfully use this fallout meter to measure dose rates and to calculate radiation doses received, permissible times of exposure, etc.

The KFM (Kearny Fallout Meter) was developed at Oak Ridge National Laboratory. It is understandable, easily repairable, and as accurate as most civil defense fallout meters. In the United States in 1979 a commercially available, dependable fallout meter that has as high a range as a KFM for radiation dose-rate measurements retailed for around $1000.

Before a nuclear attack occurs is the best time to build, test and learn how to use a KFM. However, this instrument is so simple that it could be made even after fallout arrives provided that all the materials and tools needed (see lists given in Sections V, VI, and VII) and a copy of these instructions have been carried into the shelter.

II. Survival Work Priorities During a Crisis

Before building a KFM, persons expecting a nuclear attack within a few hours or days and already in the place where they intend to await attack should work with the following priorities: (1) build or improve a high-protection-factor shelter (if possible, a shelter covered with 2 or 3 feet of earth and separate from flammable buildings). At the same time, make and install a KAP (a homemade shelter-ventilating pump) -- if instructions and materials are available. Also store at least 15 gallons of water for each shelter occupant -- if containers are available. (2) Assemble all materials for one or two KFM's. (3) Make and store the drying agent (by heating wallboard gypsum, as later described) for both the KFM and its dry-bucket.

III. How to Use These Instructions to Best Advantage

1. Read ALOUD all of these instructions through Section VII, "Tools Needed," before doing anything else.

2. Next assemble all of the needed materials and tools.

3. Then read ALOUD ALL of each section following Section VII before beginning to make the part described in that section.

A FAMILY THAT FAILS TO READ ALOUD ALL OF EACH SECTION DESCRIBING HOW TO MAKE A PART, BEFORE BEGINNING TO MAKE THAT PART, WILL MAKE AVOIDABLE MISTAKES AND WILL WASTE TIME.

4. Have different workers, or pairs of workers, make the parts they are best qualified to make. For example, a less skilled worker should start making the drying agent (as described in Section VIII) before other workers start making other parts. The most skilled worker should make and install the aluminum-foil leaves (Sections X and XI).

5. Give workers the sections of the instructions covering the parts they are to build--so they can follow the step-by-step instructions, checking off with a pencil each step as it is completed.

6. Discuss the problems that arise. The head of the family often can give better answers if he first discusses the different possible interpretations of some instructions with other family members, including teenagers.

7. After completing one KFM and learning to use it, if time permits make a second KFM--that should be a better instrument.

IV. What a KFM Is and How It Works

A KFM is a simple electroscope fallout meter with which fallout radiation can be measured accurately. To use a KFM, an electrostatic charge must first be placed on its **two** separate aluminum-foil leaves. These leaves are insulated by being suspended separately on clean, dry insulating threads.

To take accurate readings, the air inside a KFM must be kept very dry by means of drying agents such as dehydrated gypsum (easily made by heating gypsum wallboard, "sheetrock") or silica gel. (Do not use calcium chloride or other salt.) Pieces of drying agent are placed on the bottom of the ionization chamber (the housing can) of a KFM.

An electrostatic charge is transferred from a homemade electrostatic charging device to the two aluminum-foil leaves of a KFM by means of its charging-wire. The charging-wire extends out through the transparent plastic cover of the KFM.

When the two KFM leaves are charged electrostatically, their like charges (both positive or both negative) cause them to be forced apart. When fallout radiations (mainly gamma rays, that are similar to X rays but more energetic) penetrate the can and strike the air inside the can, they produce charged ions in this enclosed air. The covered can is an ionization chamber. These enclosed charged ions cause part or all of the electrostatic charge on the aluminum-foil leaves to be discharged. As a result of losing charge, the two KFM leaves move closer together.

To read the separation of the **lower** edges of the two KFM leaves with one eye, look straight down on the leaves and the scale on the clear plastic cover. Keep the reading eye 12 inches above the SEAT. The KFM should be resting on a horizontal surface. To be sure the reading eye is always at this exact distance, place the lower end of a 12-inch ruler on the SEAT, while the upper end of the ruler touches the eyebrow above the reading eye. It is best to hold the KFM with one hand and the ruler with the other. Using a flashlight makes the reading more accurate.

If a KFM is made with the specified dimensions and of the specified materials, its accuracy is automatically and permanently established. Unlike most radiation measuring instruments, a KFM never needs to be calibrated or tested with a radiation source, if made and maintained as specified and used with the following table that is based on numerous calibrations made at Oak Ridge National Laboratory.

The millimeter scale is cut out and attached (see photo illustrations on the following page) to the clear plastic cover of the KFM so that its zero mark is directly above the two leaves in their discharged position when the KFM is resting on a horizontal surface. A reading of the separation of the leaves is taken by noting the number of millimeters that the **lower edge** of one leaf appears to be on, on one side of the zero mark on the scale, and almost at the same time noting the number of millimeters the **lower edge** of the other leaf appears to be on, on the other side of the zero mark. The **sum** of these two apparent positions of the lower edges of the two leaves is called a KFM reading. The drawing appearing after the photo illustrations shows the **lower** edges of the leaves of a KFM appearing to be 9 mm on the right and zero and 10 on the left, giving a KFM reading of 19 mm. (Usually the lower edges of the leaves are not at the same distance from the zero mark.)

As will be fully explained later, the radiation dose rate is determined by:

1. charging and reading the KFM before exposure;

2. exposing it to radiation for a specified time in the location where measurement of the dose rate is needed -- when outdoors, holding the KFM about 3 ft. above the ground;

3. reading the KFM after its exposure;

4. calculating, by subtraction, the **difference** between the reading taken before exposure and the reading taken after exposure;

5. using this table to find what the dose rate was during the exposure -- as will be described later.

Instructions on how to use a KFM are given after those detailing how to make and charge this fallout meter.

TABLE USED TO FIND DOSE RATES (R/HR) FROM KFM READINGS

*DIFFERENCE BETWEEN THE READING BEFORE EXPOSURE AND THE READING AFTER EXPOSURE (8-PLY STANDARD FOIL LEAVES)

DIFF** IN READINGS	TIME INTERVAL OF AN EXPOSURE				
	15 SEC. R/HR	1 MIN. R/HR	4 MIN. R/HR	16 MIN. R/HR	1 HR. R/HR
2 mm	6.2	1.6	0.4	0.1	0.03
4 mm	12.	3.1	0.8	0.2	0.06
6 mm	19.	4.6	1.2	0.3	0.08
8 mm	25.	6.2	1.6	0.4	0.10
10 mm	31.	7.7	2.0	0.5	0.13
12 mm	37.	9.2	2.3	0.6	0.15
14 mm	43.	11.	2.7	0.7	0.18

To get a clearer idea of the construction and use of a KFM, look carefully at the following photos and read their captions.

A. An Uncharged KFM. The charging wire has been pulled to one side by its adjustment-thread. This photo was taken looking straight down at the upper edges of the two flat, 8-ply aluminum leaves. At this angle the leaves are barely visible, hanging vertically side by side directly under the zero mark, touching each other and with their ends even. Their suspension-threads insulate the leaves. These threads are almost parallel and touch (but do not cross) each other where they extend over the top of the rim of the can.

B. Charging a KFM by a Spark-Gap Discharge from a Tape That Has Been Electrostatically Charged by Being Unwound Quickly. Note that the charged tape is moved so that its surface is perpendicular to the charging-wire.

The high-voltage electro-static charge on the un-wound tape (that is an insulator) jumps the spark-gap between the tape and the upper end of the charging-wire, and then flows down the charging-wire to charge the insulated aluminum-foil leaves of the KFM. (Since the upper edges of the two leaves are ¾ inch below the scale and this is a photo taken at an angle, both leaves appear to be under the right side of the scale.)

C. A Charged KFM. Note the separation of the upper edges of its two leaves. The charging-wire has been raised to an almost horizontal position so that its lower end is too far above the aluminum leaves to permit electrical leakage from the leaves back up the charging-wire and into the outside air.

Also note the SEAT, a piece of pencil taped to the right side of the can, opposite the charging wire.

D. Reading a KFM. A 12-inch ruler rests on the SEAT and is held vertical, while the reader's eyebrow touches the upper end of the ruler. The lower edge of the right leaf is under 8 on the scale and the lower edge of the left leaf is under 6 on the scale, giving a KFM reading of 14.

For accurate radiation measurements, a KFM should be placed on an approximately horizontal surface, but the charges on its two leaves and their displacements do not have to be equal.

177

ORNL-DWG 75-11588R

2½-in. ADJUSTMENT THREAD
(NYLON IS BEST)

STICKY PART
OF TAPE

2½-in.
ADJUSTMENT-
THREAD

¼-in. TAPE (VERTICAL)
SNUG TO COVER OF CAN

mm SCALE

¾ in.

2⅝ in.

¾ in.

¼ in.

TAPE COLLAR

TRANSPARENT
PLASTIC COVER

INSULATED WIRE

¼ in.

1 in.

SKIRT OF COVER CUT
SHORTER FOR ½ in.
TO FIT OVER SEAT
ON CAN

¼-in. TAPE
AROUND EDGE
OF SKIRT OF COVER

REMOVABLE TRANSPARENT COVER
AND CHARGING WIRE

TOGGLE
DETAIL

THREAD TIED TO
TOGGLE (SMALL SLIVER
OF WOOD ⅜ in. LONG)

TAPE TOGGLE TO
OUTSIDE OF CAN

⅝ in.   SEAT   ⅝ in.

TOGGLE

TOGGLE
TIED TO
THREAD AND
TAPED SECURE
(SEE DETAIL)

15 10 5 0 5 10 15 mm

STOP-THREAD

⅝ in.   ⅝ in.

TOP VIEW
(COVER AND CHARGING WIRE NOT SHOWN)

RUBBER BAND

mm SCALE

½ in.

2½-in. THREADS
(ENDS NOT SHOWN)

TRANSPARENT PLASTIC COVER
(DETAILS ON LEFT)

¾ in.

1 in.
THREAD

1 in.
THREAD

1⅞ in.

TOGGLE
(SEE
DETAIL)

SEAT
(PIECE OF PENCIL)

1 in.

REGULAR
ALUMINUM FOIL

LEAF (8-PLY)

1½ in.

STOP-
THREAD

HOLE FOR
STOP-
THREAD

ANHYDRITE
CaSO₄

1¼ in.

"HEM"
⅜ in.

2⅞ in. INSIDE

HOLES FOR STOP-THREADS

INSIDE DIAM 2 9/16 in.

BOTTOM OF CAN

1 INCH

(This is not a Full Scale Drawing).

178

V. Materials Needed

A. For the KFM: (In the following list, when more than one alternative material is given, the **best** material is listed first.)

1. Any type metal can, approximately 2-9/16 inches in diameter inside and 2-7/8 inches high inside, washed clean with soap. (This is the size of a standard 8-ounce can. Since most soup cans, pop cans, and beer cans also are about 2-9/16 inches in diameter inside, the required size of can can also be made by cutting down the height of more widely available cans -- as described in Section IX of these instructions.)

2. Standard aluminum foil -- 2 square feet. (In 1977, 2 square feet of a typical American aluminum foil weighed about 8.2 grams -- about 0.29 oz.) (If only "Heavy Duty" or "Extra Heavy Duty" aluminum foil is available, make 5-ply leaves rather than 8-ply leaves of standard foil; the resultant fallout meter will be almost as accurate.)

3. Doorbell-wire, or other light insulated wire (preferably but not necessarily a single-strand wire inside the insulation -- 6 inches.

4. Any type of lightweight thread (preferably but not necessarily nylon). (Best is twisted nylon thread; next best, **unwaxed** lightweight nylon dental floss; next best, silk; next best, polyester.) -- 3 feet. (Thread should be CLEAN, preferably not having been touched with fingers. Monofilament nylon is too difficult to see, handle, and mark.)

5. **A piece of clear plastic -- a 6 x 6 inch square. Clear vinyl (4 mils thick) used for storm-proofing windows is best, but any reasonably stout and rather clear plastic will serve. The strong clear plastic used to wrap pieces of cheese, if washed with hot water and soap, is good. Do not use weak plastic or cellophane. Plastic film made from cellulose (such as Flex-O-Pane) and roasting bags are too permeable to water vapor.**

6. Cloth duct tape ("silver tape"), or masking tape, or freezer tape, or Scotch-type tape -- about 10 square inches. (Save at least 10 feet of Scotch Magic Transparent Tape for the charging device.)

7. Band-Aid tape, or masking tape, or freezer tape, or Scotch transparent tape, or other thin and very flexible tapes -- about 2 square inches.

8. Gypsum wallboard (sheetrock) -- about 1/2 square foot, best about 1/2 inch thick. (To make the essential drying agent.)

9. Glue -- not essential, but useful to replace Band-Aid and other thin tapes. "One hour" epoxy is best. Model airplane cement is satisfactory.

10. An ordinary wooden pencil and a small toothpick (or split a small sliver of wood).

11. Two strong rubber bands, or string.

12. Several small, transparent plastic bags, such as sandwich bags, to cover the KFM when it is exposed where fallout particles may get on it and contaminate it. Or pieces of thin, transparent plastic film, such as that from bread bags. Also small rubber bands, or string.

B. For the Charging Devices:

1. Most hard plastic rubbed on **dry** paper. This is the best method.

   a. Plexiglas and most other hard plastics, such as are used in draftsmen's triangles, common smooth plastic rulers, etc. -- at least 6 inches long.

   b. **Dry** paper -- **Smooth** writing or typing paper. Tissue paper, newspaper, or facial tissue such as Kleenex, or toilet paper are satisfactory for charging, but not as durable.

2. Scotch Magic Transparent Tape (3/4 inch width is best), or Scotch Transparent Tape, or P.V.C. (Polyvinyl chloride) insulating electrical tapes, or a few of the other common brands of Scotch-type tapes. (Some plastic tapes do not develop sufficiently high-voltage electrostatic charges when unrolled quickly.) This method cannot be used for charging a KFM inside a dry-bucket, needed for charging when the air is very humid.

C. For Determining Dose Rates and Recording Doses Received:

1. A watch -- preferably with a second hand.

2. A flashlight or other light, for reading the KFM in a dark shelter or at night.

3. Pencil and paper -- preferably a notebook.

D. For the Dry-Bucket: (A KFM must be charged inside a dry-bucket if the air is very humid, as it often is inside a crowded, long-occupied shelter lacking adequate forced ventilation.)

1. A large bucket, pot, or can, preferably with a top diameter of at least 11 inches.

2. Clear plastic (best is 4-mil-thick clear plastic used for storm windows). A square piece 5 inches wider on a side than the diameter of the bucket to be used.

3. Cloth duct tape, one inch wide and 8 feet long (or 4 ft., if 2 inches wide). Or 16 ft. of freezer tape one inch wide.

VIII. Make the Drying Agent
-- The Easiest Part to Make, but Time Consuming --

1. For a KFM to measure radiation accurately, the air inside its ionization chamber must be kept **very dry**. An excellent drying agent (anhydrite) can be made by heating the gypsum in ordinary gypsum wallboard (sheetrock). Do NOT use calcium chloride.

2. Take a piece of gypsum wallboard approximately 12 inches by 6 inches, and preferably with its gypsum about 3/8 inches thick. Cut off the paper and glue, easiest done by first wetting the paper. [Since water vapor from normal air penetrates the plastic cover of a KFM and can dampen the anhydrite and make it ineffective in as short a time as two days, fresh batches of anhydrite must be made before the attack and kept ready inside the shelter for replacement. The useful life of the drying agent inside a KFM can be greatly lengthened by keeping the KFM inside an airtight container (such as a peanut butter jar with a 4-inch-diameter mouth) with some drying agent, when the KFM is not being used.]

3. Break the white gypsum filling into small pieces and make the largest no more than 1/2 in. across. (The tops of pieces larger than this may be too close to the aluminum foil leaves.) If the gypsum is dry, using a pair of pliers makes breaking it easier. Make the largest **side** of the largest pieces no bigger than this.

4. Dry gypsum is **not** a drying agent. To drive the water out of the gypsum molecules and produce the drying agent (anhydrite), heat the gypsum in an oven at its **highest** temperature (which should be above 400 degrees F) for one hour. Heat the gypsum after placing the small pieces no more than two pieces deep in a pan. Or heat the pieces over a fire for 20 minutes or more in a pan or can heated to a dull red.

5. If sufficient aluminum foil and time are available, it is best to heat the gypsum and store the anhydrite as follows:

   a. So that the right amount of anhydrite can be taken quickly out of its storage jar, put enough pieces of gypsum in a can with the same diameter as the KFM, measuring out a batch of gypsum that almost covers the bottom of the can with a single layer.

   b. Cut a piece of aluminum foil about 8 in. x 8 in. square, and fold up its edges to form a bowl-like container in which to heat one batch of gypsum pieces.

   c. Measure out 10 or 12 such batches, and put each batch in its aluminum foil "bowl."

   d. Heat all of these filled "bowls" of gypsum in hottest oven for one hour.

4. Two plastic bags 14 to 16 inches in circumference, such as ordinary plastic bread bags. The original length of these bags should be at least 5 inches greater than the height of the bucket.

5. About one square foot of wall board (sheetrock), to make anhydrite drying agent.

6. Two 1-quart Mason jars or other airtight containers, one in which to store anhydrite and another in which to keep dry the KFM charging devices.

7. Strong rubber bands -- enough to make a loop around the bucket. Or string.

VI. Useful but not Essential Materials
--Which Could be Obtained Before a Crisis--

1. An airtight container (such as a large peanut butter jar) with a mouth at least 4 inches wide, in which to keep a KFM, along with some drying agent, when it is not being used. Keeping a KFM very dry greatly extends the time during which the drying agent **inside** the KFM remains effective.

2. Commercial anhydrite with a color indicator, such as the drying agent Drierite. This granular form of anhydrite remains light blue as long as it is effective as a drying agent; it turns pink when it becomes ineffective. Heating in a hot oven or in a can over a fire reactivates it as a drying agent and restores its light blue color. Obtainable from laboratory supply sources.

3. Four square feet of aluminum foil, to make a moisture-proof cover for the dry-bucket.

VII. Tools Needed

Small nail - sharpened
Stick, or a wooden tool handle (best 2-2½ inch diameter and at least 12 inches long)
Hammer
Pliers
Scissors
Needle - quite a large sewing needle, but less than 2½ inches long
Knife with a small blade -- sharp
Ruler (12 inches)

TABLE USED TO FIND DOSE RATES (R/HR) FROM KFM READINGS

*DIFFERENCE BETWEEN THE READING BEFORE EXPOSURE AND THE READING AFTER EXPOSURE (8-PLY STANDARD. FOIL LEAVES)

DIFF.* IN READINGS	TIME INTERVAL OF AN EXPOSURE				
	15 SEC. R/HR	1 MIN. R/HR	4 MIN. R/HR	16 MIN. R/HR	1 HR. R/HR
2 mm	6.2	1.6	0.4	0.1	0.03
4 mm	12.	3.1	0.8	0.2	0.06
6 mm	19.	4.6	1.2	0.3	0.08
8 mm	25.	6.2	1.6	0.4	0.10
10 mm	31.	7.7	2.0	0.5	0.13
12 mm	37.	9.2	2.3	0.6	0.15
14 mm	43.	11.	2.7	0.7	0.18

PAPER PATTERN TO WRAP AROUND KFM CAN (GLUE OR TAPE SECURELY TO CAN)

CUT OUT THESE PATTERNS, EACH OF WHICH IS THE EXACT SIZE FOR A KFM.

CAUTION: XEROX COPIES OF THESE PATTERNS WILL BE TOO LARGE.

PATTERN PAGE (A)

PATTERN FOR CLEAR-PLASTIC COVER FOR KFM CAN

POSITION TO ATTACH THE PAPER SCALE TO THE COVER OF CAN, <u>PERPENDICULAR</u> TO THE KFM LEAVES

CENTER LINE BETWEEN THE TWO LEAVES

CUT OUT APPROXIMATELY ALONG THIS LINE

CENTER OF CAN

APPROXIMATE RIM OF CAN

HOLE FOR CHARGING-WIRE

1/2 in.

SAVE THESE PATTERNS FOR PRINTING REPRODUCTIONS OF THE COMPLETE INSTRUCTIONS DURING A POSSIBLE CRISIS. FOR PRE-CRISIS PRACTICE CUT OUT PATTERNS FROM THE TWO EXTRA PATTERN-PAGES AT THE END OF THESE INSTRUCTIONS.

SHORT SIDE
OPEN EDGE
THREAD LINE
8-PLY LEAF
THIRD-FOLD EDGE

LONG SIDE

FINISHED-LEAF PATTERN
(CUT OUT EXACTLY ON SIDE LINES)

PATTERN PAGE (B)

CUT ALONG ENDS OF MARKS ALSO CUT ON THIS LINE

20 15 10 5 O 5 10 15 20

CUT ALONG ENDS OF MARKS ALSO CUT ON THIS LINE

20 15 10 5 O 5 10 15 20

PAPER SCALE (TO BE CUT OUT)

CAUTION: XEROX COPIES OF THE FINISHED-LEAF AND THE SCALE PATTERNS WILL BE SLIGHTLY TOO LARGE.

e. As soon as the aluminum foil is cool enough to touch, fold and crumple the edges of each aluminum foil "bowl" together, to make a rough aluminum-covered "ball" of each batch of anhydrite.

f. Promptly seal the batches in airtight jars or other airtight containers, and keep containers closed except when taking out an aluminum-covered "ball."

6. Since anhydrite absorbs water from the air very rapidly, quickly put it in a **dry** airtight container while it is still quite hot. A Mason jar is excellent.

7. To place anhydrite in a **KFM**, drop in the pieces one by one, being careful not to hit the leaves or the threads. The pieces should almost cover the bottom of the can, with no piece on top of other pieces.

8. To remove anhydrite from a **KFM**, it is best to use a pair of scissors or tweezers as forceps, holding them in a vertical position and not touching the leaves. Or carefully pour the anhydrite out of the can while with your forefinger and thumb you carefully hold the aluminum leaves out of the way. Avoid touching threads.

IX. **Make the Ionization Chamber of the KFM**
(To Avoid Mistakes and Save Time,
Read All of This Section ALOUD Before Beginning Work.)

1. Remove the paper label (if any) from an ordinary 8-ounce can from which the top has been smoothly cut. Wash the can with soap and water and dry it. (An 8-ounce can has an inside diameter of about 2-9/16 inches and an inside height of about 2-7/8 inches.)

2. Skip to step 3 if an 8-ounce can is available. If an 8-ounce can is not available, reduce the height of any other can having an inside diameter of about 2-9/16 inches (such as most soup cans, most pop cans, or most beer cans). To cut off the top part of a can, first measure and mark the line on which to cut. Then to keep from bending the can while cutting, wrap newspaper tightly around a stick or a round wooden tool handle, so that the wood is covered with 20 to 30 thicknesses of paper and the diameter (ideally) is only slightly less than the diameter of the can.

One person should hold the can over the paper-covered stick while a second person cuts the can little by little along the marked cutting line. If leather gloves are available, wear them. To cut the can off smoothly, use a file, or use a hacksaw drawn backwards along the cutting line. Or cut the can with a sharp, short blade of a pocketknife by: (1) repeatedly stabbing downward vertically through the can into the paper, and (2) repeatedly making a cut about 1/4 inch long by moving the knife into a sloping position, while keeping its point still pressed into the paper covering the stick.

Next, smooth the cut edge, and cover it with small pieces of freezer tape or other flexible tape.

3. Cut out the PAPER PATTERN TO WRAP AROUND KFM CAN. (Cut one pattern out of the following Pattern Page A.) Glue (or tape) this pattern to the can, starting with one of the two short sides of the pattern. Secure this starting short side directly over the side seam of the can. Wrap the pattern snugly around the can, gluing or taping it securely as it is being wrapped. (If the pattern is too wide to fit flat between the rims of the can, trim a little off its lower edge.)

4. Sharpen a small nail, by filing or rubbing on concrete, for use as a punch to make the four holes needed to install the stop-threads in the ionization chamber (the can). (The stop-threads are insulators that stop the charged aluminum leaves from touching the can and being discharged.)

5. Have one person hold the can over a horizontal stick or a round wooden tool-handle, that ideally has a diameter about as large as the diameter of the can. Then a second person can use the sharpened nail and a hammer to punch four very small holes through the sides of the can at the points shown by the four crosses on the pattern. Make these holes just large enough to run a needle through them, and then move the needle in the holes so as to bend back the obstructing points of metal.

6. The stop-threads can be installed by using a needle to thread a single thread through all four holes. Use a **very clean** thread, preferably nylon, and do not touch the parts of this thread that will be inside the can and will serve as the insulating stop-threads. Soiled threads are poor insulators. (See illustrations.)

CAN

END OF STICK

PUNCH SMALL HOLE WITH SHARPENED SMALL NAIL

END OF STICK OR WOODEN HANDLE INSIDE CAN

TABLE

THREAD CONTINUES TO NEEDLE

TOGGLE THIS SMALL, TIED ABOUT 1/2 in. FROM CAN; LATER THREAD IS PULLED TIGHT AND TAPED TO SIDE OF CAN

STOP-THREAD

SMALL TOGGLE TIED TO END OF THREAD

TOP VIEW OF CAN

STOP-THREAD

SINGLE THREAD THREADED THROUGH 4 HOLES TO MAKE 2 STOP-THREADS

185

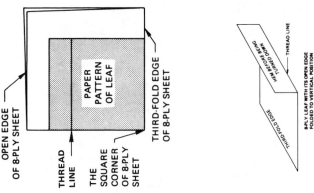

Before threading the thread through the four holes, tie a **small** toggle (see the preceding sketch) to the long end of the thread. (This toggle can easily be made of a very small sliver of wood cut about 3/8 in. long.) After the thread has been pulled through the four holes, attach a second toggle to the thread, about 1/2 inch from the part of the thread that comes out of the fourth hole. Then the thread can be pulled tightly down the side of the can and the second small toggle can be taped securely in place to the side of the can. (If the thread is taped down without a toggle, it is likely to move under the tape.)

The first toggle and all of the four holes also should be covered with tape, to prevent air from leaking into the can after it has been covered and is being used as an ionization chamber.

X. Make Two Separate 8-Ply Leaves of Standard [Not Heavy Duty*] Aluminum Foil

Proceed as follows to make each leaf:

1. Cut out a piece of standard aluminum foil approximately 4 inches by 8 inches.

2. Fold the aluminum foil to make a 2-ply (= 2 thicknesses) sheet approximately 4 inches by 4 inches.

3. Fold this 2-ply sheet to make a 4-ply sheet approximately 2 inches by 4 inches.

4. Fold this 4-ply sheet to make an 8-ply sheet (8 sheets thick) approximately 2 inches by 2 inches, being **sure** that the two halves of the second-fold edge are exactly together. This third folding makes an 8-ply aluminum foil sheet with **one corner exactly square.**

5. **Cut out** the FINISHED-LEAF PATTERN, found on the following Pattern Page B. Note that this pattern is **NOT** a square and that it is **smaller** than the 8-ply sheet. Flatten the 8 thicknesses of aluminum foil with the fingers until they appear to be a single thin, flat sheet.

6. Hold the FINISHED-LEAF PATTERN **on top of** the 8-ply aluminum foil sheet, with the pattern's THIRD-FOLD EDGE on top of the third-fold edge of the 8-ply aluminum sheet. Be sure that one lower **corner** of the FINISHED-LEAF PATTERN is on top of the **exactly square corner** of the 8-ply aluminum sheet.

7. While holding a straight edge along the THREAD LINE of the pattern, press with a sharp pencil so as to make a shallow groove for the THREAD LINE on the 8-ply aluminum sheet. Also using a sharp pencil, trace around the top and side of the pattern, so as to indent (groove) the 8-ply foil.

8. Remove the pattern, and cut out the 8-ply aluminum foil leaf.

9. While holding a straight edge along the indented THREAD LINE, lift up the OPEN EDGE of the 8-ply sheet (keeping all 8 plies together) until this edge is vertical, as illustrated. Remove the straight edge, and fold the 8-ply aluminum along the THREAD LINE so as to make a **flat-folded** hem.

10. Open the flat-folded hem of the finished leaf until the 8-ply leaf is almost flat again, as shown by the FIN-ISHED-LEAF PATTERN, from which the FINISHED-LEAF PATTERN has already been cut.

11. Prepare to attach the aluminum-foil leaf to the thread that will suspend it inside the KFM.

___

*If only heavy duty aluminum foil (sometimes called "extra heavy duty") is available, make 5-ply leaves of the same size, and use the table for the 8-ply KFM to determine radiation dose rates. To make a 5-ply leaf, start by cutting out a piece of foil approximately 4 inches by 4 inches. Fold it to make a 4-ply sheet approximately 2 inches by 2 inches, with one corner exactly square. Next from a single thickness of foil cut a square approximately 2 inches by 2 inches. Slip this square into a 4-ply sheet, thus making a 5-ply sheet. Then make the 5-ply leaf, using the FINISHED-LEAF PATTERN, etc. as described for making an 8-ply leaf.

ORNL-DWG 76-6542

HEM ON OUTSIDE OF LEAF

LEAF-SUSPENDING THREAD

THREAD ON OUTSIDE OF CAN

5 PIECES OF 1/8 IN. × 1/4 IN. BAND-AID TAPE ON EACH LEAF

TAPE STUCK TO END OF THREAD, AND LATER TO CAN

ALUMINUM-FOIL LEAF

8-oz. CAN

8-PLY LEAF

SIDE VIEW

END VIEW

SHOWING THE TWO LEAVES CHARGED (WHEN NOT CHARGED, THE LEAVES HANG PERPENDICULAR AND TOUCHING.)

17. Loosen the sec nd two small pieces of tape from the pattern paper, but leave these tapes stu k to the thread.

18. Cut 5 pieces of Band-Aid tape, each approximately 1/8 inch by 1/4 inch, this small.

Use 2 of these pieces of tape to secure the centers of the side edges of the leaf. Place the 5 pieces as illustrated in the SIDE VIEW sketch below.

*If using epoxy or other glue, use only a **very** little to hold down the hem, to attach the thread securely to the leaf and to glue together any open edges of the plied foil. Most convenient is "one hour" epoxy, applied with a toothpick. Model airplane cement requires hours to harden when applied between sheets of aluminum foil. To make sure no glue stiffens the free thread beyond the upper corners of the finished leaf, put no glue within 1/4 inch of a point where thread will go out from the folded hem of the leaf.

The instructions in step 11 are for persons lacking "one hour" epoxy or the time required to dry other types of glue. Persons using glue instead of tape to attach the leaf to its shield should make appropriate use of the pattern on the following page and of some of the procedures detailed in steps 12 through 18.

If no epoxy glue* is available to hold down the hem and prevent the thread from slipping in the hem, cut two pieces of tape (Band-Aid tape is best; next best is masking or freezer tape; next best, Scotch tape). After first peeling off the paper backing of Band-Aid tape, cut each piece of tape 1/8 inch by 1 inch long. Attach these two pieces of tape to the finished 8-ply aluminum leaf with the sticky sides up, except for their ends. As shown by the pattern on the following pattern page, secure 1/8 inch of one end of a tape strip near one corner of the 8-ply aluminum foil leaf by first turning under this 1/8-inch end; that is, with this end's sticky side down. Then turn under the other 1/8-inch-long end, and attach this end below the THREAD LINE. **Slant** each tape strip as illustrated on Pattern (C).

Be sure you have read through step 18 before you do anything else.

12. Cut an 8-1/2-inch piece of fine, unwaxed, **very clean** thread. (Fine nylon twisted thread, unwaxed extra-fine nylon dental floss, or fine silk thread are best in this order. However, any kind of fine, flexible **clean** thread will do quite well. Nylon monofilament "invisible" thread is an excellent insulator but is too difficult for most people to handle.)

Cut out Pattern (C), the guide sheet used when attaching a leaf to its suspending thread. Then tape Pattern (C) to the top of a work table. Cover the two "TAPE HERE" rectangles on Pattern (C) with pieces of tape, each piece the size of the rectangle. Then cut two other pieces of tape each the same size and use them to **tape the thread ONTO the guide sheet**, on top of the "TAPE HERE" rectangles.

Be very careful **not to touch** the two 1-inch parts of the thread next to the outline of the finished leaf, since oil and dirt even on clean fingers will reduce the electrical insulating value of the thread between the leaf and the top rim of the can.

13. With the thread still taped to the paper pattern and while slightly lifting the thread with a knife tip held under the center of the thread, slip the finished leaf **under** the thread and into position exactly on the top of the leaf outlined on the pattern page. Hold the leaf in this position with two fingers.

14. While keeping the thread straight between its two taped-down ends, lower the thread so that it sticks to the two plastic strips. Then press the thread against the plastic strips.

15. With the point of the knife, hold down the center of the thread against the center of the THREAD LINE of the leaf. Then, with two fingers, carefully fold over the hem and press it almost flat. Be sure that the thread comes out of the corners of the hem. Remove the knife, and press the hem down completely flat against the rest of the leaf.

16. Make **small** marks on the thread at the two points shown on the pattern page. Use a ballpoint pen if available.

187

COVER THE TWO "TAPE HERE" RECTANGLES WITH SAME-SIZED PIECES OF TAPE, IN ORDER TO KEEP FROM TEARING THIS PAPER WHEN REMOVING TWO ADDITIONAL PIECES OF TAPE. THEN, BY PUTTING TWO OTHER PIECES OF TAPE THIS SAME SIZE ON TOP OF THE FIRST TWO PIECES, TAPE THE THREAD ONTO THIS GUIDE SHEET, AND LATER ATTACH A LEAF TO THE TAPED-DOWN THREAD.

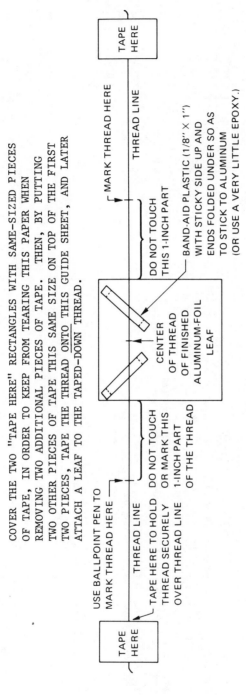

USE BALLPOINT PEN TO MARK THREAD HERE

TAPE HERE

MARK THREAD HERE

THREAD LINE

TAPE HERE TO HOLD THREAD SECURELY OVER THREAD LINE

DO NOT TOUCH OR MARK THIS 1-INCH PART OF THE THREAD

CENTER OF THREAD OF FINISHED ALUMINUM-FOIL LEAF

DO NOT TOUCH THIS 1-INCH PART

BAND-AID PLASTIC (1/8" X 1") WITH STICKY SIDE UP AND ENDS FOLDED UNDER SO AS TO STICK TO ALUMINUM (OR USE A VERY LITTLE EPOXY.)

MARK THREAD HERE

THREAD LINE

TAPE HERE

PATTERN (C)

(Cut out this guide along its border lines and tape to the top of a work table.)

WARNING: The parts of the thread that will be inside the can and on which the leaf will be suspended must serve to insulate the high-voltage electrical charges to be placed on the leaf. Therefore, the suspended parts of the thread must be kept very clean.

XI. Install the Aluminum-Foil Leaves

1. Use the two small pieces of tape stuck to the ends of a leaf-suspending thread to attach the thread to the outside of the can. Attach the tapes on opposite sides of the can, so as to suspend the leaf inside the can. See END VIEW sketch. Each of the two **marks** on the attached thread MUST **rest exactly on the top of the rim of the can**, preferably in two **very small** notches filed in the top of the rim of the can. Each of these two marks on a thread should be positioned exactly above one of the two points shown on the pattern wrapped around the can. Be sure that the hem-side of each of the two leaves faces outward. See END VIEW sketch.

2. Next, the suspending thread of the first leaf should be taped to the top of the rim. Use a piece of Band-Aid only about 1/8 in. x 1/4 in., sticking it to the rim of the can so as barely to cover the thread on the side where the second leaf will be suspended. Make sure no parts of the tapes are inside the can.

3. Position and secure the second leaf, being sure that:

   a. The smooth sides of the two leaves are smooth (not bent) and face each other and are flush (= "right together") when not charged. See END VIEW sketch and study the first photo illustration, "An Uncharged KFM".

   b. The upper edges of the two leaves are suspended side by side and at the same distance below the top of the can.

   c. The leaf-suspending threads are taped with Band-Aid to the top of the rim of the can (so that putting the cover on will not move the threads).

   d. No parts of the leaf-suspending threads inside the can are taped down to the can or otherwise restricted.

   e. The leaf-suspending parts of the threads inside the can do not cross over, entangle or restrict each other.

   f. The threads come together on the top of the rim of the can, and that the leaves are flat and hang together as shown in the first photo illustration, "An Uncharged KFM."

   g. If the leaves do not look like these photographed leaves, make new, better leaves and install them.

4. Cover with tape the parts of the threads that extend down the **outside** of the can, and also cover with more tape the small pieces of tape near the ends of the threads on the outside of the can.

5. To make the SEAT, cut a piece of a wooden pencil, or a stick, about one inch long and tape it securely to the side of the can along the center line marked SEAT on the pattern. Be sure the upper end of this piece of pencil is at the same position as the top of the location for the SEAT outlined on the pattern. The top of the SEAT is 3/4 inch below the top of the can. Be sure not to cover or make illegible any part of the table printed on the paper pattern.

6. Cut out one of the "Reminders for Operators" and glue and/or tape it to the unused side of the KFM. Then it is best to cover all the sides of the finished KFM with clear plastic tape or varnish. This will keep sticky-tape on the end of an adjustment thread or moisture from damaging the "Reminders" or the table.

XII. Make the Plastic Cover

1. Cut out the paper pattern for the cover from the Pattern Page (B).

2. From a piece of clear, strong plastic, cut a circle approximately the same size as the paper pattern. (Storm-window vinyl film, 4 mils thick, is best.)

3. Stretch the center of this circular piece of clear plastic over the open end of the can, and pull it down close to the sides of the can, making small tucks in the "skirt," so that there are no wrinkles in the top cover. Hold the lower part of the "skirt" in place with a strong rubber band or piece of string. (If another can having the same diameter as the KFM can is available, use it to make the cover -- to avoid the possibility of disturbing the leaf-suspending threads.)

4. Make the cover so it fits snugly, but can be taken off and replaced readily.

   Just below the top of the rim of the can, bind the covering plastic in place with a 1/4-inch-wide piece of strong tape. (Cloth duct tape is best. If only freezer or masking tape is available, use two thicknesses.)

   Keep vertical the small part of the tape that presses against the rim of the can while pulling the length of the tape horizontally around the can so as to bind the top of the plastic cover snugly to the rim. If this small part of the tape is kept vertical, the lower edge of the tape will not squeeze the plastic below the rim of the can to such a small circumference as to prevent the cover from being removed quite easily.

COVER (CLEAR PLASTIC)

INSIDE OF CAN

KEEP THIS SMALL PART OF THE 1/4 IN. TAPE VERTICAL WHILE PULLING TAPE AROUND RIM OF CAN

RUBBER BAND OR STRING

EDGE OF PLASTIC COVER

REMINDERS FOR OPERATORS

THE DRYING AGENT INSIDE A KFM IS O.K. IF WHEN THE CHARGED KFM IS NOT EXPOSED TO RADIATION, ITS READINGS DECREASE BY 1 MM OR LESS IN 3 HOURS.

READING: WITH THE READING EYE 12 INCHES VERTICALLY ABOVE THE SEAT, NOTE ON THE MM SCALE THE SEPARATION OF THE LOWER EDGES OF THE LEAVES. IF THE RIGHT LEAF IS AT 10 MM AND THE LEFT LEAF IS AT 7 MM, THE KFM READS 17 MM. NEVER TAKE A READING WHILE A LEAF IS TOUCHING A STOP-THREAD; NEVER USE A KFM READING THAT IS LESS THAN 5MM.

FINDING A DOSE RATE: IF BEFORE EXPOSURE A KFM READS 17 MM AND IF AFTER A 1-MINUTE EXPOSURE IT READS 5 MM, THE DIFFERENCE IN READINGS IS 12 MM. THE ATTACHED TABLE SHOWS THE DOSE RATE WAS 9.6 R/HR DURING THE EXPOSURE.

FINDING A DOSE: IF A PERSON WORKS OUTSIDE FOR 3 HOURS WHERE THE DOSE RATE IS 2 R/HR, WHAT IS HIS RADIATION DOSE? ANSWER: 3 HR x 2 R/HR = 6 R.

FINDING HOW LONG IT TAKES TO GET A CERTAIN R DOSE: IF THE DOSE RATE IS 1.6 R/HR OUTSIDE AND A PERSON IS WILLING TO TAKE A 6 R DOSE, HOW LONG CAN HE REMAIN OUTSIDE? ANSWER: 6 R ÷ 1.6 R/HR = 3.75 HR = 3 HOURS AND 45 MINUTES.

FALLOUT RADIATION GUIDES FOR A HEALTHY PERSON NOT PREVIOUSLY EXPOSED TO A TOTAL RADIATION DOSE OF MORE THAN 100 R DURING A 2-WEEK PERIOD:

6 R PER DAY CAN BE TOLERATED FOR UP TO TWO MONTHS WITHOUT LOSING THE ABILITY TO WORK.

100 R IN A WEEK OR LESS IS NOT LIKELY TO SERIOUSLY SICKEN.

350 R IN A FEW DAYS IS LIKELY TO PROVE FATAL UNDER POST-ATTACK CONDITIONS.

600 R IN A WEEK OR LESS IS ALMOST CERTAIN TO CAUSE DEATH WITHIN A FEW WEEKS.

REMINDERS FOR OPERATORS

THE DRYING AGENT INSIDE A KFM IS O.K. IF WHEN THE CHARGED KFM IS NOT EXPOSED TO RADIATION, ITS READINGS DECREASE BY 1 MM OR LESS IN 3 HOURS.

READING: WITH THE READING EYE 12 INCHES VERTICALLY ABOVE THE SEAT, NOTE ON THE MM SCALE THE SEPARATION OF THE LOWER EDGES OF THE LEAVES. IF THE RIGHT LEAF IS AT 10 MM AND THE LEFT LEAF IS AT 7 MM, THE KFM READS 17 MM. NEVER TAKE A READING WHILE A LEAF IS TOUCHING A STOP-THREAD; NEVER USE A KFM READING THAT IS LESS THAN 5MM.

FINDING A DOSE RATE: IF BEFORE EXPOSURE A KFM READS 17 MM AND IF AFTER A 1-MINUTE EXPOSURE IT READS 5 MM, THE DIFFERENCE IN READINGS IS 12 MM. THE ATTACHED TABLE SHOWS THE DOSE RATE WAS 9.6 R/HR DURING THE EXPOSURE.

FINDING A DOSE: IF A PERSON WORKS OUTSIDE FOR 3 HOURS WHERE THE DOSE RATE IS 2 R/HR, WHAT IS HIS RADIATION DOSE? ANSWER: 3 HR x 2 R/HR = 6 R.

FINDING HOW LONG IT TAKES TO GET A CERTAIN R DOSE: IF THE DOSE RATE IS 1.6 R/HR OUTSIDE AND A PERSON IS WILLING TO TAKE A 6 R DOSE, HOW LONG CAN HE REMAIN OUTSIDE? ANSWER: 6 R ÷ 1.6 R/HR = 3.75 HR = 3 HOURS AND 45 MINUTES.

FALLOUT RADIATION GUIDES FOR A HEALTHY PERSON NOT PREVIOUSLY EXPOSED TO A TOTAL RADIATION DOSE OF MORE THAN 100 R DURING A 2-WEEK PERIOD:

6 R PER DAY CAN BE TOLERATED FOR UP TO TWO MONTHS WITHOUT LOSING THE ABILITY TO WORK.

100 R IN A WEEK OR LESS IS NOT LIKELY TO SERIOUSLY SICKEN.

350 R IN A FEW DAYS IS LIKELY TO PROVE FATAL UNDER POST-ATTACK CONDITIONS.

600 R IN A WEEK OR LESS IS ALMOST CERTAIN TO CAUSE DEATH WITHIN A FEW WEEKS.

EXACT SIZE

**Labels (left diagram):**

BARE-ENDED ADJUSTMENT-THREAD

FINGER HOLD

1/4 IN.

1/4 IN.

END OF 2-1/2 IN. THREAD

3/4 IN. SQUARE

STICKY-ENDED ADJUSTMENT-THREAD (ACTUAL SIZE)

2 INCHES

BARE WIRE

BAND-AID TAPE

2-1/2 INCHES TO END

BAND-AID-TAPE STOP

INSULATION

BARE WIRE

TIE POINT FOR ONE THREAD WHOSE TWO-ENDS ARE THE ADJUSTMENT-THREADS

TAPE SECURELY

INSULATION

THIS PART GOES INSIDE THE KFM CAN

CHARGING-WIRE

(= LIGHT INSULATED WIRE)
(BELL-WIRE IS BEST)

STICKY—ENDED ADJUSTMENT—THREAD (OVERSIZED DRAWING)

**Labels (right diagram):**

FINGER HOLD MADE OF $\frac{3}{4}$ BY $1\frac{1}{4}$ TAPE

STICKY SIDE DOWN

$\frac{1}{8}$

$\frac{3}{4}$ SQUARE

$\frac{3}{4}$

FINGER HOLD

$\frac{1}{8}$

$\frac{3}{4}$

$3''$ SQUARE

END

THREAD

THREAD HELD BY $\frac{1}{8}''$ BY $\frac{3}{4}$ TAPE STUCK TO STICKY SIDE OF $\frac{3}{4}''$ BY $\frac{3}{4}''$ TAPE.

---

5. With scissors, cut off the "skirt" of the plastic cover until it extends only about one inch below the top of the rim of the can.

6. Make a notch in the "skirt," about one inch wide, where it fits over the pencil SEAT attached to the can. The "skirt" in this notched area should be only about 5/8 of an inch long, measured down from the top of the rim of the can.

7. Remove the plastic cover, and then tape the lower edges of the "skirt," inside and out, using short lengths of 1/4-inch-wide tape. Before securing each short piece of tape, slightly open the tucks that are being taped shut on their edges, so that the "skirt" flares slightly outward and the cover can be readily removed.

8. Put the plastic cover on the KFM can. From the Pattern Page (B) cut out the SCALE. Then tape the SCALE to the top of the plastic cover, in the position shown on the pattern for the cover, and also by the drawings. Preferably use transparent tape.

   Be careful not to cover with tape any of the division lines on the SCALE between 20 on the right and 20 on the left of 0.

9. Make the charging-wire by following the pattern given below which is **exactly the right size.**

   Doorbell wire with an outside diameter of about 1/16 inch is best, but any lightweight insulated wire, such as part of a lightweight two-wire extension cord split in half, will serve. The illustrated wire is much thicker than bell wire. To stop tape from possibly slipping up or down the wire, use a very little glue.

   If a very thin plastic has been used for the cover, a sticky piece of tape may need to be attached to the end of the bare-ended adjustment thread, so both threads can be used to hold the charging wire in a desired position.

   The best tape to attach to an end of one of the adjustment-threads is cloth duct tape. A square piece 3/4 inch by 3/4 inch is the sticky base. To keep this tape sticky (free of paper fibers), the paper on the can should be covered with transparent tape or varnish. A piece about 1/8 inch by 3/4 inch serves to stick under one end of the sticky base, to hold the adjustment-thread. A 3/4 inch by 1-1/4 inch rectangular piece of tape is used to make the finger hold -- important for making adjustments inside a dry-bucket.

   With a needle or pin, make a hole in the plastic cover 1/2 inch from the rim of the can and directly above the upper end of the CENTER LINE between the two leaves. The CENTER LINE is marked on the pattern wrapped around the can. Carefully push the CHARGING-WIRE through this hole (thus stretching the hole) until all of the CHARGING-WIRE below its Band-Aid-tape stop is inside the can.

191

XIII. Two Ways to Charge a KFM

When preparing to charge a KFM, be sure its anhydrite is fresh. (Under humid conditions, sometimes in only 2 days enough water vapor will go through the plastic cover to make the drying agent ineffective.) Be sure no piece of anhydrite is on top of another piece. Re-read VIII 7 and VIII 8.

1. Charging a KFM with Hard Plastic Rubbed on **Dry Paper.**

a. Adjust the charging-wire so that its lower end is about 1/16 inch above the upper edges of the aluminum-foil leaves. Use the sticky-tape at the end of one adjustment-thread to hold the charging-wire in this position. Stick this tape approximately in line with the threads suspending the leaves, either on the side of the can or on top of the plastic cover. (If the charging-wire is held loosely by the cover, it may be necessary to put a piece of sticky-tape on the end of each adjustment-thread in order to adjust the charging-wire securely. If a charging-wire is not secure, its lower end may be forced up by the like charge on the leaves before the leaves can be fully charged.)

b. Select a piece of Plexiglas, a draftsman's plastic triangle, a smooth plastic ruler, or other piece of hard, smooth plastic. (Unfortunately, not all types of hard plastic can be used to generate a sufficient electrostatic charge.) Be sure the plastic is dry.

For charging a KFM inside a dry-bucket, cut a rectangular piece of hard plastic about 1-1/2 by 5 inches. Sharp corners and edges can be smoothed by rubbing on concrete. To avoid contaminating the charging end with sweaty, oily fingers, it is best to mark the other end with a piece of tape.

c. Fold **DRY** paper (typing paper, writing paper, or other smooth, clean paper) to make an approximate square about 4 inches on a side and about 20 sheets thick. (This many sheets of paper lessens leakage to the fingers of the electrostatic charges to be generated on the hard plastic and on the rubbed paper.)

d. Fold the square of paper in the middle, and move the hard plastic rapidly back and forth so that it is rubbed **vigorously** on the paper in the middle of this folded square -- while the outside of this folded square of paper is squeezed firmly between thumb and the ends of **two** fingers. To avoid discharging the charge on the plastic to the fingers, keep them away from the edges of the paper. See photo.

e. Move the electrostatically charged part of the rubbed plastic rather slowly past the upper end of the charging-wire, while looking straight down on the KFM. Keep the hard plastic approximately perpendicular to the charging-wire and about 1/4 to 1/2 inch away from its upper end. The charge jumps the spark gaps and charges the leaves of the KFM.

f. Pull down on an insulating adjustment-thread to raise the lower end of the charging-wire. (If the charging-wire has been held in its charging position by its sticky-ended adjustment-thread being stuck to the top of the clear plastic cover, to avoid possibly damaging the threads: (1) pull down a little on the bare-ended adjustment-thread; and (2) detach, pull down on, and secure the sticky-ended adjustment-thread to the side of the can, so as to raise and keep the lower end of the charging-wire close to the underside of the clear plastic cover.) **Do not touch the charging-wire.**

g. Put the charging paper and the hard plastic in a container where they will be kept dry -- as in a Mason jar with some drying agent.

2. Charging a KFM from a Quickly Unwound Roll of Tape. (Quick unwinding produces a harmless charge of several thousand volts on the tape.)

a. Adjust the charging-wire so that its lower end is about 1/16 inch above the upper edges of the aluminum-foil leaves. Use the sticky-tape at the end of one adjustment-thread to hold the charging-wire in this position. Stick this tape approximately in line with the leaves, either on the side of the can or on the plastic cover. (If the plastic cover is weak, it may be necessary to put a piece of sticky-tape on the end of each adjustment-thread, in order to hold the charging-wire securely. If a charging-wire is not secure, its lower end may be forced up by the like charge on the leaves before the leaves can be fully charged.)

b. The sketch shows the "GET SET" position, preparatory to unrolling the Scotch Magic Transparent Tape, P.V.C. electrical tape, or other tape. Be sure to first remove the roll from its dispenser. Some of the other kinds of tape will not produce a high enough voltage.

c. **QUICKLY** unroll 10 to 12 inches of tape by pulling its end with the left hand, while the right hand allows the roll to unwind while remaining in about the same "GET SET" position only an inch or two away from the KFM.

d. While holding the unwound tape tight, about perpendicular to the charging-wire, and about 1/4 inch away from the end of the charging-wire, **promptly** move both hands and the tape to the right **rather slowly** -- taking about 2 seconds to move about 8 inches. The electrostatic charge on the unwound tape "jumps" the spark gaps from the tape to the upper end of the charging-wire and from the lower end of the charging-wire to the aluminum leaves, and charges the aluminum leaves.

Be sure neither leaf is touching a stop-thread.

Try to charge the leaves enough to spread them far enough apart to give a reading of at least 15 mm.

e. Pull down on an insulating adjustment-thread to raise the lower end of the charging-wire. If the charging-wire has been held in charging position by its sticky-ended adjustment-thread being stuck to the top of the clear plastic cover, it is best first to pull down a little on the bare-ended adjustment-thread, and then to move, pull down on, and secure the sticky-ended adjustment-thread to the side of the can so that the lower part of the charging-wire is close to the underside of the clear plastic cover.

Do not touch the charging-wire.

"GET SET" POSITION

TRANSFERRING CHARGE

¼ in. SPARK GAP

f. Rewind the tape **tight** on its roll, for future use when other tape may not be available.

If charging does not separate the two leaves sufficiently, take these corrective actions:

1. Be sure the pieces of anhydrite in the bottom of the ionization chamber (the can) are in a single layer, with no piece on top of another and the top of no piece more than ½ inch above the bottom of the can.

2. Check to be sure that the threads suspending the leaves are not crossed; then try to charge the KFM again.

3. If the KFM still cannot be charged, replace the used anhydrite with fresh anhydrite.

4. If you cannot charge a KFM when the air is very humid, charge it inside its dry-bucket.

5. If you cannot charge a KFM while in an area of heavy fallout, take it to the place affording the best protection against radiation, and try to charge it there. (A dose rate of several hundred R/hr will neutralize the charges on both the charging device and the instrument so rapidly that a KFM cannot be charged.)

If a KFM or other radiation measuring instrument gives unexpectedly high readings inside a good shelter, wipe all dust off the outside of the instrument and repeat the radiation-measurements. Especially when exposing a fallout meter outdoors where there is fresh fallout, keep the instrument in a lidded pot, plastic bag, or other covering to avoid the possibility of having it contaminated with fallout particles and afterwards getting erroneously high radiation measurements.

3/4 in.

A CENTER PIECE ABOUT 1 1/2 in. BY 1 in. IS FIRST CUT OUT OF THE CLEAR PLASTIC COVER. THEN CUTS ARE MADE TO PRODUCE FLAPS, INDICATED BY THE DOTTED LINES.

FLAPS BEFORE BEING TURNED UP TO VERTICAL POSITION, BEFORE TAPING

1 in.

2 3/4 in.

3 3/4 in.

90°

1 in.

2 3/4 in.

3 3/4 in.

XIV. Make and Use a Dry-Bucket

By charging a KFM while it is inside a dry-bucket with a transparent plastic cover (see illustration), this fallout meter can be charged and used even if the relative humidity is 100% outside the dry-bucket. The air inside the dry-bucket is kept very dry by a drying agent placed on its bottom. About a cupful of anhydrite serves very well. The pieces of this dehydrated gypsum need not be as uniform in size as is best for use inside a KFM, but do not use powdered anhydrite.

A dry-bucket can be readily made in about an hour by proceeding as follows:

1. Remove the handle of a large bucket, pot, or can preferably with a top diameter of at least 11 inches. A 4-gallon bucket having a top diameter of about 14 inches and a depth of about 9 inches is ideal. A plastic tub approximately this size is satisfactory. If the handle-supports interfere with stretching a piece of clear plastic film across the top of the bucket, remove them, being sure no sharp points remain.

2. Cut out a circular piece of clear plastic with a diameter about 5 inches larger than the diameter of the top of the bucket. Clear vinyl 4 mils thick, used for storm windows, etc., is best. Stretch the plastic smooth across the top of the bucket, and tie it in place, preferably with strong rubber bands looped together to form a circle.

3. Make a plastic top that fits snugly but is easily removable, by taping over and around the plastic just below the top of the bucket. One-inch-wide cloth duct tape, or one-inch-wide glass-reinforced strapping tape, serves well. When taping, do not permit the lower edge of the tape to be pulled inward below the rim of the bucket.

194

4. Cut two small holes (about 1 inch by 2 inches) in the plastic cover, as illustrated. Then make the radial cuts (shown by dotted lines) outward from the small holes, out to the solid-line outlines of the 3 inch by 4 inch hand-holes, so as to form small flaps.

5. Fold the small flaps upward, so they are vertical. Then tape them on their outer sides, so they form a vertical "wall" about 3/4 inch high around each hand-hole.

6. Reduce the length of two ordinary plastic bread bags (or similar plastic bags) to a length that is 5 inches greater than the height of the bucket. (Do not use rubber gloves in place of bags; gloves so used result in much more humid outside air being unintentionally pumped into a dry-bucket when it is being used while charging a KFM inside it.)

7. Insert a plastic bag into each hand-hole, and fold the edge of the plastic bag about 1/2 inch over the taped vertical "wall" around each hand-hole.

8. Strengthen the upper parts of the plastic bags by folding 2-inch pieces of tape over the top of the "wall" around each hand-hole.

9. Make about a quart of anhydrite by heating small pieces of wall-board gypsum, and keep this anhydrite dry in a Mason jar or other airtight container with a rubber or plastic sealer.

10. Make a circular aluminum-foil cover to place over the plastic cover when the dry-bucket is not being used for minutes to hours. Make this cover with a diameter about 4 inches greater than the diameter of the top of the bucket, and make it fit more snugly with an encircling loop of rubber bands, or with string. Although not essential, an aluminum-foil cover reduces the amount of water vapor that can reach and pass through the plastic cover, thus extending the life of the drying agent.

11. Charge a KFM inside a dry-bucket by:

a. Taking off wrist watch and sharp-pointed rings that might tear the plastic bags.

b. Placing inside the dry-bucket:

(1) About a cup of anhydrite or silica gel;
(2) the KFM, with its charging-wire adjusted in its charging position; and
(3) dry, folded paper and the electrostatic charging device, best a 5-inch-long piece of Plexiglas with smoothed edges, to be rubbed between dry paper folded about 4 inches square and about 20 sheets thick. (Unrolling a roll of tape inside a dry-bucket is an impractical charging method.)

c. Replacing the plastic cover, that is best held in place with a loop of rubber bands.

d. Charging the KFM with your hands inside the plastic bags, operating the charging device. Have another person illuminate the KFM with a flashlight. When adjusting the charging-wire, move your hands very slowly. See the dry-bucket photos.

12. Expose the KFM to fallout radiation either by:

a. Leaving the KFM inside the dry-bucket while exposing it to fallout radiation for one of the listed time intervals, and reading the KFM before and after the exposure while it remains inside the dry-bucket. (The reading eye should be a measured 12 inches above the SEAT of the KFM, and a flashlight or other light should be used.)

b. Taking the charged KFM out of the dry-bucket to read it, expose it, and read it after the exposure. (If this is done repeatedly, especially in a humid shelter, the drying agent will not be effective for many KFM chargings, and will have to be replaced.)

XV. **How to Use a KFM after a Nuclear Attack**

A. Background Information

If during a rapidly worsening crisis threatening nuclear war you are in the place where you plan to take shelter, postpone studying the instructions following this sentence until after you have:

(1) built or improved a high-protection-factor shelter (if possible, a shelter covered with 2 or 3 ft of earth and separate from flammable buildings), and

(2) made a KAP (homemade shelter-ventilating pump) if you have the instructions and materials, and

(3) stored at least 15 gallons of water for each shelter occupant if you can obtain containers.

Having a KFM or any other dependable fallout meter and knowing how to operate it will enable you to minimize radiation injuries and possible fatalities, especially by skillfully using a high-protection-factor fallout shelter to control and limit exposures to radiation. By studying this section you first will learn how to measure radiation dose rates (roentgens per hour = R/hr), how to calculate doses [R] received in different time intervals, and how to determine time intervals (hours and/or minutes) in which specified doses would be received. Then this section lists the sizes of doses (number of R) that the average person can tolerate without being sickened, that he is likely to survive, and that he is likely to be killed by.

Most fortunately for the future of all living things, the decay of radioactivity causes the sandlike fallout particles to become less and less dangerous with the passage of time. Each fallout particle acts much like a tiny X ray machine would if it were made so that its rays, shooting out from it like invisible light, became weaker and weaker with time.

Contrary to exaggerated accounts of fallout dangers, the radiation dose rate from fallout particles when they reach the ground in the areas of the heaviest fallout will decrease quite rapidly. For example, consider the decay of fallout from a relatively nearby, large surface burst, at a place where the fallout particles are deposited on the ground one hour after the explosion. At this time one hour after the explosion, assume that the radiation dose rate (the best measure of radiation danger at a particular time) measures 2,000 roentgens per hour (2,000 R/hr) outdoors. Seven hours later the dose rate is reduced to 200 R/hr by normal radioactive decay. Two days after the explosion, the dose rate outdoors is reduced by radioactive decay to 20 R/hr. After two weeks, the dose rate is less than 2 R/hr. When the dose rate is 2 R/hr, people can go out of a good shelter and work outdoors for 3 hours a day, receiving a daily dose of 6 roentgens, without being sickened.

In places where fallout arrives several hours after the explosion, the radioactivity of the fallout will have gone through its time period of most rapid decay while the fallout particles were still airborne. If you are in a location so distant from the explosion that fallout arrives 8 hours after the explosion, two days must pass before the initial dose rate measured at your location will decay to 1/10 its initial intensity.

B. Finding the Dose Rate

1. Reread Section IV, "What a KFM Is and How it Works." Also reread Section XIII, "Two Ways to Charge a KFM," and actually do each step immediately after reading it.

2. Charge the KFM, raise the lower end of its charging-wire and read the apparent separation of the lower edges of its leaves while the KFM rests on an approximately horizontal surface. Never take a reading while a leaf is touching a stop-thread.

3. To prevent possible contamination of a KFM (or of any other fallout meter) with fallout particles, keep it inside a plastic bag or other covering when there is risk of fallout particles being deposited or blown onto it. An instrument contaminated with fallout particles can give too high readings, especially of the low dose-rate measurements made inside a good shelter.

4. Expose the KFM to fallout radiation for one of the time intervals shown in the vertical columns of the table attached to the KFM. (Study the following table.) If the dose rate is not known even approximately, first expose the fully charged KFM for one minute. For dependable measurements outdoors, expose the charged KFM about 3 feet above the ground. The longer outdoor exposures usually are best made by attaching the KFM with 2 strong rubber bands to a stick or pole, being careful never to tilt the KFM too much.

5. Read the KFM after the exposure, while the KFM rests on an approximately horizontal surface.

6. Find the time interval that gives a dependable reading -- by exposing the fully charged KFM for one or more of the listed time intervals until the reading after the exposure is;

   (a) Not less than 5 mm.

   (b) At least 2 mm less than the reading before the exposure.

7. Calculate by simple subtraction the difference in the apparent separation of the lower edges of the leaves before the exposure and after the exposure. An example: If the reading before the exposure is 18 mm and the reading after the exposure is 6 mm, the difference in readings is 18 mm - 6 mm = 12 mm.

8. If an exposure results in a difference in readings of less than 2 mm, recharge the KFM and expose it again for one of the longer time intervals listed. (If there appears to be no difference in the readings taken before and after an exposure for one minute, this does not prove there is absolutely no fallout danger.)

9. If an exposure results in the reading after the exposure being less than 5 mm, recharge the KFM and expose it again for one of the shorter time intervals listed.

10. Use the table attached to the KFM to find the dose rate (R/hr) during the time of exposure. The dose rate (R/hr) is found at the intersection of the vertical column of numbers under the time interval used and of the horizontal line of numbers that lists the calculated difference in readings at its left end.

    An example: If the time interval of the exposure was 1 MIN. and the difference

TABLE USED TO FIND DOSE RATES (R)/HR. FROM KFM READINGS

DIFF. IN READINGS *DIFFERENCE BETWEEN THE READING BEFORE EXPOSURE AND THE READING AFTER EXPOSURE IS AT STANDARD FOIL LEAVES	TIME INTERVAL OF AN EXPOSURE				
	15 SEC R/HR	1 MIN R/HR	4 MIN R/HR	16 MIN R/HR	1 HR. R/HR
2 mm	6.2	1.6	0.4	0.1	0.03
4 mm	12.	3.1	0.8	0.2	0.06
6 mm	19.	4.6	1.2	0.3	0.08
8 mm	25.	6.2	1.6	0.4	0.10
10 mm	31.	7.7	2.0	0.5	0.13
12 mm	37.	9.2	2.3	0.6	0.15
14 mm	43.	11.	2.7	0.7	0.18

ORNL-DWG 76-6535

PATTERN PAGE (A)

PAPER PATTERN TO WRAP AROUND KFM CAN (GLUE OR TAPE SECURELY TO CAN)

CUT OUT THESE PATTERNS, EACH OF WHICH IS THE EXACT SIZE FOR A KFM.

CAUTION: XEROX COPIES OF THESE PATTERNS WILL BE TOO LARGE.

TABLE USED TO FIND DOSE RATES (R/HR)
FROM KFM READINGS

*DIFFERENCE BETWEEN THE READING BEFORE EXPOSURE AND THE READING AFTER EXPOSURE (8-PLY STANDARD FOIL LEAVES)

DIFF.* IN READINGS	TIME INTERVAL OF AN EXPOSURE				
	15 SEC. R/HR	1 MIN. R/HR	4 MIN. R/HR	16 MIN. R/HR	1 HR. R/HR
2 mm	6.2	1.6	0.4	0.1	0.03
4 mm	12.	3.1	0.8	0.2	0.06
6 mm	19.	4.6	1.2	0.3	0.08
8 mm	25.	6.2	1.6	0.4	0.10
10 mm	31.	7.7	2.0	0.5	0.13
12 mm	37.	9.2	2.3	0.6	0.15
14 mm	43.	11.	2.7	0.7	0.18

197

PATTERN FOR CLEAR-PLASTIC COVER FOR KFM CAN

POSITION TO ATTACH
THE PAPER SCALE TO
THE COVER OF CAN,
<u>PERPENDICULAR</u> TO
THE KFM LEAVES

CENTER LINE BETWEEN
THE TWO LEAVES

CUT OUT ALONG THIS LINE

CENTER
OF CAN

APPROXIMATE RIM OF CAN

HOLE FOR
CHARGING-
WIRE

1/2 in.

CUT OUT APPROXIMATELY ALONG THIS LINE

SAVE THESE PATTERNS FOR PRINTING REPRODUCTIONS OF THE COMPLETE INSTRUCTIONS
DURING A POSSIBLE CRISIS. FOR PRE-CRISIS PRACTICE CUT OUT PATTERNS FROM THE TWO
EXTRA PATTERN-PAGES AT THE END OF THESE INSTRUCTIONS.

SHORT SIDE

| OPEN EDGE |
| THREAD LINE |
| 8-PLY LEAF |
| THIRD-FOLD EDGE |

LONG SIDE

FINISHED-LEAF PATTERN
CUT OUT EXACTLY ON SIDE LINES)

PATTERN PAGE (B)

CUT ALONG
ENDS OF MARKS
ALSO CUT ON
THIS LINE

20 15 10 5 0 5 10 15 20

CUT ALONG
ENDS OF MARKS
ALSO CUT ON
THIS LINE

20 15 10 5 0 5 10 15 20

PAPER SCALE (TO BE CUT OUT)

CAUTION: XEROX COPIES OF THE FINISHED-LEAF AND THE
SCALE PATTERNS WILL BE SLIGHTLY TOO LARGE.

table shows that the **dose rate** during the time interval of the exposure was **9.2 R/HR** (9.2 roentgens per hour).

Another example: If the time interval of the exposure was **15 SEC.** and the difference in readings was **11 mm,** the table shows that the dose rate during the exposure was halfway between **31 R/HR** and **37 R/HR** that is, the **dose rate** was 34 R/hr.

11. Note in the table that if an exposure for one of the listed time intervals causes the **difference** in readings to be 2 mm or 3 mm, then an exposure 4 times as long reveals the same dose rate. An example: IF a 1 - min exposure results in a difference in readings of 2 mm, the table shows the dose rate was 1.6 R/hr; then if the KFM is exposed for 4 minutes at this same dose rate of 1.6 R/hr, the table shows that the resultant difference in readings is 8 mm.

The longer exposure results in a more accurate determination of the dose rate.

12. If the dose rate is found to be greater than 0.2 R/hr and time is available, recharge the KFM and repeat the dose-rate measurement -- to avoid possible mistakes.

C. Calculating the **Dose Received**

The **dose** of fallout radiation -- that is, the **amount** of fallout radiation received -- determines the harmful effects on men and animals. Being exposed to a high **dose rate** is not always dangerous -- provided the exposure is short enough to result in only a small **dose** being received. For example, if the **dose rate** outside an excellent fallout shelter is 1200 R/hr and a shelter occupant goes outside for 30 seconds, he would be exposed for 1/2 of 1 minute, or 1/2 of 1/60 of an hour, which equals 1/120 hour. Therefore, since the dose he would receive if he stayed outside for 1 hour would be 1200 R, in 30 seconds he would receive 1/120 of 1200, which equals 10 R (1200 R divided by 120 = 10 R). A total daily **dose** of 10 R (10 roentgens) will not cause any symptoms if it is not repeated day after day for a week or more.

In contrast, if the average dose rate of an area were found to be 12 R/hr and if a person remained exposed in that particular area for 24 hours, he would receive a **dose** of 288 R (12 R/hr x 24 hr = 288 R). Even assuming that this person had been exposed previously to very little radiation, there would still be a serious risk that this 288 **R dose** would be fatal under the difficult conditions that would follow a heavy nuclear attack.

Another example: Assume that three days after an attack the occupants of a dry, hot cave giving almost complete protection against fallout are in desperate need of water. The dose rate outside is found to be 20 R/hr. To backpack water from a source 3 miles away is estimated to take 2-1/2 hours. The cave occupants estimate that the water backpackers will receive a dose in 2-1/2 hours of 50 R (2.5 hr x 20 R/hr = 50 R). A dose of 50 R will cause only mild symptoms (nausea in about 10% of persons receiving a 50 R dose) for persons who previously have received only very small doses. Therefore, one of the cave occupants makes a rapid radiation survey for about 1-1/2 miles along the proposed route, stopping to charge and read a KFM about every quarter of a mile. He finds no dose rates much higher than 20 R/hr.

So, the cave occupants decide the risk is small enough to justify some of them leaving shelter for about 2-1/2 hours to get water.

D. Estimating the **Dangers** from Different Radiation Doses

Fortunately, the human body -- if given enough time -- can repair most of the damage caused by radiation. An historic example: A healthy man accidentally received a daily **dose** of 9.3 R (or somewhat more) of fallout-type radiation each day for a period of 106 days. His total accumulated **dose** was at least 1000 R. A dose of 1000 roentgens, if received in a few days, is almost three times the dose likely to kill the average man if he receives the whole dose in a few days and after a nuclear attack cannot get medical treatment adequate rest, etc. However, the only symptom this man noted was serious fatigue.

The occupants of a high-protection-factor shelter (such as a trench shelter covered with 2 or 3 feet of earth and having crawlway entrances) would receive less than 1/200 of the radiation dose they would receive outside. Even in most areas of very heavy fallout, persons who remain continuously in such a shelter would receive a total accumulated **dose** of less than 25 R in the first day after the attack, and less than 100 R in the first two weeks. At the end of the first two weeks, such shelter occupants could start working outside for an increasing length of time each day, receiving a **daily dose** of no more than **6 R** for up to two months without being sickened.

The risk of developing cancer years later will be greatly reduced if the daily radiation dose is restricted to 3R. A healthy person who has not received a recent dose that has sickened him can tolerate a daily dose of 3R for many months without becoming incapacitated. If a person is in an area of very heavy fallout, he may need at least to sleep in a high-protection-factor shelter for months to be able to restrict his daily dose to 3R. Or he could move to a less contaminated area.

To control radiation exposure in this way, each shelter must have a fallout meter, and a daily record must be kept of the approximate total dose received each day by every shelter occupant, both while inside and outside the shelter. The long-term penalty which would result from a dose of 100 R received within a few weeks is much less than many Americans fear. If 100 average persons received an external dose of 100 R during and shortly after a nuclear attack, the studies of the Japanese A-bomb survivors indicate that no more than one of them is likely to die during the following 30 years as a result of this 100 R radiation dose. These delayed radiation deaths would be due to leukemia and other cancers. In the desperate crisis period following a major nuclear attack, such a relatively small shortening of life expectancy during the following 30 years should not keep people from starting recovery work to save themselves and their fellow citizens from death due to lack of food and other essentials.

A healthy person who previously has received a total accumulated dose of no more than 100 R distributed over a 2-week period should realize that:

100 R, even if all received in a day or less, is unlikely to require medical care--provided during the next 2 weeks a total additional dose of no more than a few R is received.

350 R received in a few days or less is likely to prove fatal after a large nuclear attack when few survivors could get medical care, sanitary surroundings, a well-balanced diet, or adequate rest.

600 R received in a few days or less is almost certain to cause death within a few days.

E.   Using a KFM to Reduce the Doses Received Inside a Shelter

Inside most shelters, the dose received by an occupant varies considerably, depending on the occupant's location. For example, inside an expedient covered-trench shelter the dose rate is higher near the entrance than in the middle of the trench. In a typical basement shelter the best protection is found in one corner. Especially during the first several hours after the arrival of fallout, when the dose rates and doses received are highest, shelter occupants should use their fallout meters to determine where to place themselves to minimize the doses they receive.

They should use available tools and materials to reduce the doses they receive, especially during the first day, by digging deeper (if practical) and reducing the size of openings by partially blocking them with earth, water containers, etc. -- while maintaining adequate ventilation. To greatly reduce the slight risk of fallout particles entering the body through nose or mouth, shelter occupants should cover nose and mouth with a towel or other cloth while the fallout is being deposited outside their shelter, if at the same time ventilating air is being blown or pumped through their shelter.

The air inside an occupied shelter often becomes very humid. If a good flow of outdoor air is flowing into a shelter -- especially if pumped by briefly operating a KAP or other ventilating pump -- a KFM usually can be charged at the air intake of the shelter room without putting it inside a dry-bucket. However, if the air to which a KFM is exposed has a relative humidity of 90% or higher, the instrument cannot be charged, even by quickly unrolling a roll of tape.

In extensive areas of heavy fallout, the occupants of most home basements, that provide inadequate shielding against heavy fallout radiation, would be in deadly danger. By using a dependable fallout meter, occupants would find that persons lying on the floor in certain locations would receive the smallest doses, and that, if they improvise additional shielding in these locations, the doses received could be greatly reduced. Additional shielding can be provided by making a very small shelter inside the basement where the dose rate is found to be lowest. Furniture, boxes, etc. can be used for walls, doors for the roof, and water containers, books, and other heavy objects for shielding -- especially on the roof. Or, if tools are available, breaking through the basement floor and digging a shelter trench will greatly increase available protection against radiation. If a second expedient ventilating pump, a KAP, is made and used as a fan, such an extremely cramped shelter inside a shelter usually can be occupied by several times as many persons.

END OF INSTRUCTIONS

COVER THE TWO "TAPE HERE" RECTANGLES WITH SAME-SIZED PIECES OF TAPE, TO KEEP FROM TEARING THE PAPER WHEN REMOVING OTHER PIECES OF TAPE. THEN, USING TWO OTHER PIECES OF TAPE THIS SAME SIZE, TAPE THE THREAD ONTO THIS GUIDE SHEET, AND LATER ATTACH A LEAF TO THE TAPED DOWN THREAD.

TAPE HERE

MARK THREAD HERE

THREAD LINE

DO NOT TOUCH THIS 1-INCH PART

BAND-AID PLASTIC (1/8" X 1") WITH STICKY SIDE UP AND ENDS FOLDED UNDER SO AS TO STICK TO ALUMINUM (OR USE A VERY LITTLE EPOXY.)

THREAD LINE

CENTER OF THREAD OF FINISHED ALUMINUM-FOIL LEAF

USE BALLPOINT PEN TO MARK THREAD HERE

THREAD LINE

TAPE HERE TO HOLD THREAD SECURELY OVER THREAD LINE

DO NOT TOUCH OR MARK THIS 1-INCH PART OF THE THREAD

TAPE HERE

WARNING: The parts of the thread that will be inside the can and on which the leaf will be suspended must serve to insulate the high-voltage electrical charges to be placed on the leaf. Therefore, the suspended parts of the thread must be kept very clean.

203

REMINDERS FOR OPERATORS

THE DRYING AGENT INSIDE A KFM IS O.K. IF, WHEN THE CHARGED KFM IS NOT EXPOSED TO RADIATION, ITS READINGS DECREASE BY 1 MM OR LESS IN 3 HOURS.

READING: WITH THE READING EYE 12 INCHES VERTICALLY ABOVE THE SEAT, NOTE ON THE MM SCALE THE SEPARATION OF THE LOWER EDGES OF THE LEAVES. IF THE RIGHT LEAF IS AT 10 MM AND THE LEFT LEAF IS AT 7 MM, THE KFM READS 17 MM. NEVER TAKE A READING WHILE A LEAF IS TOUCHING A STOP-THREAD. NEVER USE A KFM READING THAT IS LESS THAN 5MM.

FINDING A DOSE RATE: IF BEFORE EXPOSURE A KFM READS 17 MM AND IF AFTER A 1-MINUTE EXPOSURE IT READS 5 MM, THE DIFFERENCE IN READINGS IS 12 MM, THE ATTACHED TABLE SHOWS THE DOSE RATE WAS 9.6 R/HR DURING THE EXPOSURE.

FINDING A DOSE: IF A PERSON WORKS OUTSIDE FOR 3 HOURS WHERE THE DOSE RATE IS 2 R/HR, WHAT IS HIS RADIATION DOSE? ANSWER: 3 HR x 2 R/HR = 6 R.

FINDING HOW LONG IT TAKES TO GET A CERTAIN R DOSE: IF THE DOSE RATE IS 1.6 R/HR OUTSIDE AND A PERSON IS WILLING TO TAKE A 6 R DOSE, HOW LONG CAN HE REMAIN OUTSIDE? ANSWER:

6 R ÷ 1.6 R/HR = 3.75 HR = 3 HOURS AND 45 MINUTES.

FALLOUT RADIATION GUIDES FOR A HEALTHY PERSON NOT PREVIOUSLY EXPOSED TO A TOTAL RADIATION DOSE OF MORE THAN 100 R DURING A 2-WEEK PERIOD:

6 R PER DAY CAN BE TOLERATED FOR UP TO TWO MONTHS WITHOUT LOSING THE ABILITY TO WORK.

100 R IN A WEEK OR LESS IS NOT LIKELY TO SERIOUSLY SICKEN.

350 R IN A FEW DAYS IS LIKELY TO PROVE FATAL UNDER POST-ATTACK CONDITIONS.

600 R IN A WEEK OR LESS IS ALMOST CERTAIN TO CAUSE DEATH WITHIN A FEW WEEKS.

REMINDERS FOR OPERATORS

THE DRYING AGENT INSIDE A KFM IS O.K. IF, WHEN THE CHARGED KFM IS NOT EXPOSED TO RADIATION, ITS READINGS DECREASE BY 1 MM OR LESS IN 3 HOURS.

READING: WITH THE READING EYE 12 INCHES VERTICALLY ABOVE THE SEAT, NOTE ON THE MM SCALE THE SEPARATION OF THE LOWER EDGES OF THE LEAVES. IF THE RIGHT LEAF IS AT 10 MM AND THE LEFT LEAF IS AT 7 MM, THE KFM READS 17 MM. NEVER TAKE A READING WHILE A LEAF IS TOUCHING A STOP-THREAD. NEVER USE A KFM READING THAT IS LESS THAN 5MM.

FINDING A DOSE RATE: IF BEFORE EXPOSURE A KFM READS 17 MM AND IF AFTER A 1-MINUTE EXPOSURE IT READS 5 MM, THE DIFFERENCE IN READINGS IS 12 MM, THE ATTACHED TABLE SHOWS THE DOSE RATE WAS 9.6 R/HR DURING THE EXPOSURE.

FINDING A DOSE: IF A PERSON WORKS OUTSIDE FOR 3 HOURS WHERE THE DOSE RATE IS 2 R/HR, WHAT IS HIS RADIATION DOSE? ANSWER: 3 HR x 2 R/HR = 6 R.

FINDING HOW LONG IT TAKES TO GET A CERTAIN R DOSE: IF THE DOSE RATE IS 1.6 R/HR OUTSIDE AND A PERSON IS WILLING TO TAKE A 6 R DOSE, HOW LONG CAN HE REMAIN OUTSIDE? ANSWER:

6 R ÷ 1.6 R/HR = 3.75 HR = 3 HOURS AND 45 MINUTES.

FALLOUT RADIATION GUIDES FOR A HEALTHY PERSON NOT PREVIOUSLY EXPOSED TO A TOTAL RADIATION DOSE OF MORE THAN 100 R DURING A 2-WEEK PERIOD:

6 R PER DAY CAN BE TOLERATED FOR UP TO TWO MONTHS WITHOUT LOSING THE ABILITY TO WORK.

100 R IN A WEEK OR LESS IS NOT LIKELY TO SERIOUSLY SICKEN.

350 R IN A FEW DAYS IS LIKELY TO PROVE FATAL UNDER POST-ATTACK CONDITIONS.

600 R IN A WEEK OR LESS IS ALMOST CERTAIN TO CAUSE DEATH WITHIN A FEW WEEKS.

Appendix D
Expedient Blast Shelters

INCREASING IMPORTANCE

The majority of urban and suburban Americans would need blast shelters to avoid death or injury if they did not evacuate before an all-out nuclear attack. As nuclear arsenals continue to grow, an increasing majority would need the protection of blast shelters. As much as 3% of the total area of the 48 states could be subjected to blast severe enough to destroy or damage homes—depending on targeting, weapon reliability, etc. If blast shelters affording protection up to the 15-pounds-per-square-inch (15 psi) overpressure range were available and occupied, people could survive the blast, fire, and radiation effects in about 85% of this extensive threatened area. Blast tests have indicated that the Small-Pole Shelter (the most blast-resistant of the earth-covered shelters described in Appendix A) should enable occupants to survive all blast effects at the 50-psi overpressure range—if built with the blast doors and other protective features described on the following pages. Calculations show that it also would give adequate protection against the intense initial nuclear radiation if improved in the ways outlined later in this appendix.

The life-saving potential of well designed, well built blast shelters is a demonstrated fact. Millions of Americans living in high-risk areas would be able to build expedient blast shelters within only a few days—provided they make some preparations before a crisis arises. The following information is given in the hope of encouraging more Americans to make preparations for blast protection. Also, it may serve to increase the number who realize the need for *permanent* blast shelters in high-risk blast areas.

Some informed citizens—particularly those who live near large cities or in their outer suburbs—may choose to build earth-covered expedient blast shelters in their backyards, rather than to evacuate. Going into a strange area and trying to build or find good shelter and other essentials of life would entail risks that many people might hesitate to take, particularly if they live outside the probable areas of severe blast damage. For such citizens, the best decision might be to stay at home, build earth-covered expedient blast shelters, supply them with the essentials for long occupancy, and remain with their possessions.

Persons in 15-psi blast shelters would not be injured by blast, fire, or radiation effects from a 1-megaton surface burst $1\frac{1}{2}$ miles away, or from a 20-megaton surface burst 4 miles away. If an attack occurs, the area in which persons in 15-psi blast shelters would be killed by blast, fire, or radiation would be only about $\frac{1}{7}$ as large as the area in which most people sheltered in average homes would die from blast and fire effects alone.

The following descriptions of the characteristics and components of expedient blast shelters should enable many readers to use locally available materials to provide at least 15-psi blast protection. Pre-crisis preparations are essential, as well as the ability to work very hard for two to four days. (Field-tested instructions are not yet available; to date only workers who were supervised have built expedient blast shelters.[5])

PRACTICALITY OF EXPEDIENT BLAST SHELTERS

At Hiroshima and Nagasaki, simple wood-framed shelters with about 3 feet of earth over wooden roofs were undamaged by blast effects in areas where substantial buildings were demolished.[4]

Figure D.1 shows a Hiroshima shelter that people with hand tools could build in a day, if poles or timber were available. This shelter withstood blast and fire at an overpressure range of about 65 psi. Its narrow room and a 3-foot-thick earth cover brought about effective earth arching; this kept its yielding wooden frame from being broken.

Fig. D.1. A small, earth-covered backyard shelter with a crude wooden frame—undamaged, although only 300 yards from ground zero at Hiroshima.

Although the shelter itself was undamaged, its occupants would have been fatally injured because the shelter had no blast door. The combined effect of blast waves, excessive pressure, blast wind, and burns from extremely hot dust blown into the shelter (the popcorning effect) and from the heated air would have killed the occupants. For people to survive in areas of severe blast, their shelters must have strong blast doors.

In nuclear weapons tests in the Nevada desert, box-like shelters built of lumber and covered with sandy earth were structurally undamaged by 10- to 15-psi blast effects. However, none had blast doors, so occupants of these open shelters would have been injured by blast effects and burned as a result of the popcorning effect. Furthermore, blast winds blew away much of the dry, sandy earth mounded over the shelters for shielding; this resulted in inadequate protection against fallout radiation.

Twelve different types of expedient shelters were blast-tested by Oak Ridge National Laboratory during three of Defense Nuclear Agency's blast tests.[5] Two of these tests each involved the detonation of a million pounds or more of conventional explosive; air-blast effects equivalent to those from a 1-kiloton

nuclear surface burst were produced by these chemical explosions.

Several of these shelters had expedient blast doors which were closed during the tests. Figure D.2 shows the undamaged interior of the best expedient blast shelter tested prior to 1978, an improved version of the Small-Pole Shelter described in Appendix A. Its two heavy plywood blast doors excluded practically all blast effects; the pressure inside rose only to 1.5 psi—an overpressure not nearly high enough to break eardrums. The only damage was to the expedient shelter-ventilating pump (a KAP) in the stoop-in entryway. Two men worked about 5 minutes to replace the 4 flap-valves that were blown loose.

Fig. D.2. Undamaged interior of a Small-Pole Shelter after blast testing at the 53-psi overpressure range. Large buildings would have been completely demolished.

When blast-tested at 5-psi overpressure, not even the weakest covered-trench shelters with unsupported earth walls (described in Appendix A) were damaged structurally. However, if the covering earth were sandy and dry and if it were exposed to the blast winds of a megaton explosion at the 5-psi overpressure range, so much earth would be blown away that the shelter would give insufficient protection against fallout radiation. Much of the **dry,** shielding earth mounded over some of the above-ground shelters was, in fact, removed by the blast winds of these relatively small test explosions, even at the lower overpressure ranges at which homes would be wrecked. In contrast, in blast tests where the steeply mounded earth was damp, little blast-wind erosion resulted. (The reader should remember that even if shelters without blast doors are undamaged, the occupants are likely to suffer injuries.)

CONSTRUCTION PRINCIPLES

Millions of Americans—if given good instructions, strong motivation, and several days to work—should be able to build blast shelters with materials found in many rural areas and suburban neighborhoods. During a crisis, yard trees could be cut down for poles and sticks, and a garage or part of a house could be torn down for lumber. Many average citizens could build expedient blast shelters if they learn to:

● **Utilize earth arching by making a yielding shelter.** The remarkable protection that earth arching gives to those parts of a shelter designed to use it is illustrated by Fig. D.3.

This picture shows the unbroken roof of a 4-foot-wide Pole-Covered Trench Shelter that was

Fig. D.3. Effective earth arching in the earth covering of this 4-ft-wide Pole-Covered Trench Shelter prevented a single pole from being broken by blast forces that exerted a downward force of 53 psi (over 3½ tons per square foot) on the overlying earth.

built in rock-like soil and blast tested where the blast pressure outside was 53 psi. Its strong blast doors prevented the blast wave from entering. Without the protection of earth arching that developed in the 5 feet of earth cover over the yielding roof poles, the poles would have been broken like straws. In contrast, the ground shock and earth pressure produced by 1-kiloton blast effects almost completely collapsed the unsupported, rock-like earth walls.

Fig. D.4. Post-blast interior of an Above-ground, Door-Covered Shelter that survived 1-kiloton blast effects at the 5.8-psi overpressure range. The shelter walls were made of bedsheets containing earth, as described in Appendix A.

Figure D.4 also indicates the effectiveness of earth arching. This photo shows the roof of a small, earth-covered fallout shelter, as it appeared after surviving blast effects severe enough to demolish most homes. The roof was made of light, hollow-core, interior doors and looks as though it had been completely broken. In fact, only the lower sheets of $\frac{1}{8}$-inch-thick veneer of the hollow-core interior doors were broken. (These breaks were caused by a faulty construction procedure—a front-end loader had dumped several tons of earth onto the uncovered doors.) The upper $\frac{1}{8}$-inch-thick sheets of veneer were bowed downward, unbroken, until an earth arch formed in the 2-foot-thick earth covering and prevented the thin sheets from being broken. Earth arching also prevented this roof from being smashed in by blast overpressure that exerted a pressure of 5.8 psi (835 pounds per square foot) on the surface of the earth mounded over this open shelter. (See Appendix A for details of construction.)

● **Make shelters with the minimum practical ceiling height and width.** Most of the narrow covered-trench shelters used by tens of thousands of Londoners during the World War II blitz were built with only $4\frac{1}{2}$-foot ceilings, to maximize blast protection and minimize high water-table problems. These shelters were found to be among the safest for protection against nearby explosions. The Chinese also have a good understanding of this design principle and skillfully utilize the protection provided by earth arching. A Chinese civil defense handbook states: "... the height and width of tunnel shelters should be kept to the minimum required to accommodate the sheltering requirements," and "The thicker the protective layer of earth, the greater the ability to resist blast waves."[21]

● **Shore earth walls to prevent their caving in as a result of ground shock and earth pressure.** Most unshored (that is, unsupported) earth walls are partially collapsed by ground shock at much lower blast overpressures than those at which a flexible roof protected by earth arching is damaged. Figure D.5 is a picture of a seated dummy taken by a high-speed movie camera mounted inside an unshored, Pole-Covered Trench Shelter of the Russian type tested at the 20-psi range. (A second dummy was obscured by blast-torn curtains made of blankets.) The shelter had an open stairway entryway, positioned at right angles to the stand-up-height trench and facing away from the targeted "city" so as to minimize the entry of blast waves and blast wind.

Fig. D.5. A dummy in an unshored Pole-Covered Trench Shelter as it is struck by collapsing rock-like earth walls. The photo also shows the shelter's blanket-curtains as they are torn and blown into the shelter by the 180-mph blast wind. (Immediately after this photo was taken, the dummies were hit by the airborne blast wave and blast wind. Outside, the blast wind peaked at about 490 mph.)

Figure D.6 is a post-blast view of the essentially undamaged earth-covered roof poles and the disastrously collapsed, unshored shelter walls of the Russian shelter tested at 20 psi.[21] Russian civil defense books state that unshored fallout shelters do not survive closer to the blast than the 7-psi overpressure range. This limitation was confirmed by an identical shelter tested at 7 psi; parts of its unshored walls were quite badly collapsed by the ground shock from an explosion producing merely 1-kiloton blast effects.

Fig. D.6. Dummies after ground shock from 1-kiloton blast effects at the 20-psi range had collapsed the rock-like walls of a hardened desert soil called caliche. The dummies' steel "bones" and "joints" prevented them from being knocked down and buried. The fallen caliche all around them kept them from being blown over by the air blast wave and 180-mph blast wind that followed.

Unsupported earth walls should be sloped as much as practical. The length and strength of available roofing material should be considered and, in order to attain effective earth arching, the thickness of the earth cover should be **at least** half as great as the distance between the edges of the trench.

The stability of the earth determines the proper method for shoring the walls of a trench shelter.

Methods for shoring both loose, unstable earth and firm, stable earth are described below:

*In loose, unstable earth such as sand, the walls of all underground shelters must be shored. First, an oversized trench must be dug with gently sloping sides. Next, the shoring is built, often as a freestanding, roofless structure. Then earth must be backfilled around the shoring to a level a few inches higher than the uppermost parts of the shoring, as in Fig. D.7. Finally, the roof poles or planks must be placed so that they are supported only by the backfilled earth. Blast tests have indicated that a Pole-Covered Trench Shelter thus proportioned and lightly shored should protect its occupants against disastrous collapse of its walls at overpressure ranges up to 15 psi.

 * **In firm, stable earth,** it is best first to dig a trench a few inches wider than 7 feet (the length of the roof poles) and 1 foot deep. Next, dig the part to be shored, down the center of this shallow trench, using

the dimensions given for the shoring in Fig. D.7. The trench walls should be sloped and smoothed quite accurately, so that the shoring can be tightened against the earth. If the shoring does not press tightly against the trench walls, large wedges of earth may be jarred loose, hit the shoring, and cause it to collapse.

A different, comparatively simple way to tighten shoring is indicated by Fig. D.8. This sketch shows a 4-pole frame designed to be installed every $2\frac{1}{2}$ feet along a trench in stable earth and to be tightened against trench-wall shoring with the same dimensions as those shown in Fig. D.7. Note that the two horizontal brace poles have shallow "V" notches

ORNL—DWG 78-14430R

Fig. D.7. An illustration of several ways to shore a trench in unstable earth, using various materials. A 4-piece frame (consisting of 4 poles, or 4 boards, installed as shown above) should be installed every $2\frac{1}{2}$ feet along the length of the trench, including the horizontal parts of the entryways. All parts of the shoring should be at least 2 inches below the roof poles, so that the downward forces on the roof will press only on the earth.

209

ORNL DWG 78-17246R

TOP VIEW
BRACE POLE
WALL POLE
SIDE VIEW
WALL POLE
BOTTOM OF SHALLOW V
SAWED AT SAME SLOPE AS WALL POLE

Fig. D.8. A 4-pole frame designed so that it can be tightened against the shoring materials that must press firmly against the walls of a trench dug in stable earth. (In this sketch, the middle sections of three poles have been removed, so that the upper brace pole may be seen more clearly.)

sawed in both ends. If these brace poles are driven downward when positioned as shown, the two wall poles are forced outward against the shoring materials placed between them and the earth walls. An upper brace pole should be cut to the length needed to make it approximately the same height as the roof poles on each side of it (no higher) after the shoring is tightened. Finally, each "V"-notched end should be nailed to its wall pole.

Light, yielding poles can serve simultaneously both to roof and to shore a shelter. A good example is the Chinese "Man" Shelter illustrated in Fig. D.9, requiring comparatively few poles to build.[21] This shelter is too cramped for long occupancy, and its unshored, lower earth walls can be squeezed in by blast pressure. Therefore, it is not recommended if sufficient materials are available for building a well-shored, covered-trench shelter. It is described here primarily to help the reader understand the construction of similarly designed entryways, outlined later in this appendix. The room and the horizontal entryway of the model tested were made of $6\frac{1}{2}$-foot poles averaging only 3 inches in diameter. It had two vertical, triangular entries of ORNL design. Each was protected by an expedient triangular blast door made of poles. In Fig. D.9, note the two small

horizontal poles at the top of the triangle, one tied inside and the other tied outside the triangle, to hold the wall poles together. Before covering this shelter with earth, a 6-inch-thick covering of small limbs was placed horizontally across the approximately 3-inch-wide spaces between the $6\frac{1}{2}$-foot wall poles; the limbs were then covered with bedsheets.

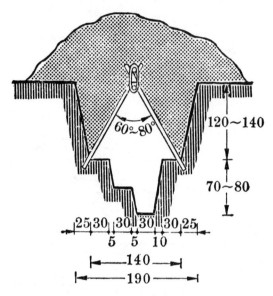

图 3-107　人字形骨架避弹所

Fig. D.9. Chinese "Man" Shelter tested at 20 psi, and undamaged because the thin poles yielded and were protected by earth arching. This drawing was taken from a Chinese civil defense manual. The dimensions are in centimeters.

When blast-tested in loose, unstable soil, the unsupported earth walls of the trench below the wall poles were squeezed in. The 12-inch width of the foot trench was reduced to as little as 4 inches by the short-duration forces produced by 0.2-kiloton blast effects at 50 psi. The much longer duration forces of a megaton explosion would be far more damaging to the shelter at lower overpressure ranges, due to destabilizing and squeezing-in unshored earth at depths many feet below ground level.

Calculations based on blast-test findings indicate that the unsupported earth walls of a shelter are likely to fail if the aboveground maximum overpressure is greater than 5 to 7 psi and this overpressure is caused by an explosion that is a megaton or more.

210

(Most homes would be severely damaged by the 3-psi blast effects from a 1-megaton or larger weapon. This damage would result one mile closer to ground zero of a 1-megaton surface burst than the distance at which the unshored earth walls of some shelters would be collapsed. For a 20-megaton surface burst, the corresponding reduction in distance would be about 2.7 miles.)

● **Build sufficiently long and strong entryways.** Blast shelters need longer horizontal entryways, taller vertical entryways, and thicker earth cover than do most fallout shelters; these are needed primarily for increased protection against high levels of initial nuclear radiation. The entryways of the Small-Pole Shelter described in Appendix A.3 (with the improvements for increased blast protection outlined in the following section of this appendix) afford protection against both blast and radiation up to the 50-psi overpressure range. However, these entryways require straight poles 14 feet long; these may be difficult to find or transport.

In contrast, both the horizontal and the vertical parts of the triangular entry pictured in Figs. D.10, D.11, and D.12 require only small-diameter, short poles. Triangular entries of this type were undamaged by 1-kiloton blast effects at the 20-psi overpressure range[5] and by 0.2-kiloton blast effects at

50 psi. This type of entry and its blast door (also triangular and made of short poles) can be used with a wide variety of expedient blast shelters and should withstand megaton blast effects at 25 psi. Therefore, their construction is described in considerable detail.

* **The horizontal part of a triangular entry:** If the Chinese "Man" Shelter shown in Fig. D.9 is made without excavating the unshored lower trench that forms its earth seats, it will serve as a horizontal, shored crawlway-entry affording blast protection up to at least the 25-psi overpressure range. Two horizontal entries, one at each end of the shelter, should be provided. Each entry should be 10 feet long. This length is needed to reduce the amount of initial nuclear radiation reaching the blast shelter room while assuring adequate through-ventilation. The outer part of such a horizontal entry is pictured in the background of Fig. D.10.

* **The vertical part of a triangular entry:** The *lower section* of the vertical part is made in a similar manner to the horizontal shelter shown in Fig. D.9. Figure D.10 shows $4\frac{1}{2}$-foot horizontal poles (1) forming a "V", with one end of each pole laid on top of the adjacent lower pole. The other ends of these poles (1) are pressed against the two pairs of vertical posts (2). (After this photo was taken, the tops of these two pairs of vertical posts were sawed off as

PHOTO 2954-77R

Fig. D.10. Uncompleted lower section of a vertical triangular entry.

SPACER BLOCKS OF 8–12 in. LONG POLES

5-ft-LONG HORIZONTAL ENTRYWAY OF CHINESE SHELTER

OUTSIDE 2 POLES LARGER DIA AND LOG-CABIN NOTCHED

SPACER POLE (WIRED TO ADJACENT POLE)

6 ft 6 in.   6 ft 6 in.

3½ in. DIA

6 in. DIA – 7 ft 6 in.

4" AND 5" DIA

43 in.

2½ in. AT TOP 4 ft 6 in.

30 in.

43 in.

CONSTRUCTION OF THE PART OF THE VERTICAL ENTRY OPPOSITE THE CRAWLWAY OPENING

STEP (1 ft–4 in.; 2½ in. DIA) SPACED ~ 1 ft APART

TOP VIEW

"BURIED ROOF" OF POLYETHYLENE (4 mil)

48 in. COVER

7 ft 0 in.

LIMBS OR BRUSH

2½ in. DIA

CLOTH OR PLASTIC

5 in. DIA

SHALLOW DITCH

6 in. DIA

7 ft 6 in.

WIRE POSTS TOGETHER, TOP AND BOTTOM

DIG SLOTS IN SIDE OF TRENCH FOR ENDS OF HORIZONTAL POLES

6 ft 6 in.

30 in.

30 in.

TRENCH 54 in. DEEP

6 in. DIA

7 ft 6 in.

5 ft 6 in. ENTRYWAY TRENCH BOTTOM

VIEW LOOKING INTO SHELTER FROM A–A

Fig. D.11. Lower part of a vertical triangular entry, showing its connection to the horizontal part of the shelter entry.

212

Fig. D.12. Completed frame of Chinese "Man" Shelter showing its two ORNL-designed entryways (one at each end) and triangular blast doors made of poles. Before covering the triangular vertical entries with earth, tree branches were placed vertically over the sides; the branches then were covered with bedsheets. Horizontal branches, also covered with bedsheets, were laid over the rest of the shelter frame. After being covered with earth, this shelter was subjected to 1-kiloton blast effects. Multiple earth arching over and around this yielding structure prevented both the small poles and the bedsheets from being damaged at 20 psi.

shown in Fig. D.11.) The $4\frac{1}{2}$-foot horizontal poles (1) were kept level by the short spacer-poles (3) that were wired or nailed in place.

Each pair of vertical posts (2) was securely wired together at top and bottom. The two pairs were held apart at top and bottom by two horizontal brace-poles toenailed in place to frame the rectangular 30-$\times$30-inch crawlway "doorway" between the vertical entry and the horizontal entry. Only the upper pole (4) of these two 30-inch-long horizontal brace-poles is shown.

The two pairs of vertical posts (2) were positioned so that they pressed against two $7\frac{1}{2}$-foot horizontal poles (5); only the uppermost is shown. These in turn pressed against the outermost two poles (6) of the horizontal entry and against the earth in two slot-trenches dug in the sidewalls of the excavation. These two $7\frac{1}{2}$-foot poles (5) should be at least 6 inches in diameter.

Additional details of the lower section of this vertical triangular entry are given in Fig. D.11. If horizontal poles considerably larger in diameter than those illustrated are used, fewer poles are required and strength is increased. However, the space inside

the entry is decreased unless the larger-diameter horizontal poles that form the "V" are made longer than $4\frac{1}{2}$ feet.

As shown on the left in Fig. D.10, a small, vertical pole (7) was placed in the small "V" between the outer ends of the horizontal poles that form the lower section of the vertical entry. After this photo was taken, a second small, vertical pole was positioned in the adjacent large "V", inside the entry. These two poles (7) were then tightly wired together so as to make a strong, somewhat yielding, outer-corner connection of the horizontal poles (1)—in the same way that the tops of the side-wall poles of the Chinese "Man" Shelter are bound together.

The **upper section** of the vertical part of this entry (the section above the tops of the two pairs of vertical posts shown in Fig. D.10 and Fig. D.11) is made by overlapping the ends of its nearly horizontal poles (Fig. D.12). These poles [marked with a (1) in Fig. D.10] were each 4 feet 6 inches long and varied uniformly in diameter from about $2\frac{1}{2}$ inches just above the two pairs of wired-together posts, to 4-inch diameters just below the triangular door frame of poles. The triangular-shaped blast door was hinged to and closed against this door frame. The hinges were strips cut from worn auto tires, to be described shortly.

The upper section is formed by laying poles in a triangular pattern, ends crossing at the angles, with large ends and small ends placed so that the poles are as nearly horizontal as is practical. Each of its three corners is held together by strong wires that tightly bind an outside and an inside small vertical pole, in the same manner as the top of the Chinese "Man" Shelter (shown in Fig. D.9) is secured. (Instead of No. 9 soft steel wire, rope or twisted strips of strong fabric could be used.)

Before starting to install the upper section of a vertical triangular entry, the three outermost of the six small vertical poles that will hold the three corners together should be connected temporarily with three small horizontal poles. Connect them at the height of the door frame planned for the triangular blast door, and space them so as to be the same size as this door frame.

Next, all the horizontal poles should be laid out on the ground in the order of their increasing diameters. The triangular entry then should be started with the smallest poles at the base, with increasingly large-diameter poles used toward the top—so that the three pairs of small vertical poles will press securely against all the horizontal side poles of the entry.

To prevent the negative overpressure ("suction") phase of the blast from yanking out and carrying away the blast door and the upper part of the vertical entry to which it is hinged, the uppermost 4 or 5 horizontal poles of each of the three sides of the vertical entry should be wired or tied securely together. Rope or strips of strong cloth can be used if strong wire is not available.

Before placing earth around this lightly constructed blast-protective entry, the vertical walls must be covered to a thickness of about 6 inches with a yielding, crushable covering of limbs, brush, or innerspring mattresses. Limbs or brush should be placed in three layers, with the innermost layer at right angles to the underlying poles. The yielding thickness then is covered with strong cloth, such as 50% dacron bedsheets, or two thicknesses of 4-mil polyethylene film. This outermost covering keeps loose earth or sand from filling spaces inside the yielding layer or running into the entry. Thus protected, this vertical entry should be undamaged by 25-psi blast effects of megaton weapons.

A vertical blast-protective entry can also be made like a strong box, using 2-inch-thick boards. Such entries afford blast protection up to 50 psi if made as small as shown here and protected with yielding materials such as a 6-inch-thick layer of brush covered with strong cloth.

• **Install blast doors** to keep out airborne blast waves, blast wind, overpressure, blast-borne debris, burning-hot dust and air, and fallout.

A fast-rising overpressure of as little as 5 psi will break some people's eardrums. At overpressures of 15 to 20 psi, 50% of the people who are exposed will have their eardrums broken. However, persons near a shelter wall may have their eardrums broken by somewhat less than half of these unreflected overpressures. (Any wall may reflect blast waves and greatly increase overpressures near it.) Broken eardrums are not serious in normal times, but after a nuclear attack this injury is likely to be far more dangerous to persons in crowded shelters without effective medical treatment. Lung damage, that can result from overpressures as low as 10 to 12 psi, would also be more serious under post-attack conditions.

A blast door must withstand blast waves and overpressure. Not only must the door itself be sufficiently strong to withstand forces at least as great as those which the shelter will survive, but in addition the door frame and the entranceway walls must be equally as strong. The expedient blast door pictured in Fig. D.13 was made of rough boards, each a full 2 inches thick. It had a continuous row of hinges made of 18-inch-long strips cut from the treads of worn car tires.

The strips were nailed to the vertical poles on one side of the vertical entry. These and other details of construction are shown in Fig. D.14. Although the two center boards were badly cracked by the shock wave and overpressure at the 17-psi range, the door

Fig. D.13. Blast door surrounded by 4 blast-protector logs that were notched and nailed together. The wet, mounded soil had been compacted by the blast but not blown away.

pictured in Fig. D.13 afforded good protection against all blast effects from a surface explosion of a million pounds of TNT. In Fig. D.14, note the *essential,* strong tie-down attachment of the wires at the bottom of the vertical entry, to prevent the blast door from being yanked open by the negative pressure ("suction") that follows the overpressure.

Blast doors must be protected against reflected pressures from blast waves that could strike an edge of an unprotected door and tear it off its hinges. Note the blast-protector logs installed around the door pictured in Fig. D.14. When the door was closed, the tops of these four logs were about 2 inches higher than the door, thus protecting its edges on all sides.

The closed door must be prevented from rebounding like a spring and opening a fraction of a second after being bowed down by overpressure, or from being opened and perhaps torn off its hinges by the partial vacuum ("suction") that follows the overpressure phase. Figure D.14 gives the details of such a hold-down system for a blast door. Note that near the bottom of the vertical entry the 6 strong wires must encircle a horizontal pole that is flattened on one side and nailed to the vertical wall poles with at least a dozen 6-inch (60-penny) nails. Blast tests up to the 53-psi overpressure range have proved that this hold-down system works.[5]

Figure D.15 shows a blast door made of 5 thicknesses of $^3/_4$-inch exterior plywood, well glued and nailed together with $4^1/_2$-in. nails at 4-in. spacings. This door was protected by 4 blast-protector logs, each 8 feet long and about 8 inches in diameter. The logs were notched, nailed together, and surrounded with earth. For protection against ignition by the thermal pulse from an explosion, exposed wood and rubber should be coated with thick whitewash (slaked lime) or mud, or covered with aluminum foil.

An equally strong blast door and the door base upon which it closes can be made of poles. If poles are fresh-cut, they are easy to work with ax and saw. Figure D.16 shows the best blast-tested design. This door also had a continuous row of hinges made from worn auto tire treads. The pole to which the hinges were attached was 7 inches in diameter after peeling and had been flattened on its top and outer sides. The two other poles of the equal-sided triangle were 8 inches in diameter and had been flattened with an ax on the bottom, top, and inner sides. The three poles were each 55 inches long. They were notched and spiked together with 60-penny nails so that the door would close snugly on its similarly constructed base made of three stout poles. Other poles, at least 7 inches in diameter before being hewn so that they would fit together snugly, were nailed side-by-side on top of the three outer poles.

Many Americans have axes and would be able to cut poles, but not many know how to use an ax to hew flat, square sides on a pole or log. This easily acquired skill is illustrated by Fig. D.17. The worker should first fasten the pole down by nailing two small poles to it and to other logs on the ground. Figure D.17 shows a pole thus secured. When hewing a flat side, the worker stands with his legs spread far apart, and repeatedly moves his feet so that he can look almost straight down at where his ax head strikes. First, vertical cuts with a *sharp* ax are made about 3 or 4 inches apart and at angles of about 45° to the surface of the pole, for the length of the pole. These multiple cuts should be made almost as deep as is needed to produce a flat side of the desired width. Then the worker, again beginning at the starting end, should cut off long strips, producing a flat side.

BLAST DOOR
SHOWN IN READY POSITION

BRIDLE SPACE

4ft 0in.

24 in.

8-2X6-in. X 4ft 0-in-LONG BOARDS FOR 10 psi OVERPRESSURE (ROUGH LUMBER PREFERRED).

PROP-STICK

THREE-2X6-in. BOARDS FOR 10 psi.

8-in. DIAM LOGS OF BLAST-PROTECTION FRAME ARE PLACED 5 TO 6-in. OUTSIDE ENTRYWAY.

TWO 40-PENNY NAILS PER 4-ft BOARDS.

PULL-CORD TIED TO PROP-STICK

ONE 18-in.-LONG CAR-TIRE HINGE PER VERTICAL POLE.

BLAST DOOR
SHOWING WIRE HOLD-DOWN BRIDLE AND PROP-STICK.

WIRE SAFETY LOOP

ALL NAILS BENT OVER AND CLINCHED

SHORT SECURITY-CORD TIED TO PROP-STICK.

TWO STRANDS NO 9 WIRE.

FOUR STRANDS NO 9 WIRE.

WIRE BINDING AT "Y" OF BRIDLE 4ft BELOW CONNECTIONS TO DOOR.

8 STRANDS NO. 9 WIRE

BLAST-PROTECTION FRAME (NOTCHED LOGS-LIKE LOG CABIN).

SIMPLER FRAME CORNER, REQUIRING THREE 60-PENNY NAILS.

8 STRANDS OF NO. 9 WIRE (FOR ANY BLAST OVER-PRESSURE).

CORD TIED TO LINK AND SUPPORTING LOAD-BINDER IN READY POSITION (CHEST HEIGHT).

WIRE LOOP AT END OF 8 STRANDS OF NO 9 WIRE CONTINUING INTO WIRE "Y" BRIDLE.

LINKAGE BETWEEN UPPER HOOK AND SWIVEL TAPED OR BOUND TO STIFFEN AND HOLD HOOK FACING WIRE LOOP.

LOOP OF EASILY BROKEN STRING TO HOLD HANDLE UP IN MAXIMUM TIGHTENING POSITION.

LOAD-BINDER INSTALLED FOR 4-sec HOLD-DOWN OF BLAST DOOR.

LOWER HOOK TAPED OR BOUND TO LOWER WIRE HOOP.

PUSH BOTTOM OF OPEN DOOR AWAY FROM ENTRYWAY SO IT RESTS ON HINGES, TO MAKE RAPID CLOSING POSSIBLE.

WIRE SAFETY LOOP HOOKED OVER 3 TO 4-in. DIAM SAFETY POST.

TOP OF PROTECTOR-LOGS 2-in. ABOVE TOP OF CLOSED DOOR.

FIRST EACH CAR-TIRE HINGE IS NAILED TO DOOR WITH SIX 16-PENNY NAILS (CLINCHED); THEN A 2X6-in. BOARD IS NAILED OVER HINGES WITH 40-PENNY NAILS (CLINCHED)

6 STRANDS OF NO. 9 SOFT STEEL WIRE.

STICK DRAIN UNDER PROTECTOR LOGS – BUNDLE OF CLEAN STICKS WITH PLASTIC WRAPPED AROUND OUTSIDE.

CAR-TIRE HINGE, 4-in. X 18-in. LONG

OUTSIDE 12 in. OF EACH VERTICAL POLE IS FLATTENED FOR HINGE, ATTACHMENT WITH NINE 20-PENNY NAILS PER POLE.

5-in DIAM POLE, FLATTEN ONE SIDE BY REMOVING 1½ in AND NAIL WITH TWO 60-PENNY NAILS TO EACH VERTICAL POLE.

CROSS SECTION
SHOWING HINGE OFF-SET AND BLAST DOOR SHOWN IN SAFETY POSITION.

BOTTOM OF ENTRYWAY

Fig. D.14. Expedient blast door that can be closed and secured in 4 seconds.

Fig. D.15. Tire-strip hinges nailed to an expedient, 4-inch-thick blast door made of plywood, designed to withstand 50-psi blast effects of very large weapons and undamaged by blast at the 53-psi range.

Fig. D.16. Blast-tested triangular blast door made of hand-hewn pine poles, notched and nailed together. This door closed on a triangular pole base that is concealed in this photo by two of the three blast-protector logs that also withstood 53-psi blast effects.

Fig. D.17. Hewing flat sides on a pole with a sharp ax.

To hew a second flat side at right angles to the first side, rotate the pole 90°, secure it again, and repeat—as pictured in Fig. D.17.

● **Provide blast closures for an adequate ventilation system.** The following two expedient closure systems permit adequate volumes of ventilating air to be pumped through a shelter:

1. **Install two blast doors,** one on each end of the shelter, designed to be left open until the extremely bright light from a large blast is seen. Figure D.14 shows a door held open by a prop-stick that can be yanked away by the attached pull-cord. While propped open, one blast door serves as an extremely low-resistance air-intake opening, and the other serves as an air-exhaust opening. A large KAP can pump air at the rate of several thousand cubic feet per minute through such open doors.

When an attack is expected, each pull-cord should be held by a shelter occupant who stays ready at all times to yank out the prop-stick as soon as he sees the light of an explosion. After the door has fallen closed, the loop at the end of its wire bridle is close to the upper hook of the load-binder and at the same height (Fig. D.14). The person who closes the door should quickly hook the upper hook of the load-binder into the wire loop and pull down on the handle of the load-binder. The door will then be tightly shut. (Sources during an emergency would be the millions of load-binders owned by truckers and farmers.)

At distances from a large explosion where blast wave and overpressure effects are not destructive enough to smash most good expedient blast shelters, there is enough time between the instant the light of the explosion is seen and the arrival of its blast wave for an alert person to shut and securely fasten a well-designed blast door. The smaller the explosion and the greater the overpressure range, the shorter the warning time. Thus at the 15-psi overpressure range from a 1-megaton surface burst (1.5 miles), the blast wave arrives about 2.8 seconds after the light; whereas at the 10-psi overpressure range from a 1-megaton surface burst (1.9 miles), the blast wave arrives about 4.5 seconds after the light. For a 20-megaton surface burst, the warning time at the 15-psi range is about 8 seconds, and at the 30-psi overpressure range, about 4 seconds. Experiments have shown that even people who react quite slowly can close and secure this door within 4 seconds after seeing a spotlight shine on the door without warning.

2. Install in the vertical entries two expedient blast valves, one on each end of the shelter, to protect both the vertical air-intake and air-exhaust ducts, which should be installed outside the vertical entries. Figure D.18 illustrates the construction of a fast-closing expedient blast valve, a design that was undamaged by the 65-psi shock wave and other effects produced by the explosion of a million pounds of TNT. When blast-tested in a shock-tube at 100-psi, the flaps were undamaged; they closed in 6/1000 of a second (0.006 sec.). This is as fast as the best factory-made blast valves close.

Fig. D.19. Installation of a 50-psi Overlapping-Flaps Blast Valve in such a way that it will not be blown into a shelter by the blast overpressure, nor pulled out by the following negative pressure ("suction") phase.

Fig. D.18. Overlapping-Flaps Blast Valve, made of boards, plywood, and strips cut from the treads of worn car tires.

To withstand 50 psi, the load-bearing "2-inch" boards (actually $1\frac{1}{2}$ inches thick) of the valve should be at least 6 inches wide, if the 1-in.-high air openings are each made 12 in. wide, measured between two vertical poles of a shelter entry. See Fig. D.19, that gives the dimensions of a valve that has been blast tested.[5] Note that there are 5 inches of solid wood at each end of each 1-in.-high air opening. If there are 5 such air openings to a valve, a properly installed KAP (Appendix B) can pump air at about 125 cubic feet

per minute (125 cfm) through a shelter equipped with such valves. This ventilation rate is ample for at least 40 people in cold weather. Except in hot and humid weather, a constant air supply of about 10 cfm per shelter occupant is enough to maintain tolerable conditions during continuous shelter occupancy for many days.

If a factory-made blower capable of pumping several hundred cfm is available, use it. Such a hand-operated blower can pump against much higher air flow resistances than a KAP can. It can pump its full-rated volume of outdoor air through a shelter equipped with two Overlapping-Flaps Blast Valves—each with only 2 air openings—providing 24 square inches of openings per valve.

Remember that a pressure of 7200 pounds pushes against each square foot of the exposed face of a blast valve when it is subjected to a 50-psi blast overpressure. Also keep in mind that the "suction" that follows can exert an outwardly directed force of up to 700 pounds per square foot on the valve face and can yank it out of position unless it is securely installed. Figure D.19 shows how to securely install a blast valve. (Merely nailing a blast valve in its opening will not enable it to withstand severe blast forces.)

● **Minimize aboveground construction and the mounding of shielding earth.** At high overpressure ranges, the shock wave and the blast-wind drag can wreck an aboveground shelter entry. For example, the 5-ft-high earth mound over a shelter built with its pole roof at ground level was moved enough by 1-kiloton air-blast effects at the 53-psi overpressure range to break one of the poles of a blast-door frame. The forces of a 1-megaton explosion at the same overpressure range would have operated 10 times as long, and probably would have smashed the vertical entryways of this shelter. Whenever practical, a blast shelter should be built far enough belowground so that the top of its shielding earth cover is at ground level. Avoiding aboveground construction and earth mounds also greatly reduces the chances of damage from blast-hurled, heavy debris, such as tree trunks and pieces of buildings.

Dry earth, steeply mounded over a shelter which is subjected to blast winds from a big explosion, will be mostly blown away. However, blast-wind "scouring" of **wet** earth is negligible. The blast winds from a 1-kiloton explosion at the 31-psi overpressure range scoured away 17 inches of **dry,** sandy soil mounded at a slope of 32°.

If it is impractical to build a blast shelter with its roof belowground, good protection can be attained by mounding even dry earth at slopes not steeper than 10°.

● **Provide adequate shielding against initial nuclear radiation.** Good expedient blast shelters require a greater thickness of earth cover than is needed on good fallout shelters, for these reasons:

* Blast shelters should also protect against initial nuclear radiation emitted by the fireball. This radiation is reduced by half when it penetrates about 5 inches of packed earth (as compared to a halving-thickness of only about $3\frac{1}{2}$ inches of earth against radiation from fallout).

* The initial radiation, in some areas where good blast shelters will survive, can be much greater than the fallout radiation is likely to be.

* Initial nuclear radiation that comes through entryways is more difficult to attenuate (reduce) than fallout radiation. Therefore, longer entryways or additional right-angle turns must be provided.

For these reasons, good blast shelters should be covered with at least 4 ft of well-packed, average-weight earth, or 5 ft of unpacked or light earth. (A 3-ft thickness gives excellent protection against radiation from fallout.)

A 50-PSI SMALL-POLE SHELTER

This expedient blast shelter is described in detail to enable the reader to build this model. The details will help him better understand the design principles of other expedient blast shelters that are capable of preventing injuries from blast effects severe enough to destroy all ordinary buildings and kill the occupants. Blast tests and calculations have indicated that the Small-Pole Shelter described and illustrated in Appendix A.3 will afford protection against all weapon effects at overpressure ranges up to 50 psi that are produced by an explosion of 1 megaton, or *larger,* provided the shelter is:

● Made with horizontal entryways each with ceilings no higher than 7 ft, 2 in., no wider than 3 ft, and each at least 10 ft long—to lessen the radiation coming through the entries (see Fig. D.20). Lower and narrower entryways would give better protection but would increase the time required for entry.

● Constructed with a floor of poles that are 4 in. or more in diameter, laid side-by-side, with the wall poles resting on the floor poles. The ground shock and earth pressures at a depth of 10 ft or more resulting from an overpressure on the surface of more than about 35 psi, if caused by a large explosion, may destabilize and squeeze earth upward into the shelter through an unprotected earth floor. The Small-Pole Shelter described in Appendix A.3 has an earth floor.

● Installed in an excavation about 13 feet deep, with the shelter's vertical entrances appropriately increased in height so that the blast doors are only about one foot above the original ground level.

Fig. D.20. Entryway of Small-Pole Blast Shelter shielded against initial nuclear radiation. This sketch is a simplified vertical section through the centerline of one end of the shelter.

- Made with 4 rectangular horizontal braces in each vertical entry, in addition to the ends of the two long, ladder-like braces. The detailed drawings in Appendix A show such braces. The lowest rectangular brace should be positioned $3\frac{1}{2}$ feet above the flooring at the bottom of the vertical entry (see Fig. D.20).

- Equipped with blast doors each made of 5 sheets of $\frac{3}{4}$-inch exterior plywood (see Fig. D.15) bonded with resin glue and nailed together with $4\frac{1}{2}$ in. nails. The nails should be driven on 4-in. spacings and their protruding ends should be clinched (bent over). The blast doors must be secured against being yanked open by negative pressure ("suction") by securing

them with a strong wire bridle (see Fig. D.14), and with the lower, fixed wire strongly connected near the bottom of the entry to all of the vertical poles on one side, as shown in Fig. D.14.

- Provided with an adequate ventilation pump and with ventilation openings protected against blast by expedient blast-valves (Fig. D.18) installed in the vertical entries as shown in Fig. D.19, to protect the air-intake and the air-exhaust openings. (Ventilation openings should be as far as practical from buildings and combustible materials. Manually closed ventilation openings are NOT effective at the 50-psi overpressure range of most weapons, because there is insufficient time to close them between the arrival of the warning light from the explosion and the arrival of the blast wave.)

- Made with the roof poles covered by a yielding layer of brush or limbs about 6 inches thick, or of innerspring mattresses. This yielding layer in turn should be covered with bedsheets or other strong cloth, to increase the effectiveness of protective earth arching. Brush or limbs should be laid in 3 layers with sticks of the middle layer perpendicular to those of the other two layers.

- Covered with 5 feet of earth, sloped no steeper than 10°.

- Provided with additional shielding materials in the entryways, as shown in Fig. D.20. Such shielding would be needed to prevent occupants from receiving possibly incapacitating or fatal doses of initial nuclear radiation through the entryways at the 50-psi overpressure range, if the shelter is subjected to the effects of a weapon that is one megaton, *or larger,* in explosive yield.

Damp earth serves better for neutron shielding material than dry earth and can be substituted for water as shielding material if sufficient water containers are not available. (At the 50-psi overpressure range from explosions *smaller* than one megaton, the entry and shielding shown in Fig. D.20 may not provide adequate protection against initial nuclear radiation.)

When the shelter is readied for rapid occupancy, the shelter-ventilating KAP is secured against the ceiling, and the bags of earth in the doorway (under the KAP) are removed. Persons entering the shelter would stoop to go under the platform adjacent to the vertical entry. This platform is attached to vertical wall-poles of the horizontal entry and supports shielding water and earth. When all except the person who will shut and secure the blast door are inside the shelter room, occupants should quickly begin to place bags of earth in the doorway. When the attack has begun, the whole doorway can be closed with bags of earth or other dense objects until ventilation is necessary.

The entries of other types of blast shelters can be shielded in similar ways.

- Protected against fire by being built sufficiently distant from buildings and flammable vegetation and by having its exposed wood covered. For maximum expedient protection against ignition by the thermal radiation from a large explosion, all exposed wood should be free of bark, coated with wet mud or damp slaked lime (whitewash), and covered with aluminum sheet metal or foil to reflect heat. (Most of the thermal radiation from an explosion that was 1 megaton or larger would reach the 50-psi overpressure range after the blast wave had arrived and had torn the expedient protective coverings from the wood. However, as has been observed in megaton nuclear weapon tests, the dust cloud first produced by the popcorning effect and later by the blast winds would screen solid wood near the ground so effectively against thermal radiation that it would not be ignited, provided it had been initially protected as described above.)

PRECAUTIONS FOR OCCUPANTS OF BLAST SHELTERS

Although a well constructed blast shelter may be undamaged at quite high overpressure ranges, its occupants may be injured or killed as a result of rapid ground motions that move the whole shelter several inches in a few thousandths of a second. Rapid ground motions are not likely to cause serious injuries unless the shelter is in an area subjected to 30-psi or greater blast effects. To prevent possible injury, when the occupants of high-protection blast shelters are expecting attack they should avoid:

- Having their heads close to the ceiling. The "air slap" of the air-blast wave may push down the earth and an undamaged shelter much more rapidly than a person can fall. If one's head were to be only a few inches from the ceiling, a fractured skull could result.

- Leaning against a wall, because it may move very rapidly, horizontally as well as vertically.

- Sitting or standing on the floor, because ground shock may cause the whole shelter (including the floor) to rise very fast and injure persons sitting or standing on the floor. The safest thing to do is to sit or lie in a securely suspended, strong hammock or chair, or on thick foam rubber such as that of a mattress, or on a pile of small branches.

In dry areas or in a dry expedient shelter, ground shock may produce choking dust. Therefore, shelter occupants should be prepared to cover their faces with towels or other cloth, or put on a mask. If an attack is expected, they should keep such protective items within easy reach.

SELECTED REFERENCES

1. *Radiobiological Factors in Manned Space Flight,* Space Radiation Study Panel of the Life Sciences Committee, Space Science Board, National Academy of Sciences, National Research Council, 1967.

2. Personal communication with Dr. C. C. Lushbaugh, Chairman, Medical and Health Science Division, Oak Ridge Associated Universities, in June 1977.

3. *The Effects of Nuclear Weapons,* 1962, Samuel Glasstone, Editor, published by U.S. Atomic Energy Commission, April 1962.

4. "Adequate Shelters and Quick Reactions to Warning: A Key to Civil Defense," Francis X. Lynch, *Science,* Vol. 142, pp. 665–667, 1963.

5. *Blast Tests of Expedient Shelters in the DICE THROW Event,* Cresson H. Kearny and Conrad V. Chester, Oak Ridge National Laboratory Report No. 5347, February 1978.

6. *The Effects of Nuclear Weapons,* 1977, Third Edition, Samuel Glasstone and Philip J. Dolan, Editors, U.S. Department of Defense and U.S. Department of Energy, 1977. This most authoritative publication has numerous sections written for non-technical educated readers. In 1979, a paperback copy can be purchased for $7.00 from the Superintendent of Documents, U.S. Government Printing Office, Washington, D.C. 20402. When ordering, ask for *The Effects of Nuclear Weapons, 1977,* Stock No. 008-046-00093-0. (Since the price may be increased in future years, a buyer should first write requesting the current price.)

7. *The 900 Days,* Harrison E. Salisbury, Harper Row, New York, N.Y., 1969.

8. *Expedient Shelter Construction and Occupancy Experiments,* Cresson H. Kearny, Oak Ridge National Laboratory Report No. 5039, March 1976.

9. *Biological Tolerance to Air Blast and Related Biomedical Criteria,* Clayton S. White et al., Lovelace Foundation for Medical Education and Research, Albuquerque, N.M., April 1965.

10. *Instrument Requirements for Radiological Defense of the U.S. Population in Community Shelters,* Carsten M. Haaland and Kathy S. Gant, Oak Ridge National Laboratory Report No. 5371, August 1978.

11. *Field Testing and Evaluation of Expedient Shelters in Deeply Frozen Ground,* Ren Read, College of Environmental Design, University of Colorado, Denver, Colo., July 1978.

12. "Construction of Hasty Winter Shelters," Cresson H. Kearny, *Annual Progress Report,* Oak Ridge National Laboratory Report No. 4784, March 71–March 72, December 1972.

13. *Shelter Occupancy Studies at the University of Georgia, Final Report,* J. A. Hammes and Thomas R. Ahearn, OCD Contract No. OCD-PS-66-25, 1966.

14. "Environmental Physiology of Shelter Habitation," A. R. Dasler and D. Minard, paper presented at the ASHRAE Semiannual Meeting in Chicago, January 1965.

15. *Studies of the Bureau of Yards and Docks Protective Shelter,* NRL Report 5882, U.S. Naval Research Laboratory, Washington, D.C., December 1962.

16. *Winter Ventilation Tests,* Guy B. Panero, Inc., Subcontract No. B-64212-US for Office of Civil Defense, February 1965.

17. "Interim Standards for Ventilating Systems and Related Equipment for Fallout Shelters," Office of Civil Defense, Washington, D.C., 1962.

18. *Response to DCPA Questions on Fallout,* DCPA Research Report No. 20, prepared by Subcommittee on Fallout, Advisory Committee on Civil Defense, National Academy of Sciences, November 1973.

19. *Personnel Shelters and Protective Construction,* NAVDOCKS P-81, Department of Navy, Bureau of Yards and Docks, September 1961.

20. *The Destruction of Dresden,* David Irving, Wm. Kimber and Co., London, May 1963.

21. *Chinese Civil Defense,* excerpts from *Basic Military Knowledge, Shanghai 1975,* ORNL/tr-4171, edited by Conrad V. Chester and Cresson H. Kearny, Oak Ridge National Laboratory translation, August 1977.

22. *The Effects of Mass Fires on Personnel in Shelters,* A. Broido and A. W. McMasters, Technical Paper 50, Pacific Southwest Forest and Range Experiment Station, Berkeley, Calif., August 1960.

23. *Civil Defense,* N. I. Alabin, et al., Moscow 1970, ORNL/tr-2793, Oak Ridge National Laboratory translation, December 1973.

24. *Manual of Individual Water Supply Systems,* Environmental Protection Agency, Water Supply Division, Washington, D.C., 1973.

25. "Solubility of Radioactive Bomb Debris," D. C. Linsten, et al., *Journal of American Water Work Association,* 53, pp. 256–62, 1961.

26. *Maintaining Nutritional Adequacy During A Prolonged Food Crisis,* Kay B. Franz and Cresson H. Kearny, Oak Ridge National Laboratory Report No. ORNL-5352, July 1979.

27. *Livestock, Fallout and a Plan for Survival,* W. F. Byrne and M.C. Bell, UT-AEC Agricultural Research Laboratory, Oak Ridge, Tenn., R-CD-3, April 1973.

28. "Availability and Shipment of Grain for Survival of the Relocated Population of the U.S. After a Nuclear Attack," Carsten M. Haaland, *American Journal of Agricultural Economics,* May 1977.

29. Personal Communication with Kathy S. Gant and Conrad V. Chester, January 1979.

30. *Food Stockpiling for Emergency Shelters,* Food and Materials Division, Commodity Stabilization Service, U.S. Department of Agriculture, April 1961.

31. *The KFM, a Homemade Yet Accurate and Dependable Fallout Meter,* Cresson H. Kearny, Paul R. Barnes, Conrad V. Chester, and Margaret W. Cortner, Oak Ridge National Laboratory Report No. ORNL-5040 (corrected), January 1978.

32. *Where There Is No Doctor,* David Werner, Hesperian Foundation, Palo Alto, Calif., 1977.

33. Personal communications from Colonel C. Blanchard Henry, M.D., Binghamton, N.Y., to Cresson H. Kearny in 1963.

34. *Emergency Medical Treatment,* TM-11-8, Federal Civil Defense Administration, U.S. Government Printing Office, April 1953.

35. "The Radiation Studies Begin," *Science,* Vol. 204, p. 281, 1979.

36. *Protection of the Thyroid Gland in the Event of Releases of Radioiodine,* National Council on Radiation Protection and Measurements, NCRP Report No. 55, Washington, D.C. 20014, August 1, 1977.

37. *Accidental Radioactive Contamination of Human and Animal Feeds and Potassium Iodide as a Thyroid-Blocking Agent in a Radiation Emergency,* Food and Drug Administration, Federal Register, December 15, 1978, pp. 58790-58800.

38. *Civil Defense,* N. I. Akimov et al., Moscow, 1969, ORNL/tr-2306, Oak Ridge National Laboratory translation, April 1971.

39. "Frantic Team Efforts Brought Vital Chemical to Stricken Plant," Robert Reinhold, *New York Times,* April 4, 1979, p. A16.

40. *Trans-Pacific Fallout and Protective Countermeasures,* Cresson H. Kearny, Oak Ridge National Laboratory Report No. 4900, November 1973.

41. Letter dated May 23, 1979 from William H. Wilcox, Administrator, Federal Disaster Assistance Administration, Washington, D.C. to Robert A. Levetown, Washington Representative of the American Civil Defense Association.

42. *Historical Instances of Extreme Overcrowding,* Bureau of Social Science Research, Inc., Report No. 354-5, March 1963.

43. *After-Action Report, Operation Laboratory Shelter,* Headquarters U.S. Army XXIV Airborne Corps, Ft. Bragg, N.C., 1970.

ACKNOWLEDGMENTS

The author takes this opportunity to thank the following persons for their special contributions:

L. Joe Deal, James L. Liverman, and W. W. Schroebel for the essential support they made possible over the years, first by the U.S. Atomic Energy Commission, then by the Energy Research and Development Administration, and currently by the Department of Energy. This support was the basis of the laboratory work and field testing that produced most of the survival instructions given in this book. Mr. Schroebel also reviewed early and final drafts and made a number of improvements.

John A. Auxier, Ph.D., health physicist, Director of Industrial Safety and Applied Health Physics Division, Oak Ridge National Laboratory (ORNL)—for manuscript review and especially for checking statements regarding the effects of radiation on people.

Conrad V. Chester, Ph.D., chemical engineer, civil defense researcher, developer of improved defenses against exotic weapons and unconventional attacks, nuclear strategist, and currently Head of the Solar and Special Studies Section, Energy Division, ORNL—for advice and many contributions, starting with the initial organization of material for this book and continuing through all the drafts.

William K. Chipman, LLD, Deputy Assistant Director for Plans, Defense Civil Preparedness Agency—for review of the final draft.

George A. Cristy, M.S., chemical engineer and civil defense researcher at ORNL—for contributions to the planning of this book and editing of early drafts.

Kay B. Franz, Ph.D., nutritionist, Assistant Professor, Food Science and Nutrition Department, Brigham Young University—for information and advice used extensively in the food chapter.

Samuel Glasstone, Ph.D., physical chemist and the leading authority on the effects of nuclear weapons—for overall review and constructive recommendations, especially regarding simplified explanations of the effects of nuclear weapons.

Carsten M. Haaland, M.S., physicist and civil defense researcher at ORNL—for scientific advice and mathematical computations of complex nuclear phenomena.

Robert H. Kupperman, Ph.D., physicist, Chief Scientist, U.S. Arms Control and Disarmament Agency, Department of State—for review of the final draft.

David B. Nelson, Ph.D., electrical engineer and mathematician, civil defense and thermonuclear energy researcher at ORNL, an authority on electromagnetic pulse (EMP) problems—for manuscript review and contributions to sections on electromagnetic pulse phenomena and communications.

Lewis V. Spencer, Ph.D., physicist, Radiation Physics Division, Center for Radiation Research, National Bureau of Standards—for his calculations and advice regarding needed improvements in the design of blast shelters to assure adequate protection of occupants against excessive exposure to initial nuclear radiation.

Eugene P. Wigner, Ph.D., physicist and mathematician, Nobel laureate, Professor Emeritus of Theoretical Physics, Princeton University, a principal initiator of the Nuclear Age and a prominent leader of the civil defense movement—for encouraging the writing of this book, contributing the Foreword section, and improving drafts, especially of the appendix on expedient blast shelters.

Edwin N. York, M.S. Nuclear Physics, Research Specialist in Survivability/Vulnerability with the Boeing Aerospace Company, and designer of blast-protective structures—for overall review and recommendations, particularly those based on his extensive participation in nuclear and conventional blast tests.

Civil defense officials in Washington and several states for information concerning strengths and weaknesses of official civil defense preparations.

Helen C. Jernigan for editing the manuscript, and especially for helping to clarify technical details for non-technical readers.

May E. Kearny for her work on the index and assistance with editing.

Ruby N. Thurmer for advice and assistance with editing.

Marjorie E. Fish for her work on the photographs and drawings.

Debra A. Swaggerty for initial typing and word processing of the manuscript.

CIVIL DEFENSE and the SURVIVAL OF AMERICAN SOCIETY

An overview of civil defense in America since World War II

NWS RESEARCH BUREAU

INTRODUCTION

The survival of American society is a subject which arouses minimal interest, especially among Americans. Survival is assumed. For hundreds of years Americans enjoyed a unique isolation which conditioned them to take the continuance of their society for granted. There was never any potential risk or combination of dangers which seriously threatened the survival of American society. This is no longer true. Today, nuclear weapons and intercontinental delivery systems stand ready to destroy the majority of our economic base and as many as 75% of our population. If this were to occur the remaining populace would be unable to rebuild their society in a short period of time. It is unlikely that the survivors would be allowed to rebuild an independent America. If a disaster like this should occur there would be surviving Americans, but American society as we know it today would cease to exist.

Stated simply: the means exist today to bring an end to American society. Few Americans understand that our country may not survive the 1980's. We have created this vulnerability ourselves and have repeatedly ignored advice to reduce our nuclear exposure. It is critically important to understand that America's present danger is not opinion but a distinct fact. Many, perhaps most, people lose sight of this alarming situation by immediately propounding one theory or another which they believe guarantees that the awful event can never take place. While these "can't happen" theories may be comforting they in no way mitigate the extent of the potential disaster. In other words, if these theories are wrong, then the victims will still be 100% dead. A more positive approach would be a movement in the direction of reducing the damage if the theories of "can't happen" turn out to the inaccurate.

The process of limiting damage and loss of life is unpopular. It is known as civil defense. This study will present a history of what has transpired in the last 35 years of American civil defense and what must be done in the future. It is possible that the survival of American society will depend upon the civil defense actions taken in the 1980's.

1946-1950

This period witnessed the end of World War II and the start of the international political tension which became known as the Cold War. We frequently hear that this was the time of maximum American military strength. In many people's minds it follows that this was also the time of maximum safety for U.S. citizens. Actually this was not true. We dismantled our military structure in a short period of time and quickly reoriented ourselves to a peacetime economy. While these events took place foreign nuclear weapons were being developed which would, for the first time, threaten American lives. The territorial safety which Americans had enjoyed for 200 years ended with the successful detonation of the first Russian atomic bomb on September 23, 1949—three years sooner that our experts had predicted. The American civil defense effort at this time consisted of two full-time federal workers and a small part-time contingent.

Atomic weapons were a dangerous mystery in the minds of most U.S. citizens during this five year period. American film studios produced numerous atomic fantasies involving giant ants and other improbable consequences of nuclear explosions. A view of life in the atomic age developed which was far from reality. Who could have imagined that thirty years later between 60%-80% of Americans would face the possibility of nuclear destruction?

1951-1955

Any thoughts that the world had entered a new era of peace were dispelled during this five year period. A costly war in Korea and numerous world disruptions were ample proof that international tensions would remain. On January 12, 1951, the Federal Civil Defense Administration was created to take over the duties of the Office of Civil Defense Planning which had originated in 1947. By 1954 America was ready for its first "World War III" drill. The country learned that fallout, as well as blast damage, was a significant factor to be considered.

By 1955 the United States had a credible

nuclear weapons inventory and the bomber force to assure a high degree of damage to any hostile country. Basically, we were "buying" protection for our people with a threatening retaliatory force. We could inflict such damage that no sane government would consider full scale war. Yet, the trends in effect by 1955 guaranteed that this situation would not persist. The American government would lose its overwhelming nuclear advantage in little more than a decade.

During this period strategic planners began to critically analyze the possibility of nuclear war. Informed Congressmen, military leaders and others came to the realization that a dangerous vulnerability existed. It was becoming obvious that something more than air raid sirens was necessary. America was strong offensively but weak in terms of civilian defense.

1956-1960

This five year period could be viewed as the time when a realistic assessment of the nuclear was question was finally made in the United States. In 1956 the Rockefeller Brothers Study contained astute civil defense observations, developed in part by the 33-year-old Henry Kissinger. The report strongly urged a shelter program and Nelson Rockefeller declared that the next war's victory could go to the nation with the best civil defense. In the last 24 years nothing has altered the truth of this observation. However, the Rockefeller study was largely ignored.

The question of defense in the nuclear age soon prompted President Eisenhower to commission a special report on strategic issues. In 1957 this group, the Gaither Committee, handed the President its recommendations. The report was read by top administration officials, marked "Top Secret", and withheld from public view until 1973. We now know that on page one the report said:

> "We have found no evidence in Russian foreign and military policy since 1945 to refute the conclusion that USSR intentions are expansionist, and that her great efforts to build military power go beyond any concepts of Soviet defense."

On page five:

> "In case of nuclear attack against the continental United States: (1) active defense for the future will not give adequate assurance of protection to the civil popula-

tion...(2) passive defense programs now in being and programmed for the future will afford no significant protection to the civil population."

The Gaither Report went on to recommend a nationwide fallout shelter program and came to the conclusion that a protected populace was not an attractive target. This report represented the conclusions of the best informed minds in the country. Its recommendations regarding civil defense were ignored, however, because Secretary of State Dulles felt that shelters would create a defensive attitude that could impede his efforts to build mutual security arrangements with our allies. In addition, President Eisenhower rejected the Gaither cost estimate of twenty five billion dollars for nationwide shelters. Hindsight reveals this to have been a very significant decision. If ever there was an ideal time to proceed with civil defense, this was it. It can only be hoped that history does not record this as the greatest, perhaps ultimate, error in judgement made by any U.S. administration. The rejection of the Gaither civil defense recommendations was the first indication that the U.S. government considered policy matters and budgets as more important than the lives of U.S. citizens. Equally disturbing was the effort to conceal the report's recommendations from the American people.

The 1950's ended with the United States strong in nuclear weapons and interlocking foreign defense treaties. Yet, an uneasiness existed in the minds of many people. In 1959 the film "On The Beach" depicted the fate of nuclear war victims. Though totally inaccurate in its presentation of fallout dangers, the film summed up the growing concern of a population that knew, perhaps subconsciously, that something very dangerous was growing closer each year.

The newly formed Federal Civil Defense Administration knew that protection as needed and started the decade (1951-1953) with budget requests averaging $500 million per year.

Actual budget appropriations in these years were about $50 million annually; only 10% of what was requested. Congress had decided not to fund civil defense in a serious manner. Between 1951 and 1959 the Federal government spent, on the average, about $54 million each year on the civil defense of its citizens...about 35¢ per year per person. The situation was made worse when a significant portion of these expenditures were diverted to non-nuclear areas. While non-nuclear programs were useful, it was obvious that the primary danger which threatened the survival of the American people was being ignored.

The record of the fifties clearly shows a recognized national survival problem which received inadequate governmental support. The protection of American lives was assigned a low priority. Many thoughtful observers began to ask why such an important program had so little support. The maintenance of an ineffective, underbudgeted agency appeared to be a cosmetic attempt to show the taxpayers that something was being done. The need was real; the response inadequate.

1961-1965

The early sixties were another grim confirmation that America could not look forward to a period of international calm. The Kennedy administration was disturbed when it recognized the critical nature of the threat of U.S. citizens from nuclear war. In January of 1961 President Kennedy asked Congress for $312 million to build shelters for Americans. The Berlin and Cuban crises highlighted the urgent need for adequate nuclear protection. In the sumer of 1963, a six week civil defense conference was held at Woods Hole, Massachusetts. This top level assembly of 63 scientists and engineers plus 88 briefers was directed by the Nobel prize winner, Dr. Eugene Wigner and the National Academy of Sciences. The result was the Harbor Study which received wide attention. The report's recommendations for immediate and sustained civilian protection greatly encouraged civil defense advocates. It should be remembered that the earlier Rockefeller and Gaither reports were unavailable to the public. With the release of the Harbor Study, however, all the facts were available to the public for the first time. The quality and extent of this undertaking suggested that constructive civil defense efforts would finally begin in America. A recognized need was given the highest possible level of scientific endorsement. No one could have known that fateful events would soon crush these encouraging developments.

The civil defense budget rose to $228 million in 1963, but a reduction to $97 million was seen in 1964. Protection for U.S. citizens from nuclear war died with President Kennedy in Dallas. By 1965 President Johnson had quietly withdrawn plans for national civilian shelters. Many asked, what happened? The need for civilian nuclear shelter was documented. The Eisenhower administration had ignored the issue. The Johnson administration proceeded with its plans for a Great Society and the war in Vietnam. Unfortunately, there was no money for civil defense. The United States ultimately poured approximately three times the assets which would have sheltered every American man, woman and child, into the Asian war effort.

Governments, like individuals, display their true priorities through their spending habits. The lives of American civilians were judged to be worth something less than 40¢ per year in expenditures. The Asian war effort would consume about $1,000 per American citizen. By 1965 a trend had developed which indicated that U.S. policy did not put a substantial premium on American life, military or civilian.

1966-1970

The hopefulness, in regard to civil defense, which was present when the decade began had vanished by 1966. Knowledgeable observers knew the nuclear threat grew more ominous each year. Yet, nothing was done. Expedient politics, misdirected priorities and turbulent domestic issues seemed to have doomed American citizens to an existence of nuclear uncertainty. A small segment of both Congress and the academic community maintained the struggle for adequate civil defense funding, which in 1966 was only $90 million. By this time both of the communist super-powers were well ahead in sound civil defense programs. Sweden and Switzerland also had comprehensive shelter programs underway. The realities of the nuclear age seemed to be obvious, but not to the American government. In 1967 an update of the Harbor Study (Little Harbor) was released. Its conclusions said in part:

> "...that a very substantial expansion in civil defense and other preparedness programs is consistent with a national strategy whose primary emphasis is on deterrence of nuclear war".

Nothing was done. A ray of hope shone through when the newly elected president said on March 14, 1969:

> "Congressman Holified, in the meeting this morning strongly urged that the administration look over the shelter program, and he made the point that he thought it has fallen somewhat into disarray due to lack of attention over the past few years. I

have directed that General Lincoln, the head of the Office of Emergency Preparedness, conduct such a survey. We're going to look at the shelter program to see what we can do there to minimize American casualties''.

The result was the Lincoln Report, an in-depth study which confirmed all the prior reports and recommended immediate action to meet the nuclear danger threatening American citizens. Nothing was done. In 1970 seven members of President Nixon's ''Blue Ribbon Defense Panel'', as a matter of conscience, submitted an unasked-for supplemental report expressing their shock at America's defense laxity. They warned that:

> ''...the mood of the people and much of Congress is almost one of precipitous retreat from the challenge. This paradox in response to possible national peril is without precedent in the history of the country.''

Nothing was done. The civil defense budget was $49 million in 1969 and $51 million in 1970. By this time the American government had demonstrated its disinterest in civil defense. As the 1960's ended, two developments had begun to haunt concerned individuals. First: the fifties had ended with a clear superiority in the U.S. offensive weapons posture; the 1960's ended with this advantage going to the USSR. Second: during the 1960's the deliberate exposure of U.S. citizens to nuclear elimination became the official policy of the American government. The name of this new policy was Mutually Assured Destruction, or MAD. From our vantage point in 1980 we can see that this policy was the unannounced repudiation of effective civil defense efforts by the Federal government.

1971-1975

The unexpected and awesome buildup of nuclear weapons targeted on the United States by 1970 forced the U.S. government to develop a concept of defense which would rationalize the precarious state of the civil population. What good is defense, many asked, if no one is being defended? The new defense theory which emerged by 1971 made the American people, in effect, ''hostages'' of the Russian military. This policy had become known as the theory of Mutually Assured Destruction. Our defense policy was to be one of response only; if we were attacked we would retaliate and inflict unacceptable losses on our enemy. Therefore, this theory declared, no one would ever attack. In addition, our government decided to leave the American people exposed to show our good faith to potential enemies. Our unprotected civilians were supposed to guarantee that the U.S. would never attack first. Critics warned that this policy would encourage aggressive enemies to enlarge their first strike capability and accelerate civil defense measures for their own population. This is exactly what has happened in the last ten years. It was not surprising that strategic planners around the world referred to the Mutually Assured Destruction theory as ''immoral'', ''bankrupt'', ''unconscionable'' and worst of all...a policy which ''increases the chances of war.'' A few voices were raised against this theory in the early seventies but they were ignored as the bureaucracy focused on a dramatic new foreign policy effort.

The 1971-1975 period saw the growth of ''detente'' and disarmament negotiations. The American people began to hear of ''overkill'' and other grisly concepts which conveyed the impression that each side possessed so many nuclear weapons that war was no longer possible. Unfortunately, government and private studies which contradicted these ''doomsday'' predictions were ignored. In the early seventies, civil defense was ''out''; disarmament was ''in''. This was the mood of government as our representatives bargained for the future of America at European disarmament conferences. The official thinking of this time can best be seen in the statement by a high official of the Arms Control and Disarmament Agency:

> ''The favorite apothegm of Washington's assured destruction school of strategy (is): Offense is defense, killing people is good, killing weapons is bad.''

This policy is still in effect today. It is difficult for most Americans to understand that their government has embraced the concept of civilian nuclear vulnerability. To put the lives of an estimated 100 million Americans at risk, on purpose, cannot be justified in the minds of most U.S. citizens.

1976-1980

No recognized expert denies the fact that the USSR pulled ahead of the U.S. in overall military capabilities by 1976. This does not tell the real story, however, as the realities of nuclear war give a profound advantage to the side striking first.

Few Americans realize this, and government officals are reluctant to confirm it publicly. This is unfortunate because the American public deserves to know the truth. Most defense planners do not believe that Americans could adjust to the actual danger which confronts them. Unfortunately, the facts are very grim. Government surveys indicate that the U.S. casualties in a nuclear war would be ten times higher than those of the Soviet Union. Between 50%-80% of these nuclear casulaties would survivie if a nationwide shelter plan were instituted. Thus, our present policies (of no civil defense) doom about 100 million Americans to perish unnecessarily if our planners have made a mistake. The reason Soviet losses would be so small is clear: civil defense in Russia is a five billion dollar per year program of the highest priority. Russian civilians are trained and protected in a sensible manner. If current trends continue the ratio of American to Russian casualties in a nuclear war could be 20 to 1 by 1985.

This was the situation which greeted the administration that had promised . . . "to never lie to the American people." By 1976 many of our highest officials believed that something had to be done quickly. The result has been a half-hearted attempt to design a civilian evacuation plan. Needless to say, no one has taken this effort seriously. In 1977 our Secretary of State went to Moscow and proposed to the Russians that both countries avoid spending large sums on civilian defense. The Russians refused.

At this point it was clear that a change in policy was in order. Like a ship frozen in the ice, our government seemed unable to break out of the policies of recent decades. Congress did begin to take notice of the sickly state of civil defense and the seventies drew to a close with a new name on the government's civil defense activities. The administration reshuffled all natural disaster and civil defense activities into FEMA . . . the Federal Emergency Management Agency. In reality, there is no capability of managing a nuclear attack emergency in America. Thrity years of neglect will not vanish because new titles appear on Washington stationery.

The situation is close to being desperate. The Secretary of Defense has admitted that a Russian first strike would eliminate our Minuteman missile force. The extreme vulnerability of our ancient bomber force is well known. Also, it became known that the Soviets had constructed a formidable air defense and ABM system. Equally dis-turbing has been the gradual admission that the USSR had a civil defense program which far surpassed earlier expectations. All of these developments reached a climax in 1979. It was then that the facts regarding the SALT II treaty (Strategic Arms Limitation Talks) and our overall defense capabilities were made public. While civil defense was only a minor consideration, the deterioration of U.S. defenses shocked many congressmen and informed citizens. It was painfully obvious that changes were in order. The events in Afghanistan have since confirmed the need for a new course in the 1980's. Unfortunately, the dangerous world situation finds American citizens without nuclear war protection of any kind.

The great majority of Americans do not realize their degree of vulnerability. They have not been told the truth. Most would find it hard to believe that their government could allow a situation of this magnitude to develop.

Several years ago the head of the Russian government said: "Capitalism is a system without a future." Few Americans took him seriously. Today, the question is simple and direct; can thirty five years of neglect be overcome in time? If not, American society as we know it today has a distinct, and growing, chance of not surviving the 1980's.

SUMMARY

THE BASIC FACTS

If nuclear war broke out today approximately 100 million Americans would die unncessarily. Our country has never faced such a critical problem. A solution is possible, and can be set in motion, if we face up to three questions which must be answered. (1) Why has it happened? (2) What can we do at this late date? (3) What can individuals do?

1. WHY HAS IT HAPPENED? There are three reasons:

Poor Priorities: This is not pleasant for Americans to face, but it is unavoidable. Our political leadership has not provided a program which will protect American lives, the most important asset in this country. The seeds for this oversight were planted in the 1950's when policies and budgets took precedence over the protection of American lives. Imagine that a virulent disease had begun to infect the U.S. in 1950 and that it threatened to kill 50% of the American population. What would have happened? Clearly, we would have spent any amount and explored any answer to avoid this fate. Politicians ignoring the problem would have been quickly returned to private life. In 1981, the United States faces a far more dangerous threat than this; yet, nothing is being done. The obligation incumbent upon leaders is that they lead. They lead by telling the people the truth and meeting the high priority needs of the country. The facts regarding civil defense were known in the 1950's and are obvious today. Leadership fails when these facts are kept from public view and other more politically expedient courses followed. We must, immediately, get our priorities in order.

Poor Policies: Since the 1960's the cynical policy of Mutually Assured Destruction has gripped our government. In effect, our leaders began to rationalize **not** protecting citizens. This policy was neither understood nor accepted by the people. Policy-makers were forced to conduct defense planning without fully explaining the enormous risks to American citizens. Secrecy bred bad policy. Bad policies had to be covered up or hidden behind a smokescreen of technical defense statistics. The process became self-generating. It is likely, if the American people had been given the facts, that the proponents of these muddled policies would have had shorter bureaucratic careers. Americans are a trusting people. We naturally have faith in our leaders. The people deserved to know the truth but it was not forthcoming. New policies must be instituted without delay.

Poor Judgement: During the 1970's our leaders were preoccupied with disarmament negotiations. Anyone who understands the need for civil defense knows that realistic arms limitations are the only ultimate answer in a tense world. However, both sides must negotiate in good faith. In the 1970's our leaders cut back on defense spending, dismantled our ABM (Anti-Ballistic Missile) system and virtually ignored civil defense. On the other hand, the Soviets increased defense spending, constructed a viable ABM system and accelerated their efforts to establish an effective civil defense program. If this is disarmament, it must be viewed as somewhat one sided.

Each administration in the 1970's ignored the truth about civil defense and those who recommended telling the facts to the American people. Seemingly, each administration tried to grab the

"brass ring" of disarmament. It was hoped that if arms limitations took place then civil defense would not be needed. If the Russians would cooperate then civil defense would not be needed. If the Russians would cooperate then the growing risk to American lives would recede. Washington officials have been unable to see that an effective civil defense program is necessary with or without disarmament. Who can predict the future? What will technology bring in the 1980's? Does history teach us to be ever-vigilant? Who can rationalize the intentional exposure of 100 million Americans to unnecessary nuclear termination? The time has come to replace wishful thinking with common sense.

2. WHAT CAN BE DONE AT THIS LATE DATE?

There is only one answer. We must tell the truth to the American people. Recent surveys indicate that 77% of Americans believe the country is on the "wrong track." Almost as many, 64%, believe the country is in "deep and serious trouble." In addition, a majority of Americans harbor a distrust for politicans. Are these views justified? Would Americans still feel this way if they were told the truth? Could the fundamental reason for public distrust of politicans be that Americans know, subconsciously, that some basic breach of confidence has separated them from their elected representatives? If the government cannot be trusted to provide survival . . .what can it be trusted for?

If each Congressman, Governor and Mayor told the public where we stood in regard to civil defense the changes would not be long delayed. A wave of support would launch the long overdue shelter program. There can be no reason why Americans should have less hope for their survival than do the Swiss, the Swedes. or the Chinese. Only the truth can solve this central problem facing America today.

3. WHAT CAN YOU DO NOW?

First, learn everything you can about the present situation. Get the facts; they will upset you but it's better to know the truth. Contact your civil defense department and ask for available materials. Devise a family survival plan on the assumption that no one will be able to help you but yourself. Prepare your family for whatever might come. If your ancestors had not done this, you wouldn't be here. Make some sacrifices, examine your priorities and meet the future with confidence and resolve. Americans may be gullible but they are not quitters. Second, work within the system for positive change. Everyone should write to his elected officials stating his or her beliefs. Then write again, and again. Confront your school board, the editor of your local paper, your church, your fellow workers and your neighbors with the facts. One person's voice can be clearly heard in Washington if the facts are correct. Third, pray for peace. Pray for your country and its leaders. Pray for the enemies of your country as well. Pray for wisdom so that you can help solve this national problem instead of being a part of it.

APPENDIX

COMMON EXCUSES GIVEN TO EXPLAIN THE LACK OF CIVIL DEFENSE MEASURES

An overview of civil defense between 1946 and 1980 raises many serious questions. Once Americans have learned the facts they look to their elected representatives for an explanation. Some leaders have worked faithfully to institute civil defense measures and these men deserve their constituent's support. Most officials, however, will say nothing or respond with a statement like, "I have always supported a strong defense for the American people." To be fair, most Congressmen and government officials are not against civil defense, they simply do not know enough to have an informed opinion. Their interests lie in other areas and they are, like the public, unaware of the problem. For those who admit that they are against civil defense, one of the five following excuses will usually be given to explain their opposition. We will examine each of them in detail.

EXCUSE #1 We maintain peace through civilian vulnerability

Though this is the official U.S. government policy it is very difficult to get an official to publicly commit himself or even comment on this excuse. This excuse assumes that both the U.S. and the USSR have an exposed populace and that the theory of Mutually Assured Destruction is valid. Anyone using this excuse as a reason for not supporting civil defense must close his eyes to the facts of Soviet civil defense and our very unequal nuclear war "fatality" ratio vs. the Russians. Any theory based on killing millions of Russians is morally questionable. If the same theory assures the destruction of 100 million Americans, unne-

cessarily, it is obviously absurd. This excuse cannot survive a careful analysis and many in the government are abandoning it quietly. Logic would indicate that the United States cannot maintain a policy of citizen vulnerability on one hand and effective civil defense on the other.

EXCUSE #2 Civil defense cannot work; nuclear war kills everyone

This excuse will be seen most often among those who are idealistic and subject to emotional opinions. To sincerely espouse this type of opposition to civil defense requires a tendency towards black-or-white judgements without benefit of supporting facts. This is the "On The Beach" attitude which was repudiated years ago. Even opponents of civil defense realize that the most serious major effects of a nuclear war would not persist for an extended period. With sound protection and good planning a nation's populace can rebuild after a nuclear war in a short period of time. Fortunately for Soviet citizens, this is exactly the type of civil defense planning seen in Russia today. One soon learns that "doomsday" prophecies and similar end-of-the-world predictions numb our initiative and delay needed civil defense measures. The lessons of history clearly tell us that wars are not avoided by the adoption of unrealistic assumptions.

EXCUSE #3 We cannot afford civil defense

This is the reason most politicians do not support civil defense. Hundreds of billions have been spent on non-essential programs over the years. Obviously, Congress would rather spend our money on programs other than civil defense. Few Americans know that the U.S. government spends about 40¢ annually for their civil defense. On the other hand, the Russians spend at least $20 per year per person, the Chinese $5 and the Swiss $10. Of course, if official U.S. policy is to expose American citizens, why spend money to protect them? The United States desperately needs a comprehensive shelter program that will cost about $500 per person. We need to spend this $500 over a five year period. Thereafter, we need to maintain a perpetual program with an annual budget of about $10 per year per American. To suggest that we cannot afford $500 per citizen is a position which is difficult to justify. People are the greatest asset in America. Are you worth $500? Is your child? Public officials who say we cannot afford the survival of the population should be encouraged to seek other employment.

231

EXCUSE #4 Civil defense is provocative: if we shelter our people the Russians will think we are preparing for war

The Russians, Chinese and others have good civil defense programs. We do not regard these efforts as provocative, nor should anyone else. Protecting the citizens of a country is not debatable; it is the clear obligation and first priority of government. At all levels, public officials take oaths of office which clearly state this obligation. These oaths are being ignored or misunderstood; there is no other explanation.

In effect, present U.S. policy is provocative because it makes the populace an attractive target. Our leaders maintain a policy which increases, rather than decreases, the chances of a nuclear war. Is it not true that a protected country is one that an aggressor will hesitate attacking? Excuse number four is more commonly heard from academics whose education has elevated their thinking into a world of theories. Unfortunately, many of these individuals lack a durable connection with the real world of common sense.

EXCUSE #5 The American people are apathetic

This is the excuse given by those who confuse expedience with duty. It represents an attitude which degrades our civilian population. It assumes Americans to be so blind and materialistic that continued existence as a free people is not important. Obviously, no population gets excited over civil defense, highways or income taxes. This does not mean that the people do not want these programs. The government's duty is to implement what individuals cannot do for themselves. Why then does government fail to provide for civil defense? The problem is not inactivity; our Congress is voting and spending at record levels. The problem is improper government priorities, not public apathy.

The American people need to hear the truth. The truth is that civil defense is needed more than all the pork barrel expenditures which each Congress passes to perpetuate its stay in office. We must reorder our priorities. Numerous opinion polls have exposed the following facts about the attitudes of Americans in regard to civil defense.

1. Over 80% of Americans favor fallout shelters

2. Over 60% favor shelters in new construction

3. Over 50% would volunteer to work on civil defense projects

4. Americans believe the civil defense budget to be much higher than it actually is. Most are surprised to learn it is so small

5. Most Americans believe the civil defense program of the U.S. government includes supplies of food and medicines

It is untrue that the public does not know what it wants; it wants civil defense. Neither is it true that the public is apathetic. The public seems apathetic because it assumes that normal, prudent precautions have already been taken. The public does not know that the government has failed to provide the civil defense program which will preserve our society in the event of a nuclear war.